THIRD EDITION

Learning iOS Programming

Alasdair Allan

O'REILLY®

Beijing · Cambridge · Farnham · Köln · Sebastopol · Tokyo

Learning iOS Programming, Third Edition

by Alasdair Allan

Copyright © 2013 Alasdair Allan. All rights reserved.

Printed in the United States of America.

Published by O'Reilly Media, Inc., 1005 Gravenstein Highway North, Sebastopol, CA 95472.

O'Reilly books may be purchased for educational, business, or sales promotional use. Online editions are also available for most titles (*http://my.safaribooksonline.com*). For more information, contact our corporate/institutional sales department: 800-998-9938 or *corporate@oreilly.com*.

Editor: Rachel Roumeliotis	**Cover Designer:** Randy Comer
Production Editor: Kristen Borg	**Interior Designer:** David Futato
Proofreader: Rachel Leach	**Illustrator:** Rebecca Demarest
Indexers: Fred Brown and Meghan Jones	

March 2013:   Third Edition

Revision History for the Third Edition:

2013-03-05:   First release

See *http://oreilly.com/catalog/errata.csp?isbn=9781449359348* for release details.

ISBN: 978-1-449-35934-8

[LSI]

Table of Contents

Preface

The arrival of the iPhone changed everything. Or, at the very least, it changed the direction of software development for mobile platforms, which is a pretty big thing. It has spawned an entire generation of copycat devices and brought an entire multibillion-dollar industry to its knees. Despite this, it still fits in your pocket.

Third Edition

There have been a lot fewer changes between the release of iOS 5 and iOS 6 than between the release of iOS 3 and iOS 5, especially since changes to Xcode 4 have now slowed as it has matured. Consequently the changes here in the third edition are less sweeping than they were in the second. Nonetheless, the book you now hold in your hands has been updated to reflect the changes Apple has made to Xcode to support the arrival of the iPhone 5 and iOS 6, as well as discussing the changes in iOS 6 that seemed interesting or relevant to mention as part of a introductory title.

Notes from the Second Edition

The changes made in the second edition reflected the fact that a lot had happened since the first edition was published: the release of the iPad, a major release of Xcode, two revisions of the operating system itself, and the arrival of Apple's iCloud. That book had therefore been refreshed, renewed, and updated to reflect these fairly fundamental changes to the platform, and all of the example code was rewritten from the ground up for Xcode 4 and iOS 5 using ARC.

Who Should Read This Book?

This book gives a rapid introduction to programming for the iPhone, iPod touch, and iPad for those with some programming experience. If you are developing on the Mac for the first time, drawn to the platform because of the iPhone, or alternatively are an experienced Mac programmer making the transition to the iOS, this book is for you.

What Should You Already Know?

The book assumes some knowledge of C, or at least passing knowledge of a C-derived language. Additionally, while I do give a crash course, some familiarity with object-oriented programming concepts would be helpful.

What Will You Learn?

This book will guide you through developing your first application for the iOS from opening Xcode for the first time to submitting your application to the App Store. You'll learn about Objective-C and the core frameworks needed to develop for the iOS by writing applications that use them, giving you a basic framework for building your own applications independently.

What's in This Book?

Here's a short summary of the chapters in this book and what you'll find inside:

Chapter 1, Why Go Native?
> This chapter discusses the need for native applications and compares building native applications to building web applications.

Chapter 2, Becoming a Developer
> This chapter walks you through the process of registering as an iOS developer and setting up your work environment, from installing Xcode and the iOS SDK to generating the developer certificates you'll need to build your applications and deploy them onto your own iPhone, iPod touch, or iPad.

Chapter 3, Your First iOS App
> This chapter allows you to get hands-on as quickly as possible and walks you through building your first Hello World application, including how to deploy and run the application on your iPhone, iPod touch, or iPad.

Chapter 4, Coding in Objective-C
> This chapter provides a crash course in the basics of the Objective-C language, and if you're familiar with another C-derived language (and perhaps with object-oriented programming), it should be enough to get you up and running with Objective-C and the Cocoa Touch frameworks.

Chapter 5, Table View-Based Applications
> The UITableView and associated classes are perhaps the most commonly used classes when building user interfaces for iOS applications. Due to the nature of the

applications, these classes can be used to solve a large cross section of problems, and as a result, they appear almost everywhere. In this chapter, we dive fairly deeply into the table view classes.

Chapter 6, Other View Controllers

After discussing the table view controller in detail, we discuss some of the other view controllers and classes that will become useful when building your applications: simple two-screen views, single-screen tabbed views, modal view controllers, and a view controller for selecting video and images.

Chapter 7, Connecting to the Network

This chapter discusses connecting to the Internet, browsing the Web, sending email, and retrieving information.

Chapter 8, Handling Data

This chapter discusses how to handle data input, both from the application user and programmatically, and how to parse XML and JSON documents. The chapter also covers storing data in flat files and storing data with the SQLite database engine.

Chapter 9, Using Sensors

This chapter discusses how to determine what hardware is available and illustrates how to deal with the major sensors on iOS devices: the accelerometer, magnetometer, camera, and GPS.

Chapter 10, Geolocation and Mapping

This chapter walks you through the process of building applications that make use of the Core Location and MapKit frameworks.

Chapter 11, Introduction to iCloud

This chapter provides a brief introduction to integrating Apple's iCloud service into your own applications. iCloud is a service that helps you synchronize your data across devices, making documents and data available to all of your subscribed devices.

Chapter 12, Integrating Your Application

This chapter shows you some of the tricks to integrate your application with iOS's software ecosystem, how to present user preferences with Settings Bundles, and how to use custom URL schemes to launch your application. It also discusses how to make use of the Media Player and Address Book.

Chapter 13, Distributing Your Application

This chapter talks about how to add some final polish to your application and walks you through the process of building your application for distribution, either via ad hoc distribution or for the App Store.

Chapter 14, Going Further

This chapter provides a collection of pointers to more advanced material on the topics we covered in the book, as well as material covering some of those topics that we didn't manage to talk about in the book.

Conventions Used in This Book

The following typographical conventions are used in this book:

Italic

Indicates new terms, URLs, email addresses, filenames, and file extensions

`Constant width`

Used for program listings, as well as within paragraphs to refer to program elements such as variable or function names, databases, data types, environment variables, statements, and keywords

`Constant width bold`

Shows commands or other text that should be typed literally by the user

`Constant width italic`

Shows text that should be replaced with user-supplied values or by values determined by context

This icon signifies a tip, suggestion, or general note.

This icon signifies a warning or caution.

Using Code Examples

This book is here to help you get your job done. In general, if this book includes code examples, you may use the code in your programs and documentation. You do not need to contact us for permission unless you're reproducing a significant portion of the code. For example, writing a program that uses several chunks of code from this book does not require permission. Selling or distributing a CD-ROM of examples from O'Reilly books does require permission. Answering a question by citing this book and quoting example code does not require permission. Incorporating a significant amount of example code from this book into your product's documentation does require permission.

We appreciate, but do not require, attribution. An attribution usually includes the title, author, publisher, and ISBN. For example: "*Learning iOS Programming (3rd ed)* by Alasdair Allan. Copyright 2013 Alasdair Allan, 978-1-44935-934-8 (O'Reilly)."

If you feel your use of code examples falls outside fair use or the permission given here, feel free to contact us at *permissions@oreilly.com*.

How to Contact Us

Please address comments and questions concerning this book to the publisher:

O'Reilly Media, Inc.
1005 Gravenstein Highway North
Sebastopol, CA 95472
800-998-9938 (in the United States or Canada)
707-829-0515 (international or local)
707-829-0104 (fax)

We have a web page for this book, where we list errata, examples, and any additional information. You can access this page at *http://oreil.ly/learn-ios-programming-3e*. Supplementary materials are also available at *http://www.learningiosprogramming.com/*.

To comment or ask technical questions about this book, send email to *bookquestions@oreilly.com*.

For more information about our books, conferences, Resource Centers, and the O'Reilly Network, see our website at *http://www.oreilly.com*.

Find us on Facebook: *http://facebook.com/oreilly*

Follow us on Twitter: *http://twitter.com/oreillymedia*

Watch us on YouTube: *http://www.youtube.com/oreillymedia*

Safari® Books Online

Safari Books Online (*http://my.safaribooksonline.com/?portal=oreilly*) is an on-demand digital library that delivers expert content (*http://www.safaribooksonline.com/content*) in both book and video form from the world's leading authors in technology and business. Technology professionals, software developers, web designers, and business and creative professionals use Safari Books Online as their primary resource for research, problem solving, learning, and certification training.

Safari Books Online offers a range of product mixes (*http://www.safaribooksonline.com/subscriptions*) and pricing programs for organizations (*http://www.safaribookson*

line.com/organizations-teams*), government agencies (*http://www.safaribookson
line.com/government*), and individuals (*http://www.safaribooksonline.com/individu
als*). Subscribers have access to thousands of books, training videos, and prepublication manuscripts in one fully searchable database from publishers like O'Reilly Media, Prentice Hall Professional, Addison-Wesley Professional, Microsoft Press, Sams, Que, Peachpit Press, Focal Press, Cisco Press, John Wiley & Sons, Syngress, Morgan Kaufmann, IBM Redbooks, Packt, Adobe Press, FT Press, Apress, Manning, New Riders, McGraw-Hill, Jones & Bartlett, Course Technology, and dozens more (*http://www.safar
ibooksonline.com/publishers*). For more information about Safari Books Online, please visit us online (*http://www.safaribooksonline.com/*).

Acknowledgments

Books do not write themselves, especially the third editions, and especially the third edition of your first book. After fixing everything you felt was wrong with it in the second edition, at least to your own satisfaction, the prospect of doing it all again to keep up with moving technology is daunting. It's a horrifying prospect, and a harder job than just sitting down and writing a new book from scratch. I'd therefore like to thank my editors, Brian Jepson and Shawn Wallace, for prodding and poking until I actually picked up the manuscript once more and wrote something. I'd also like to thank my long-suffering wife, Gemma Hobson. I'm not entirely sure why she lets me keep writing; it's almost certainly nothing to do with the royalty checks. Finally to my son Alex, who is still young enough that he's not entirely sure what Daddy is doing, although he's moved on a fair way since the first edition was written and can now read and write a few words of his own. Sorry for being so grumpy while I went about the whole business.

CHAPTER 1

Why Go Native?

When the iPhone was originally introduced back in 2007, there was no native SDK. Apple claimed that one wasn't needed and that applications for the device should be built as web applications using JavaScript, CSS, and HTML. This didn't go down well with the developer community; they wanted direct access to the hardware and integration with Apple's own applications.

Only a few months after the iPhone's release, the open source community had accomplished something that many thought impossible. Despite Apple locking the device down, developers had gained access, reverse-engineered the SDK, and gone on to build a free open source tool chain that allowed them to build native applications for the device. At one point, it was estimated that more than one-third of the iPhones on the market had been "jailbroken" by their users, allowing them to run these unsanctioned third-party applications.

However, the book you hold in your hands isn't about the open source "hacker" SDK, because in March 2008, less than a year after the release of the first iPhone, Apple publicly changed its mind and released a native SDK to a waiting developer community. Whether this release was in response to the open source community's efforts, or perhaps because it was just the plan by a notoriously secretive Apple all along, we'll probably never know.

The Pros and Cons

When the native SDK was introduced, a number of people in the industry argued that it was actually a step backward for developers. They felt that web-based applications were good enough. By writing code specifically for the iPhone in Objective-C, you were making it more difficult to port your applications, and porting a web application more or less consisted of simply restyling it using a new CSS template.

It seemed that the users of the applications disagreed. It's arguable why this is the case, but it's very hard to make native-looking web applications that can be reused across many different platforms, though it is possible. Just as applications on the Mac desktop that have been ported from Windows tend to stand out like a sore thumb by not quite working as the user expects, web applications, especially those that are intended to be used across different platforms, tend to do the same.

Just to be clear, this isn't a criticism of HTML, CSS, and JavaScript. The Web's technology stack is solid and maturing, and the attraction of having a cross-platform code base is going to be immediately obvious to you as a developer. However, to your users, it's not so obvious. Most of the arguments that are put forth in support of using web technologies, or other non-native frameworks, are from a developer's perspective. While that doesn't make them invalid, you should take a serious look at those arguments from a user's perspective, because none of them really address their main concern: usability.

Consumers won't buy your application on their platform just because you support other platforms; instead, they want an application that looks like the rest of the applications on their platform, that follows the same interface paradigms as the rest of the applications they're used to, and that is integrated into their platform.

If you integrate your application into the iOS ecosphere, make use of the possibilities that the hardware offers, and make sure your user interface is optimised for the device, the user experience is going to be much improved. All of this is possible using web technologies, but most of the time it's actually really hard to write non-native applications that work well across multiple platforms. It's harder still to make them look native on half a dozen different platforms.

Why Write Native Applications?

The obvious reason to use the native SDK is to do things that you can't do using web technologies. The first generation of augmented reality applications is a case in point; these needed close integration with the iPhone's onboard sensors (e.g., GPS, accelerometer, digital compass, and camera) and wouldn't have been possible without that access.

Although the Safari browser on iOS supports the geolocation capabilities HTML 5 provides (*http://www.w3.org/TR/geolocation-API/*), this doesn't alleviate the problem entirely. It's doubtful that all platform-specific hardware is going to get the same sort of treatment in HTML 5, so it's unlikely that you will see the arrival of augmented reality web applications.

If you are coming from a web development background, you may be interested in the cross-platform PhoneGap framework (*http://phone gap.com/*). This framework provides native wrapper classes and allows you to build native applications in HTML/JavaScript on a range of mobile platforms. One of the platforms it targets is the iOS.

Sometimes it's not about doing things that can't be done; it's about doing things faster, and doing client-side error handling. For instance, the Apple iTunes and App Store applications that are provided with the iOS are actually web applications wrapped inside native applications. Just like the iTunes and App Stores on the Mac desktop, the main panel you see is actually just a web page, but the surrounding infrastructure is a native application. This means that while the application can't do a lot without an Internet connection, it can at least start up cleanly.

But those are extreme examples. A lot of the applications in the App Store combine remote data and native interfaces. Without access to the network, some of the UI is generally disabled. However, native applications can be built to degrade gracefully when the device's network connection disappears or if it was never present in the first place. The user can still use the bits of the application that don't need a network connection to work.

Sometimes it's also about what an application doesn't need. If it doesn't need a network connection, the idea that your phone needs to be connected to the network to use it, sucking extra battery power in the process, is wasteful. Even when it is connected, the device isn't always connected to a fast Internet connection. Anything you can do to minimize the amount of data you need to suck down the data connection will improve users' interaction with your application. That means generating your user interface locally, and populating it with data pulled from the Internet.

Network performance will affect the user's perception of speed; rendering your user interface while a web request is made to populate it allows your application to remain responsive to user interaction even while it's waiting for the network. That can only be a good thing.

I haven't even mentioned game development yet, and with Apple pitching the iPod touch as "the funnest iPod ever," that's important. You cannot develop the sorts of games now starting to appear on the App Store using web-based technologies. While this book covers the basics of how to program for iOS devices, if you want to delve deeply into game programming on the platform, I recommend *Tap, Move, Shake: Turning Your Game Ideas into iPhone & iPad Apps* by Todd Moore (O'Reilly).

The Release Cycle

Paul Graham, one of my favorite dispensers of wisdom, argues that the arrival of web-based software has changed not just the user experience, but the developer experience as well:

> One of the most important changes in this new world is the way you do releases. In the desktop software business, doing a release is a huge trauma, in which the whole company sweats and strains to push out a single, giant piece of code. Obvious comparisons suggest themselves, both to the process and the resulting product.
>
> — From "The Other Road Ahead" by Paul Graham

He is exactly right. Working in the cloud, you rarely make a software release in the old sense of the word. Despite the benefits, I must admit I actually somewhat miss the "big push" where, usually with a great deal of trepidation, you roll out a new, improved version of a piece of software. However, one problem with writing native applications is that we've made a return to the release cycle.

With web-based software you can make incremental releases, fixing bugs when and if they occur. Native applications are far more like desktop software.

I cover the details of how to submit applications to the App Store in Chapter 13. However, you should prepare yourself now for some amount of pain. The review process is notoriously opaque, and it can and does take time. Plus, each of your applications must go through it, not just when you initially submit it to the store, but also for each new version you release. Typically, it can take up to seven days from submitting your application for it to be approved (or rejected) by the review team, although it can take much longer. While some of my applications have sailed through the submission process in only a couple of days, I have had applications in the review process for up to four months before receiving approval.

 If you're interested in how the average review time for iOS and OS X applications changes with time, look at Average App Store Review Times (*http://reviewtimes.shinydevelopment.com/*). The site, written by Dave Verwer, a well known iOS developer, tracks the average App Store review times for apps submitted to both the iOS and the Mac App Store using data crowdsourced from developers on Twitter.

Build It and They Will Come

Earlier in the chapter, I argued against web applications because they require an Internet connection; of course, that's not entirely the whole truth. You can write an offline web application using the Offline Application Cache available in HTML5, although there are obvious limitations to that approach. However, the big advantage of a native application, even with today's crowded App Store, is exposure. If nobody can find your application, nobody can pay for it, and the Web is a big place.

One big advantage a native application has over a web application is that it's easier for potential users to find, and much easier to pay for when they find it. That is, if you can get people to pay for web applications at all. People don't impulse-subscribe to a web service; they impulse-buy from the App Store.

However, don't assume that if you build it, users will appear. Unless you're really lucky and your application goes viral, you still need to market your application. The App Store may be a lot smaller than the Web, but it's still a pretty big place.

Marketing your application is like marketing any product; you need to make use of the tools available and your contacts to get news of your software to your target market. Apple provides promotional codes for your application (although at the time of this writing, these work only in the US App Store) that will give free downloads of your applications. Many developers reach out to high-profile blogs or the many application catalog sites and offer them review copies in hopes that they will publicize the application. If it's well designed and useful, they might well be interested in reviewing it.

Produce a screencast showing how your application works and how to use it. Also, applications with good support resources (such as forums and trouble-ticket systems) sell more copies. Applications with good design stand out in the store and sell more copies.

Good design often means that you do things "the Apple way." Integrate your application well with the other applications on the phone. Don't reinvent the wheel—use the standard widgets and interface elements familiar to iOS users.

CHAPTER 2

Becoming a Developer

Before you start writing code, you'll need to do some housekeeping. First, you'll need to install Xcode, Apple's development environment, as well as the iOS SDK. Both of these are available directly from Apple via the Mac App Store.

However, if you want to distribute your applications, or even just deploy them onto your own device, you will also need to register with Apple as a developer and then enroll in one of the developer programs. You'll then need to create, download, and install a number of certificates and profiles to allow you to deploy your applications onto your iPhone, iPod touch, or iPad.

> Developing applications for iOS requires an Intel Mac, and while it's possible to develop applications for iOS using OS X 10.6 (Snow Leopard). it is now very difficult to obtain the tools that allow you to do so. It's highly recommended that you upgrade to the latest version of OS X, currently OS X 10.8 (Mountain Lion), before starting development work. This is a requirement if you want to develop applications that make use of iCloud or other features introduced in iOS 5 and iOS 6. We'll talk about iCloud in more detail later in the book, in Chapter 13.

Let's get these housekeeping tasks out of the way now so that you can get to the interesting bit—the code—as quickly as possible.

Registering as an iOS Developer

Until recently, the only way to obtain Xcode was to become a registered Apple developer. However, you can now download the current release of Xcode and the iOS SDK directly from the Mac App Store.

If you are still running OS X 10.6 (Snow Leopard), then you need to register as an Apple developer, become a member of the iOS Developer Program, and then download Xcode 4 and the iOS SDK from the iOS Dev Center. The version of Xcode available on the Mac App Store is for OS X 10.7 (Lion) and 10.8 (Mountain Lion) only. However, it's likely that in the near future support for OS X 10.7 (Lion) will be dropped from the public release in the Mac App Store.

Nevertheless, before you can obtain access to the developer documentation, you'll need to register as an iOS developer. Additionally, while the current release version of the SDK is distributed via the Mac App Store, when beta releases are made available, they are usually only distributed as *.dmg* files via the iOS Dev Center.

If you want to be able to test your applications on your own iPhone, iPod touch, or iPad, you will have to enroll in the iOS Developer Standard or Enterprise Program (both these programs have a yearly fee), and we will discuss how to enroll in these programs in the next section.

If you choose the free account, you won't be able to install your applications onto your hardware, nor will you be able to sell applications on Apple's App Store (Standard Program) or distribute them to people within your own company (Enterprise Program). If you stick with a free account, you also won't have access to prerelease versions of the iOS SDK or iOS releases.

You can sign up at *http://developer.apple.com/ios/*.

 If you have an existing Apple ID, such as for an iTunes or iCloud account, you can use this identity to register as an iOS developer. However, if you intend to sell software commercially, you may want to create a new identity for use with the developer program to keep it separate from your existing Apple ID.

You'll initially be asked to either choose an existing Apple ID or create a new one. If you create a new ID, you'll be asked for some details (e.g., email and physical addresses); if you choose an existing Apple ID, you'll still need to confirm some of these details, although they should be filled in with the most recent information Apple has.

You'll also be asked to provide a professional profile, indicating what sort of applications you'll be developing and whether you also develop for other mobile platforms.

Finally, you'll need to agree to the developer license. After you do, a verification code may be sent to the email address you registered with Apple, although this doesn't happen in all cases. However, if this happens to you, the final step of registering as an iOS developer will be to verify your email address. While this email is, in most cases, dispatched fairly quickly (within an hour or two), I have known of cases where there have been several days' delay before this email was dispatched. If you need to set up a new developer account, don't leave it until the last minute.

Apple Websites

You'll use three main websites as part of the iOS development process:

iOS Dev Center (http://developer.apple.com/ios/)
> This site is where you can get access to the latest versions of the iOS SDK, along with background technical information, API documentation, sample code, and instructional videos. You need to be a registered iOS developer to access the site.

iOS Provisioning Portal (http://bit.ly/XYsFAX)
> This site is where you can generate and manage the certificates, provisioning profiles, approved devices, and other housekeeping tasks necessary to test your applications on your device and prepare them for distribution. You'll need to be both a registered iOS developer and enrolled in one of the iOS Developer Programs to access this site.

iTunes Connect (https://itunesconnect.apple.com/)
> This site provides you with the tools to manage your applications on the iTunes App Store and your contracts with Apple. You'll need to be both a registered iOS developer and enrolled in the iOS Developer Standard Program to access this site.

Apple also provides extensive online documentation about the developer program. Two sites that are especially helpful are:

Developer Support Center (https://developer.apple.com/support/ios/)
> This site provides support for managing and dealing with the developer program and your developer account, including if you have a problem concerning the developer program enrollment. You'll need to be a registered iOS developer to access this site.

App Store Resource Center (http://developer.apple.com/iphone/appstore/)
> This site provides help and advice on how to distribute your application on the App Store, including preparing your app for submission, understanding the App Store approval process, and learning how to manage your apps on the App Store. You'll need to be both a registered iOS developer and enrolled in the iOS Developer Standard Program to access this site.

Finally, Apple provides a discussion forum for developers:

Apple Developer Forums (https://devforums.apple.com/)
> This site is the only place where you are allowed by your non-disclosure agreement to discuss certain aspects of iOS development, including features, issues, and installation of pre-release software and tools.

Enrolling in the iOS Developer Program

If you intend to sell your applications on the App Store, or you just want to be able to deploy them onto your own iPhone, iPod touch, or iPad, you'll also need to enroll in the iOS Developer Program. If you've not already registered as an iOS developer, you can do that during this process.

> Your iOS Developer Program membership lasts for one year and can be renewed starting 60 days before the expiration date of your existing membership. If you do not renew your membership, your ability to distribute your applications will be curtailed. In addition, your developer and distribution certificates will be revoked. Finally, any applications you have on the iTunes App Store will be removed.

You have two options when enrolling in the iOS Developer Program. Most people will want to register for the Standard Program, which costs $99 per year. This will allow you to create free—or, once you've filled out some paperwork, commercial—applications for the iPhone, iPod touch, and iPad and distribute them either via the App Store or via the ad hoc distribution channel where you provide both the application binary and a provisioning certificate to the end user.

> Ad hoc distribution allows you to distribute your application directly to your users, bypassing the App Store. However, distribution is limited to just 100 devices during the course of your one-year membership and, at least for the end user, is more complicated than distributing your application via the App Store. It's mainly intended for beta testing programs, and it isn't a substitute for publishing your application to the store. If you need to conduct large-scale rollouts to a specific group of users and you want to avoid the App Store, you should probably look at the Enterprise Program. If you are interested in developing for enterprise, I'd recommend *Developing Enterprise iOS Applications* by James Turner (O'Reilly).

The more expensive Enterprise Program, at $299, is intended for companies with more than 500 employees that wish to create applications for in-house distribution. While this program allows you to distribute your applications inside your own company, it does not allow you to publish them for sale on the App Store. If you're thinking about selling your applications to the public, you need the Standard Program.

An iOS Developer University Program (*http://developer.apple.com/programs/ios/university/*) is also available. This program is designed specifically for higher education institutes looking to introduce iOS development into their curricula. However, unless you're an academic at such an institute, it's unlikely that this program will be applicable to you.

 If you want to register as a company in the Standard Program, rather than as an individual, or as a member of the Enterprise Program, you will need to be an official representative of your company (and be able to prove that with the relevant documentation) and know your company DUNS Number.

The Mac Developer Program

As well as enrolling as a member of the iOS Developer Program, you may also wish to register as a member of the Mac Developer Program. Doing so is a good idea if you're serious about developing with iOS. You can sign up for the Mac Developer Program here (*http://developer.apple.com/programs/mac/*).

Like the iOS Developer Program, the Mac Developer Program costs a $99 a year for enrollment. If you sign up for the program, it's a good idea to use the same Apple ID you used when signing up for the iOS Developer Program.

Installing the iOS SDK

At the time of this writing, the current release of both Xcode and the iOS SDK are available as a single download from the Mac App Store. Open the store and search for Xcode. Navigate to the download page, shown in Figure 2-1, and click on the blue "Free" button, then click "Install App."

The combined download of the Xcode development tools and the iOS SDK from the Mac App Store is around 1.5 GB in size. You can monitor the download from the Purchased tab in the Mac App Store. When the download successfully completes, you'll find a new application in the */Applications* folder on your machine, called *Xcode*.

Starting Xcode for the first time you'll (probably) be presented with a dialog asking you to install some additional components; the nature of these is going to vary with the precise version of Xcode you've just downloaded. For me, it's the support for legacy iOS Simulators—see Figure 2-2.

Figure 2-1. Xcode in the Mac App Store

Figure 2-2. Installing additional system components when starting Xcode for the first time

After installing the necessary system components you should be presented with the New Project window, as shown in Figure 2-3.

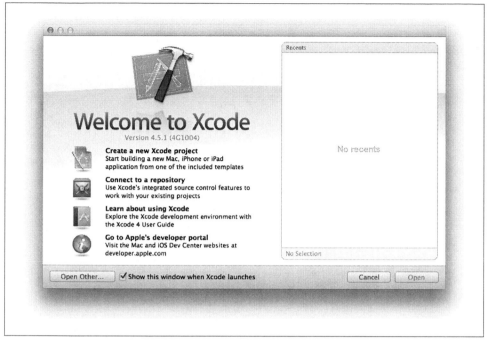

Figure 2-3. The Xcode New Project window

However, we're not quite done yet. Select Preferences from the Xcode menu and open the Downloads section. Under the Components tab you'll see that there are items like the command line tools, and some legacy simulators, that are not installed by default. You'll probably want those. Go ahead and click on each item to download it—see Figure 2-4. Then switch to Documentation tab and go ahead and download all the relevant documentation. You'll probably want to check the "Check for an install updates automatically" tickbox.

Figure 2-4. Downloading additional components and documentation from the Xcode Preferences menu

You now have everything you need to write applications and test them in the simulator.

 If you want to test your code on an actual iOS device, you will need to enroll in either the Standard or Enterprise iOS Developer Program. However, the amount of time it takes to be accepted into the program varies, so after you enroll and have been accepted, you should bookmark this page and finish the steps in this chapter. You can use iPhone and iPad simulators for the examples in this book while you wait to be accepted.

While the simulator is very good, it's not perfect. Code runs much faster on the simulator than it does on the device. If you're dealing with applications that have a complicated UI or consume a great deal of processor power, the difference in performance between the simulator and the device could become important. On several occasions, I've had to go back and rewrite my code and refactor the way in which my UI functions; when I tested my application on the simulator it worked fine, but on real hardware it just ran too slowly. You can also allocate much more memory in the simulator than is available on the real hardware.

Additionally, some frameworks are available to you in the simulator—notably the NSPredicate and NSXMLDocument classes—that just don't exist on the device. Code that uses these missing classes will compile and run on the simulator, but not on the device. In addition to regularly building your application in iPhone Simulator, it's therefore a good idea to perform regular device builds. If you accidentally use one of these "missing" classes, it will show up as a link error at compile time for such a build. After all, you don't want to get too far down the road of developing your application only to discover (hours, or worse yet, days later) that you're using classes or frameworks that aren't actually present on the device.

Both NSPredicate and NSXMLDocument are commonly used classes. For instance, NSXMLDocument is the class most people programming in Objective-C on the Mac (rather than the iPhone) would use to perform an XQuery on an XML document. The lack of NSXMLDocument is something that most developers notice quite quickly.

While I've seen some complaints that the simulator can sometimes be slightly off on pixel alignment of UIKit elements, I've not yet come across this myself. However, when using lower-level graphics libraries, such as OpenGL ES, the renderer used on the device is slightly different from the one used in the simulator, so when a scene is displayed on the simulator it may not be identical to the actual device at the pixel level.

Additionally, the simulator has some built-in limitations. For instance, if your application's UI is designed to respond to touch events with more than two fingers, it's harder to test it in the simulator.

While it doesn't allow you to simulate gestures requiring many fingers, iPhone Simulator does allow you to test applications that require two-finger (multitouch) touch gestures. You can use Option-click (for pinch) or Option-Shift-click (for drag) while using the mouse to get two "fingers."

Furthermore, you will not have access to the accelerometer, GPS, Bluetooth, or digital compass when running your application in the simulator. If your application relies on these hardware features, you have no choice but to test it on your device.

What Happens When There Is a Beta?

In the past, Apple has made development (beta) releases of these tools available in different ways. Normally they are distributed as *.dmg* files via the iOS Dev Center; however, some betas are distributed using redemption codes via the Mac App Store, linked to the Apple ID you used to register as an Apple developer. This code can be redeemed to gain access to the beta release. Additionally, while most recently the tools have been distributed as a single download, there have been some previous distributions where you first needed to download Xcode and then install the iOS SDK from a separate installer.

Preparing Your iOS Device

Before you can install applications onto your iOS device, you must follow a number of steps, and you'll need to do so in the order shown in Figure 2-5.

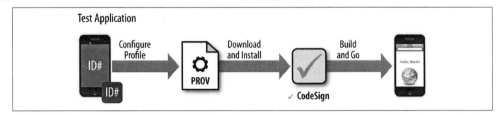

Figure 2-5. The workflow for creating certificates and mobile provisioning profiles

So, if you have enrolled in either the Standard or Enterprise iOS Developer Program, now is the time to generate the appropriate certificates and provisioning profiles so that you will be able to deploy the test application from the next chapter onto your device.

Certificates and Provisioning Profiles

You must have a development certificate for Xcode to sign your application binaries. This certificate also identifies you as a developer. When you build your iPhone application, Xcode will look in your Mac OS X keychain for this certificate and the corresponding certificate from Apple, called the WWDR Intermediate certificate, which you'll also need to download from the Developer Portal.

Provisioning profiles associate a development certificate, and hence a developer, with a hardware device and an iOS application ID, which is a unique identifier for your application. To install an application that you've signed with your development certificate onto your iOS device, you need to install the associated provisioning profile onto your device.

While recent releases of Xcode have automated creating and updating the certificates and provisioning profiles you'll need to develop for iOS to some extent, I think it is a good idea that, at least the first time you create these profiles, you do so manually so that you have some idea of what Xcode is doing behind the scenes. It'll also come in handy when, as is often the case, Xcode gets confused and you have to fix its mistakes by hand.

Creating a Development Certificate

The first thing you need is a development certificate and Apple's WWDR Intermediate certificate. To request a development certificate from the Provisioning Portal, you need to generate a certificate-signing request (CSR) using the Keychain Access application.

You can find the Keychain Access application in the */Applications/Utilities* folder. Launch the application and select Keychain Access→Preferences from the menu. Go to the Certificates Preferences pane to confirm that the Online Certificate Status Protocol (OCSP) and Certificate Revocation List (CRL) options are turned off, as shown in Figure 2-6.

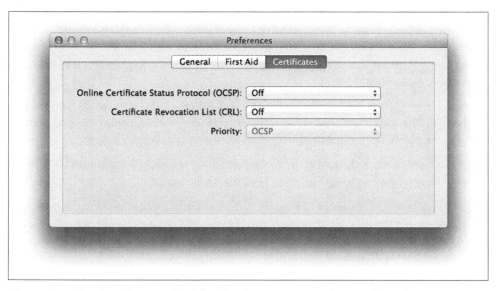

Figure 2-6. The Certificates tab of the Keychain Access application's Preferences pane

Next, select Certificate Assistant→Request a Certificate from a Certificate Authority from the Keychain Access menu, and enter the email address that you selected as your Apple ID during the sign-up process along with your name, as shown in Figure 2-7. Click the "Saved to disk" and the "Let me specify key pair information" radio buttons and then click Continue. You'll be prompted for a filename for your certificate request.

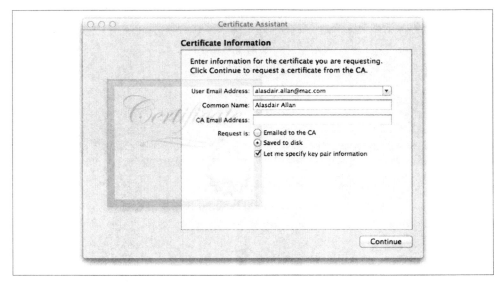

Figure 2-7. The Keychain Access.app Certificate Assistant

Accept the defaults (a key size of 2,048 bits using the RSA algorithm) and click Continue. The application will proceed to generate a CSR file and save it to disk. The file will be saved to the location you specified when you were prompted to choose a filename (the default is usually your desktop).

Next, log in to the iOS Dev Center (*http://developer.apple.com/ios/*) and click on the link to the iOS Provisioning Portal. This will take you to the main portal used to manage certificates and devices associated with your developer program account.

Click the Certificates link, then go to the Development tab and click Request Certificate. Follow the instructions to upload your CSR file to the portal.

If you joined the iOS Developer Program as an individual, your certificate request will be automatically approved. However, if you are part of a development team, your nominated team admin must approve your certificate request before it will be generated and made available for download.

 If you don't see the Download option appear after you click Approve, click the Development tab link to refresh the page, and it should appear.

After approval, you need to download your personal certificate and the WWDR Intermediate certificate and install them in your Mac OS X keychain. Still on the Development tab, click the Download button to download your personal certificate, then right-click on the link to the WWDR Intermediate certificate and save the linked file to disk.

Once both of these certificates have downloaded to your local machine, you need to install them in your Mac OS X keychain. Double-click on the certificate files to install them into your keychain. This will activate the Keychain Access application and ask you to confirm that you want to add the certificates to your Mac OS X keychain.

If you have more than one keychain, you need to make sure the certificates are installed in the default keychain, normally called *login*. The default keychain is highlighted in bold in the list of keychains at the top left of the *Keychain Access.app* application. It's normally best to keep the *login* keychain the default, but if this is not the case, you can make it the default by selecting the File→Make Keychain "login" Default option from the menu bar. If the certificates are not installed into the default keychain, Xcode will be unable to find them, and hence will be unable to sign binaries with them. This means you will not be able to install your applications onto your iOS device.

You can check that the two certificates have been correctly installed in your keychain by clicking on the Certificates category in the Keychain Access application. You should see both your own developer certificate and Apple's WWDR certificate in the *login* keychain, as shown in Figure 2-8.

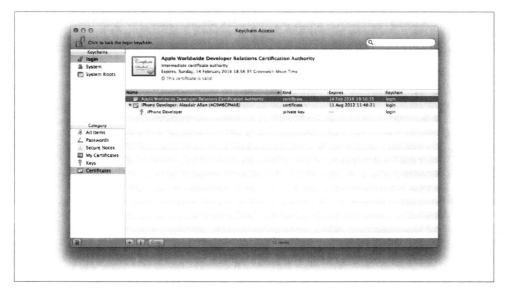

Figure 2-8. The Keychain Access application showing the newly installed certificates necessary for Xcode to sign your binaries and deploy them onto your iOS device

Getting the UDID of Your Development Device

Plug the iOS device you intend to use for development into your Mac. Open Xcode and select the Window→Organizer item from the menu bar. The Organizer window will open, showing the list of connected devices (see Figure 2-9).

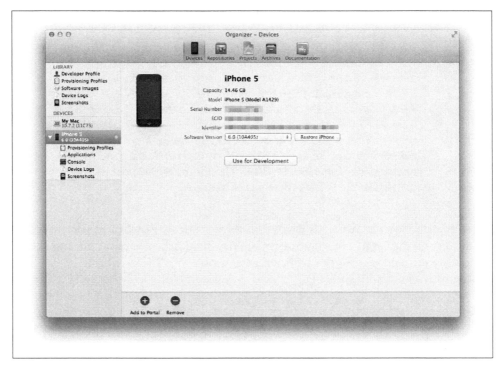

Figure 2-9. The Xcode Organizer window

You'll need the unique device identifier (UDID) of your development device so that you can create a mobile provisioning profile for this device. Right-click or Control-click on the 40-character string labeled Identifier (see Figure 2-9) and select Copy.

Return to the Provisioning Portal, click Devices, select the Manage tab, and click Add Devices. Enter the device name in the appropriate box and the UDID in the box labeled Device ID, and click Submit. You have now registered your device.

Creating an App ID

The App ID is also used as part of the mobile provisioning profile. The mobile provisioning profile is different from the certificate you generated earlier. Certificates stay in the keychain on your Mac and are used by Xcode to digitally sign the iOS application binaries. The mobile provisioning profile you're about to generate is tied to one or more devices and is transferred by Xcode onto your iOS device. This allows the applications you create to run on that device.

Go to the App IDs section of the iOS Developer Program Portal, select the Manage tab, and click on New App ID. Enter a name for your App ID; this should be a human-readable name used to refer to this particular App ID. It's entirely arbitrary what you use as the name for the App ID. Since this is your first App ID, for the Bundle Seed ID select Generate New.

Finally, enter a Bundle Identifier. This must be unique, and most developers use a reversed version of their domain name so that this is the case. For instance, my domain name is *babilim.co.uk*, so I entered **uk.co.babilim.*** as my Bundle Identifier.

The asterisk (*) that appears at the end of my Bundle Identifier is the *wildcard* symbol. Using a * in the Bundle Identifier means you will be able to use this App ID for multiple applications. If you did not use a wildcard here, you'd have to generate a new App ID for each of your applications, and a new provisioning profile for each of these applications, before you could deploy your application onto your iOS device. Using a wildcard means you can generate a single mobile provisioning profile that will allow you to deploy multiple applications onto your developer device.

Technically, this means that all the applications created using this Bundle Identifier will share the same portion of the keychain on your iOS device. I discuss the implications of this later. Using a wildcard in the Bundle Identifier also means that the applications you create using this App ID, and the mobile provisioning profile(s) associated with it, will not be able to use the Apple Push Notification and in-app purchase services.

Click Submit. The portal will now generate a new 10-character Bundle Seed ID and prepend it to the Bundle Identifier you provided. This is your App ID.

You need to make a note of your Bundle Identifier as you'll need to supply it to Xcode, as described near the end of Chapter 3, to allow you to deploy the application you are developing onto your iOS device.

Creating a Mobile Provisioning Profile

Now you're ready to create a mobile provisioning profile. Go to the Provisioning section of the Provisioning Portal, select the Development tab, and click on New Profile.

Enter a profile name. While it's more or less arbitrary what you put here, I recommend using "Developer Profile" somewhere in the name. You may be generating a number of provisioning profiles, including ones later on for distribution (both ad hoc and to the App Store), so it's helpful to know that this profile is to be used for development.

Check the relevant certificate box: if you're an independent developer, you'll have only one choice here—the certificate you generated earlier using the Keychain Access application.

Select the App ID you generated in the previous section, and then select the development device (or devices if you have more than one available) for which this profile will be valid. As I mentioned before, Xcode will transfer the provisioning profile onto your iOS device, and application binaries built by Xcode using a provisioning profile will run successfully only on devices for which this profile is valid. If you don't select the correct device here, your code will not run on it. Don't worry, though: you can add additional devices to the profile at any time, but you'll need to regenerate a provisioning profile inside the Provisioning Portal.

Click Submit to generate the new mobile provisioning profile that you'll use during development. I discuss provisioning profiles needed for distributing your applications later in the book. The status will appear as pending; click the Development tab to reload it until it is no longer pending.

When the profile is ready, click Download and download the provisioning profile to your Mac. You can install it in a number of ways, but the easiest way is to drag the *.mobileprovision* file you downloaded onto the Xcode icon in the dock. This will install it in Xcode and make it available for development.

Making Your Device Available for Development

The final step before you can start coding is to make your device available for development. Return to Xcode and click Window→Organizer from the menu. Select your development device from the lefthand pane and click Use for Development. If Xcode doesn't manage to correctly register your device, you may have to disconnect and reconnect it so that Xcode can find it correctly. If that fails to work, you should try turning your device off and then on again. Depending on the version of the SDK you installed and the version of the OS currently on your device, you may have to restore your device from the Organizer window inside Xcode. In the process, you'll lose any data you have on it. If this is necessary, you can back up your data by syncing with iTunes or iCloud as normal before restoring the OS using Xcode.

If you can afford the extra cost, I recommend using a separate device for development than you use as your day-to-day device. In the future, you may wish to install prerelease versions of iOS onto your development device, and by definition, these are always unstable. For instance, if you're relying on your personal iPhone to keep you in touch with the world, you may not want to use it for development.

Once you've installed the profiles, you can verify that Xcode should automatically sync it with your iOS device. You can verify that the profile has been installed by going to Settings→General→Profile on your iOS device and checking that the profile has been correctly installed and verified, as shown in Figure 2-10.

Figure 2-10. The development provisioning profile installed on my iPhone 5

You can now confirm that everything has worked correctly by noting the status light next to your device in the Xcode Organizer window. If Xcode has managed to connect to the device, and it is correctly enabled for development, the status light next to the listing on the lefthand pane will be green. You'll also see your mobile provisioning profile listed in the center box in the main pane, as shown in Figure 2-11.

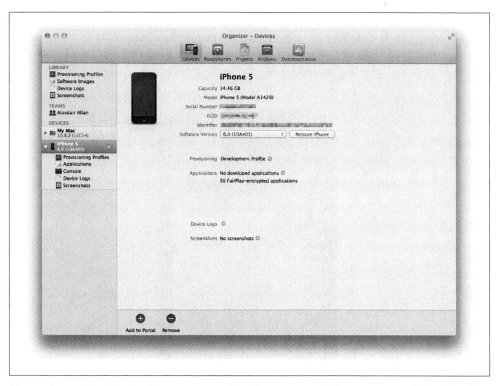

Figure 2-11. The Xcode Organizer window showing my iPhone 5 is ready for development with my development provisioning profile installed

Congratulations, you now have all the certificates and profiles in place to allow you to start running code on your iOS device.

CHAPTER 3

Your First iOS App

In this chapter, you'll build a small Hello World application and run it in iPhone Simulator. If you're enrolled in the iOS Developer Program, you'll even get to run the application on your iOS device. I'm going to take you through this step by step, just to give you an idea of how Xcode and Interface Builder work together.

> Enrolling in the iOS Developer Program is separate from registering as an iOS developer. Enrollment ($99 or $299 per year, depending on which program you join) provides you with the software certificates and online provisioning tools needed to run your own apps on your own iOS device and submit them for approval to the App Store. See Chapter 2 for more information on registering and enrolling.

Objective-C Basics

I talk in detail about how Objective-C applications are normally structured in Chapter 4. However, in this chapter, although I do get into Objective-C's sometimes-quirky syntax, I'm going to give you a higher-level overview of the language to get you going quickly.

Object-Oriented Programming

If you've heard someone explain object orientation before, the distinction between the terms *class* and *object* may not be totally clear. However, there is a difference. A class is the blueprint for objects; each time you create an object, the class definition determines its structure. An object is a collection of operations (*methods*) and information (*data*) that occupies space in memory and can be instructed to perform operations (*invoke methods*) on that information.

For those of you who are new to programming, the following list defines some of the terms you'll come across frequently:

Objects and classes

A class consists primarily of two things: variables that can store data and methods that can perform operations. The methods are used to retrieve, set, and manipulate the variables. Objects—sometimes referred to as *instances* of a class—have specific values associated with these variables. For example, you might use Apple's UIView Controller class to manage the view (i.e., UI) you present to the user of your application. You also might create an instance of that class named myView Controller to actually carry out the work of managing the view presented to the user. This would then be referred to as the myViewController object. An *instance* of a class should not be confused with its *implementation*, which is the realization of the class in code.

Subclasses

Classes can also inherit functionality from an existing class (the parent or base classes, commonly known as the *superclass*); classes that inherit functionality in this way are referred to as subclasses. This means you can invoke a method of the parent class on an object that is an instance of a subclass of the parent. Subclassing is normally done so that you can extend the functionality of that class with additional methods or data. For example, when writing applications for iOS devices, you commonly define a subclass of the UIViewController class to manage your views, instead of using the class directly. The subclass of the standard view controller inherits all of the properties of its parent class, but in addition, it allows you to implement code to handle the specific view presented to the user, such as data entry and validation.

Instance and class variables

Both instance and class variables are defined as part of the class declaration. However, every object (instance of the class) holds a separate copy of an instance variable. In other words, if a class defines a variable foo, the value of foo can be different for objects for the same class. Changing the value of an instance variable in one object will not affect the value of the same variable in all the other objects of that class. Conversely, only a single copy of a class variable exists. If you change the value of a class variable from one object, the value of that variable will change for all the objects of that class.

Accessor methods

Accessor methods, sometimes called *getters* and *setters*, are usually fairly simple methods used to get and set instance variables in a class. They are used to provide an abstraction layer between variables and the outside world so that the implementation of the class can change without having to change any code outside of the class itself. In Objective-C, the compiler can generate these commonly used functions for you.

Class methods

Class methods (also known as *static methods*) are similar in nature to class variables. These are methods that are associated directly with the class rather than the object instance; they therefore will not have access to object instance variables.

Events and messages

An event is a message generated by the user interacting with your application's controls. For instance, if you tap the screen of your iOS device, this generates a UI event in your application that is passed via a message from the application to an object that has been delegated to deal with that specific type of event.

Protocols

A protocol definition declares methods that any class can implement. If your class declares that it abides by a particular protocol definition, you are announcing that you have implemented the minimum mandatory methods declared in the protocol definition, and may optionally have implemented some nonmandatory methods.

Delegate classes

A delegate class is a class that implements a protocol for handling events. Each delegate protocol specifies a number of methods that must be implemented, and additionally methods that may optionally be implemented. Declaring your class a delegate implies that it (at least) implements the mandatory methods. For instance, if your UI has a button, you can declare your class a delegate to handle events generated by the button.

Event loop

The main event loop is the principal control loop for your application. This loop is the process that receives and then passes external events, such as the user tapping the iPhone's screen or changes in the device's orientation, to the appropriate delegate classes that you've included in your application.

Frameworks and libraries

A framework is a collection of related classes, protocols, and functions collected together within a cohesive architecture. When you make use of a framework, many of the design decisions about how you as a developer will use the code it includes have been taken out of your hands. However, by using the standard frameworks, you inherit standard behavior. For example, when Apple introduced Copy & Paste to the iPhone with the release of version 3.0 of the firmware, it was enabled by default in most third-party applications because the developers made use of the standard UIKit framework to build those applications.

The Objective-C Object Model

For those of you coming from an object-oriented background, there are a number of differences between the Objective-C model of object orientation and the one implemented by Simula-derived languages such as C++, Java, and C#.

While its nonobject operations are identical to C, Objective-C derives its object syntax almost directly from the Smalltalk language. Its object model is based on sending messages to object instances; in Objective-C you do not invoke a method, but instead send a message. What's the difference? Invoking a method implies that you know something about that method. Sending a message leaves it up to the receiver of the message to figure out what to do with it.

This kind of loosely coupled chain of command means that Objective-C is much more dynamic at runtime than the Simula-derived languages, but it also means it might appear to be insubordinate.

That's because in Simula-derived languages, you must know the type of an object before you can call a method on it. In Objective-C, this is not the case. You simply send the object a message. The receiving object then attempts to interpret the message, but there is no guarantee of a response. If it doesn't understand the message, it will ignore it and return nil. Among other things, this kind of model does away with the need to continually cast objects between types to ensure that you are sending a message that will be understood.

 Casting is the process whereby you represent one variable as a variable of another type. This is done both for primitive types (suppose you want to change a float to an integer as part of an integer arithmetic operation), as well as for objects. An object can be cast to another object type if it is a subclass of that type. In Objective-C, objects can be represented by the generic id type, and you can cast objects to this type without regard for their parent class.

The other main difference is in the way memory is managed. While languages such as Java use garbage collection to handle memory management, in Objective-C memory is managed using reference counting. In the past this was done by hand (see the alloc-retain-release cycle discussion in Chapter 4), but with the introduction of Automatic Reference Counting (ARC) with the arrival of iOS 5, this manual procedure has been much simplified.

While the examples in this book will make use of ARC, it is important to understand what is going on behind the scenes. ARC is a compiler-level feature that simplifies the previous manual management of Objective-C objects; it automatically inserts the appropriate calls into your code at compile time.

Because of this, it is still important to understand manual memory management, especially during the transition from the existing legacy code bases to ARC-native code, as many external libraries will not be compatible with ARC. We're therefore going to be discussing manual memory management in Chapter 4.

Garbage Collection and Reference Counting

In the simplest case, memory management must provide a way to allocate a portion of memory and then free that memory when it is no longer needed. Garbage collection is a form of memory management that automatically attempts to free memory that is no longer in use. While garbage collection frees the developer from having to worry about manually managing memory, the point where memory is automatically freed can be unpredictable, and the garbage collection routines consume additional computing resources.

Reference counting is a form of garbage collection, which counts the number of references to an object (or portion of memory) and frees the associated memory when the number of references reaches zero. The main advantage of reference counting over "classic" garbage collection is that memory is freed as soon as it is no longer in use. Although most programmers wouldn't necessarily class it as such, reference counting is among the simplest garbage collection algorithms, as it frees the developer from having to manually manage memory at a low level.

Finally, the applications are almost invariably based on the Model-View-Controller (MVC) design pattern, which is pervasive in the Cocoa Touch and other frameworks that you'll use to build iOS applications. Rather than encouraging you to create subclasses, the MVC pattern makes use of *delegate classes*. A pattern is a reusable solution to a commonly occurring problem; in object-oriented programming, patterns usually describe how the developer should model the application in terms of the classes that are used, and how the developer should structure the interactions and relationships between these classes.

For example, the root `UIApplication` class implements the behavior necessary for an application, but instead of forcing you to subclass the `UIApplication` class for your own application and add your own code to the subclass, it delivers notification messages of events to an assigned delegate class that implements the `UIApplicationDelegate` protocol. The `UIApplication` class asks the delegate class to respond to events when they occur.

The Basics of Objective-C Syntax

I'll dive a bit deeper into Objective-C as we go through the book, but to make it through this chapter, all you really need to know is that while variable declarations look much the same as variable declarations do in other languages, method calls are surrounded by square brackets. So, for example, both of the following lines of code are method calls:

```
[anObject someMethod]; ❶
[anObject someMethod: anotherObject]; ❷
```

❶   The someMethod message is sent to the anObject object.

❷   The someMethod message is sent to the anObject object and passes anotherOb
ject as an argument.

Despite the sometimes-quirky syntax (including the square brackets and colon shown in the preceding code) that Objective-C has inherited from Smalltalk, the logic of what is going on should be clear, and we'll discuss the syntax in much greater detail in the next chapter.

Creating a Project

Now let's create our first application in Xcode. Launch Xcode by double-clicking its icon (it's located in the /Applications folder on your hard drive). Click "Create a new Xcode project" in the Xcode welcome window.

If you don't see a welcome window when you start up Xcode, you can create a new project by choosing File→New Project.

This will open an Xcode Project window with a drop-down window that will allow you to choose the type of project we'll be building. We want to build a "Single View Application," which is one of iOS Application templates supplied by Xcode (see Figure 3-1).

If it's not already selected, click on the Single View Application template, and then click on the "Next" button. You should then be presented with something that looks a lot like Figure 3-2. In the Product Name box, enter *HelloWorld*; this will be the name of both the Xcode project and the application target.

You should make sure you don't put a space between *Hello* and *World* as part of your Project Name, as this can confuse some versions of Xcode.

In the Company Identifier box, enter the root part of your Bundle Identifier [see the section on "Creating an App ID" (page 20) in Chapter 2 for more details]. For me, this is **uk.co.babilim**. You should leave the Class Prefix box blank, and ensure that the

Device Family is set to iPhone and the checkbox for ARC is ticked, and the boxes for storyboard and unit tests are not (see Figure 3-2).

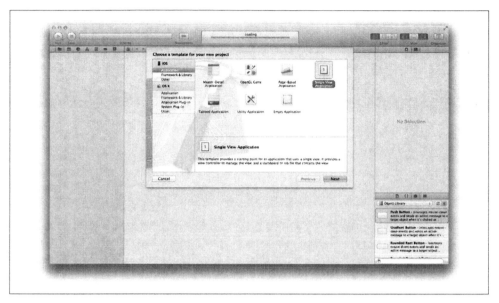

Figure 3-1. The initial project window opened by Xcode

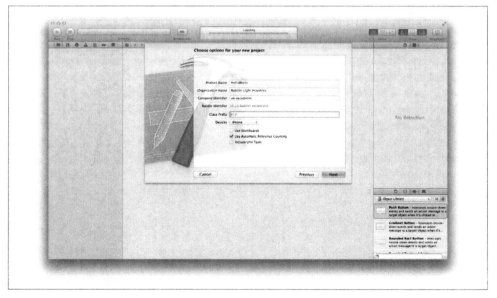

Figure 3-2. Configuring the HelloWorld project

Once you've filled in the Configuration panel, click on the Next button to proceed. You should then be presented with another dialog to save your new project (see Figure 3-3). You'll notice that Xcode will create a local Git repository for your project if you want it to. For now at least, let's ignore that option. Click Create to create and save your first Xcode project.

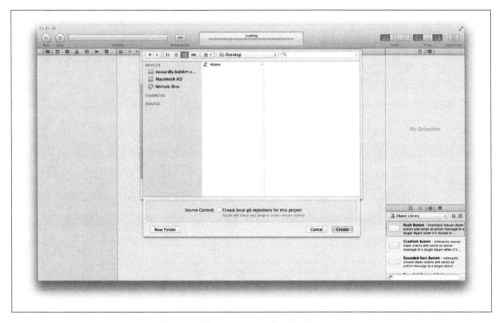

Figure 3-3. Saving your HelloWorld project to the desktop

Xcode will now open a project window, as shown in Figure 3-4. The left pane shows the classes and other files associated with the project, organized into groups in what's called the Project Navigator. If you click on the arrow next a group icon (represented as yellow folders), the group will expand to show you the files it contains.

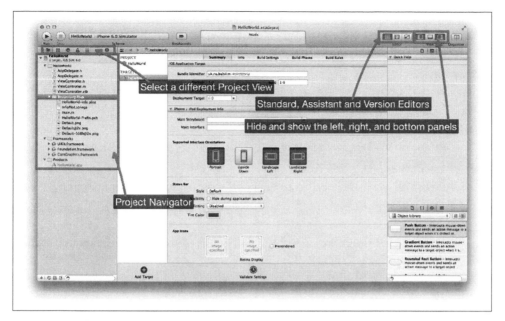

Figure 3-4. The initial Project window

The application template you choose determines how the groups are arranged, but you can move the files around and create your own groups if you prefer to organize things differently. The main group at the top of the Project Navigator window is named after your project, and it contains all the classes that make up the application including the *.xib* files that the Interface Builder application uses to describe your application's user interface.

The Navigator Window

The Navigator window gives you access to different aspects of your project. Along the top of the area is the Navigator selector bar (see Figure 3-4) with seven icons that will allow you to change the view of your project. In order, these are:

Project Navigator
> This view (see Figure 3-4) shows the files in your project and allows you to add, delete, group, and manage them while also allowing you to select the file you are currently editing.

Symbol Navigator
> This allows you to browse the symbols in your project and navigate through the available Classes, Protocols, Functions, Structs, Unions, Enums, Types, and Globals.

Search Navigator

Possibly the most self explanatory of the available views. This allows you to search your project and carry out find and replace operations over the entire project.

Issue Navigator

This will display diagnostics, warnings, and errors found when Xcode opens or attempts to build your project.

Debug Navigator

Allows you to examine the running threads and the current stack.

Breakpoint Navigator

Allows you to see the location of each of the debugging breakpoints you have inserted into your code.

Log Navigator

Allows you to inspect the current and past builds of your application as well as the build log for each of these builds.

The middle pane is the Editor window; by default, the project will open with the Editor window showing the contents of the Project file (the blue document at the top of the Navigator window). This project file contains all the metadata associated with your project. If you click on one of the source code files, which have postfixes *.m* or *.h*, you'll see that the Editor window fills with more familiar source code.

The righthand pane is the Utilities window. Right now, this is empty, but it gives access to Quick Help and other inspectors as well as resources to use in your project. For now, you may want to minimize the utility view by using the Show/Hide button in the Xcode toolbar. See Figure 3-4 above.

Exploring the Project in Xcode

When you created the project, Xcode generated a number of files and, along with them, a lot of the boilerplate code you'd otherwise have to laboriously type in. In fact, the project that Xcode generates for you is a complete (if boring) iPhone application. You know those flashlight applications that have proliferated on the App Store? You've just written one…

If you click the button in the Xcode toolbar (see Figure 3-4 again), Xcode will compile the application, deploy it into the iPhone Simulator, and then run it. After the application opens, what you see in the simulator should look very similar to Figure 3-5—a simple, blank, gray view.

Figure 3-5. Our Xcode template compiled and running inside iPhone Simulator

Let's look at the files Xcode has generated as part of the template and how it has divided them into separate groups in the Project Navigator view:

HelloWorld

The main HelloWorld group contains the classes and header files we're most interested in and will be working with in this chapter. These are *AppDelegate.h*, *AppDelegate.m*, *ViewController.h*, *ViewController.m*, and *ViewController.xib*. These are the classes that do most of the heavy lifting in the application; in particular, the *.xib* file is what Interface Builder uses to describe your application's user interface.

Supporting Files

This subgroup contains four main files: *HelloWorld-Prefix.pch*, *HelloWorld-Info.plist* along with the associated *InfoPlist.strings* file, and *main.m*.

The Supporting Files group also contains three launch images: *Default.png*, *Default@2x.png* and *Default-568h@2x.png*. We'll talk about these in more detail later in "Adding a Launch Image" (page 390).

The *HelloWorld-Prefix.pch* prefix header file is implicitly included by each of your source files when they're built; if you need to include a header file in all of the classes in your project, you can add it here. However, it's unlikely that you'll need to do this, so you can safely ignore it for the time being. The *HelloWorld-Info.plist* (property list) file also plays a role in defining the UI. This property list is an XML file that describes basic information about your application for Xcode and the compiler. The *main.m* file contains the main() routine; this is the place where your program begins. In this project, the *main.m* file handles some memory management duties (discussed in Chapter 4) and then calls the UIApplicationMain function, which is the main controller, responsible for handling the event loop. You'll almost never have to change anything in the Supporting Files group, as the boilerplate code the template generated should serve you fairly well.

Frameworks

> The Frameworks group contains a list of external frameworks that your application links to. These frameworks provide the headers and libraries you need to write software for the iPhone OS.

Products

> The Products group contains the application binary that is generated when you compile your application. At first the *HelloWorld.app* file is shown in red. Xcode knows this file should exist, but since you haven't yet compiled the application, the file currently doesn't exist.

 If you open the Mac OS X Finder and navigate to where you saved the project, you'll be able to see how the project files are organized on disk. Xcode groups do not necessarily correspond to folders on disk.

Overview of an iPhone application

Figure 3-6 shows a high-level overview of an iOS application life cycle. This illustrates the main elements of a typical iOS application. Most iOS applications make use of the MVC pattern (see Chapter 4 for more details).

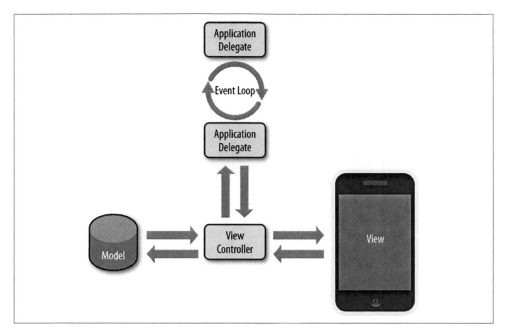

Figure 3-6. A block diagram of a typical iPhone application

When the user launches your application by tapping its icon on the Home screen, the application's `main()` function is called. The `main()` routine calls the `UIApplication Main` function, which is the main application controller responsible for handling the event loop. From this point, the heavy lifting is done by the UIKit framework, which loads the UI and starts the main event loop. During this loop, UIKit dispatches events, such as notification of touches and orientation changes, to your objects and responds to commands issued by your application. When the user performs an action that would cause your application to quit, UIKit notifies your application and begins the termination process.

The application delegate is the core class in your application and receives messages from the main event loop. It is responsible for handling critical system messages. For example, the application delegate handles both the `applicationDidFinishLaunching:` and the `applicationWillTerminate:` messages. Every iOS application must contain an application delegate object.

The view controller class is responsible for providing views, or a set of views, and presenting them to the user. The class also acts as a delegate and manages your application's response to some of the standard system behaviors (e.g., a change in device orientation), rearranging and resizing the views it manages in response to these system events.

Declarations, Interfaces, and Implementation

The declaration of a class announces its existence to the compiler, while the implementation of a class consists of the actual code that is the realization of the declaration. Just like the UI the application presents to the world, the class declaration presents an interface to the developer. The declaration declares an interface to your code, and the implementation carries out the task the code has been written to perform.

It's a common practice to separate the declaration of the class and the implementation into separate header and implementation files. This is done because header files can be, and usually are, included in multiple source files. Therefore, if we separate the class declaration from its implementation, we make the resultant code more flexible and increase reusability. We can change the underlying implementation of the class without having to recompile the (possibly many) source files that make use of that class.

The application delegate

Let's begin at the beginning, with the definition of the application delegate class. Click on the *AppDelegate.h* file, which contains the declaration of the class:

```
#import <UIKit/UIKit.h>

@class ViewController;

@interface AppDelegate : UIResponder <UIApplicationDelegate>

@property (strong, nonatomic) UIWindow *window;
@property (strong, nonatomic) ViewController *viewController;

@end
```

Here we see the app delegate class declaration, also known as the class header file, begins with the @interface directive and ends with the @end directive. This is the delegate class that implements the UIApplicationDelegate protocol and receives messages from the UIApplication class. Breaking down this interface directive, we see that the class is called AppDelegate, it's a subclass of UIResponder, and it implements the UIApplicationDelegate protocol.

We declare a UIWindow object as part of the class, and after telling the compiler that ViewController is a class using the @class directive further up, we also declare a ViewController object. The UIWindow class defines an object that coordinates the views (the user interface) that we see on the iPhone's screen. Both of these objects are declared

---

as class properties using the @*property* name directive. Properties are a generic way of declaring the data that a class provides.

Let's look at the corresponding implementation. Click on the *AppDelegate.m* file to open it in the Standard Editor:

```
#import "AppDelegate.h" ❶
#import "ViewController.h"

@implementation AppDelegate ❷

- (BOOL)application:(UIApplication *)application
  didFinishLaunchingWithOptions:(NSDictionary *)launchOptions {

    self.window =
        [[UIWindow alloc] initWithFrame:[[UIScreen mainScreen] bounds]]; ❸
    self.viewController = [[ViewController alloc] initWithNibName:
                                        @"ViewController" bundle:nil]; ❹
    self.window.rootViewController = self.viewController; ❺
    [self.window makeKeyAndVisible]; ❻
    return YES;
}

- (void)applicationWillResignActive:(UIApplication *)application {

}

- (void)applicationDidEnterBackground:(UIApplication *)application {

}

- (void)applicationWillEnterForeground:(UIApplication *)application {

}

- (void)applicationDidBecomeActive:(UIApplication *)application {

}

- (void)applicationWillTerminate:(UIApplication *)application {

}

@end ❼
```

❶ The header files are imported with the class declarations for both the App Delegate and the ViewController classes.

❷ This is the beginning of the declaration of the Hello World application delegate class.

❸ This statement allocates and initializes the main UIWindow object.

❹ Likewise for the `ViewController` object.

❺ Here is the view managed by the `viewController` object as the root view of the window.

❻ This makes the window visible using the `makeKeyAndVisible` method.

❼ This is the end of the declaration of the Hello World application delegate class.

Quick Access to Class and Method Documentation

In Xcode 4.5, if you Option-click on a class or method name, information about that class or method will appear in a small pop-up window. On most Apple keyboards, the Option key is also labeled as the Alt key, is positioned between the Control and Command keys, and may have the | symbol on it.

Click the *Reference* link at the bottom of the pop-up, and you'll get to see the full documentation. Click on the *Declared* link to go to the header file where that class or method is declared. The trick still works in previous versions of Xcode, but the pop-up window might look a bit different, or for even older versions you may be taken directly to the class documentation.

Option-click on the `UIApplicationDelegate` in the app delegate header file, then click on the Reference link to go to the full documentation, and you'll see the protocol reference. This shows you the methods the app delegate must implement as well as the optional methods (which are marked as such in the protocol documentation). These represent the messages the `UIApplication` class sends to the application delegate.

 When looking at the Xcode documentation, you may on occasion be asked to log in to the Apple Developer site, and when attempting to do so receive the error:

```
"index.HTML" is locked for editing and you may not be able
to save your changes. Do you want to unlock it?
```

Followed by a second error,

```
The file "index.HTML" could not be unlocked. The file is a remote
resource. Try making a local copy.
```

If you receive this warning, open the Xcode Preferences, click on the Downloads button in the Preferences toolbar, select the Documentation tab, and then the iOS 5.0 Library. Click on the check box, then click the Install Now button. This will download and install the needed documentation locally.

Now let's examine the implementation's `application:DidFinishLaunchingWithOp tions:` method. This is where we can insert our own code to customize the application after it launches. See Chapter 5 and the City Guide application for an example of this sort of customization. At the moment, it contains the following:

```
self.window = [[UIWindow alloc] initWithFrame:
    [[UIScreen mainScreen] bounds]];
self.viewController = [[ViewController alloc] initWithNibName:
                                   @"ViewController" bundle:nil];
self.window.rootViewController = self.viewController;
[self.window makeKeyAndVisible];
```

You make an object perform an operation by sending a message to the object. Messages are enclosed in square brackets. Inside the brackets, the object receiving the message is on the left side and the message (along with any parameters the message requires) is on the right. The parameters follow the colon [see "The Basics of Objective-C Syntax" (page 29) for another example].

The view controller

Next, let's look inside the ViewController class. The interface file for this class is called *ViewController.h*; the implementation file is called *ViewController.m*.

Let's start with the interface file. Click on the *ViewController.h* file in the Classes group to open the file in the Standard Editor.

Back in *AppDelegate.h*, the application delegate declared a viewController property of the class ViewController (note the capitalization) that right now doesn't contain any methods or properties of its own:

```
#import <UIKit/UIKit.h>

@interface ViewController : UIViewController

@end
```

However, looking at the header file, you'll see that the ViewController class is a subclass of the UIViewController class. This is the class that provides the fundamental view-management model for iOS applications, and this class is associated in Interface Builder with a nib file (when you create a view-based project, Xcode automatically creates the associated nib file). That nib file contains the UI that will be displayed when we make this view visible.

 Although the Interface Builder files end with the *.xib* extension, Cocoa programmers still refer to them by their old name, nibs.

Next, click on the *ViewController.m* file in the Classes group and look at the implementation of the class. For now, bear in mind that this subclass relies on its parent class to handle the messages that are left undefined by virtue of being not implemented.

```
#import "ViewController.h"

@interface ViewController ()

@end

@implementation ViewController

- (void)viewDidLoad {
    [super viewDidLoad];
}

- (void)didReceiveMemoryWarning {
    [super didReceiveMemoryWarning];
}

@end
```

Our Project in Interface Builder

I've talked about Interface Builder quite a bit so far, but we haven't looked at it. Let's do that now. Interface Builder allows you to create and lay out the UI for your iOS application visually; it stores your application's interface in a bundle (an XML file that, for historic reasons, is generally referred to as a nib file) containing the interface objects and their relationship with your own code. However, unlike almost all other similar design systems that generate code, nib files are *serialized* (also known as *freeze-dried*) objects. In other words, the files contain the ready-to-run object instances, rather than code to generate these objects at compile time.

We can use Interface Builder to associate the laid out UI elements with our own code by connecting outlets, actions, and delegates to the UI elements inside the Interface Builder application. However, to do so, we must first declare the objects and methods in our code as either IBOutlets, or IBActions where appropriate, and the classes as delegates.

This IBOutlet or IBAction symbol doesn't affect how the code is compiled, but it is a place marker to tell Xcode that this object in the code can be connected to a UI component in Interface Builder. This allows the UI constructed in Interface Builder to receive messages from the code. The corresponding IBAction declaration on method declarations, which we'll meet later, is yet another place marker for Interface Builder, allowing us to connect calling actions in response to events happening in the UI to a method. In many instances, a UI element will also have an associated delegate protocol, and we can declare classes to act as delegates to specific UI elements. Our class will then receive messages when the UI element generates events. For instance, in Chapter 5, you'll see the UITableView class and associated delegate protocols in action.

Click on the *ViewController.xib* file. This will open Interface Builder and display the nib file, as shown in Figure 3-7.

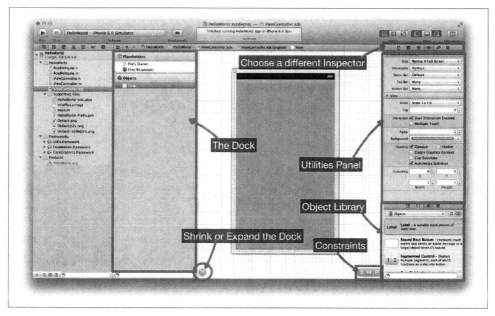

Figure 3-7. The basic ViewController.xib in Interface Builder

When you click on a nib file, the Standard Editor will change to become a visual representation of your user interface. To the left of this, sandwiched between the editing area and the Project Navigator pane, is the dock. The dock shows the Interface Builder objects and placeholders in the nib file (or if using storyboards, the *.storyboard* file); you can shrink and expand the dock using the button near the bottom of the Editor window (see Figure 3-7).

The Utilities panel to the right provides access to the Inspector tabs, which will allow you to manipulate your objects in the editor, as well as to inspect the connections and other properties of a specific object.

The Constraints button allows us to modify the constraints governing the positioning of user interface items. The left button aligns items, and is the equivalent of choosing Editor→Align. The center button pins items, equivalent of choosing Editor→Pin, while the right button lets you control how constraints are applied when resizing views.

We'll discuss the details of what's going on inside Interface Builder in later chapters; for now, we're just going to add a button and a label to the view. Then we'll modify our code so that it knows about those elements, and connect those elements to objects in the code. At that point, we'll have a working Hello World application.

Building the User Interface

Click on the View icon in the dock, or directly on the view in the Editor panel, to select it, and then pick the Attributes Inspector from the tab bar along the top of the Utilities panel. The Attributes Inspector is the fourth icon along, as shown in Figure 3-8.

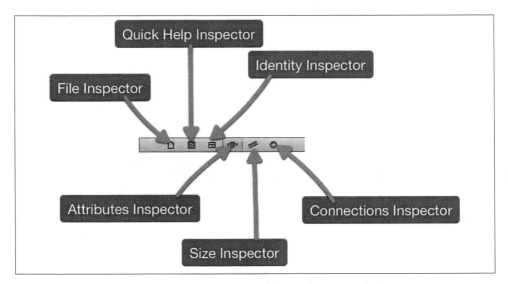

Figure 3-8. The Inspector tab bar at the top of the Utilities panel

Let's start by changing the rather dull gray background of the view to white. Click on the Background Color box in the View section of the Attributes Inspector to bring up the standard Mac OS X color picker. Push the opacity slider to 100% and change the color to something more interesting. In my case, I picked white, which is only marginally more interesting than gray. Close the color picker; the background of your View window should now be a more interesting color.

Now go to the Object Library (see Figure 3-7) and click and drag a label and a button, Label (`UILabel`) and Round Rect Button (`UIButton`), onto your view and drop them in a sensible place.

Delete the placeholder text in the label by double-clicking on the label text to select it and then pressing the Backspace key. This will make the label invisible in the view; however, you can see it's still there as it's shown in the dock. If you lose track of where you put it, just click on the Label icon in the dock to select it and it'll be selected in the view.

You should then add some appropriate replacement text for the button. Just double-click on the button as you did for the label, but this time add some text —"Push me!" perhaps (see Figure 3-9).

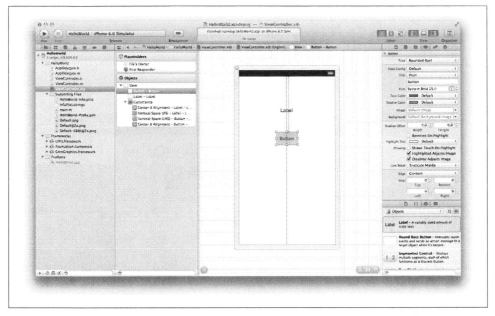

Figure 3-9. Adding user interface elements to our view

In Figure 3-9 you can see some blue vertical lines, these are (some of) the constraints dictating how our user interface will be displayed on different shaped screens.

Connecting the User Interface to the Code

At this point, we need to tell our code about the user interface elements we added to the view. In the Xcode toolbar, change the Editor type from Standard to Assistant (see Figure 3-10). If you're short of screen space, for instance, if you're working on a laptop as I am, you might want to shrink the dock and hide the Utilities panel at the same time to give yourself some extra room to work.

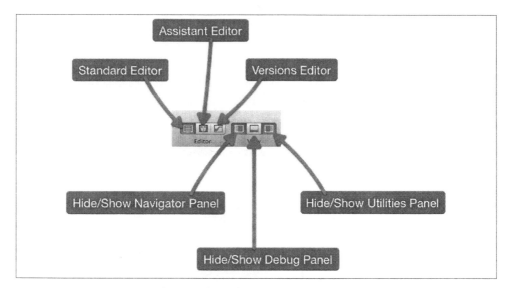

Figure 3-10. Buttons to change the Editor type and hide/show panels in the Xcode toolbar

You'll see that changing from the Standard to the Assistant Editor brings up the interface file that corresponds to the nib file we're modifying inside Interface Builder (see Figure 3-11).

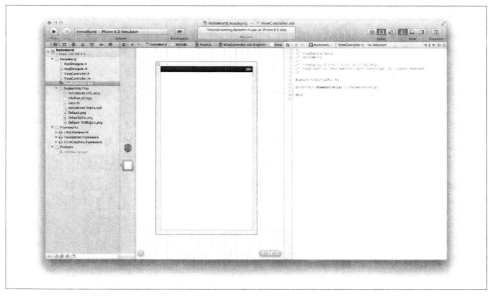

Figure 3-11. The Assistant Editor in Interface Builder

Now Control-click and drag from the label element you dropped into your view, or from the icon representing the label in the dock, to the header file (between the @interface and @end markers). A pop-up window will appear to create an outlet. Name your outlet "label" and click on the Connect button (see Figure 3-12).

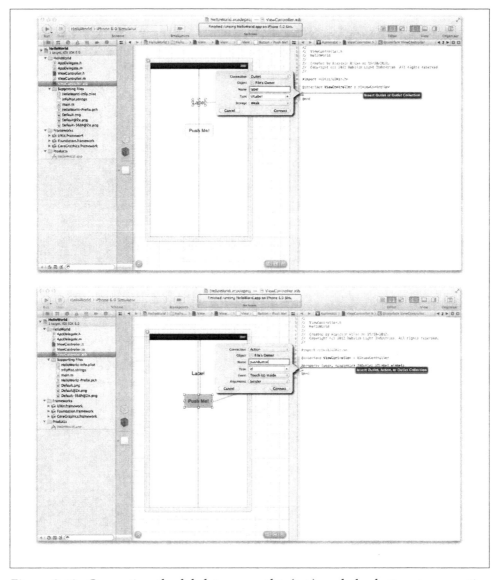

Figure 3-12. Connecting the label to an outlet (top) and the button to an action (bottom)

Afterward, Control-click and drag from the button to your code. This time, change the connection type from Outlet to Action before naming your action **pushButton**. This will not only both define and create a method called pushButton: in your View Controller object, but also connect the button element in Interface Builder to your code. The pushButton: method will be called when the "Touch Up Inside" event (which corresponds to a user tapping on and then releasing the button) is triggered in the interface. We'll use this to change the text associated with the label and tell the world "Hello!".

After making these connections, your *ViewController.h* interface code should look something like this (with the changes highlighted for clarity):

```
#import <UIKit/UIKit.h>

@interface ViewController : UIViewController

@property (weak, nonatomic) IBOutlet UILabel *label;
- (IBAction)pushButton:(id)sender;

@end
```

For now, you should just follow along; we'll discuss the layout of Objective-C methods in the next chapter.

Debugging Using NSLog

If you have problems developing this application, or any of the other applications we talk about in the rest of the book, you may want to make use of the NSLog function. You can use this function to print debugging statements to the Debug Console, which you can bring up by clicking on the appropriate button in the Xcode toolbar (see Figure 3-10).

Here's how an NSLog is used in your code:

```
NSLog( @"Prints this string to the console." );
```

The NSLog function understands the conventions used by the standard C library printf function, including %f for floats and %d for integers, but in addition uses %@ for objects:

```
NSLog( @"Prints the UILabel object %@ to the console.", label);
```

This works by asking the object to describe itself and produces sensible output for many standard objects. This is done by calling the description: method in the object, which returns a string describing the receiving class. The default implementation gives the name of the class, although many objects override this implementation. For example, with the NSArray object, it prints out a list of values.

If you click on the *ViewController.m* file, you'll see that in addition to adding code to the interface file, Interface Builder has modified our implementation. The changes it made are highlighted:

```
#import "ViewController.h"

@interface ViewController ()

@end

@implementation ViewController

- (void)viewDidLoad {
    [super viewDidLoad];
        // Do any additional setup after loading the view, typically from a nib.
}

- (void)didReceiveMemoryWarning {
    [super didReceiveMemoryWarning];
    // Dispose of any resources that can be recreated.
}

- (IBAction)pushButton:(id)sender {

}

@end
```

Interface Builder has automatically synthesized our `label` property for us, which will in turn automatically generate accessor methods. Additionally, it has added a `pushBut ton:` method to the code; this is the hook we're going to use to change the text of the label.

If you look at the documentation for the `UILabel` class, you'll see that all you need to do is to set the `text` property to change the text displayed by the label:

```
- (IBAction)pushButton:(id)sender {
    self.label.text = @"Hello World!";
}
```

Here `@"Hello World"` is a constant `NSString` object.

Running the Application in the Simulator

We're done! Make sure the Scheme in Xcode's toolbar is set to HelloWorld→iPhone 6.0 Simulator, and click on the Run button. If all goes well, this will start iPhone Simulator and run the code. If there are any issues, the build will fail and you'll see something like Figure 3-13. Xcode will list the problems in the Navigation panel on the left and automatically jump to the first issue in the Editor window. Here, for instance, I've

"accidentally typed" self.label.foo rather than self.label.text in the pushBut
ton: method.

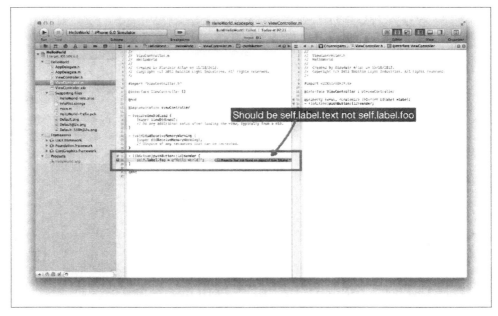

Figure 3-13. Problems building the application

However, if all goes well, the application should start in the iPhone Simulator, and you
should see something more like Figure 3-14.

Congratulations, you've written your first iPhone application. Once you're done, click
on the Stop button in the Xcode toolbar to stop the application running. Now let's get
it to work on your iPhone and iPod touch.

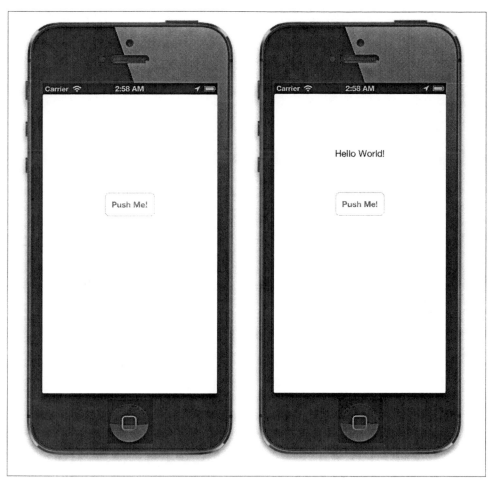

Figure 3-14. Our Hello World application running in the iPhone Simulator at startup (left) and after pushing the button (right)

Putting the Application on Your iPhone

Plug your phone into your Mac. After all the work we did in the previous chapter, Xcode should recognize it. Go ahead and change the Scheme from targeting the simulator to targeting your device (see Figure 3-15). As you can see from the figure, in my case, I'm using an iPhone 5.

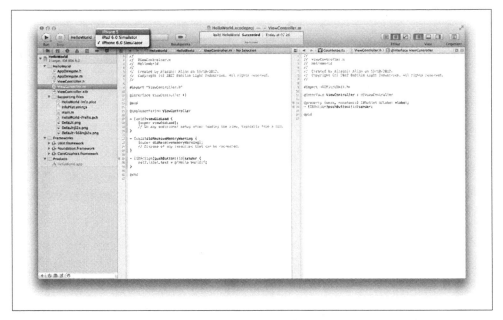

Figure 3-15. Changing the scheme in the Xcode toolbar

Click on the Run button in the Xcode toolbar. If all goes well, Xcode should build and deploy onto your iPhone automatically at this stage. You can monitor this process using the Organizer window. When you're done with the application, remember to click the Stop button in the Xcode toolbar.

Congratulations, you've written and deployed your first iPhone application.

 If there is a problem, make sure you have completed all the steps needed to use your iPhone or iPod touch for development that we talked about in the preceding chapter, and make sure your device is plugged in and Xcode is aware of it by opening the Organizer window. You should see a green light next to the name of your device in the lefthand pane.

CHAPTER 4

Coding in Objective-C

Thus far, you've built a simple iPhone application and discovered that it's not that hard to build apps for iOS. Let's step back and take a broader look at the Objective-C language.

Objective-C is an object-oriented language that adds Smalltalk-style messaging to C. The language is a superset of the C language, providing constructs to allow you to define classes and objects. Once you get the hang of the Smalltalk-style syntax, if you've programmed in an object-oriented language before, things should look fairly familiar. However, there are some differences, and I discuss them in this chapter. One of the bigger differences, especially for those who are coming from a Java background, is in how Objective-C deals with memory management, although this has been massively simplified with the arrival of iOS 5.

Declaring and Defining Classes

As is the case in almost all other object-oriented languages, in Objective-C, classes provide the building blocks to allow encapsulation of data and methods that act on that data. Objects are specific instances of a class, and they contain their own instance data and pointers to the methods implemented by the class. Classes are specified in two pieces: the *interface* and the *implementation*. The interface contains the declaration of the class and is normally contained in a *.h* file. The implementation contains your actual code (the definition) and is normally contained in a *.m* file. We briefly discussed this in Chapter 3, but let's take some time to look at it in more detail here.

Declaring a Class with the Interface

Let's return to the declaration of the ViewController class from Chapter 3, which illustrates a typical class interface. The interface begins with the @interface keyword, followed by the name of the class being declared, and ending with a colon followed by the name of the base (or parent) class:

```
@interface ViewController : UIViewController
```

An Objective-C class cannot inherit from multiple classes; however, the class it inherits from may in turn inherit from another class. In the case of ViewController, its base class is UIViewController, which itself inherits from UIResponder, which inherits from NSObject, the root class of most Objective-C class hierarchies.

Objective-C allows objects to descend from any root class. Although NSObject is the most common root class, it is not the only one. For instance, NSProxy is also a root class. So, you cannot always assume that a given class is derived from NSObject.

After that first line, the instance variable declarations appear within curly braces, although in the case of the view controller class, we do not declare any and can omit the curly braces. Following that, we have the declaration of properties and methods associated with the class. The class declaration is wrapped up with the @end keyword:

```
#import <UIKit/UIKit.h> ❶

@interface ViewController : UIViewController
@property (weak, nonatomic) IBOutlet UILabel *label;

- (IBAction)pushButton:(id)sender;

@end
```

❶   The #import statement is not technically part of the class declaration. Instead, this is a C preprocessor directive that avoids multiple inclusions of the same header file and is effectively equivalent to the C preprocessor directive #include <UIKit/UIKit.h>.

Dynamically creating instance variables using properties is a feature of Objective-C 2.0, and not a result of preprocessing magic done on your behalf by Xcode.

In this class, we are relying on the instance variables for the properties to be automatically created when they are synthesized inside the implementation of the class. Dynamically creating the instance variables in this manner works on both the modern runtimes (Intel 64-bit and ARM) you are likely to encounter but not on older platforms.

Before the release of iOS 4, the iPhone Simulator was an Intel 32-bit application, and the dynamic addition of properties at runtime was not possible. This is no longer the case.

If instead we wished to manually create the instance variables, we would do as below:

```
#import <UIKit/UIKit.h>

@interface ViewController : UIViewController {
    UILabel *label;
}

@property (weak, nonatomic) IBOutlet UILabel *label;
- (IBAction)pushButton:(id)sender;

@end
```

…which is entirely interchangeable with the initial code.

Defining a Class with the Implementation

The ViewController implementation from Chapter 3 begins by importing the class interface in the .h file. The implementation begins with the @implementation declaration and ends with the @end declaration:

```
@implementation ViewController

    ...

@end
```

We must ensure that all declared properties have the accessor (getter and setter) methods declared as part of the implementation. In most cases this is done for us by the compiler, vastly reducing the amount of code we need to write ourselves.

Now that you've taken a quick look at the structure of an interface and implementation, let's take a detailed look at the individual parts.

Object Typing

When instance variables are themselves objects—for instance, when the View Controller class declares a UILabel variable—you should always use a pointer type. However, Objective-C adds an interesting twist: it supports both strongly typed and weakly typed declarations. Here's a strongly typed declaration:

```
UILabel *label;
```

Here we declare `anObject`. In the first instance, we use strong typing, declaring it as an object of the class `SomeClass`.

Here's a weakly typed version of the declaration, where it is declared as an object of class `id`:

```
id label;
```

The `id` class is a generic C type that Objective-C uses to represent an arbitrary object; it's a general type representing any type of object regardless of class and can be used as a placeholder for both a class and a reference to an object instance. All objects therefore are of type `id`. This can prove very useful; you can imagine that if you wanted to build a generic class implementing a linked list, the type of object held in each node would be of type `id`, since you'd then be able to store any type of object.

Properties

The declaration of properties using the `@property` compiler directive is a convenience to avoid the declaration and, usually, the implementation of accessor methods for member variables. You can think of a property declaration as the equivalent of declaring accessor methods. You can also dictate how the automatically generated accessor methods behave by declaring custom attributes [see the sidebar "Declaring Custom Attributes for Properties" (page 56)]. In the `ViewController` class, we declare the property to be (`weak, nonatomic`):

```
@property (weak, nonatomic) IBOutlet UILabel *label;
```

We can also declare the property to be an `IBOutlet`. While not formally part of the list of attributes for an `@property` declaration, `IBOutlet` denotes that this property is an Interface Builder outlet. I talked about outlets briefly in Chapter 3 and will discuss them in more detail later.

Declaring Custom Attributes for Properties

Accessor methods

By default, the automatically generated accessor methods created when you `@syn thesize` a property are `propertyName:` and `setPropertyName:`. You can change this by using the `getter=getterName` and `setter=setterName` custom attributes. Bear in mind that changing the default names will invariably break the *dot syntax* syntactic sugar [see "The Dot Syntax" (page 58)] that Objective-C normally provides.

Writability

You can choose whether the property has an associated setter accessor method by specifying the `readonly` custom attribute. If this is set, only a getter method is generated when you `@synthesize` the property in your implementation.

Setter semantics

The assign, retain, copy, weak, and strong custom attributes govern the setter accessor method and are mutually exclusive. The assign attribute is the default and implies that the generated setter uses simple assignment. The retain attribute specifies that a retain should be invoked on the object when it is assigned, and the previous value should be sent a release message. See "Memory Management" (page 60) for the implications of this constraint. The copy attribute implies that a copy of the object should be used when the object is assigned, rather than a straight assignment. This attribute is valid only for objects that implement the NSCopying protocol.

The weak attribute specifies there is a weak (nonowning) relationship to the object. If the object is deallocated, the property value is automatically set to be nil. Typically a child object should not own its parent, so we would use a weak reference in that case.

Conversely, the strong attribute indicates an owning relationship—the class instance takes ownership of the referenced object and it will not be deallocated until the owner is likewise deallocated in turn.

Atomicity

The nonatomic custom attribute specifies that the accessor method is nonatomic. Properties are atomic by default so that the accessor methods are robust in multi-threaded environments. Note that while the accessor is robust, it is not necessarily thread-safe. Specifying nonatomic implies that the accessor is conversely not robust in such environments, and that the generated accessor method returns the object directly. However, it does result in considerably faster code and is generally recommended for iPhone applications.

Synthesizing Properties

When you declare an @property in the class interface the property will usually be automatically synthesized by the compiler. This means the accessor methods, along with an underlying instance variable, are automatically generated. However this isn't always the case and we may sometimes have to manually use the @synthesize directive to do this task.

You'll know you need to do this because your code will fail to build with an error that may look something like,

```
Property 'foo' requires method 'foo' to be defined - use @synthesize,
@dynamic or provide a method implementation in this class implementation
```

However in most cases, at least since the release of Xcode 4.5, you no longer have to worry about this sort of detail.

If you must manually synthesize the property, you do so using the `@synthesize` declaration, which should directly follow the `@implementation` declaration, e.g.

```
@synthesize label;
```

This asks the compiler to generate the accessor methods according to the specification in the property declaration. You can use the form:

```
@synthesize label = _label;
```

to indicate that a particular instance variable (in this case `_label`) should be used for the property. This is a useful form to ensure that the values of the property are always accessed using the generated accessor methods and not directly via the instance variable backing the property, which can lead to problems.

 You may want to implement the getter and setter methods yourself, and forego using the automatically generated versions. You can go right ahead and do that. If you implement these methods they'll replace the automatically generated versions.

The Dot Syntax

When you declare a member variable as a property and synthesize the declared accessors using the `@synthesize` declaration in the `@implementation` of the class, you can (entirely optionally) make use of some syntactic sugar that Objective-C provides, called the *dot syntax*, as an alternative to using the automatically generated accessor methods directly. For instance, this lets us do the following:

```
label.text = @"Hello World";
```

instead of doing this (note that Objective-C capitalized the *t* in *text* when it generated the accessor method):

```
[label setText:@"Hello World"];
```

The dot syntax is arguably somewhat neater and easier to read.

Declaring Methods

We declare one method in the `HelloWorldViewController` class, called `pushButton`:

```
#import <UIKit/UIKit.h>

@interface ViewController : UIViewController

@property (weak, nonatomic) IBOutlet UILabel *label;
- (IBAction)pushButton:(id)sender;

@end
```

The minus sign in front of the method indicates the method type, in this case an instance method. A plus sign would indicate a class method. For example:

```
+(void)aMethod:(id) anObject;
```

The `pushButton:` method takes an `id` object as an argument and is flagged as an `IBAction` for Interface Builder. When compiled, `IBAction` is replaced with `void` and `IBOutlet` is removed; these compiler directives are simply used to flag methods and variables to Interface Builder. This method is passed a generic `id` object as an argument since we intended it to be triggered by a UI event, and we want to leave it open as to what sort of UI element will be used. Under the UI, it's triggered when the user clicks the Push me! button in the UI, and this `id` object will be the `UIButton` that the user clicked to trigger the event. We can recover the `UIButton` object by casting the `sender` object to a `UIButton`:

```
UIButton * theButton = (UIButton *)sender;
```

It's a standard practice in Objective-C to call such objects `sender`. If we were unsure of the underlying type of an `id` object, we could check the type using the `isKindOfClass` method:

```
if([thisObject isKindOfClass:[anotherObject class]]) { ... }
```

Calling Methods

If you want to call a method exposed by an object, you do so by sending that object a message. The message consists of the method signature, along with the parameter information. Messages are enclosed in square brackets; the object receiving the message is on the left and the parameters are on the right, with each parameter following a colon. If the method accepts more than one argument, this is explicitly named, and the second parameter follows a second colon. This allows multiple methods with the same name and argument types to be defined:

```
[anObject someMethod];
[anObject someMethod: anotherObject];
[anObject someMethod: anotherObject withAnotherArgument: yetAnotherObject];
```

The name of the method is the concatenation of the method name and any additional named arguments. Hence in the preceding code we have `someMethod:` and `someMethod: withAnotherArgument:`. This may seem odd to people coming in from other languages, which usually have much terser naming conventions, but in general, Objective-C method names are substantially more self-documenting than in other languages. Method names contain prepositions and are made to read like sentences. The language also has a fairly entrenched naming convention, which means that method names are fairly regular.

While Objective-C method names are long, Xcode will perform code completion as you type. A pop-up list of suggested methods will appear automatically. You can select a method using the up and down arrow keys, pressing Return to accept a suggestion. Pressing Control-/ will step you through the parameters of the method.

Methods can return output, as shown here:

```
output = [anObject someMethodWithOutput: anotherObject];
```

And they can be nested, as in the following:

```
output = [anObject someMethodWithOutput: [anotherObject someOtherMethod]];
```

When I originally started writing in Objective-C, one of the main problems I had with the language was the way it dealt with method calls. For those of us who are coming from more utilitarian languages, the behavior of Objective-C in this regard does seem rather strange. Although Objective-C code can be valid and not follow the rules I've described here, modern Objective-C is not really separable from the Cocoa framework, and Cocoa rules and conventions have become Objective-C's rules and conventions.

Calling Methods on nil

In Objective-C, the nil object is functionally equivalent to the NULL pointer found in many other C-derived languages. However, unlike most of these languages, it is permissible to call methods on nil without causing your application to crash. If you call a method on (although, in Objective-C we are actually passing a message to) the nil object type, you will get nil returned.

Memory Management

The way memory is managed in Objective-C on the iPhone and the iPad is probably not what you're used to if you're coming in from a language such as Java, Perl, Ruby, or even JavaScript. If you're writing an application in Objective-C for the Mac, you have the option of enabling garbage collection; however, on the iPhone and iPad, you are restricted to using reference counting. This isn't as bad as it seems, especially with the arrival of Automatic Reference Counting (ARC), which we will talk about a little later on in the chapter.

Reference counting is a memory management technique where a running count of the number of references to a particular object is kept and used to deallocate the memory when the count reaches zero. See the section "The alloc, retain, copy, and release Cycle" (page 62) later in the chapter.

Creating Objects

You can create an object in two ways. As shown in the following code, you can manually allocate the memory for the object with `alloc` and initialize it using `init` or an appropriate `initWith` method (e.g., `NSString` has an `initWithString` method):

```
NSString *string = [[NSString alloc] init];
NSString *string = [[NSString alloc] initWithString:@"This is a string"];
```

Alternatively, you can use a convenience constructor method. For instance, the `NSString` class has a `stringWithString` class method that returns an `NSString` object:

```
NSString *string = [NSString stringWithString:@"This is a string"];
```

In the preceding two cases, you are responsible for releasing the memory you allocated with `alloc`. If you create an object with `alloc`, you need to `release` it later. However, in the second case, the object will be *autoreleased*. You should never manually release an autoreleased object, as this will cause your application to crash. An autoreleased object will, in most cases, be released at the end of the current function unless it has been explicitly retained.

The Autorelease Pool

The autorelease pool is a convenience that defers sending an explicit `release` message to an object until "later," with the responsibility of freeing the memory allocated to objects added to an autorelease pool devolved onto the Cocoa framework. All iOS applications require a default autorelease pool, and the Xcode template inside the *main.m* file creates it for us:

```
int main(int argc, char *argv[]) {
    @autoreleasepool {
        return UIApplicationMain(argc, argv, nil,
                        NSStringFromClass([AppDelegate class]));
    }
}
```

Here, the call to the `UIApplicationMain` routine is held within the autorelease block, with the default autorelease pool set up prior to entering the main event loop, and then drained after exiting the loop.

An additional inner autorelease pool is created at the beginning of each event cycle (i.e., iteration through your application's event loop) and is released at the end.

The need for and existence of autorelease makes more sense once you appreciate why it was invented, which is to transfer control of the object life cycle from one owning object to another without immediately deallocating the object.

The alloc, retain, copy, and release Cycle

Although the autorelease pool is handy, you should be careful when using it, because you unnecessarily extend the time over which the object is instantiated, thereby increasing your application's memory footprint. Sometimes it makes sense to use autoreleased objects. However, beginning Cocoa programmers often overuse convenience constructors and autoreleased objects.

 Apple, writing in its Cocoa Fundamentals guide, officially discourages the use of autorelease objects on the iOS due to the memory-constrained environment on the device, stating that "Because on iOS an application executes in a more memory-constrained environment, the use of autorelease pools is discouraged in methods or blocks of code (for example, loops) where an application creates many objects. Instead, you should explicitly release objects whenever possible."

When handling memory management manually using the retain count and the `alloc`, `retain`, and `release` cycle (see Figure 4-1), you should not release objects you do not own. You should always make sure your calls to `retain` are balanced by your calls to `release`. You own objects that you have explicitly created using `alloc` or `copy`, or that you have added to the retain count of the object using `retain`. However, you do not own objects you have created using convenience constructors such as `stringWith String`.

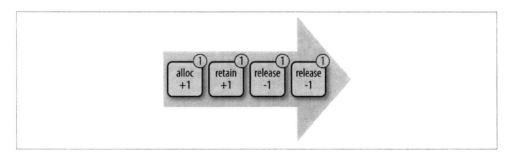

Figure 4-1. The alloc-retain-release cycle; an object is allocated, retained, and then released twice, bringing the reference count back to zero and freeing the memory

When releasing the object, you have the option of sending it either a release message or an autorelease message:

```
[anObject release];
[anObject autorelease];
```

Sending a release message will immediately free the memory the object uses if that release takes the object's retain count to zero, while sending an autorelease message adds the object to the local autorelease pool. The object will be released when the pool is destroyed, normally at the end of the current function.

If your object is a delegate of another object, you need to set the delegate property of that object to nil before you release your original object.

Automatic Reference Counting

While it's vital to understand how the underlying memory management works if you're going to be building applications in Objective-C, the arrival of Automatic Reference Counting with the release of iOS 5 has simplified memory management on the iOS platform a great deal.

Instead of you having to remember when to use retain, release, and autorelease, ARC evaluates the requirements of your objects and automatically inserts the appropriate method calls for you at compile time. The compiler also generates appropriate dealloc methods for you.

 As iOS 4 is supported as a target for ARC-based applications, non-ARC-based code is really only needed when targeting iOS 3.x. Additionally, Apple notes that, "ARC interoperates with manual reference counting code on a per-file basis. If you want to continue using manual reference counting for some files, you can do so." This is important when making use of legacy libraries that are not ARC ready in ARC-based code. We'll talk about this later in the book.

It's really important to realize that ARC is a precompilation step that adds retain, release, and autorelease statements to your code for you, and reference counting has not disappeared, it has simply been automated.

With ARC enabled in your project, the following code:

```
NSObject *anObject = [[NSObject alloc] init];

// ... code which calls methods on the object
```

will be transformed during a precompilation step into:

```
NSObject *anObject = [[NSObject alloc] init];

// ... code which calls methods on the object

[anObject release];
```

All of the projects we'll look at in this book use ARC-based templates.

The dealloc Method

The dealloc method is called when an object is released. You should never call this method directly, but instead send a release message to the object, because the object may contain references to other objects that will not be deallocated. Inside an application making use of ARC, there shouldn't be much reason to override the dealloc method, and of course ARC inserts the release messages for you automatically.

 Even though ARC releases instance variables automatically, there may still be legitimate reasons to override the dealloc method in your own classes. In such cases, and unlike other superclass methods that you may have overridden, you should never call the dealloc method in the superclass directly. ARC will add this for you.

Responding to Memory Warnings

Your code must respond to memory warnings. Let's look at the HelloWorldViewCon troller implementation from Chapter 3 again. It implements the didReceiveMemory Warning method:

```
- (void)didReceiveMemoryWarning {
    [super didReceiveMemoryWarning];
}
```

This is where you should release any large blocks of memory—for instance, image or web caches—that you are using. If you ignore a memory warning, your application may crash. Since iOS devices do not have any sort of virtual memory or swap file, when the device runs out of memory, there really is no more memory to allocate. It's possible, and advisable, to test your application by simulating a memory warning in iOS Simulator, which you can do by selecting Hardware→Simulate Memory.

Fundamental iOS Design Patterns

When you write code, you're probably already using patterns, although possibly you're doing so without realizing it. A design pattern is just a reusable solution, a template, for how to approach commonly occurring problems. A pattern is not code, but instead describes how you should model the application in terms of the classes that are used, and how they should structure the interactions and relationships between these classes.

The Cocoa Touch framework underlying your iOS applications is based on one of the oldest design patterns, the Model-View-Controller (MVC) pattern, which dates from the 1970s. The MVC pattern is used to separate the program logic from the UI, and is the generally accepted way to build iOS applications. As it is used so extensively inside Apple's own frameworks, including the UIKit framework, it would be quite hard to write an iOS application without using this pattern in your implementation. While you could write an iOS application without referencing the MVC pattern, it is enormously difficult to fight the underlying frameworks; you should instead work with them. Attempting to write iOS applications while ignoring the underlying MVC patterns is a pointless exercise in make-work.

The Model-View-Controller Pattern

The MVC pattern divides your application into three functional pieces:

Model
> The model manages the application state (and associated data) and is usually persistent. It is entirely decoupled from the UI or presentation of the application state to the user.

View
> The view is what the user sees, and it displays the model for the user. It allows the user to manipulate it and respond and generate events. In iOS applications, the view is normally built inside Interface Builder rather than programmatically.

Controller
> The controller coordinates updates of the view and the model when user interaction with the view makes changes to the model, and vice versa. This is typically where most of the application logic lives.

We implemented the Hello World application from Chapter 3 using this pattern. We created the view using Interface Builder, and the ViewController class managed the view. The application was too simple to require an explicit class to manage the application's state; effectively, the model was embedded in the ViewController class. If we were strictly adhering to the design pattern, we would have implemented a further class that the pushButton: method would have queried to ask what text should have been displayed.

The model class is usually a subclass of NSObject and has a set of instance variables and associated accessor methods, along with custom methods to associate the internal data model.

Views and View Controllers

I've talked about both views and view controllers quite a lot, and while so far we've built the views in Interface Builder and then handled them using the own view controller code, that isn't the only way to build a view. You can create views programmatically; in fact, in the early days of iOS development, you had to do things that way.

However, Interface Builder has made things a lot easier, and I recommend that in most cases you build your views using it if you can. When you used Interface Builder to construct your view, you edited a nib file, an XML serialization of the objects in the view. Using Interface Builder to create these objects, and to define the relationship between them and your own code, saves you from writing large amounts of boilerplate code that you would otherwise need to manage the view.

 Using Interface Builder and storyboards with iOS 5, it's now actually possible to build a moderately complicated application with little or no code at all. We're not going to cover Storyboarding in this book. While on the face of things, using Storyboards appears simpler than using nib files, you can quickly get into trouble. While Storyboards have a lot of potential, at least in my opinion, they aren't yet mature technology. At the time of writing, there are some severe issues that make the current implementation burdensome to use in practice.

If you want to create your view manually, you should override the `viewDidLoad:` method of your `ViewController` class, as this is the method the view controller calls when the `view` property is requested but is currently set to `nil`. Don't override this method if you've created your view using the `initWithNibName:` method, or set the `nibName` or `nibBundle` properties. If you're creating your view manually and you do override this method, however, you must assign the root view you create to the `view` property of your `ViewController` class:

```
-(void) viewDidLoad {
    UIView* view = [[UIView alloc] initWithFrame:CGRectMake(0,0,320,480)];
        .
        .
        .
    self.view = view;
    [view release];
}
```

Your implementation of this method should not call `[super viewDidLoad]`, as the default implementation of this method will create a plain `UIView` if no nib information is present and will make this the main view.

The Delegates and DataSource Pattern

I talked briefly about delegates in Chapter 3. An object that implements a delegate protocol is one that acts on behalf of another object. To receive notification of an event to which it must respond, the delegate class needs to implement the notification method declared as the delegate protocol associated with that event. The protocol may, and usually does, specify a number of methods that the delegate class must implement.

Data sources are similar to delegates, but instead of delegating control, if an object implements a `DataSource` protocol, it must implement one or more methods to supply data to requesting objects. The delegating object, typically something such as a `UITable View`, will ask the data source what data it should display; for instance, in the case of a table view, what should be displayed in the next `UITableViewCell` when it scrolls into the current view.

Declaring that a class is a data source or a delegate flags the object for Interface Builder so that you can connect the relevant UI elements to your code. (We'll be talking about `UITableView` in Chapter 5.) To declare that `AnObject` was *both* a table view data source and a delegate, we would note this in the `@interface` declaration:

```
@interface AnObject: UIViewController &lt;UITableViewDataSource,
                                       UITableViewDelegate&gt; {
   . . .
}
```

This would mean that the `AnObject` object, a `UIViewController`, is responsible for both populating the table view with data and responding to events the table view generates. Another way to say this is that this object implements both the `UITableViewData Source` and the `UITableViewDelegate` protocols.

At this point, you would use Interface Builder, and we'll be doing that in the next chapter when we build a table-view-based application to connect the `UITableView` in the view to the data source and delegate object in the code.

Conclusion

This has been a dense chapter and fairly heavy going. However, the discussion of the MVC pattern should show you that this delegation of event handling and of populating data into the UI from the view to a controller class makes sense inside the confines of the pattern, and the availability of these features in Objective-C is one of the reasons why the MVC pattern has been widely adopted.

In this chapter, I was able to give you only a brief overview of Objective-C and the Cocoa Touch framework. Added levels of subtlety are involved in many of the things I covered, but I didn't have the space to cover them here. My coverage of the basics should give you enough information so that you can pick up the rest as we go along. However, if you intend to develop for the iOS on a serious level, you should read up on the language in more detail. Apple provides some excellent tutorial material on its Developer website (*http://developer.apple.com/iphone/*), and that should certainly be your first port of call. However, I also suggest several other books for further reading in Chapter 14.

CHAPTER 5

Table View-Based Applications

The UITableView and associated classes are perhaps the most commonly used classes when building user interfaces for your iOS applications, especially for the iPhone and iPod touch. Due to the nature of the applications, you can use these classes to solve a large cross section of problems, and as a result, they appear almost everywhere. In this chapter, we're going to dive fairly deeply into the table view classes, and by the end of it, you'll be able to produce UITableView-based applications on your own. We'll also discuss some features of Xcode and Interface Builder as we go along.

We're going to write a simple guidebook application. We'll start by displaying a list of cities in a table (using the UITableView class). Then we'll add the ability to click on the city name inside each table cell (each cell is a UITableViewCell object), which will take you to a page describing the city. Later in the chapter, I'll show you how to add and delete cities to and from the guidebook. By the end of the chapter, we will have a working application.

Creating the Project

Open Xcode and select "Create a new Xcode project" in the startup window, choosing a Single View Application template from the template pop-up window—the same template we used for the Hello World application back in Chapter 3.

In the Product Name box, enter **CityGuide**, and then in the Company Identifier box enter the root part of your Bundle Identifier [as we did in Chapter 3; also see the section "Creating an App ID" (page 20) in Chapter 2 for more details]. For me, this is uk.co.ba bilim.

This time, we're going to make use of the class prefix, by entering **CG** in its respective box. The class prefix is prepended to all the class files. Objective-C doesn't have namespaces, so we prefix the class names with initials. This avoids namespace collision, where two pieces of code have the same name but do different things.

 Most core classes in the iOS SDK are prefixed with the letters *NS* for historical reasons, as the Cocoa Touch frameworks grew out of the NeXTStep/OpenStep API that came out of NeXT computing, the company Steve Jobs founded after he left Apple in 1985.

Ensure that Device Family is set to iPhone and that the checkbox for ARC is ticked, but the boxes for storyboard and unit tests are not ticked, as we don't require them for this project.

Once you've filled in the Configuration panel, click on the Next button to proceed. You should then be presented with another dialog to save your new project. You'll notice that Xcode will by default create a local Git repository for your project if you want it to; let's ignore that option for now. Untick the box. Click Create to create and save your first Xcode project.

Creating a Table View

Let's begin by building a simple table view. Click on the *CGViewController.xib* file in Xcode to open it in Interface Builder. Go to the Object Library and click and drag a table view (UITableView) onto your view and drop it in place; it should automatically resize to fill the view, as shown in Figure 5-1.

At this point, we need to tell the code about the user interface elements we added to the view. In the Xcode toolbar, change the Editor type from Standard to Assistant (the middle of the three buttons in the Editor group in the toolbar). Changing from the Standard to the Assistant Editor brings up the interface file that corresponds to the nib file we're modifying inside Interface Builder; see Figure 5-2.

If you're short of screen space, you might want to hide the Utilities panel at the same time to give yourself some extra room to work (using the right-most button in the View group of buttons in the toolbar).

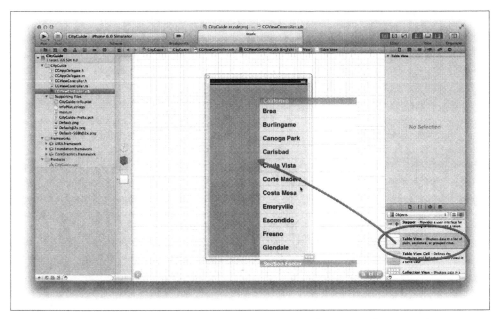

Figure 5-1. Dragging a UITableView from the Object Library window into the view

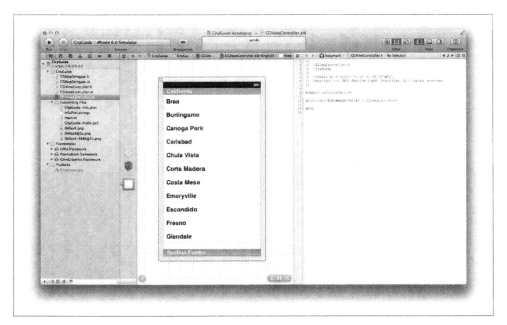

Figure 5-2. The Assistant Editor in Interface Builder

Now Control-click and drag from the table view you dropped into your view, to the header file (between the @interface and @end markers). A pop-up window will appear to create an outlet; name the outlet **tableView** and click on the Connect button (see Figure 5-3).

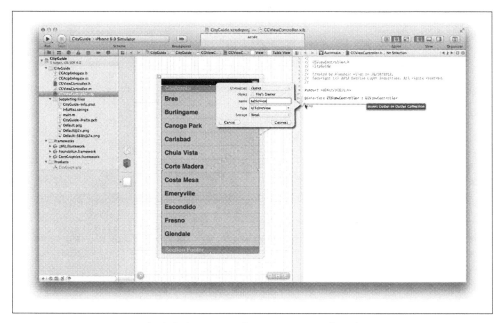

Figure 5-3. Connecting the label to an outlet in your interface file

Next, right-click and drag from the UITableView in the central View panel to the icon representing File's Owner (the top icon in the dock that looks like a transparent cube) and release the mouse button. A small, black pop-up window will appear, as shown in Figure 5-4.

Click on **dataSource** to connect the table view to the File's Owner (the CGViewControl ler class) as its data source. Right-click and drag again, this time clicking on **dele gate** in the pop-up window to make the File's Owner class the table view's delegate class.

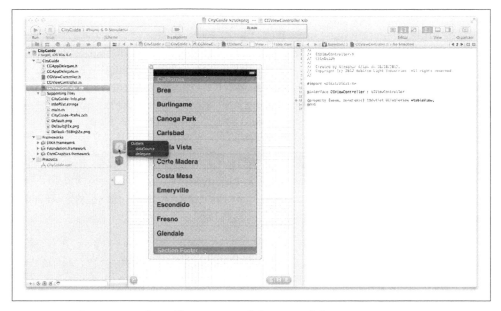

Figure 5-4. Connecting the table view as a delegate and data source

In the Assistant Editor, modify the corresponding interface file to reflect these connections and declare that the class implements both the UITableViewDataSource and the UITableViewDelegate protocols.

Once you've done this, the *CGViewController.h* file should look like this:

```
#import <UIKit/UIKit.h>

@interface CGViewController : UIViewController <UITableViewDataSource,
                                                UITableViewDelegate>

@property (weak, nonatomic) IBOutlet UITableView *tableView;

@end
```

What we've done here is indicate that the CGViewController class both provides the data to populate the table view and handles events generated by user interaction with the table view.

If you Option-double-click UITableViewDataSource in the declaration and then click the Documentation icon in the upper-right corner of the window that appears (or ⌘-Option-double-click to go directly there), you'll see that the protocol has a number of optional methods, as well as two mandatory methods (you must implement the methods that aren't labeled as "optional").

Having declared that the view controller is a UITableViewDataSource, the CGViewCon troller implementation must implement these two mandatory methods. These methods are tableView:cellForRowAtIndexPath: and tableView:numberOfRowsInSec tion:. The first of these methods returns a UITableViewCell object; the table view will ask the data source for a cell each time a new cell is displayed in the view. The second method returns an NSInteger determining how many sections are in the table view. Table views can be divided into sections, and a title is added to the top of each section. For now, we'll use just one section (the default).

Despite what the documentation for UITableViewDelegate seems to suggest, there aren't any mandatory methods. However, to obtain any sort of functionality from the table view, we will at least have to implement the tableView:didSelectRowAtIndex Path: method.

Now we must add the implementation of those two mandatory data source methods to the CGViewController class (*CGViewController.m*). Once we have the code up and running, we'll look at the tableView:cellForRowAtIndexPath: method in detail. This method returns a populated table view cell for each entry (index) in the table, and it's called each time the view controller wants to display a table view cell. For example, it's called as the table view is scrolled and a new cell appears in the view.

Change back to the Standard Editor, click on the *CGViewController.m* file, and add the delegate and datasource methods to the code.

Here are the contents of *CGViewController.m*. I marked in bold the lines I added to the file that was generated by the Xcode template:

```
#import "CGViewController.h"

@interface CGViewController ()

@end

@implementation CGViewController

- (void)viewDidLoad {
    [super viewDidLoad];
}

- (void)didReceiveMemoryWarning {
    [super didReceiveMemoryWarning];

}

#pragma mark UITableViewDataSource Methods

- (UITableViewCell *)tableView:(UITableView *)tv
    cellForRowAtIndexPath:(NSIndexPath *)indexPath {
    UITableViewCell *cell = [tv dequeueReusableCellWithIdentifier:@"cell"];
```

```
        if( nil == cell ) {
            cell = [[UITableViewCell alloc] initWithStyle:UITableViewCellStyleDefault
                                    reuseIdentifier:@"cell"];
        }
        return cell;
    }

    - (NSInteger)tableView:
        (UITableView *)tv numberOfRowsInSection:(NSInteger)section {
                                        return 3;
    }

    #pragma mark UITableViewDelegate Methods

    @end
```

I've implemented only the required bare bones of the UITableViewDataSource protocol, and not any of the delegate methods.

Organizing and Navigating Your Source Code

I introduced something new in the preceding code listing: the #pragma mark declaration. If you examine the bar along the top of the Xcode Editor, you'll see that it contains a breadcrumb trail consisting of the project, followed by the group, then the filename, and immediately to the right of that, the name of the method that you are currently editing. If you click on this, you'll see a drop-down menu showing all the method names in the implementation.

You'll also see the text of the pragma marks I added to the code. For large classes, this is a convenient way to separate the methods involved in different jobs. In this case, I've added marks for the instance, data source, and delegate methods. You can also add a horizontal bar to the method list like this:

```
    #pragma mark -
```

Do not add a space after the -, as this will make Xcode think this is a text comment.

Running the Code

We've reached a natural point at which to take a break. The code should now run without crashing, although it's not going to do very much. So click on the Run button to build and deploy the application into the iPhone Simulator. You should see something along the lines of Figure 5-5.

Figure 5-5. The empty table view inside iPhone Simulator

Remember to click on the Stop button to stop the application running in the iPhone Simulator when you're done.

Populating the Table View

Now that we have the basic table view code working, let's go back to the CGViewController implementation (in *CGViewController.m*) and look at that tableView:cellForRowAtIndexPath: method where we were creating and then returning table view cells. For performance reasons, the UITableView can reuse cells to enhance scroll performance by minimizing the need to allocate memory during scrolling. However, to take advantage of this ability, we need to specify a *reuse identifier string*. The UITableView uses this to look up existing cells with the same identifier using the dequeueReusableCellWithIdentifier: method. If it can't find an unused cell with the correct identifier, it will create one, but if an unused cell is available (perhaps it's scrolled out of the current view), it will reuse it:

```
- (UITableViewCell *)tableView:(UITableView *)tv
        cellForRowAtIndexPath:(NSIndexPath *)indexPath {
    UITableViewCell *cell = [tv dequeueReusableCellWithIdentifier:@"cell"];
    if( nil == cell ) {
        cell = [[UITableViewCell alloc]
                    initWithStyle:UITableViewCellStyleDefault
                    reuseIdentifier:@"cell"];
    }
    return cell;
}
```

So far, the table view isn't that interesting, so let's push forward and add some content and some event handling. To do this, add an implementation for the tableView:didSelectRowAtIndexPath: delegate method to *CGViewController.m*. As the name suggests, this method is called when a user clicks on a table view cell. Because the cells are empty at the moment, we'll also add some text to a cell before returning it from this method. Added lines of code are shown in bold:

```
#pragma mark UITableViewDataSource Methods

- (UITableViewCell *)tableView:(UITableView *)tv
        cellForRowAtIndexPath:(NSIndexPath *)indexPath {
    UITableViewCell *cell = [tv dequeueReusableCellWithIdentifier:@"cell"];
    if( nil == cell ) {
        cell = [[UITableViewCell alloc]
                    initWithStyle:UITableViewCellStyleDefault
                    reuseIdentifier:@"cell"];
    }
    cell.textLabel.text = @"Testing";❶
    return cell;
}

- (NSInteger)tableView:(UITableView *)tv numberOfRowsInSection:
    (NSInteger)section {
    return 3;
}
```

```
#pragma mark UITableViewDelegate Methods

- (void)tableView:(UITableView *)tv
                  didSelectRowAtIndexPath:(NSIndexPath *)indexPath {❷
    [tv deselectRowAtIndexPath:indexPath animated:YES];❸
}
```

❶   This is where we added text to the cell we're returning from the `tableView:cell`
     `ForRowAtIndexPath:` method.

❷   Here's where we implemented the `tableView:didSelectRowAtIndexPath:`
     delegate method.

❸   Here we just told the table view to deselect the cell every time the user touches it
     and selects it. Because the `animated` argument is set to `YES`, the cell fades out as
     it deselects itself. Previously, if you touched the cell, it would have stayed
     permanently selected.

You can see the results of these additions in Figure 5-6.

Figure 5-6. The new code running inside iPhone Simulator

Building a Model

At this point, you should have a working UITableView. So far, you've implemented both the view and the controller parts of the MVC pattern. Now we're going to return to Xcode and implement the model. This needs to be separate from the view and the view controller, since we want to decouple the way the data is stored from the way it is displayed as much as possible. This will increase the reusability of both the classes that handle the user interface and the classes that store the data behind the scenes, allowing us to change how parts of the application work while affecting as little code as possible.

Right-click on the CityGuide group in the Project navigator, and select New File from the menu. A drop-down window will then appear, allowing you to select a template for the new file you want to add to the project (see Figure 5-7).

Figure 5-7. The New File template chooser that allows you to select the template Xcode will use to generate the new class interface and implementation file

Select "Objective-C class" if it is not already selected by default, and click on Next. You will be prompted for the name of the class; you should enter **City** when prompted, as this class will be holding the model describing a city in the guide (see Figure 5-8). Ensure that the class is a subclass of NSObject (rather than UIViewController which is the default option presented by Xcode) in the drop-down, and click on Next.

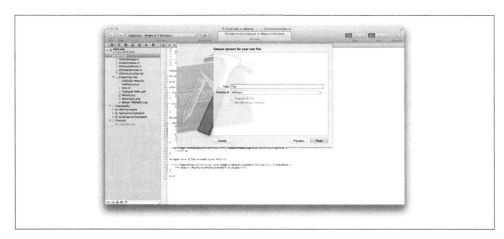

Figure 5-8. Naming the new class

You'll then be presented with something that looks a lot like Figure 5-9, prompting you to save the file onto disk. You can optionally change where the file is created on disk inside the project, but for now you should probably just accept the defaults. Click on the Create button.

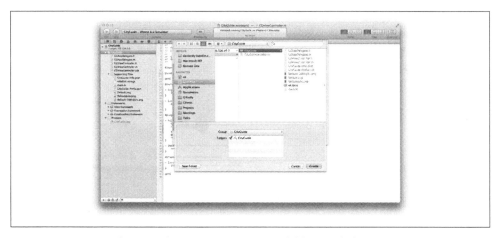

Figure 5-9. Saving the new class into your Project folder on disk

Xcode will generate a pair of files, *City.h* and *City.m*, containing the template interface and the implementation of the new class, and will put them in the CityGuide group in the Project navigator. If you look at these files, you can see that since you specified that the class was a subclass of the base NSObject class, Xcode really hasn't created a lot of code. It didn't know what you wanted the object for, so you'll have to write the code yourself.

Open the *City.h* file and add variables to hold the name of the city, a short descriptive paragraph, and an image. Declare these variables as properties.

```
#import <Foundation/Foundation.h>

@interface City : NSObject {

}

@property (nonatomic, strong) NSString *cityName;
@property (nonatomic, strong) NSString *cityDescription;
@property (nonatomic, strong) UIImage *cityPicture;

@end
```

I'm declaring the name and description as an NSString, and I'm declaring the variable used to hold the picture as a UIImage. UIImage is a fairly high-level class that can be directly displayed in a UIImageView that we can create inside Interface Builder.

 I could have decided to use an NSMutableString rather than an NSString. An NSMutableString is a subclass of NSString that manages a *mutable string*, which is a string whose contents can be edited. Conversely, an NSString object manages an *immutable string*, which, once created, cannot be changed and can only be replaced. Using mutable strings here might give us a bit more flexibility later on, and if you decide you need it, you can always go back and change these definitions to mutable strings later. Changing from using an NSString to an NSMutableString is easy since mutable strings are a subclass and implement all of the methods provided by the NSString class. Going in the opposite direction is more difficult, unless you have not made use of the additional functionality offered by the mutable string class.

Because we're making use of properties, the accessor methods will be generated for us automatically. So, we're actually done now. Admittedly, this is just a fairly small class to hold some data, but it illustrates how useful properties will be for larger, more complex classes.

Use the keyboard shortcut ⌘-S to save your changes, and return to the *City.h* interface file, where you should see that the warning triangles have disappeared.

Adding Cities to the Guide

Let's go into the CGAppDelegate class and prepopulate it with a few cities. After doing so, the *CGAppDelegate.h* file should look very much like the code below (added lines are shown in bold):

```
#import <UIKit/UIKit.h>

@class CGViewController; ❶

@interface CityGuideDelegate : NSObject <UIApplicationDelegate>

@property (strong, nonatomic) UIWindow *window;
@property (strong, nonatomic) CGViewController *viewController;
@property (strong, nonatomic) NSMutableArray *cities;

@end
```

❶   You should #import the header files for any classes you're using in the implementation. But if you need to reference a class in your header file, you should use the @class forward declaration instead of importing the class header file. Apple says in its documentation that the @class directive "minimizes the amount of code seen by the compiler and linker, and is therefore the simplest way to give a forward declaration of a class name. Being simple, it avoids potential problems that may come with importing files that import still other files."

Here in the application delegate interface file, we are simply creating an NSMutable Array to hold the list of cities, and declaring this mutable array to be a property.

The changes to the application delegate implementation are slightly more extensive:

```
#import "CGAppDelegate.h"
#import "CGViewController.h"
#import "City.h" ❶

@implementation CGAppDelegate

- (BOOL)application:(UIApplication *)application
          didFinishLaunchingWithOptions:(NSDictionary *)launchOptions {

    self.window = [[UIWindow alloc] initWithFrame:[[UIScreen mainScreen] bounds]];

    City *london = [[City alloc] init]; ❷
    london.cityName = @"London";
    london.cityDescription = @"The capital of the United Kingdom and England.";
    london.cityPicture = [UIImage imageNamed:@"London.jpg"];

    City *sanFrancisco = [[City alloc] init];
    sanFrancisco.cityName = @"San Francisco";
    sanFrancisco.cityDescription = @"The heart of the San Francisco Bay Area.";
    sanFrancisco.cityPicture = [UIImage imageNamed:@"SanFrancisco.jpg"];

    City *sydney = [[City alloc] init];
    sydney.cityName = @"Sydney";
    sydney.cityDescription = @"The largest city in Australia.";
    sydney.cityPicture = [UIImage imageNamed:@"Sydney.jpg"];
```

```
    City *madrid = [[City alloc] init];
    madrid.cityName = @"Madrid";
    madrid.cityDescription = @"The capital and largest city of Spain.";
    madrid.cityPicture = [UIImage imageNamed:@"Madrid.jpg"];

    self.cities = [[NSMutableArray alloc]
                   initWithObjects:london, sanFrancisco, sydney, madrid, nil];❸

    self.viewController = [[CGViewController alloc]
                           initWithNibName:@"CGViewController" bundle:nil];
    self.window.rootViewController = self.viewController;
    [self.window makeKeyAndVisible];
    return YES;
}

- (void)applicationWillResignActive:(UIApplication *)application {

}

- (void)applicationDidEnterBackground:(UIApplication *)application {

}

- (void)applicationWillEnterForeground:(UIApplication *)application {

}

- (void)applicationDidBecomeActive:(UIApplication *)application {

}

- (void)applicationWillTerminate:(UIApplication *)application {

}

@end
```

❶ First, we imported the *City.h* interface file.

❷ Following this, we declared and populated four instances of the City class. For
   each one, we allocated and initialized the instance object and then used the
   accessor methods to populate the instance. We could also have written an init
   WithName:withDescription:andImage: method for the class and achieved the
   same result by using this method to initialize the class. I'm going to discuss that
   sort of approach to class initialization later in the book; the first time you'll read
   about this is when I talk about web views near the start of Chapter 7.

❸ Here, we initialized an NSMutableArray and populated it with the four cities. The trailing nil in the object list passed to the initWithObjects: method is essential. You must ensure that the last object in a comma-separated list of objects is the nil object; otherwise, when iterating through the array, your code will end up pointing to unallocated memory, which will lead to an exception.

 If you create a UIImage using the imageNamed: method as shown in this example, it is added to the default autorelease pool rather than the event loop autorelease pool. This means the memory associated with such images will be released only when the application terminates. If you use this method with many large images, you'll find that your application may quickly run out of memory. Since these images are part of an autorelease pool, you'll be unable to free the memory they use when the device's operating system calls the didReceiveMemoryWarning: method in the application delegate when it runs short on memory. You should use the imageNamed: method sparingly, and generally only for small images.

If you're just using it for personal testing, you can use text and images from Wikipedia for the city entries. Later in the book I'll show you how to retrieve data like this directly from the network, but for now, we'll *hardcode* (embed the data directly into the code; you will normally store your data outside the app) a few cities into the app delegate class and include the images inside the application itself rather than retrieving them from the network.

Adding Images to Your Projects

As you can see, we retrieve the UIImage by name using the imageNamed: class method, but from where are we retrieving these images? From somewhere inside the application itself. For testing purposes, I sorted through my image collection, found a representative image for each city (and then scaled and cropped the images to be the same size [1,000 × 750 pixels] and aspect ratio using my favorite image editing software), and copied them into the Xcode project. To do this yourself, drag and drop each image into the Supporting Files group in the Project Navigator panel. This brings up the copy file drop-down pane, as shown in Figure 5-10. If you want to copy the file into the project's directory rather than create a link to wherever the file is stored, click on the relevant checkbox. If you do not copy the files to the project's directory, they will still be collected in the application bundle file when Xcode compiles the application; however, if you later move or delete the file, Xcode will lose the reference to it and will no longer be able to access it. This is especially important when copying source code files. In general, I advocate always checking the box and copying the file into your project, unless you have a very good reason not to do so.

There are other ways to add a file to a project. You can also right-click
on the Supporting Files group and select Add Files to "CityGuide" to
add a file or group of files to the project.

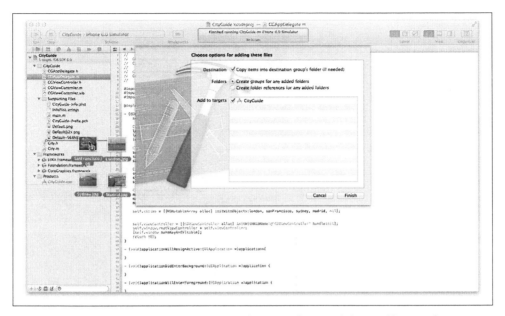

Figure 5-10. The drop-down brought up when you drag and drop a file into the project

After you copy the downloaded images into the project, they become accessible from
your code (see Figure 5-11).

It's generally advisable not to copy large images into the project. For example, if your
binary gets too large, you'll have distribution problems. Among other problems, applications above a certain size cannot be downloaded directly from the App Store onto
your iOS device unless it is connected to the Internet via WiFi. Depending on the dem-
ographic you're targeting, this may limit the market for your application. However,
despite this, bundling images into your application is a good way to get easy access to
small icons and logos that you may want to use in your project.

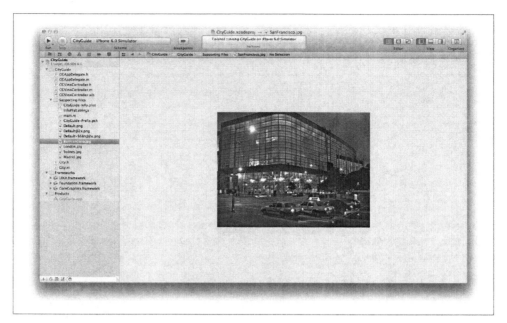

Figure 5-11. One of the copied images inside my Xcode project

Connecting the Controller to the Model

Now that we've built the model, we have to go back to the `CGViewController` class and build the bridge between the view controller and the model. To do this, we need to make only one change in the `CGViewController` interface declaration (*CGView Controller.h*). We're going to add an instance variable to an `NSMutableArray` that you'll then populate inside the `viewDidLoad:` method:

```
@interface CGViewController : UIViewController <UITableViewDataSource,
                                                UITableViewDelegate> {
    NSMutableArray *cities;
}

@property (weak, nonatomic) IBOutlet UITableView *tableView;

@end
```

We're not going to be accessing the `cities` array outside of the view controller, so there is no need to create it as a property and have accessor methods we're not going to be using. We'll just use a plain instance variable.

All instance variables are private in Objective-C by default. By default, instance variables are only visible in instance methods of a class and its subclasses (those methods beginning with a minus sign).

Changes to the implementation (*CGViewController.m*) are only slightly more extensive. You need to #import both the *City.h* and *CGAppDelegate.h* interface files, as you'll be using both of these classes inside the updated implementation:

```
#import "CGViewController.h"
#import "CGAppDelegate.h"
#import "City.h"
```

As I mentioned earlier, you must implement the viewDidLoad: method. This UIView Controller method is called after the controller's view is loaded into memory, and is the method we'll normally use to set up things that the view needs. You'll find that the Xcode template included a stub for viewDidLoad, not far from the #pragma mark labeled "View lifecycle":

```
- (void)viewDidLoad {
    [super viewDidLoad];
    CGAppDelegate *delegate =
            (CGAppDelegate *)[[UIApplication sharedApplication] delegate];
    cities = delegate.cities;
}
```

Here, we acquired a reference to the application delegate by using the [UIApplication sharedApplication] delegate] method call. Since this method returns a generic id object, we had to cast it to be a CGAppDelegate object before assigning it. We then grabbed a pointer to the array of cities managed by the app delegate.

Finally, we must use the model to populate the table view. The number of rows in the table view should now be determined by the number of cities in the NSMutableArray instead of simply returning 3 all the time. We must now change the tableView:number OfRowsInSection: method to reflect that by replacing the line return 3;. Here's how the method should look now:

```
- (NSInteger)tableView:(UITableView *)tv numberOfRowsInSection:
    (NSInteger)section {
    return [cities count];
}
```

Finally, we need to change the tableView:cellForRowAtIndexPath: method to label the cell with the correct city name. To do this, add the following code shown in bold, which figures out which row of the table we're trying to populate and looks up the appropriate element of the cities array:

```
- (UITableViewCell *)tableView:(UITableView *)tv
                cellForRowAtIndexPath:(NSIndexPath *)indexPath {
```

```
    UITableViewCell *cell = [tv dequeueReusableCellWithIdentifier:@"cell"];
    if( nil == cell ) {
        cell = [[UITableViewCell alloc]
                    initWithStyle:UITableViewCellStyleDefault
                reuseIdentifier:@"cell"];
    }
    City *thisCity = [cities objectAtIndex:indexPath.row];
    cell.textLabel.text = thisCity.cityName;
    return cell;
}
```

We've now reached a point where we have a functional, buildable application. However, while the table view now reflects the model, we still can't access any of the information we entered about the cities. When we click on a city, we want the application to tell us about the city, and for that we need to modify the `tableView:didSelectRowAtIndex Path:` method. But for now, click the Run button on the Xcode toolbar, and your iPhone Simulator should pop up, looking like Figure 5-12.

Figure 5-12. Populating the UITableView of the application using the new model

Mocking Up Functionality with Alert Windows

Before I go on to show how to properly display the city descriptions and images using the UINavigationController class, let's do a quick hack and get the application to pop up an alert window when we click on a table view cell. Go back to *RootController.m* and add the highlighted lines in the following code to the didSelectRowAtIndexPath: method:

```
- (void)tableView:(UITableView *)tv didSelectRowAtIndexPath:
        (NSIndexPath *)indexPath {
    City *thisCity = [cities objectAtIndex:indexPath.row];
    UIAlertView *alert = [[UIAlertView alloc]
                            initWithTitle:thisCity.cityName
                                message:thisCity.cityDescription
                                delegate:nil
                        cancelButtonTitle:nil
                        otherButtonTitles:@"OK", nil];
    [alert show];

    [tv deselectRowAtIndexPath:indexPath animated:YES];
}
```

In this method, we create a UIAlertView window with an OK button, and set the title to be the city name and the contents to be the city description. You can see how this looks in Figure 5-13.

Figure 5-13. After you modify the tableView:didSelectRowAtIndexPath: method, a UIAlertView pop-up appears when you click on a city name

Adding Navigation Controls to the Application

Next, back out the changes you just made to the `tableView:didSelectRowAtIndex Path:` method by deleting the lines you added in the preceding section. Be careful to not remove the call to the `deselectRowAtIndexPath:animated:` method.

Now, let's wrap this app up properly. This means we have to add a `UINavigation Controller` to the application. If you've used many iPhone apps, you'll be familiar with this interface; it's one of the most commonly used iPhone design interface patterns. Clicking on a cell in the table view makes the current view slide to the left and displays a new view. You return to the original table view by clicking on the Back button.

The first thing you need to do is add a `UINavigationController` to the app delegate interface (*CGAppDelegate.h*):

```
#import <UIKit/UIKit.h>

@class CGViewController;

@interface CGAppDelegate : UIResponder <UIApplicationDelegate>

@property (strong, nonatomic) UIWindow *window;
@property (strong, nonatomic) CGViewController *viewController;
@property (strong, nonatomic) UINavigationController *navController;
@property (strong, nonatomic) NSMutableArray *cities;

@end
```

You'll also need to make some modifications to the app delegate implementation (*CGAppDelegate.m*). You're going to have to replace the section of the code that adds the `CGViewController` main view as a root view of the main window. Delete the following line from the bottom of the `applicationDidFinishLaunching:` method:

```
self.window.rootViewController = self.viewController;
```

and replace it with the following code snippet:

```
self.navController = [[UINavigationController alloc]
                        initWithRootViewController:self.viewController];
self.window.rootViewController = self.navController;
```

This new code creates a navigation controller and adds the `CGViewController` to the `NavController`'s stack of view controllers, making its view the current view of the `NavController`. Then it sets the current `NavController` view as the root view of the main window. The end of the `applicationDidFinishLaunching:` method should look like this now:

```
        .
        .
        .
    self.viewController = [[CGViewController alloc]
                         initWithNibName:@"CGViewController" bundle:nil];
    self.navController = [[UINavigationController alloc]
                         initWithRootViewController:self.viewController];
    self.window.rootViewController = self.navController;
    [self.window makeKeyAndVisible];
    return YES;
}
```

As the current view of the `NavController` changes, it will automatically update the subview of the main window, and thus what the user sees on his screen. Let's get this working first, and afterward I'll discuss exactly how the `NavController` manipulates its stack of views.

Save your changes to the application delegate files and click the *CGViewController.m* file to open it in the Standard Editor. Go to the `viewDidLoad:` method and add the following code highlighted below:

```
- (void)viewDidLoad {
    [super viewDidLoad];
    self.title = @"City Guide";
    CGAppDelegate *delegate =
                (CGAppDelegate *)[[UIApplication sharedApplication] delegate];
    cities = delegate.cities;
}
```

We've reached another good time to take a break, so click the Run button in the Xcode toolbar to build and deploy your application into the iPhone Simulator. If you've followed all the steps, you should see what I see, something that looks a lot like Figure 5-14.

Figure 5-14. The application is starting to look more like a typical iPhone application

Adding a City View

You might have a nice navigation bar, but it doesn't do any navigation yet, and after backing out of the changes you made to the `tableView:didSelectRowAtIndexPath:` method to present a pop-up, the code doesn't tell you about the selected city anymore. Let's fix that now and implement a view controller and associated view to present the city information to the application user.

Right-click on the CityGuide group in the Project Navigator panel, select New File, and choose a `UIViewController` subclass. Name the new class **CityController** when prompted, as this will be the view controller we're going to use to present the information about the cities, making sure the checkbox asking Xcode to generate an associated nib file for the user interface is ticked, as shown in Figure 5-15.

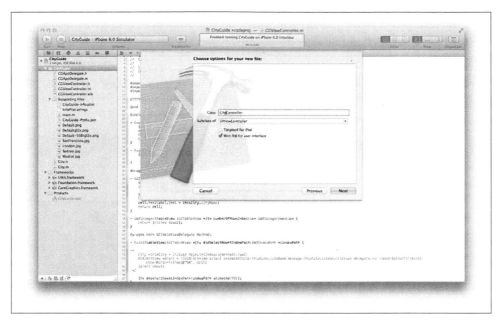

*Figure 5-15. Select a UIViewController subclass and tick the checkbox for Xcode to cre-
ate an associated XIB for the user interface*

This will generate three new files: *CityController.h*, *CityController.m*, and *CityControl-
ler.xib*.

Right now, the new nib file is just a blank view. We'll fix that later. First of all, at the top
of the *CGViewController.m* class, since we're about to make use of the `CityControl
ler` class, we'll need to import its interface file into this class:

```
#import "CityController.h"
```

Then we can go ahead and add code to the `tableView:didSelectRowAtIndexPath:`
method in the *CGViewController.m* class to open the new view when a city is selected
in the table view:

```
- (void)tableView:(UITableView *)tv didSelectRowAtIndexPath:
        (NSIndexPath *)indexPath {
    CGAppDelegate *delegate =
                  (CGAppDelegate *)[[UIApplication sharedApplication] delegate];
    CityController *city = [[CityController alloc] init];
    [delegate.navController pushViewController:city animated:YES];

    [tv deselectRowAtIndexPath:indexPath animated:YES];
}
```

Here we grabbed a reference to the application delegate and initialized a new `CityCon troller` instance. We then pushed this view controller onto the top of the `UINavigation Controller` stack, making its view the current view.

This is another good point to stop and try things out, so click the Run button in the Xcode menu bar to build and deploy your application into the iPhone Simulator. If all has gone well, when you click on a city inside your table view, it should slide neatly to the left and reveal a blank white view created by the `CityController` view controller, with a navigation bar at the top and a Back button provided by your `UINavigation Controller` that will take you back to the city table view, as shown in Figure 5-16.

Figure 5-16. The blank view generated by the CityController view controller

From here we need to modify the `CityController` class so that we can populate its view from the model held by the app delegate; then we need to build that view in Interface Builder by modifying the *CityController.xib* file. The first question we need to ask, however, is "How does the controller class know which city to display?" An easy way to make this happen is to override the `init` method. In the interface file (*CityControl- ler.h*), we'll declare the following method:

```
- (id)initWithIndexPath:(NSIndexPath *)indexPath;
```

I plan to initialize the class by passing in the index (`NSIndexPath`) of the selected `UITableViewCell` in the main table view. From this, you can figure out which `City` to use to populate the view. As you can imagine, this is one of a number of different ways to approach this problem.

Inside the view, we'll be using the navigation bar to display the city name as the view title, a `UITextView` element to display the city description, and finally a `UIImageView` to display the picture of the city that we added to the project earlier.

So far we've used Interface Builder and the Assistant Editor to link the user interface to the code, creating outlets and actions in the code directly from Interface Builder. That's only one way of doing things. This time, we're going to create the code first, and then link the user interface elements to the existing code.

Go ahead and click on the *CityController.h* interface file to open it in the Standard Editor. Modify the interface as follows:

```
#import <UIKit/UIKit.h>

@interface CityController : UIViewController {
    NSIndexPath *index;

    IBOutlet UIImageView *pictureView;
    IBOutlet UITextView *descriptionView;
}

- (id)initWithIndexPath:(NSIndexPath *)indexPath;

@end
```

We've gone ahead and created instance variables for the `UITextView` and `UIImageView` user interface elements, and made them available to Interface Builder by declaring them as an `IBOutlet`. Take note of the two empty circles that appear to the left of the outlet declarations, which indicate that these outlets are unconnected. When we connect them in Interface Builder, they will be filled in, indicating that these outlets are now connected to a specific user interface element.

You'll also notice that we declared the variables as an `IBOutlet` inside the `@interface` declaration instead of doing so while declaring them as a property. There really isn't any need to make these variables into a property, as we don't need accessor methods for them, and making the `IBOutlet` declaration as part of the variable declaration is perfectly fine.

 Even when working with properties, you can put the `IBOutlet` declaration in the property's variable declaration instead of the `@property` statement if you wish (it's a matter of style).

Switch to the implementation, and implement the `init` method inside the *CityController.m* file as follows:

```
- (id)initWithIndexPath: (NSIndexPath *)indexPath {

    if ( (self = [super init]) ) {
        index = indexPath;
    }
    return self;
}
```

This invokes the superclass `init` method—note the single equals means we're not testing for identity; instead we're assigning the result of the superclass's `init` method to the `self` variable. If the call to the superclass is unsuccessful, `self` will be set to `nil` and this will be returned by the `initWithIndexPath:` method. This is very unlikely to occur, and if it does, your application will crash. However, normally the line of custom initializer code will be executed: it sets the `index` variable to point to the `NSIndexPath` we passed into the object.

We're going to be making use of both the `CityGuideDelegate` and the `City` classes, so we need to remember to import them in the implementation. Add these lines to the top of *CityController.m*:

```
#import "CGAppDelegate.h"
#import "City.h"
```

We then initialize the view inside the `viewDidLoad:` method:

```
- (void)viewDidLoad {
    [super viewDidLoad];
    CGAppDelegate *delegate =
      (CGAppDelegate *) [[UIApplication sharedApplication] delegate];
    City *thisCity = [delegate.cities objectAtIndex:index.row];
    self.title = thisCity.cityName;

    descriptionView.text = thisCity.cityDescription;
    descriptionView.editable = NO;
    pictureView.image = thisCity.cityPicture;
}
```

Inside the `viewDidLoad:` method we grabbed a reference to the application's app delegate, and then used this and the `index` variable to retrieve the correct city. Then we set the `text` and `image` properties of the two subviews to hold the city data, and the `title` of the main view to be the city name. The title of the view will be displayed in the navigation bar. We also set the `editable` property of the `descriptionView` to `NO`, as we don't want the user to be able to edit the text describing the city.

Now we have to go back to the `CGViewController` implementation and make one quick change: substitute the new `initWithIndexPath:` method for the default `init` method call we originally used. In the `tableView:didSelectRowAtIndexPath:` method of *CGViewController.m*, replace the following line:

```
CityController *city = [[CityController alloc] init];
```

with this line, making use of the new initialization method:

```
CityController *city = [[CityController alloc] initWithIndexPath:indexPath];
```

At this point, all we need to do is go into Interface Builder and build the view, and then connect the view to the outlets we have already declared and implemented inside the `CityController` class.

Opening the *CityController.xib* file in Interface Builder will present you with a blank view. Drag an image view (`UIImageView`) and text view (`UITextView`) element from the Object Library onto the view.

Since I resized my images to be the same aspect ratio, we're going to change the size of the `UIImageView` to reflect that. In the Size tab of the Inspector panel, resize the `UIImage View` to have a width of 250 points and a height of 188 points. Next, position it at X = 160 and Y = 208.

Doing this will automatically generate Constraints on the `UIImageView` object. Go ahead and click on the button to expand the Dock and then the arrow to expand the constraints. If you click on the generated constraints you can see how they affect the positioning of the object (see Figure 5-17).

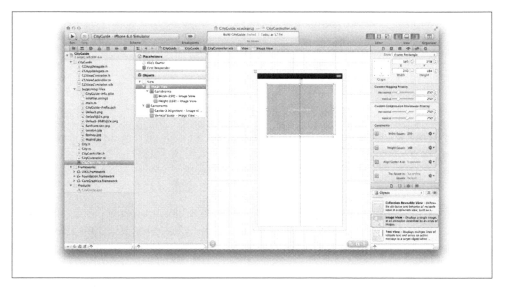

Figure 5-17. The constraints automatically generated by positioning the `UIImageView` object in our view

Points Versus Pixels

With the arrival of the iPhone 4, there were suddenly multiple screen sizes to consider when designing and building applications targeted to the iPhone. However, despite the screen size remaining unchanged, the iPhone 4's Retina display has precisely twice the number of pixels as the previous iPhone models.

Apple dealt with this in an interesting way, making it as easy as possible to support both displays from the same codebase. We no longer talk about physical pixels when defining sizes or views inside the iOS applications. Instead, iOS deals in points, not pixels. These points automatically convert to pixels as appropriate for the device. If you have an iPhone 3GS, 1 point is equivalent to 1 pixel; however, on an iPhone 4, 1 point is a 4-pixel square. This behavior leads to an important fact that you should always remember: 1 point does not necessarily correspond to 1 pixel on the screen.

The arrival of the iPhone 5 hasn't really changed things that much, the 4-inch screen is simply taller. While the aspect ratio of our display has changed, the scaling factor between pixels and points has not.

In your own drawing code, you will use points most of the time, but there are times when you might need to know how points are mapped to pixels. For example, on a high-resolution screen, you might want to use the extra pixels to provide extra detail in your content.

Since iOS 4, the `UIScreen` (*http://bit.ly/X99HvZ*), `UIView`, `UIImage`, and `CALayer` classes expose a scale factor that tells you the relationship between points and pixels for that particular object—currently, this will be 1.0 or 2.0, depending on the resolution of the underlying device.

While all current models share these two scaling factors, you should bear in mind that in the future other scale factors may also be introduced. Write your code, and design your interfaces, accordingly.

Turning to the Attributes tab of the Inspector panel, change the mode of the view from "Scale to Fill" to "Aspect Fill." This means the image will be scaled to the size of the view, and if the aspect ratio of the image is not the same as the aspect ratio of the view, some portion of the image will be clipped so that the view is filled.

Turning to the `UITextView` element, use the Size tab of the Inspector panel to position it at X = 160 and Y = 242 with a width of W = 320 and a height of H = 306. This fills the main view below the image, see Figure 5-18.

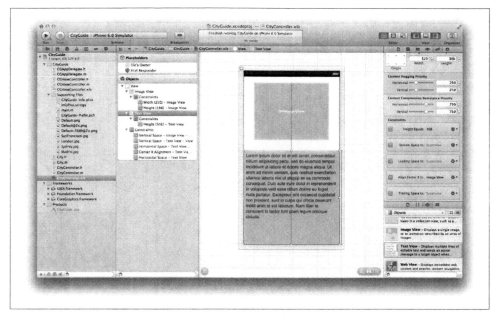

Figure 5-18. The CityController.xib with a UIImageView and UITextView added to the main view

Before the introduction of the iPhone 5 this was sufficient, and the UITextView element would be correctly sized and placed for both Retina and non-Retina displays. With the arrival of the new 4-inch display, we need to make use of the Constraints system to make sure the Text View is correctly scaled.

Select the UITextView and then open the Editor menu and select Editor→Pin→Top Space to SuperView. This will create a new constraint, see Figure 5-19.

Once you've done this, go to the Size inspector in the Utility panel and click on the cog wheel of (what should be) the top-most constraint, "Height Equals: 306." Choose Select and Edit from the drop-down menu. See Figure 5-20.

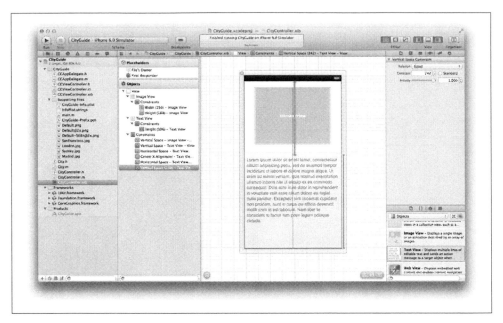

Figure 5-19. Constraining the UITextView with respect to the top of the SuperView

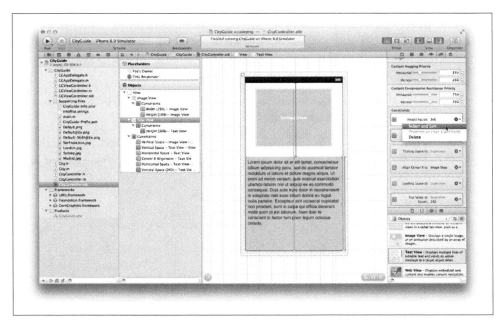

Figure 5-20. Modifying the height constraint of the the UITextView

Go ahead and change this relation to "Less Than or Equal"; after doing so, you should see something like Figure 5-21.

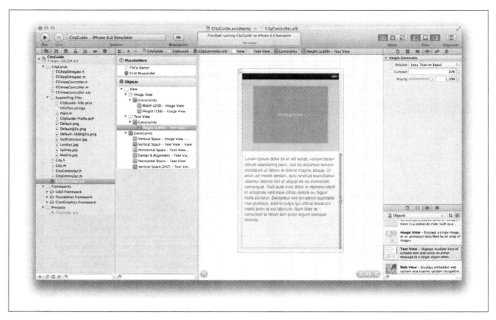

Figure 5-21. The height constraint of the the UITextView set to be ≤ 306 pixels

This is a good point to pause and try things out. Click the Run button in the Xcode menu bar to build and deploy your application into the iPhone Simulator. By default the application will deploy into the iPhone (Retina 4-inch) simulator, but we can change this by going to the iPhone Simulator menu and selecting Hardware→Device→iPhone (Retina 3.5-inch). Doing this will stop our application running, so we'll need click on the Run button in the Xcode menu to deploy our application once again. If all goes well you should see something like Figure 5-22 when you tap through to the City View.

The only thing left to do is connect the UIImageView and UITextView elements to the two IBOutlet variables we created in code. Right-click and drag from the File's Owner icon in the dock (the pale yellow wireframe cube) to the image view in the editor. Release the mouse button, and an Outlets pop-up will appear. Click on **pictureView** to connect the instance variable in your code to the image view in your interface. Right-click and drag again from the File's Owner icon to the text view in the editor. Release the mouse button, and this time, click on **descriptionView** to connect the instance variable in your code to the text view in your interface.

Figure 5-22. The iPhone (Retina 4-inch) and iPhone (Retina 3.5-inch) simulators side by side. Note that the space reserved for the UIImageView *is the same in both cases*

If you right-click on the File's Owner icon after you've made these connections, you should see something much like Figure 5-23. This pop-up window shows the connections from the owning class—in this case, the CityController class—to the user interface elements in your nib file.

At this point, we're done. Dismiss the pop-up, and click on the Run button on the Xcode toolbar to build and deploy the CityGuide application into the iPhone Simulator. After the application starts, tap one of the city names, and you should see something like Figure 5-24.

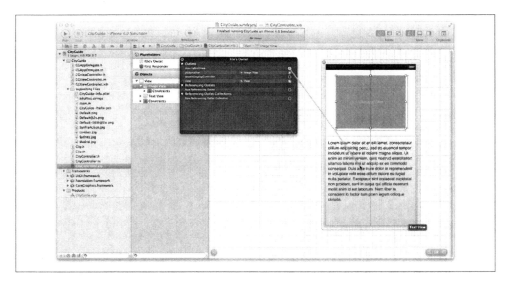

Figure 5-23. Connecting the outlets to the user interface elements in the view

Figure 5-24. The city guide to San Francisco

Edit Mode

So far, so good. But it would be nice if we could add more cities to the guide and, if we're not interested in a particular city, delete them as well. Let's implement a first cut at that using the `UITableViewController` edit mode. You'll have seen this many times when using iPhone applications such as the Mail application. There is an Edit button on the top right on the navigation bar. When tapped, it will drop the table view into edit mode, allowing you to delete mail messages. In some applications, the Edit button lets you add entries to the table view.

This is such a commonly implemented pattern that there are hooks inside the `UIView Controller` to simplify things. In the `viewDidLoad:` method of *CGViewController.m*, you need to add the following line of code:

```
self.navigationItem.rightBarButtonItem = self.editButtonItem;
```

This will add an Edit button to the navigation bar. Clicking on this button calls a method called `setEditing:animated:` on the view controller, which sets the table view into edit mode and changes the Edit button to a Done button. Clicking on the Done button will take the table view out of edit mode and call the `setEditing:animated:` method again, although this time to different effect (ending the edits and changing the button back to an Edit button).

Since we want to be able to add new cities, when the table view is put into editing mode, we're going to add another cell to the table view prompting us to "Add New City." When this is clicked, we'll open a new view that allows us to enter the details of the city.

To do that, we need to change the `tableView:numberOfRowsInSection:` method in *CGViewController.m* to return `cities.count+1` when the table view has been put into editing mode. We'll need to delete the one line (`return cities.count;`) in that method and replace it with the code shown in bold:

```
- (NSInteger)tableView:(UITableView *)tv numberOfRowsInSection:
  (NSInteger)section {
  NSInteger count = cities.count;
  if(self.editing) {
      count = count + 1;
  }
  return count;
}
```

We also need to edit the `tableView:cellForRowAtIndexPath:` method to return the extra cell when in edit mode:

```
- (UITableViewCell *)tableView:(UITableView *)tv
  cellForRowAtIndexPath:(NSIndexPath *)indexPath {

    UITableViewCell *cell =
      [tv dequeueReusableCellWithIdentifier:@"cell"];
```

```
        if( nil == cell ) {
            cell = [[[UITableViewCell alloc]
              initWithFrame:CGRectZero reuseIdentifier:@"cell"] autorelease];
        }
        if (indexPath.row < cities.count ) {
            City *thisCity = [cities objectAtIndex:indexPath.row];
            cell.textLabel.text = thisCity.cityName;
        } else {
            cell.textLabel.text = @"Add New City...";
            cell.textLabel.textColor = [UIColor lightGrayColor];
            cell.editingAccessoryType = UITableViewCellAccessoryDisclosureIndicator;
        }

        return cell;
    }
```

Next, we need to override the setEditing:animated: method to put the table view into edit mode and display the extra cell needed to prompt us to add a new city. Add this method to *CGViewController.m* somewhere above the #pragma mark labeled UITable ViewDataSource Methods:

```
    -(void)setEditing:(BOOL)editing animated:(BOOL) animated {
        [super setEditing:editing animated:animated];
        [self.tableView setEditing:editing animated:animated];
        [self.tableView reloadData];
    }
```

This code calls the super method and notifies the subview (the UITableView we are attempting to put into edit mode) that we have been put into edit mode. It then reloads the data in the table view to update the view the user sees.

By default, when you put the table view into edit mode, the edit control that appears next to the table view cell is of style UITableViewCellEditingStyleDelete, a red circle enclosing a minus sign, to signify that editing this row will delete the item in question. This is fine for the existing cities, but for the newly added "Add New City" cell, we need to set this to a different style. To do so, we need to implement the tableView:editing StyleForRowAtIndexPath: method that is part of the UITableViewDelegate protocol. This should go somewhere below the #pragma mark labeled UITableViewDelegate Methods:

```
    - (UITableViewCellEditingStyle)tableView:(UITableView *)tv
      editingStyleForRowAtIndexPath:(NSIndexPath *)indexPath {
        if (indexPath.row < cities.count ) {
            return UITableViewCellEditingStyleDelete;
        } else {
            return UITableViewCellEditingStyleInsert;
        }

    }
```

In this method, we tell the table view that for cells occupied by existing cities, we want the delete style; otherwise, we want the insert style, a green circle enclosing a plus sign.

Bearing in mind that we haven't actually implemented the backend logic for editing yet, we've reached a good point to see if everything's working. Click Run in the Xcode toolbar, and when the City Guide application starts, tap on the Edit button on the navigation bar. Your app should look just like Figure 5-25.

Figure 5-25. The City Guide table view in editing mode

You've probably noticed that putting the table view into editing mode wasn't very pretty, as no animation was carried out while the table view reloaded the view. It's actually fairly simple to change this by making use of two methods: `insertRowsAtIndexPaths:with RowAnimation:` and `deleteRowsAtIndexPaths:withRowAnimation:`.

Going back to the overridden `setEditing:animated:` method, we need to modify it to use these two methods as shown here:

```
-(void)setEditing:(BOOL)editing animated:(BOOL) animated {
    if( editing != self.editing ) {

        [super setEditing:editing animated:animated];
        [self.tableView setEditing:editing animated:animated];

        NSArray *indexes =
          [NSArray arrayWithObject:
            [NSIndexPath indexPathForRow:cities.count inSection:0]];
        if (editing == YES ) {
            [self.tableView insertRowsAtIndexPaths:indexes
               withRowAnimation:UITableViewRowAnimationLeft];
        } else {
            [self.tableView deleteRowsAtIndexPaths:indexes
               withRowAnimation:UITableViewRowAnimationLeft];
        }
    }
}
```

This code now checks to see whether we are changing editing modes; if we are, we call the `super` method and then notify the subview as before. However, instead of just calling `[self.tableView reloadData]`, we now need to build an array containing the NSIndex Path of each cell we wish to insert (or delete) with animation. In this case, the array will hold only a single object since we intend to animate only a single cell; we then insert or delete with animation depending on whether we are entering or leaving editing mode, respectively.

After clicking Run again, you should still see something that looks a lot like Figure 5-26; however, this time, the "Add New City" cell, as well as the + and – buttons, will be nicely animated and fly in and out. Note that you still won't be able to do anything with these buttons, but at least they make a nice entrance and exit.

Deleting a City Entry

To actually delete a table view cell, we need to add the table view data source method `tableView:commitEditingStyle:forRowAtIndexPath:` to the code. Add this method to *CGViewController.m* between the `#pragma` mark labeled `UITableViewDataSource` Methods and the `#pragma` mark labeled `UITableViewDelegate` Methods:

```
- (void) tableView:(UITableView *)tv
  commitEditingStyle:(UITableViewCellEditingStyle) editing
  forRowAtIndexPath:(NSIndexPath *)indexPath {
    if( editing == UITableViewCellEditingStyleDelete ) {
        [cities removeObjectAtIndex:indexPath.row];
        [tv deleteRowsAtIndexPaths:[NSArray arrayWithObject:indexPath]
          withRowAnimation:UITableViewRowAnimationLeft];
```

```
        }
    }
```

In this method, we check that the editing style is set to delete, and if that's the case, we remove the item from the `cities` array. We figure out which item to remove by checking the `indexPath.row`, and delete the relevant table view cell with animation.

You can now delete cities from the City Guide application. Click Build and Run and try it out. Tap the Edit button on the navigation bar, and then tap the edit control to the left of a city name. Tap the Delete button that appears, as shown in Figure 5-26. The city will be deleted. Tap the Done button.

Figure 5-26. Deleting a city

The nice part about implementing things in this way is that you don't have to drop the table into edit mode to delete a city; swiping from left to right will also bring up the Delete button.

Adding a City Entry

Before you can add a new city, you must implement an interface to allow the user to enter city metadata: the city name, a description, and an image. I'm going to put off adding the ability to add a picture to the city entry until the next chapter, where we look at various view controllers including the `UIImagePickerController`; for now, let's implement the basic framework to allow us to add a new city by allowing the user to enter a city name and description.

Right-click on the CityGuide group in the Project navigator and select New File. Choose to generate a `UIViewController` subclass and when prompted, name the new class `AddCityController`, making sure to tick the checkbox to ask Xcode to generate an associated XIB file.

As we did when we created the `CityController` class earlier, let's add the hooks in the code, which will allow us to open the new view when we click on the "Add New City" cell after putting the table view into edit mode.

First we need to make some changes to the `CGViewController` class. Since we're going to be using the new `AddCityController` class, we need to import the declaration into the implementation. Add this line to *CGViewController.m* near the top of the class with the rest of the `import` statements:

```
#import "AddCityController.h"
```

We also have to make some changes to the `tableView:didSelectRowAtIndexPath:` method in that same file:

```
- (void)tableView:(UITableView *)tv didSelectRowAtIndexPath:
    (NSIndexPath *)indexPath{

    CGAppDelegate *delegate =
                (CGAppDelegate *)[[UIApplication sharedApplication] delegate];

    if (indexPath.row < cities.count && !self.editing ) {❶
        CityController *city =
            [[CityController alloc] initWithIndexPath:indexPath];
        [delegate.navController pushViewController:city animated:YES];
    }
    if( indexPath.row == cities.count && self.editing ) {❷
        AddCityController *addCity = [[AddCityController alloc] init];
        [delegate.navController pushViewController:addCity animated:YES];
    }
    [tv deselectRowAtIndexPath:indexPath animated:YES];
}
```

❶   We execute the commands within this `if` statement for cells whose rows are less than the number of entries in the `cities` array, but only if the table view is *not* in editing mode.

❷   We execute the commands within this `if` statement for cells whose rows are equal to the number of entries in the `cities` array, but only if the table view *is* in editing mode.

Because Objective-C is derived from C, its array indexes start at zero. So, the only cell in the table view whose row number is *greater* than the number of entries in the `cit ies` array is the "Add New City" cell. Therefore, the code in the first `if` block uses the `cities` array to display each cell; the code in the second block uses a new city that the user is adding.

The first code branch, for city cells, is unchanged from the original implementation. While the second branch is very similar to the first, in this case, we create an `AddCity Controller` instance rather than a `CityController` instance.

Click the Run button on the Xcode toolbar. Running the application at this point shows us that we've forgotten something. Right now, clicking on any of the table view cells when the table is in edit mode, including the "Add New City" cell, doesn't do anything, even though we implemented code inside the `tableView:didSelectRowAtIndex Path:` method.

 You need to go back to the *CGViewController.xib* file inside Interface Builder, select the `UITableView` element, and in the Attributes Inspector in the Utilities panel look inside the Table View section and in the Editing drop-down menu select the "Single Selection During Editing" option from the menu.

If you rerun the application after setting this option inside Interface Builder and click on a city cell when the table view is in edit mode, you should see that it is briefly selected and then deselected. Clicking on the "Add New City" cell, however, should slide in a blank view: the one associated with the *AddCityController.xib* file.

However, the brief selection effect you get when you click on one of the normal city cells inside edit mode is annoying. These cells shouldn't be selectable in edit mode, but unfortunately there isn't a way to tell the table view that only the last cell is selectable. There are several ways to fool the user into thinking that this is the case, though. One of these is to extend the `setEditing:animated` method in the `CGViewController` class to set the selection style of these cells to `UITableViewCellSelectionStyleNone` when the table view is in edit mode, and then set the style back to `UITableViewCellSelection StyleBlue` when we leave edit mode. The changes you need to make to the `setEdit ing:animated:` method in the *CGViewController.m* file are significant, so you can simply replace the method with the following:

```
-(void)setEditing:(BOOL)editing animated:(BOOL) animated {
    if( editing != self.editing ) {
        [super setEditing:editing animated:animated];
        [self.tableView setEditing:editing animated:animated];

        NSMutableArray *indices = [[NSMutableArray alloc] init];
        for(int i=0; i < cities.count; i++ ) { ❶
            [indices addObject:[NSIndexPath indexPathForRow:i inSection:0]];
        }
        NSArray *lastIndex = [NSArray
          arrayWithObject:[NSIndexPath
                            indexPathForRow:cities.count inSection:0]]; ❷

        if (editing == YES ) {
            for(int i=0; i < cities.count; i++ ) { ❸
                UITableViewCell *cell =
                [self.tableView
```

```
              cellForRowAtIndexPath:[indices objectAtIndex:i]];
            [cell setSelectionStyle:UITableViewCellSelectionStyleNone];
        }
        [self.tableView insertRowsAtIndexPaths:lastIndex
            withRowAnimation:UITableViewRowAnimationLeft];
    } else {
        for(int i=0; i < cities.count; i++ ) { ❹
            UITableViewCell *cell =
              [self.tableView
                cellForRowAtIndexPath:[indices objectAtIndex:i]];
            [cell setSelectionStyle:UITableViewCellSelectionStyleBlue];
        }
        [self.tableView deleteRowsAtIndexPaths:lastIndex
            withRowAnimation:UITableViewRowAnimationLeft];
    }
  }
}
```

❶ Inside this loop, we build an NSMutableArray containing the NSIndexPath of all
    the cells where we want to modify the selection style; that is, normal cells that
    contain cities.

❷ Here we build an NSArray containing the NSIndexPath of the final "Add New
    City" cell.

❸ We have just entered edit mode, so inside this loop, we retrieve the UITableView
    Cell for each NSIndexPath in the array and set the selection style to None.

❹ Leaving edit mode, we do the opposite and set the selection style back to the
    default for each cell in the array.

Build and run the application, and you'll see that this gets you where you want to go:
inside edit mode, the only (apparently) selectable cell is the "Add New City" cell. None
of the other cells show any indication that they have been selected when they are clicked
on. However, outside edit mode, these cells are selectable, and will take you (as expected)
to the view describing the city.

The "Add New City" Interface

There are a number of ways we could build an interface to allow the user to enter
metadata about a new city. I'm going to take the opportunity to show you how to customize a UITableViewCell inside Interface Builder and load those custom cells into a
table view.

Open the *AddCityController.xib* file in Interface Builder. Drag and drop a table view
(UITableView) from the Object Library in the Utilities panel into the view. Next, grab
a UITableViewCell from the Library window and drag and drop that into the main

Editor panel (not into existing view). Repeat this step and drag another `UITableView` `Cell` from the Library window. You should have something that looks like Figure 5-27.

Figure 5-27. The main AddCityController nib

Here you can see the main view with its table view and the two table view cells, which are not part of the main view.

We now need to customize these two cells to give users the ability to enter text. To do this, we're going to build a table view similar to the one Apple uses when we write a new mail message. Yes, in case you didn't realize it, that's just a highly customized table view. It's actually pretty amazing how far you can get writing iOS applications just using the `UITableView` and associated classes.

Since you're going to be using these cells to enter text, you don't want them to be selectable, so you should open the Attributes Inspector in the Utilities panel for both of the cells and change the Selection type from "Blue" to "None" using the drop-down menu in both cases.

At the top of the table view, we'll have a normal-size table view cell with an embedded `UITextField` to allow users to enter the city name. Below that we'll have a super-sized table view cell with an embedded `UITextView` to allow users to enter the much longer description.

Click on the first of your two table view cells, grab a label (UILabel) from the Object Library, and drop it onto the Table View Cell window. Make sure the label is selected, and in the Attributes Inspector change the text to "City:". Then switch to the Size tab and position the label at X = 37 and Y = 11 with width W = 42 and height H = 21.

Now grab a text field (UITextField) from the Object Library and drag and drop it onto the same Table View Cell window. Click on the Text field, and in the Attributes Inspector tab of the Utilities panel, select the dotted-line Border Style for the field. This represents the "no border" style.

In the Text Input Traits section of the same tab, set Capitalize to None and Correction to No. With the Text field still selected, go to the Size tab of the Inspector window and resize the element to have origin X = 248 and Y = 0 with width W = 260 and height H = 44.

Finally, back in the Attributes Inspector, you may want to add some placeholder text to the Text field to prompt the user to enter a city name. I went with "e.g. Paris, Rome."

Next, double-click on the second of the two table view cells. You need to resize this to fill the remaining part of the main view. The navigation bar at the top of the view is 54 points high, and a standard table view cell is 44 points high. Because the 3.5-inch iPhone's screen is 460 points high, and the 4-inch iPhone's screen is 568 points high, we want the table view cell to be 362 points high to fill the view. So, go to the Size Inspector in the Utilities panel and set H = 470. The table view cell will automatically grow to reflect its new size.

 We're taking a shortcut here as it doesn't really matter for our purposes; however, instead of hardwiring the sizes of the table view cells as we have done here, in production code, you should either make use of the UIScreen class to determine the size (in points) of the main window and modify the cell sizes in code, or make more use of the Auto-Layout and Constraints options offered by Interface Builder to make sure your interface elements resize and stretch correctly.

Grab another UILabel from the Object Library and drop it onto the Table View Cell window. In the Attributes Inspector, change the text to Description and then switch to the Size Inspector. Position the label at X = 63 and Y = 1 with width W = 86 and height H = 21.

Now grab a text view (UITextView) from the Object Library, drag and drop it into this new expanded table view cell, resize it to the remaining extent of the cell using the Size tab in the Inspector window (X = 160, Y = 29, W = 297, H = 440), and delete the default text from the Attributes tab. After doing so, you should have a collection of views that resembles that seen in Figure 5-28.

Figure 5-28. Interface Builder with the two modified UITableViewCell views

Finally, click on the UITextView, and in the View section of the Attributes Inspector, set the Tag attribute to 777. Then switch back to your other table view cell and do the same for its UITextField. The Tag attribute is a UIView property that Interface Builder is exposing to us; this is used to uniquely identify views (or in this case a subview) to the application. We'll be able to grab the UITextView and UITextField easily using this tag directly from the code after setting it here in Interface Builder.

We're done with Interface Builder for now, so save your changes and open the *Add CityController.h* file. Add the code shown in bold:

```
#import <UIKit/UIKit.h>

@interface AddCityController : UIViewController
  <UITableViewDataSource, UITableViewDelegate> {
    IBOutlet UITableView *tableView;
    IBOutlet UITableViewCell *nameCell;
    IBOutlet UITableViewCell *descriptionCell;
}

@end
```

Here we declare the view controller class to be both a data source and a delegate for the table view. We also declare three variables: a UITableView variable and two UITable

ViewCell variables. We declare each of these variables to be an IBOutlet; we'll connect these variables to the views inside Interface Builder in a little while.

However, before we return to Interface Builder to do that, we need to implement a number of table view data source and delegate methods inside the *AddCityController.m* class implementation. Here is the full listing for that file:

```
#import "AddCityController.h"

@implementation AddCityController

- (id)initWithNibName:(NSString *)nibNameOrNil
               bundle:(NSBundle *)nibBundleOrNil {

    self = [super initWithNibName:nibNameOrNil bundle:nibBundleOrNil];
    if (self) {
        // Custom initialization
    }
    return self;
}

- (void)viewDidLoad {
    [super viewDidLoad];
    self.title = @"New City"; ❶

}

- (void)didReceiveMemoryWarning {
    [super didReceiveMemoryWarning];
}

#pragma mark UITableViewDataSource Methods

- (UITableViewCell *)tableView:(UITableView *)tv
        cellForRowAtIndexPath:(NSIndexPath *)indexPath {
    UITableViewCell *cell = nil;
    if( indexPath.row == 0 ) { ❷
        cell = nameCell;
    } else {
        cell = descriptionCell;
    }
    return cell;

}

- (NSInteger)tableView:(UITableView *)tv
           numberOfRowsInSection:(NSInteger)section {
    return 2; ❸
}

#pragma mark UITableViewDelegate Methods
```

```
- (CGFloat)        tableView:(UITableView *)tv
    heightForRowAtIndexPath:(NSIndexPath *)indexPath {
    CGFloat height;
    if( indexPath.row == 0 ) { ❹
        height = 44;
    } else {
        height = 440;
    }
    return height;

}

@end
```

❶ As we did for the CityController view controller, we need to add a title to the
    view inside the viewDidLoad: method. This title will be displayed in the
    navigation bar at the top of the view.

❷ Instead of using the dequeueReusableCellWithIdentifier: method to obtain
    a cell, we check which row we are being asked to display, and return either the
    custom cell to enter the city name or the custom cell to enter the city description.

❸ Since we have only two cells in the table view, we just return 2 from this method.

❹ Since the table view cells are different heights, we have to return the correct height
    in pixels based on the cell we are being asked about.

The only method you haven't seen before is the tableView:heightForRowAtIndex
Path: method. As you would expect, this delegate returns the height of the individual
table view cell in a specified location.

Click the *AddCityController.xib* file to open it in Interface Builder. Expand the dock and
then click on File's Owner and open the Connections Inspector in the Utilities panel.
I'm going to show you yet another way to connect your user interface to your code.

Left-click and drag from the descriptionCell outlet in the Connections Inspector (on
the right) to the icon representing the super-sized table view cell in the dock (on the
left) and then again for the nameCell outlet to the smaller table view cell (see
Figure 5-29). If you aren't sure which table view cell is which by looking at the dock,
you can click on the cell in the Editor panel to highlight it.

You should then connect the tableView outlet to the table view in the main View window in a similar fashion, or by click and dragging onto the Editor window.

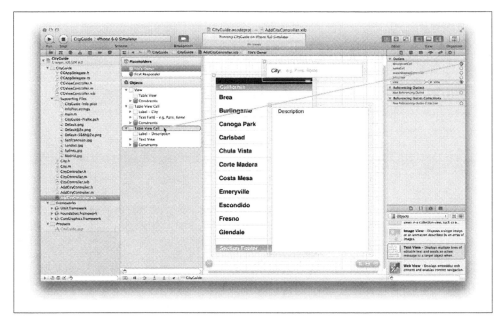

Figure 5-29. Connecting the outlets using the Connections Inspector and the dock

Finally, click on the table view in the main View window and connect both the `data Source` and the `delegate` outlets of the table view to File's Owner. After doing this, click on File's Owner, and the Connections tab of the Inspector window should look the same as in Figure 5-30.

We've reached a point where we should have a working application. Click on the Run button in the Xcode toolbar to compile and start the application in the simulator. Once it has started successfully, click on the Edit button to put your table view into edit mode and then click on the "Add New City" cell. If everything has gone according to plan, you should see something like Figure 5-31.

If we tap inside one of the custom table view cells, the keyboard will appear and we can start typing. However, right now we don't have any way to save the information we enter in these fields. Let's implement that right now.

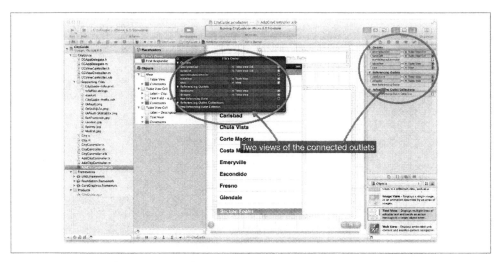

Figure 5-30. Interface Builder after making all the necessary connections between the components

Figure 5-31. The new "New City" UI in iPhone Simulator

Capturing the City Data

Both the `UITextField` and the `UITextView` we're using to capture the name and description of the city have delegate protocols. However, we don't need to look into those quite yet, although I will be talking about them later in the book. The first step is to add a Save button to the interface.

That's actually pretty easy to do from the `viewDidLoad:` method of the view controller. We can use the same technique we used to add the Edit and Done buttons to the main view controller to add the Save button to the `AddCityController`. However, instead of declaring the navigation item to be `self.editButtonItem`, we make use of the `UIBar ButtonItem` method's `initWithBarButtonSystemItem:target:action:` to create the navigation item:

```
self.navigationItem.rightBarButtonItem =
    [[UIBarButtonItem alloc] initWithBarButtonSystemItem:UIBarButtonSystemItemSave
    target:self action:@selector(saveCity:)];
```

We must add the preceding code to the `viewDidLoad:` method of *AddCityController.m*. In this method call, we declare that the button delegate is `self` (the `AddCityController` class) and that, when clicked, the event will be handled by the `saveCity:` method in this class.

Since we're going to be making use of the `CGAppDelegate`, `CGViewController`, and `City` classes in this method, we must also remember to import their definitions into the implementation. Add these lines to the top of *AddCityController.m* before proceeding:

```
#import "CGAppDelegate.h"
#import "CGViewController.h"
#import "City.h"
```

We must add the following to *AddCityController.m*:

```
- (void)saveCity:(id)sender {

    CGAppDelegate *delegate =
                    (CGAppDelegate *)[[UIApplication sharedApplication] delegate];
    NSMutableArray *cities = delegate.cities; ❶

    UITextField *nameEntry = (UITextField *)[nameCell viewWithTag:777];❷
    UITextView *descriptionEntry =
    (UITextView *)[descriptionCell viewWithTag:777];

    if ( nameEntry.text.length > 0 ) { ❸
        City *newCity = [[City alloc] init];
        newCity.cityName = nameEntry.text;
        newCity.cityDescription = descriptionEntry.text;
        newCity.cityPicture = nil;
        [cities addObject:newCity];
```

```
        CGViewController *viewController = delegate.viewController;
        [viewController.tableView reloadData]; ❹
    }
    [delegate.navController popViewControllerAnimated:YES]; ❺

}
```

❶   This gets a pointer to the `cities` array (the data model) held by the application delegate class.

❷   Here, the `Tag` property is used to obtain references to the `UITextField` and `UITextView` in the two custom table view cells.

❸   If the city name text field holds some text, we must assume there is a new city to add to the guide. We need to create a new `City` object, populate it, and push it onto the `cities` array.

❹   Because we have changed the size of the `cities` array, we need to reload the data held by the main view controller. The current view held by the object is not correct anymore.

❺   We are done with this view, so we ask the navigation controller to remove it from its stack of views. This will mean that the current (displayed) view becomes the next view down in the navigation controller's stack of views. In this specific case, this will be the previous view.

We could actually compile and run the application at this point and it would work, mostly. But there are a few UI loose ends we need to clear up before everything works correctly.

When we click the Save button and return to the main table view, we will be reusing the table view cell that previously held the "Add New City" cell to hold a city name in the newly expanded list of cities. This will cause some problems: while we explicitly set the color and accessory properties for this cell in `cellForRowAtIndexPath:`, we don't do the same for the other cells. We therefore have to make a small change to the `table View:cellForRowAtIndexPath:` method and set the `textLabel.textColor` and `edi tingAccessoryType` for the other cells as well as the "Add New City" cell. Make the changes shown here to the `tableView:cellForRowAtIndexPath:` method in *CGView-Controller.m*:

```
- (UITableViewCell *)tableView:(UITableView *)tv
  cellForRowAtIndexPath:(NSIndexPath *)indexPath
{

    UITableViewCell *cell =
    [tv dequeueReusableCellWithIdentifier:@"cell"];
    if( nil == cell ) {
        cell = [[UITableViewCell alloc]
            initWithFrame:CGRectZero reuseIdentifier:@"cell"];
```

```
    }
    NSLog( @"indexPath.row = %d, cities.count = %d", indexPath.row,
        cities.count );
    if (indexPath.row < cities.count ) {
        City *thisCity = [cities objectAtIndex:indexPath.row];
        cell.textLabel.text = thisCity.cityName;
        cell.textLabel.textColor = [UIColor blackColor];
        cell.editingAccessoryType = UITableViewCellAccessoryNone;
        if (self.editing) {
            [cell setSelectionStyle:UITableViewCellSelectionStyleNone]; ❶
        }

    } else {
        cell.textLabel.text = @"Add New City...";
        cell.textLabel.textColor = [UIColor lightGrayColor];
        cell.editingAccessoryType =
                UITableViewCellAccessoryDisclosureIndicator;
    }
    return cell;
}
```

❶ Since we are creating an extra cell while in edit mode, and as the table view has
    been flagged as allowing selection in edit mode, the selection style for this cell
    will be the default. The selection style will not be set implicitly since the setEdit
    ing:animated: method has already been called on this table view. We therefore
    have to set the selection style explicitly, to None, as the table view is already in
    edit mode when we return to it from the Add City view and the cell is created.

We're done! Click the Run button on the Xcode toolbar to compile and start the application in the simulator. Once it has started, click on the Edit button to put the table view
into edit mode and then click on the "Add New City" cell. Enter a name for the new city,
as shown in Figure 5-32, and click the Save button.

Figure 5-32. The Add New City view

You should see something that looks a lot like Figure 5-33.

Figure 5-33. The City Guide view in edit mode with the new city added to the list

Click Done, and take the table view out of edit mode. Clicking on the new city will take you to the city page; apart from the blank space where the picture will be placed, it should look the same as the other city pages in the guide.

If you don't enter a city name in the Add City view, or if you click on the Back button on the left rather than the Save button, no changes will be made to either the `cities` array or the data model held by the application delegate.

The blank space where the image should be on the newly added city is a bit annoying; the easiest way to get around this is to add a default image. The image you choose to use for this placeholder image isn't really relevant. I used the classic image of a question mark on top of a folder, the image Mac OS X would display if it could not find my boot disk, but you can use anything. Remember to keep your aspect ratio the same as you scale your image, and copy it into your project, as we did with the other city images.

You can add the image to the `viewDidLoad:` method of the `CityController` class. You'll be replacing the last line of code in the method (`pictureView.image = thisCity.cit yPicture;`) with the code shown in bold:

```
- (void)viewDidLoad {
    CityGuideDelegate *delegate = (CityGuideDelegate *)
      [[UIApplication sharedApplication] delegate];
    City *thisCity = [delegate.cities objectAtIndex:index.row];

    self.title = thisCity.cityName;
    descriptionView.text = thisCity.cityDescription;
    descriptionView.editable = NO;

    UIImage *image = thisCity.cityPicture;
    if ( image == nil ) {
        image = [UIImage imageNamed:@"QuestionMark.jpg"];
    }
    pictureView.image = image;

}
```

Here we added a check to see whether the cityPicture returned by the City object is equal to nil. If so, we simply substitute the default image; this should produce something similar to Figure 5-34.

Figure 5-34. The default image displayed in the CityController view

We're done, at least for this chapter. We'll come back to the City Guide application to fix the remaining problems later. For instance, we'll return to it briefly in the next chapter, where I'll show you how to use the `UIImagePickerController` to attach images to your new City Guide entries. We'll also come back to it again in Chapter 8, where I'll address how to store your data. At the moment, while users can add new cities and delete cities, if they quit the application and restart it, they'll be back to the original default set of cities.

CHAPTER 6

Other View Controllers

Now that we've discussed the UITableView and UINavigationController (as well as their associated classes and views) and built an iPhone application using them, you've actually come a long way toward being able to write applications on your own. With these classes under your belt, you have the tools to attack a large slice of the problem space that iOS applications normally address.

In this chapter, we'll look at some of the other view controllers and classes that will be useful when building your applications: simple two-screen views (utility applications), single-screen tabbed views (tab bar applications), view controllers that take over the whole screen until dismissed (modal view controllers), and a view controller for selecting video and images (image picker view controller). We'll also take a look at the Master-Detail Application template and see how it is implemented differently on the iPhone (using a UINavigationController) than on the iPad (using a UISplitView Controller) along wit the iPad-only Popover controller.

Utility Applications

Utility applications perform simple tasks: they have a one-page main view and another window that is brought into view with a flip animation. Both the Stocks and Weather applications that ship with the iPhone are examples of applications that use this pattern. Both are optimized for simple tasks that require the absolute minimum of user interaction. Such applications are usually designed to display a simple list in the main view, with preferences and option settings on the flip view. You access the flip view by clicking a small *i* icon from the main view.

The Xcode Utility Application template implements the main view and gives the user access to a flipside view. It is one of the most extensive templates in Xcode and it implements a fully working utility application, which is fortunate, as the documentation

Apple provides regarding this type of application is otherwise somewhat lacking in details.

Open Xcode and start a new project. Click Application under the iOS group, and then select Utility Application from the New Project window as the template (see Figure 6-1). Click Next, and enter **BatteryMonitor** when asked for the Product Name, and **BM** when asked for the class prefix for this project. We want an ARC-based template, but don't want Storyboards, Core Data support, or Unit Tests.

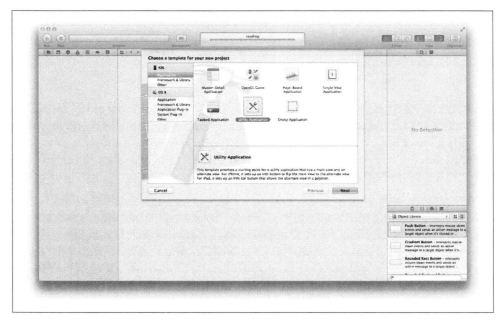

Figure 6-1. Selecting Utility Application in the New Project window

The names of the classes the Xcode template generates are meant to hint strongly at what each of them does, and since the template implements all the logic necessary to control the application's interface, we only need to implement our own user interface and some basic logic to control it.

Click the Run button in the Xcode toolbar to compile and run the application. You'll find that it's a fully working utility application, although with blank main and flipside views (see Figure 6-2).

Figure 6-2. The basic Utility Application running in the iPhone Simulator, showing the front side (left) and flipside (right) views

Making the Battery Monitoring Application

The somewhat descriptive name of the application has probably revealed its purpose already. We're going to implement a simple battery monitoring application, and to do so, I'm going to introduce you to the UIDevice class. This is a *singleton class* that provides information relating to your hardware device.

A *singleton class* is restricted so that only one instance of the class can be created. This design pattern can be used to coordinate actions or information across your application. Although some argue that because use of singleton classes introduces global state into your application, and is therefore almost by definition a bad thing, I think that when it is used correctly, the pattern can simplify your architecture considerably.

From it you can obtain information about your device such as its assigned name, device model, and operating system name and version. More important, perhaps, you can use the class to detect changes in the device's characteristics, such as physical orientation, and register for notifications about when these characteristics change.

 The UIDevice class used to return the UDID of the iOS device your application is running on, and the developer community has extensively used this ability in the past to obtain a per-device unique identifier. However, with the arrival of iOS 5, this capability was deprecated, and with the arrival of iOS 6 this capability went away.

Information—and notifications—about the device battery state weren't introduced until the 3.0 update of the SDK. Even now, the implementation is somewhat coarse-grained (notifications regarding charge level changes occur in only 5% increments).

 The UIDevice class has several limitations, and some developers have resorted to the underlying IOKit framework to obtain more information about the device (e.g., better precision to your battery measurements). However, while Apple marked the IOKit as a public framework, no documentation or header files are associated with it.

If you use this framework and try to publish your application on the App Store, it is possible that Apple will reject it for using a private framework despite its apparent public status. In the official documentation, IOKit is described as "Contain[ing] interfaces used by the device. Do not include this framework directly."

Building the interface

First we're going to build the interface. Double-click on the *BMMainViewController.xib* file to open it in Interface Builder. You'll see that the default view that Xcode generated already has the Info button to switch between the main and flipside views, and not only is it there, but it's connected to the template code so it's already working.

The UI will consist of just three `UILabel` elements, so drag and drop three labels from the Object Library onto the view, and position them roughly as shown in Figure 6-3.

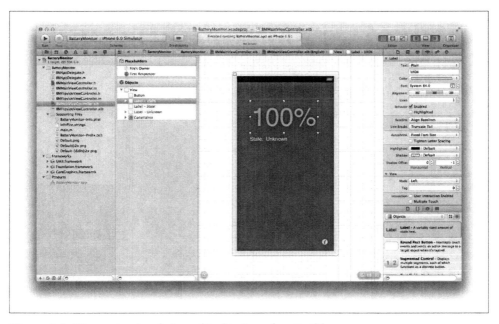

Figure 6-3. The main view being edited in Interface Builder

You can use the Attributes Inspector in the Utilities panel to change the font size and color as I have done with my view. We'll be setting the text of the labels from inside our code, but for now I've added placeholder text (100%, State:, and Unknown) using the Attributes Inspector so that I can position the labels more neatly and get a better idea of how my interface will look.

Let's connect our interface to our code. Select the Assistant Editor to open up the interface file associated with our nib file. If you're short on screen real estate, you may want to minimize the dock and close the Utilities panel at this point.

Then Control-click and drag from the 100% label into your code (just above the existing `IBAction`, which was connected to the Information button in the bottom-right of the view by the template) and name your outlet **levelLabel**. Next, Control-click and drag from the state label (which has the placeholder text Unknown) into the code and name your outlet **stateLabel**, as in Figure 6-4.

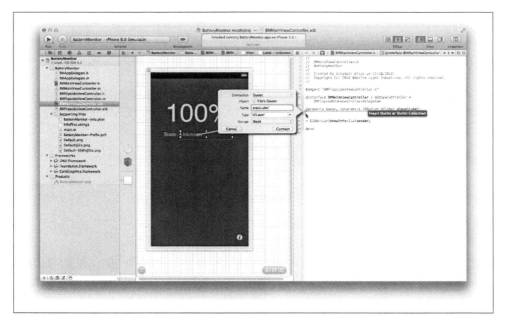

Figure 6-4. Connecting the interface elements to your code

Afterward, your interface file should look like this:

```
#import "BMFlipsideViewController.h"

@interface BMMainViewController :
    UIViewController <BMFlipsideViewControllerDelegate>

@property (weak, nonatomic) IBOutlet UILabel *levelLabel;
@property (weak, nonatomic) IBOutlet UILabel *stateLabel;

- (IBAction)showInfo:(id)sender;

@end
```

That's all we're going to do to the main view. Save the nib file and open the *BMFlip-side__ViewController.xib* file. You'll see that this time, the default view that Xcode generates already has a navigation bar and a Done button present and connected to the template code. Switch back to the Standard Editor and reopen the Utilities panel. You'll need to add a label (`UILabel`) and switch (`UISwitch`) to this interface.

Drag and drop the two elements from the Object Library into the Flipside View window and position them as shown in Figure 6-5. Set the text of the label to **Monitor Bat tery**, and use the Attributes Inspector to set the label text color to white. The default black text won't show up well against the dark gray background of the view.

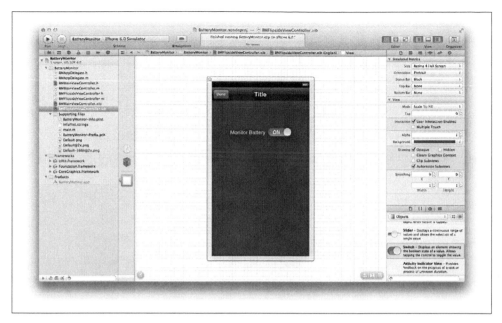

Figure 6-5. The flipside view being edited in Interface Builder

We now need to connect our switch back into our code. Reopen the Assistant Editor and Control-click and drag from the switch in the view to the associated interface file to create an outlet (see Figure 6-6). Call the outlet **toggleSwitch** when asked.

Afterward, your interface file should look like this:

```
#import <UIKit/UIKit.h>

@class BMFlipsideViewController;

@protocol BMFlipsideViewControllerDelegate
- (void)flipsideViewControllerDidFinish:(BMFlipsideViewController *)controller;
@end

@interface BMFlipsideViewController : UIViewController

@property (weak, nonatomic) IBOutlet id <BMFlipsideViewControllerDelegate>
    delegate;
@property (weak, nonatomic) IBOutlet UISwitch *toggleSwitch;

- (IBAction)done:(id)sender;

@end
```

We're going to use the switch to turn battery monitoring on and off.

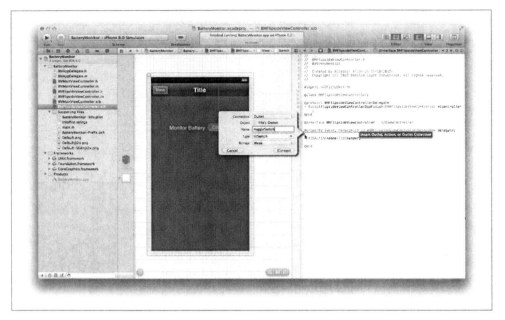

Figure 6-6. Connecting the switch to your code

Writing the code

Open up the *BMAppDelegate.h* interface file. We're going to need to add a Boolean variable that stores the flag that indicates whether the app is currently monitoring the battery state. Add the following property next to the existing @property declarations (but before the @end):

```
@property (nonatomic) BOOL monitorBattery;
```

By default, we're going to make it so that the application starts with battery monitoring turned off, so in the application:didFinishLaunchingWithOptions: method, we must set the flag to NO. Add the following to the top of the method:

```
self.monitorBattery = NO; ❶
```

❶ Note that we access the variable by using the accessor method that was automatically generated for us. It's important to realize that accessing the underlying instance variable directly using _monitorBattery and accessing the property via a call to self.monitorBattery: are completely different in Objective-C, since you are sending a message when you invoke the property, rather than directly accessing the variable.

Next, open the *BMFlipsideViewController.m* implementation file. You first need to import the application delegate header file, as we'll need access to the Boolean property we added. Add the following line to the top of *BMFlipsideViewController.m*:

```
#import "BMAppDelegate.h"
```

Next, make the changes shown in bold to the viewDidLoad: method:

```
- (void)viewDidLoad {
    [super viewDidLoad];
    self.title = @"Preferences";❶
    BMAppDelegate *appDelegate =
        (BMAppDelegate *) [[UIApplication sharedApplication] delegate];❷
    self.toggleSwitch.on = appDelegate.monitorBattery; ❸
}
```

❶   This sets the title of the view.

❷   We grab a reference to the application delegate here.

❸   Here, we set the status of the toggle switch to reflect whether we're currently monitoring the battery.

Now modify the done: method to save the status of the toggle switch back to the application delegate when you close the flipside view:

```
- (IBAction)done {
    BMAppDelegate *appDelegate =
        (BMAppDelegate *) [[UIApplication sharedApplication] delegate];
    appDelegate.monitorBattery = self.toggleSwitch.on;
    [self.delegate flipsideViewControllerDidFinish:self];
}
```

The modifications we need to make to the main view controller are a bit more extensive than those we've made thus far. Open the *BMMainViewController.h* interface file and make the changes shown in bold.

```
#import "BMFlipsideViewController.h"

@interface BMMainViewController :
    UIViewController <BMFlipsideViewControllerDelegate>

@property (weak, nonatomic) IBOutlet UILabel *levelLabel;
@property (weak, nonatomic) IBOutlet UILabel *stateLabel;

- (IBAction)showInfo:(id)sender;

- (void)batteryChanged:(NSNotification *)note; ❶

- (NSString *)batteryLevel; ❷
- (NSString *)batteryState:(UIDeviceBatteryState )batteryState; ❸

@end
```

❶   This method will be called when we receive a notification that there has been a change in the state of the battery.

❷   This is a convenience method to wrap the call to `UIDevice` to query the current battery level and return an `NSString` that we can use for the text of one of the `UILabels`.

❸   This is another convenience method to convert a `UIDeviceBatteryState` into an `NSString` that we can use for the text of one of the other `UILabels`.

Save the interface file, and then open the *BMMainViewController.m* implementation file in Xcode. We'll need to reference the application delegate in the interface file, so now we need to import the relevant header file. Add this line at the top:

```
#import "BMAppDelegate.h"
```

 You should see a small warning triangle next to the `@implementation` line in the *BMMainViewController.m* implementation file in the Xcode Editor. This is indicating that we've added methods to the interface file that we haven't yet implemented; it's safe to ignore, as we're about to go ahead and do that.

Next, we need to implement the `viewWillAppear:` method, another `UIApplication Delegate` callback method which will be called before the existing `viewDidLoad:` method.

At this point, you may be wondering what the difference is between this method and the previous `viewDidLoad:` method. The answer is that they're called at different times: `viewWillAppear:` will be called each time the view becomes visible, while `viewDid Load:` is called only when the view is first loaded. Because the changes we make to the preferences (on the flip side) affect the main view, we need to use `viewWillAppear:`, which is triggered each time we flip back from the preferences view to the main view. Add the following to *BMMainViewController.m*:

```
- (void)viewWillAppear:(BOOL)animated { [super viewWillAppear:animated];
    UIDevice *device = [UIDevice currentDevice];
    BMAppDelegate *appDelegate =
      (BMAppDelegate *) [[UIApplication sharedApplication] delegate];
    device.batteryMonitoringEnabled = appDelegate.monitorBattery; ❶

    if (device.batteryMonitoringEnabled) { ❷
        [[NSNotificationCenter defaultCenter]
          addObserver:self
            selector:@selector(batteryChanged:)
                name:@"UIDeviceBatteryLevelDidChangeNotification"
              object:nil];
        [[NSNotificationCenter defaultCenter]
          addObserver:self
            selector:@selector(batteryChanged:)
```

```
                name:@"UIDeviceBatteryStateDidChangeNotification"
              object:nil];
    } else { ❸
         [[NSNotificationCenter defaultCenter]
           removeObserver:self
                   name:@"UIDeviceBatteryLevelDidChangeNotification"
                 object:nil];
         [[NSNotificationCenter defaultCenter]
           removeObserver:self
                   name:@"UIDeviceBatteryStateDidChangeNotification"
                 object:nil];
    }
    self.levelLabel.text = [self batteryLevel]; ❹
    self.stateLabel.text = [self batteryState:device.batteryState];
    [super viewWillAppear:animated];
}
```

❶   This sets the current battery monitoring state in the singleton UIDevice object
    to correspond to our current battery monitoring state, as determined by the
    switch on the flipside view.

❷   If battery monitoring is enabled, we're going to add our object as an observer to
    receive notifications when either the battery level or the battery state changes. If
    either of these events occurs, the batteryChanged: method will be called.

❸   If battery monitoring is disabled, we're going to remove the object as an observer
    for these notifications.

❹   In either case, we'll populate the text of our two UILabels using the convenience
    methods (batteryState: and batteryLevel:, which we'll define shortly).

Since the object may be registered as an observer when we deallocate this view, we also
need to make sure we remove ourselves as an observer of any notifications in the
dealloc method (see Chapter 4 for a discussion of the dealloc method). Add the
method below to your code:

```
- (void)dealloc {
    [[NSNotificationCenter defaultCenter] removeObserver:self];
}
```

We also need to implement the batteryChanged: method, which is called when our
application is notified of a change in battery state. Here, all we're doing is updating the
text of our two labels when we receive a notification of a change. Add the following to
BMMainViewController.m:

```
- (void)batteryChanged:(NSNotification *)note {
    UIDevice *device = [UIDevice currentDevice];
    self.levelLabel.text = [self batteryLevel];
    self.stateLabel.text = [self batteryState:device.batteryState];
}
```

Finally, we need to implement those convenience methods. Add the following to *Main-ViewController.m*:

```
- (NSString *)batteryLevel {
    UIDevice *device = [UIDevice currentDevice];

    NSString *levelString = nil;
    float level = device.batteryLevel;
    if ( level == -1 ) {
        levelString = @"---%";
    } else {
        int percent = (int) (level * 100);
        levelString = [NSString stringWithFormat:@"%i%%", percent];
    }
    return levelString;
}

- (NSString *)batteryState:(UIDeviceBatteryState )batteryState {

    NSString *state = nil;
    switch (batteryState) {
        case UIDeviceBatteryStateUnknown:
            state = @"Unknown";
            break;
        case UIDeviceBatteryStateUnplugged:
            state = @"Unplugged";
            break;
        case UIDeviceBatteryStateCharging:
            state = @"Charging";
            break;
        case UIDeviceBatteryStateFull:
            state = @"Full";
            break;
        default:
            state = @"Undefined";
            break;
    }
    return state;
}
```

At this point, we're done. We've implemented everything we need to in code, and we've linked all of our outlets to our interface. Unfortunately, since this application makes use of the UIDevice battery monitoring API, and iPhone Simulator doesn't have a battery, we have to test it directly on the device.

Make sure your iPhone is plugged in and registered with Xcode, and then change the scheme in the Xcode toolbar from iPhone Simulator to your device, as shown in Figure 6-7.

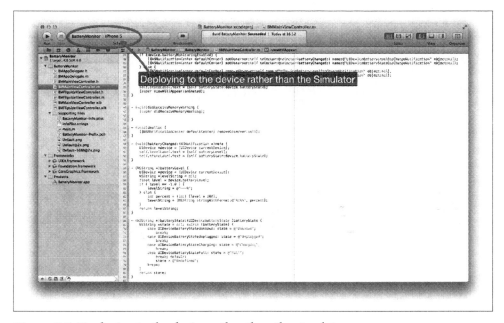

Figure 6-7. Deploying to the device rather than the simulator

Now click the Run button in the Xcode toolbar to build and deploy your application onto your iPhone. The application should automatically start and you should see something a lot like Figure 6-8.

Click the Info button in the bottom righthand corner to switch to the flipside and enable battery monitoring in the Preferences pane. Click the Done button and return to the main view. Both the battery level and the state should have changed. While the battery level only changes every 5%, you can get some immediate feedback by plugging and unplugging your device from your Mac. The state should change from Full or Charging (see Figure 6-8) to Unplugged after you unplug it from your Mac.

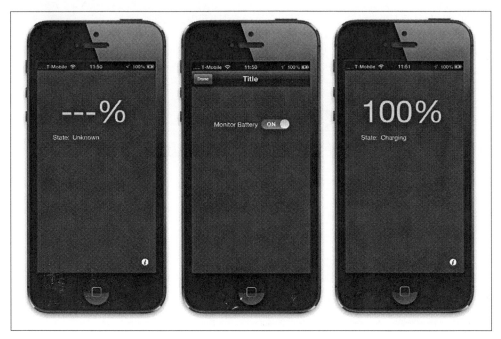

Figure 6-8. The BatteryMonitor application, as it initially starts up (left), the flipside (middle), and charging from my Mac (right)

Tab Bar Applications

If you need to provide a number of different views on the same data set, or separately present a number of different tasks relating to your application, Apple recommends using a tab bar application. Both the iTunes and the App Store applications that ship with iOS devices are examples of applications that use this pattern.

To create a tab bar application, open Xcode and start a new project. Select the Tabbed Application template from the New Project window (see Figure 6-9). When prompted, ensure the checkbox to use ARC is ticked, while the checkboxes to use storyboarding and unit tests are not. Name the project **TabExample**, and use the prefix **TE**. We're going to build a project for the iPhone once again, and we probably don't need a Git repository.

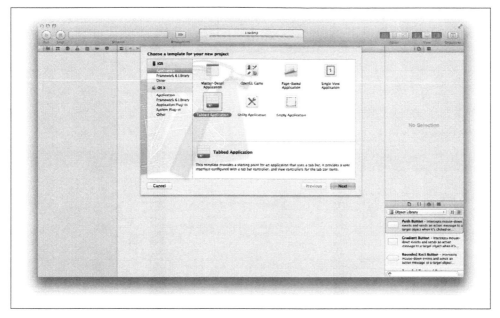

Figure 6-9. Creating a tab bar application with Xcode

The default template provides a tab bar application with the two tab items and, at least in the more recent version of Xcode, the template it uses to do so manages the tabbed views in code directly from the application delegate.

There are actually several different approaches you could take to building a tab bar application: creating and managing the tab bar directly from the application delegate, managing the tab's view entirely from a view controller, loading a individual tab's view from a secondary nib, or using a hybrid of these three approaches. The one used by Xcode is probably the simplest.

 If you are using an older version of Xcode, the tabbed application template may well be very different and could be using a hybrid approach to creating the tabbed views.

If you click the Run button in the Xcode toolbar, you should see something much like Figure 6-10 in the iPhone Simulator. If you tap the two tab bar items, you'll switch between the two tab views. Each of these views is a separate view controller.

Figure 6-10. The default tab example in the iPhone Simulator

Adding Another Tab Bar Item

Let's add another tab bar item so that you can see how to create one from scratch. The
first thing we need to do is create a new view controller. Right-click on the main TabEx
ample group and select New Files from the menu, choose a UIViewController subclass
from the template drop-down menu, and name the new class **TEThirdViewControl
ler** when prompted by Xcode. Make sure the "With XIB for User Interface" checkbox
is ticked. Three files will be created: an interface, implementation, and a corresponding
nib file.

Open up the *TEThirdViewController.m* implementation file, and in the initWithNib
Name:bundle: method, add the following code:

```
- (id)initWithNibName:(NSString *)nibNameOrNil bundle:
  (NSBundle *)nibBundleOrNil {
    self = [super initWithNibName:nibNameOrNil bundle:nibBundleOrNil];
    if (self) {
        self.title = NSLocalizedString(@"Third", @"Third");
        self.tabBarItem.image = [UIImage imageNamed:@"second"];❶
    }
    return self;
}
```

❶ We're going to reuse the icon associated with the second tab bar item for the third tab.

Although currently our tab bar item doesn't have its own image, we could easily add one. Just drag and drop the image you want to use into the project in the same way you added the images for the City Guide application in Chapter 5.

Applications need to be prepared to run on devices with different screen resolutions. To support devices with a Retina display, you should provide a high-resolution image for each image resource in your application bundle. The UIImage class will handle loading the high-resolution version of your image behind the scenes. When creating objects, you use the same filename to request both the standard and the high-resolution versions of your image. For instance:

```
self.tabBarItem.image = [UIImage mageNamed:@"second"];
```

On devices with a Retina display, the larger *second@2x.png* image will be used in place of the standard sized *second.png* image (see Chapter 12 for more details).

To look like Apple's icons, your images cannot be larger than 32×32 points in size and they must have a transparent background. I've found that PNG images between 20 and 30 points work well as tab bar icons.

You should be aware there is a difference between points and the underlying pixels on a device. One point does not necessarily correspond to one pixel on the screen. The purpose of using points is to provide a consistent size of output that is device independent. How points are actually mapped to pixels is a detail that is handled by the system. In the case of the high-resolution images you supply to your application for use in devices with a Retina display, the high-resolution image is twice the size, but since for a Retina display 4 pixels (2×2) equal 1 point, in your application, everything is laid out the same.

Creating Tab Bar Icons

Creating tab bar-based applications means you must create icons for the bar. You may be able to use the system-supplied icons, either by setting the Identifier by clicking on the UITabBarItem on the *MainWindow* nib file and changing the Identity value in the Attributes tab of the Inspector window inside Interface Builder, or directly via code inside your view controller's init: method, as shown here:

```
self.tabBarItem = [[UITabBarItem alloc]
        initWithTabBarSystemItem:UITabBarSystemItemSearch tag:0];
```

However, the selection of available icons is fairly limited and you will inevitably have to resort to creating your own. Apple has this to say on tab bar icons: "The unselected and selected images displayed by the tab bar are derived from the images that you set. The alpha values in the source image are used to create the other images—opaque values are ignored."

Effectively, the alpha channel of your image will determine the shading of your icon. Tab bar icons should therefore be in PNG format, be no larger than 30×30 points in size, and have a transparent background. Multicolor icons are ignored. The icons themselves are an opaque mask iOS will use to generate the actual tab bar icon.

One you've done that, go back and open the *TEAppDelegate.m* application delegate file in the editor and import the newly created interface file:

```
#import "TEThirdViewController.h"
```

Then, in the application:didFinishLaunchingWithOptions: method, modify the method as follows:

```
-   (BOOL)application:(UIApplication *)application
        didFinishLaunchingWithOptions:(NSDictionary *)launchOptions {
    self.window =
        [[UIWindow alloc] initWithFrame:[[UIScreen mainScreen] bounds]];
    // Override point for customization after application launch.
    UIViewController *viewController1 = [[TEFirstViewController alloc]
        initWithNibName:@"TEFirstViewController" bundle:nil];
    UIViewController *viewController2 = [[TESecondViewController alloc]
        initWithNibName:@"TESecondViewController" bundle:nil];
    UIViewController *viewController3 = [[TEThirdViewController alloc]
        initWithNibName:@"TEThirdViewController" bundle:nil];

    self.tabBarController = [[UITabBarController alloc] init];
    self.tabBarController.viewControllers =
        self.tabBarController.viewControllers =
            @[viewController1, viewController2, viewController3];❶
    self.window.rootViewController = self.tabBarController;
    [self.window makeKeyAndVisible];
```

```
        return YES;
    }
```

❶ Here we're using the new Objective-C literal support introduced with the arrival of iOS6 and Xcode 4.5. Before the arrival of support for literals you'd have had to do something like `self.tabBarController.viewControllers = [NSArray arrayWithObjects:viewController1, viewController2, view Controller3, nil];` instead.

Finally, edit the three nib files— *TEFirstViewController.xib*, *TESecondViewController.xib*, and *TEThirdViewController.xib* —and add large (say, in 144-pt font) labels saying 1, 2, and 3 to the respective views. This way you can confirm that the correct one is being activated. When you edit your new view controller, *TEThirdViewController.xib*, you'll need to add a bottom bar to the view from the Simulated Metrics section—see Figure 6-11.

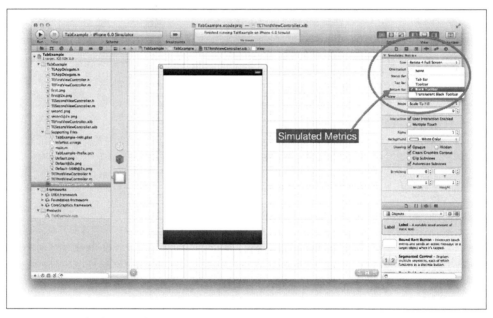

Figure 6-11. The bottom bar to the view in the TEThirdViewController.xib file

Make sure you save your changes and then click on the Run button in the Xcode toolbar to compile, deploy, and run the application in iPhone Simulator, as shown in Figure 6-12.

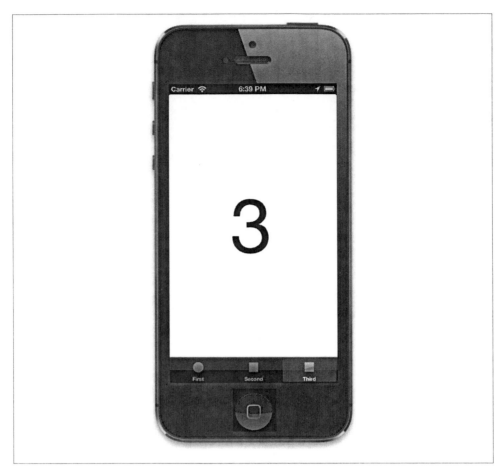

Figure 6-12. The tab bar application running in the simulator

Despite the fact that we haven't written more than a couple of lines of code in this section, you should now have a working, if rather basic, tab bar application.

Although we haven't walked through the process of building a full-blown application, you should have begun to see the commonalities and familiar patterns emerging in this application. Our application has an application delegate along with three custom view controllers with which to manage the views. This is a very similar arrangement to both the table view application we wrote in Chapter 5 and the utility application we wrote earlier in this chapter.

At this point, you may want to try building your own application on top of the infrastructure we have created so far. Start with something simple where changing something in one view affects the contents of another view. Don't worry; take your time, and I'll be here when you get back.

Combining View Controllers

It's possible to combine different types of view controllers into one application; one fairly common pattern is for each view of a tabbed application to be managed by a navigation controller. So let's take our example from the preceding section and add a navigation controller.

First, we'll modify the *TEFirstViewController.xib* by adding a table view. Click on the nib file to open it in Interface Builder, then drag and drop a table view from the Object Library into your view, and then, in the Attributes Inspector of the Utilities panel, add a simulated navigation bar from the Simulated Metrics section (see Figure 6-13).

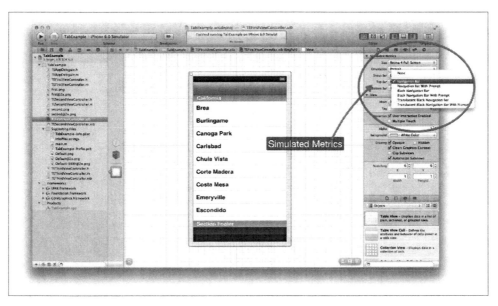

Figure 6-13. Adding a table view and a simulated navigation bar

Then switch to the Assistant Editor and Control-click and drag from the table view to the associated interface file to declare the table view as a property (see Figure 6-14) called tableView.

Finally, Control-click and drag from the UITableView in the central View panel to the icon representing File's Owner (the top icon in the dock that looks like a transparent cube) and release the mouse button. A small black pop-up window will appear, as shown in Figure 6-15.

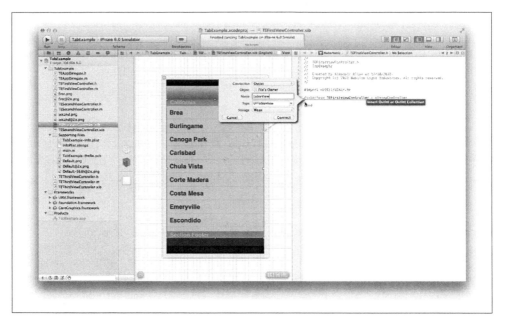

Figure 6-14. Connecting the table view outlet to the code

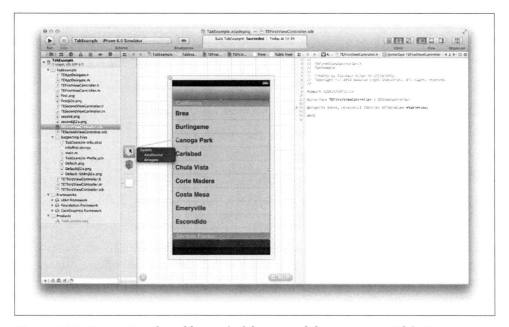

Figure 6-15. Connecting the table view's delegate and data source to File's Owner

Click on **dataSource** to connect the table view to the File's Owner (the `TEFirstView Controller` class) as its data source. Right-click and drag again, this time clicking on **delegate** in the pop-up window to make the File's Owner class the table view's delegate class.

In the Assistant Editor, modify the *TEFirstViewController.h* interface file to reflect these connections and declare that the class implements both the `UITableViewDataSource` and the `UITableViewDelegate` protocols.

Once you've done this, the *TEFirstViewController.h* file should look like this:

```
#import <UIKit/UIKit.h>

@interface TEFirstViewController :
    UIViewController <UITableViewDelegate, UITableViewDataSource>

@property (weak, nonatomic) IBOutlet UITableView *tableView;

@end
```

What we've done here is indicate that the `TEFirstViewController` class both provides the data to populate the table view and handles events generated by user interaction with the table view.

Drop back into the Standard Editor and click on the *TEFirstViewController.m* implementation file. Having declared the class as a data source and delegate, we need to implement the mandatory methods. Add the following methods to the class:

```
#pragma mark - UITableViewDataSource Methods

-   (UITableViewCell *)tableView:(UITableView *)tv
            cellForRowAtIndexPath:(NSIndexPath *)indexPath {
    UITableViewCell *cell = [tv dequeueReusableCellWithIdentifier:@"cell"];
    if( nil == cell ) {
        cell = [[UITableViewCell alloc] initWithStyle:UITableViewCellStyleDefault
                                      reuseIdentifier:@"cell"];
    }
    cell.textLabel.text = @"Test";❶
    return cell;
}

- (NSInteger)tableView:(UITableView *)tv numberOfRowsInSection:
    (NSInteger)section {
    return 3; ❷
}

#pragma mark - UITableViewDelegate Methods

- (void)tableView:(UITableView *)tv
    didSelectRowAtIndexPath:(NSIndexPath *)indexPath {
```

```
    [tv deselectRowAtIndexPath:indexPath animated:YES];
}
```

❶ We're just going to set the text of each of the table view cells to have the string Test.

❷ We'll generate three cells.

Now that we've prepared the way, let's create the navigation controller. In the *TEApp-Delegate.h* interface file, declare the property:

```
@property (strong, nonatomic) UINavigationController *navController;
```

Finally, in the `application:didFinishLaunchingWithOptions:` method, you should make the following changes:

```
- (BOOL)application:(UIApplication *)application
        didFinishLaunchingWithOptions:(NSDictionary *)launchOptions {
    self.window = [[UIWindow alloc] initWithFrame:[[UIScreen mainScreen] bounds]];
    // Override point for customization after application launch.
    UIViewController *viewController1 = [[TEFirstViewController alloc]
        initWithNibName:@"TEFirstViewController" bundle:nil];
    UIViewController *viewController2 = [[TESecondViewController alloc]
        initWithNibName:@"TESecondViewController" bundle:nil];
    UIViewController *viewController3 = [[TEThirdViewController alloc]
        initWithNibName:@"TEThirdViewController" bundle:nil];

    self.navController = [[UINavigationController alloc]
        initWithRootViewController:viewController1];
    self.navController.navigationBar.barStyle = UIBarStyleBlack;❶

    self.tabBarController = [[UITabBarController alloc] init];
    self.tabBarController.viewControllers =
        @[self.navController, viewController2, viewController3];❷
    self.window.rootViewController = self.tabBarController;
    [self.window makeKeyAndVisible];
    return YES;
}
```

❶ We're going to set the navigation bar to have a black color, rather than the default blue, as this complements the default style of the tab bar controller.

❷ Here we replace the reference to `viewController1` with the navigation controller that is now managing that view controller and other associated views.

After doing that, we've reached a good place to test the code. Save your changes and click on the Run button in the Xcode toolbar to build and deploy the application into the iPhone Simulator; you should see something much like Figure 6-16.

Figure 6-16. The navigation controller inside the first tab view

Of course if you tap on one of the table view cells, nothing, at least at the moment, is going to happen. So from here we just need to add another new view controller, fairly simple in this case, which can then be presented by the navigation controller when a cell is tapped.

Right-click on the TabExample group and select NewFile. Choose to create a UIView Controller subclass named **SimpleViewController**. When asked, make sure the checkbox to create an associated nib file is ticked (see Figure 6-17).

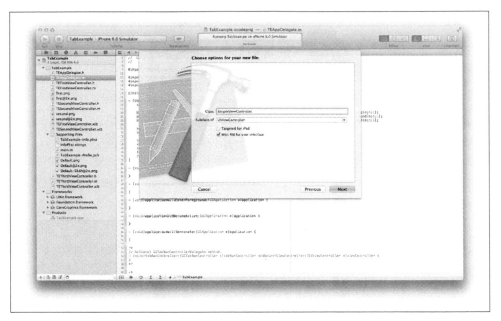

Figure 6-17. Creating a simple view controller

After creation, we're going to make just one change to the template class. In the `view DidLoad:` method of the newly created *SimpleViewController.m* implementation file, add the following line:

```
- (void)viewDidLoad {
    [super viewDidLoad];
    self.title = @"Test";
}
```

Then, returning to the *TEFirstViewController.m* implementation file once again, import both the `SimpleView` and `TEAppDelegate` classes:

```
#import "TEAppDelegate.h"
#import "SimpleViewController.h"
```

In the `tableView:didSelectRowAtIndexPath:` method, the delegate method that is called when a table view cell is tapped, add the following lines:

```
- (void)tableView:(UITableView *)tv didSelectRowAtIndexPath:
    (NSIndexPath *)indexPath {

    TEAppDelegate *delegate =
        (TEAppDelegate *)[[UIApplication sharedApplication] delegate];
    UIViewController *controller =
        [[SimpleViewController alloc] initWithNibName:@"SimpleViewController"
                                               bundle:nil];
    [delegate.navController pushViewController:controller animated:YES];
```

```
    [tv deselectRowAtIndexPath:indexPath animated:YES];
}
```

Once you've done so, save your changes and click the Run button in the Xcode toolbar to build and deploy your application back into the iPhone Simulator once again.

When the application starts, the initial tab view will look the same; however, if you now tap on a table view cell, you'll be presented with a further view (see Figure 6-18).

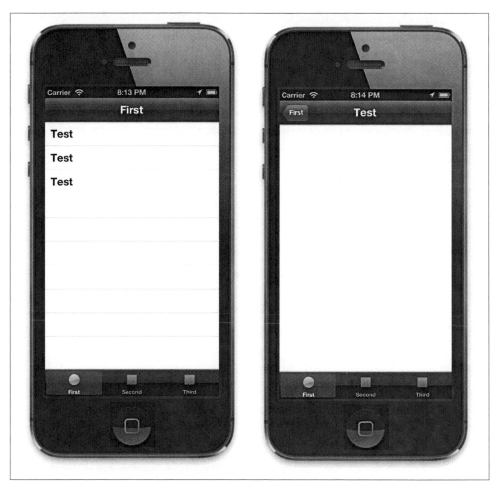

Figure 6-18. The navigation controller in a tab (left) and detail view (right)

If you tap on the second or third tabs, you'll be switched to that tab without disturbing the status of the first tab. Returning to the first tab by tapping on the relevant tab bar icon for the first tab will return you to the navigation controller in whatever state you left it when you tapped on one of the other tabs.

You've now successfully embedded a navigation controller into one of the tabs in the tab view controller; you could go on from this starting point and follow this pattern to embed a navigation controller into each of your tabs.

Modal View Controllers

So far in this chapter we've looked at two of Apple's application templates. However, in this section we're going to focus once again on an individual view controller—or rather, a way to *present* a view controller to the user. After table views and the UINavigation Controller, it's probably one of the most heavily used ways to present data: the modal view controller.

You'll have seen a modal controller in action many times when using your iPhone. A view slides in from the bottom of the screen and is usually dismissed with a Done button at the top of the screen. When dismissed, it slides back down the screen, disappearing at the bottom.

In the main controller, we would generally have a button or other UI element; tapping this would trigger an event linked to the following method in the view controller, which would bring up the modal view:

```
-(void)openNewController:(id)sender {
    OtherController *other = [[OtherController alloc] init];❶
    [self presentModalViewController:other animated:YES];❷
}
```

❶   We instantiate the view controller that manages the view we wish to display.

❷   We present the view managed by the view controller.

In the modal view itself, we would implement a button or some other way to close the view, which would call this method in the view controller:

```
-(void)doneWithController:(id)sender {
    [self dismissModalViewControllerAnimated:YES];
}
```

This dismisses the current modal view.

Modifying the City Guide Application

The best way to explain the modal view is to show it in action. For that, we're going to go back to the City Guide application we built in Chapter 5. We're going to make some fairly extensive changes to it, so you should make a copy of the project first and work with the copy while you make your modifications. In this section, I'll show you how to take your code apart and put it back together again in an organized fashion. This occurs a lot when writing applications, especially for clients who have a tendency to change their minds about what they want out of the application in the first place.

Open the Finder and navigate to the location where you saved the *CityGuide* project; see Figure 6-19.

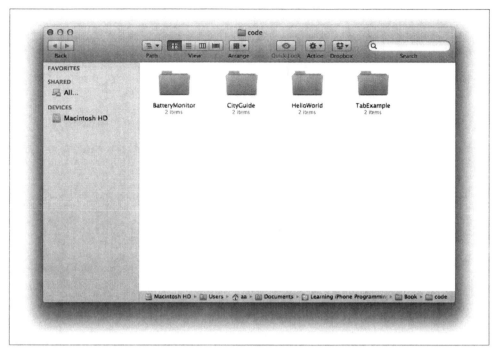

Figure 6-19. The CityGuide project folder in the Finder

Right-click or Control-click on the folder containing the project files and select Duplicate. A folder called *CityGuide copy* will be created containing a duplicate of our project. You should probably rename it to something more sensible. I suggest *CityGuide2*. Now open the new version of the project in Xcode and mouse over the blue Project icon at the top of the Project navigator and hit the Enter key, which will make the project name editable.

Enter **CityGuide2** as the new project name, and a drop-down will appear (see Figure 6-20) prompting you to approve the changes to the project. Click on Rename when prompted to do so to rename the project.

Xcode may prompt you as to whether you want to create a snapshot of the project before making a mass editing operation. While that's useful in some cases, there isn't really any need here. You can just hit "Disable."

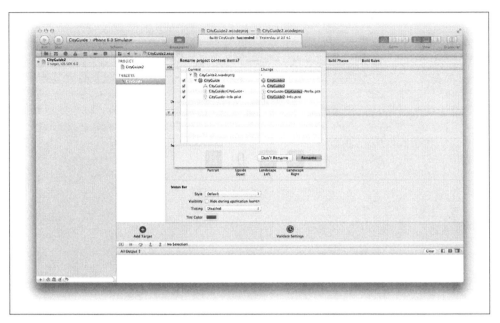

Figure 6-20. The rename project dialog window

In Chapter 5, we built an application that lets users both add and delete city entries in our table view. Incorporating the functionality to delete table view cells was fairly simple; the complicated part was allowing the ability to add cities. So, let's take a step back and look at another way to implement that functionality.

First we're going to go into the `CGViewController` implementation and back out of the changes that allowed users to edit the table view. We're going to replace the Edit button and the associated implementation with an Add button, reusing the `AddCityControl ler` code and associated view, but presenting the Add City view modally instead of using the navigation controller.

You may wonder about deleting lots of perfectly good code, but refactoring functionality like this is a fairly common task when you change your mind about how you want to present information to the user, or if the requirements driving the project change. This is good practice for you.

If you want to do a global find (and replace) over the entire project for a word or phrase, you can do so from the Search navigator tab of the lefthand pane in the Xcode window.

To remove functionality like this, first you need to figure out what needs to be removed. If you don't know the author of the original application, this can sometimes be difficult. Do a project-wide search for "editing," as shown in Figure 6-21. If you do that, you'll see that the only mention of "editing" is in the *CGViewController.m* file. The changes we'll need to make are fairly tightly constrained inside a single class. We'll have to make some minor changes elsewhere in the project. Limiting the scope of necessary changes when refactoring code in this way is one of the main benefits of writing code in an object-oriented manner.

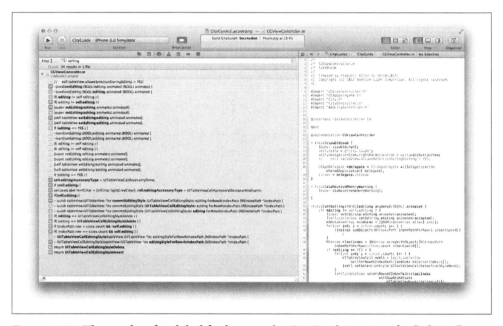

Figure 6-21. The results of a global find across the CityGuide2 project for "editing"

Open the *CGViewController.m* file in Xcode. Begin the refactoring by deleting the following methods in their entirety:

- `setEditing:animated:`
- `tableView:commitEditingStyle:forRowAtIndexPath:`
- `tableView:editingStyleForRowAtIndexPath:`

Remember that the methods as they appear in the file have longer, more complicated names. For example, `setEditing:animated:` has a prototype of `(void)setEditing:(BOOL)editing animated:(BOOL)animated`.

Next, do the following:

1. In the `viewDidLoad:` method, remove the line that adds the `self.editButtonItem` to the navigation bar.

2. In the `tableView:cellForRowAtIndexPath:` method, remove the section enclosed in the `if( self.editing )` { … } conditional statement, and the `else` { … } statement that adds the "Add New City" cell. Additionally, you should remove the line that sets the `editingAccessoryType` inside the conditional statement.

3. Similarly, remove the `if( self.editing )` { … } conditional statement in the `tableView:numberOfRowsInSection:` method.

4. Finally, in the `tableView:didSelectRowAtIndexPath:` method, remove the `&& !self.editing` expression from the first `if` block. Remove the second `if` block (which deals with what happens if we are editing) in its entirety.

We're done. If you do a global search in the project for "editing" you should now come up blank, and the class should appear as shown here:

```
#import "CGViewController.h"
#import "CGAppDelegate.h"
#import "City.h"
#import "CityController.h"
#import "AddCityController.h"


@interface CGViewController ()

@end

@implementation CGViewController

- (void)viewDidLoad {
    [super viewDidLoad];
    self.title = @"City Guide";

    CGAppDelegate *delegate =
      (CGAppDelegate *)[[UIApplication sharedApplication] delegate];
    cities = delegate.cities;
}

 - (void)didReceiveMemoryWarning {
```

```
        [super didReceiveMemoryWarning];

}

#pragma mark UITableViewDataSource Methods

- (UITableViewCell *)tableView:(UITableView *)tv
        cellForRowAtIndexPath:(NSIndexPath *)indexPath {
    UITableViewCell *cell = [tv dequeueReusableCellWithIdentifier:@"cell"];
    if( nil == cell ) {
        cell = [[UITableViewCell alloc]
            initWithStyle:UITableViewCellStyleDefault reuseIdentifier:@"cell"];
    }

    NSLog( @"indexPath.row = %d, cities.count = %d",
        indexPath.row, cities.count );
    if (indexPath.row < cities.count ) {
        City *thisCity = [cities objectAtIndex:indexPath.row];
        cell.textLabel.text = thisCity.cityName;
        cell.textLabel.textColor = [UIColor blackColor];
    }
    return cell;
}

- (NSInteger)tableView:(UITableView *)tv numberOfRowsInSection:
    (NSInteger)section {
    NSInteger count = cities.count;
    return count;
}

#pragma mark UITableViewDelegate Methods

- (void)        tableView:(UITableView *)tv
  didSelectRowAtIndexPath:(NSIndexPath *)indexPath {

    CGAppDelegate *delegate =
        (CGAppDelegate *)[[UIApplication sharedApplication] delegate];

    NSLog(@"index.row = %d", indexPath.row);
    if (indexPath.row < cities.count ) {
        CityController *city =
            [[CityController alloc] initWithIndexPath:indexPath];
        [delegate.navController pushViewController:city animated:YES];
    }
    [tv deselectRowAtIndexPath:indexPath animated:YES];
}

@end
```

Since you've now made fairly extensive changes to the view controller, you should test it to see if things are still working. Click the Build and Run button on the Xcode toolbar, and if all is well, you should see something very similar to Figure 6-22 (and in fact, looking a lot like it did back in Figure 5-14). Tapping on one of the city names should take you to its city page as before.

Figure 6-22. The stripped-down City Guide application

We've deleted a lot of code, so let's write some more. In the `viewDidLoad:` method, we need to replace the Edit button that we deleted with an Add button.

Let's add a button of style `UIBarButtonSystemItemAdd` and set things up so that when it is clicked it will call the `addCity:` method in this class. Add the following code to the `viewDidLoad:` method:

```
self.navigationItem.rightBarButtonItem = [[UIBarButtonItem alloc]
  initWithBarButtonSystemItem:UIBarButtonSystemItemAdd target:self
  action:@selector(addCity:)];
```

Since there isn't an `addCity:` method right now, we need to declare it in the *CGView-Controller.h* interface file. Open that file, and add this line after the `@property` declaration but before the `@end` directive:

```
- (void)addCity:(id)sender;
```

Now add the implementation to the *CGViewController.m* file:

```
- (void)addCity:(id)sender {
    AddCityController *addCity = [[AddCityController alloc] init];
    [self presentViewController:addCity animated:YES completion:NULL]; ❶
}
```

❶ We can pass a block to the `presentViewController:animated:completion:` method that will be called when the view controller has been successfully presented to the user, but we don't really have any use so in this case we're simply passing `NULL` as a parameter. On iPhone and iPod touch, modal view controllers are always presented full-screen, but on iPad there are several different presentation options governed by the `modalTransitionStyle` property of the view controller.

This looks almost identical to the snippet of code I showed you at the beginning of this section, but the modal view we're going to display is the one managed by our `AddCity Controller` class.

Now we need to make a couple of small changes to our `AddCityController` class. Open the *AddCityController.h* interface file in Xcode and declare the `saveCity:` method as an `IBAction`. Add this line after the `@interface { … }` statement but before the `@end` directive:

```
- (IBAction)saveCity:(id)sender;
```

Open the implementation file (*AddCityController.m*), and remove the last line (where we pop the view controller off the navigation controller) and replace it with a line dismissing the modal view controller. You'll also change the return value of the `saveCi ty:` method from `void` to `IBAction` here, just as you did in the interface file:

```
- (IBAction)saveCity:(id)sender {
    CityGuideDelegate *delegate =
      (CityGuideDelegate *)[[UIApplication sharedApplication] delegate];
    NSMutableArray *cities = delegate.cities;

    UITextField *nameEntry = (UITextField *)[nameCell viewWithTag:777];
    UITextView *descriptionEntry =
                    (UITextView *)[descriptionCell viewWithTag:777];

    if ( nameEntry.text.length > 0 ) {
        City *newCity = [[City alloc] init];
        newCity.cityName = nameEntry.text;
```

```
            newCity.cityDescription = descriptionEntry.text;
            [cities addObject:newCity];

            RootController *viewController = delegate.viewController;
            [viewController.tableView reloadData];
        }
        [self dismissViewControllerAnimated:YES completion:NULL];

    }
```

We're pretty much there at this point; however, before we finish with our changes here, we also need to go up to the `viewDidLoad:` method and delete the lines where we add the Save button to the view (it's a single statement beginning with `self.navigationI tem.rightBarButtonItem` that spans multiple lines).

Make sure you save the changes you made to the `AddCityController` class, and open the *AddCityController.xib* file inside Interface Builder.

First, drag and drop into the view a navigation bar (`UINavigationBar`) from the Object Library. Position it at the top of the view, and resize the table view so that it fits in the remaining space. While you're there, change the title of the navigation bar from "title" to Add New City.

Next, drag and drop a bar button item (`UIBarButtonItem`) onto the navigation bar and position it to the left of the title. In the Attributes Inspector, change the Identifier from Custom to Done. You'll see that this changes both the text and the style of the button, as in Figure 6-23.

Finally, right-click and drag from the Done button to File's Owner and connect the button to the `saveCity:` received action in our view controller, as in Figure 6-24.

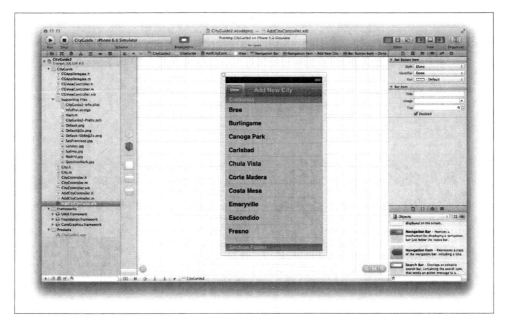

Figure 6-23. Modifying the Add City Controller nib file in Interface Builder

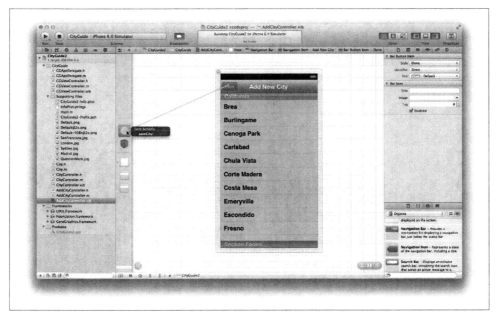

Figure 6-24. Connecting the SaveCity: received action to the Done button

Save your changes to the nib file, as we've now finished refactoring our City Guide application.

Click the Run button on the Xcode toolbar to compile and start the application in iPhone Simulator. When the application starts, you should see something like Figure 6-25. Clicking the Add button in the navigation bar should bring up our Add City view; when it does, enter some information and click the Done button. You should see your test city appear in the main table view.

Figure 6-25. The new City Guide application with the Add button on the right of the navigation bar (left) and the modified Add City view (right)

Well done. We've just taken the City Guide application apart, put it back together again, and made it work slightly differently. But what if you disliked the way we implemented the ability to add cities in the first version of the application, preferring this approach, but you still want to retain the ability to delete cities? You could still implement things so that a left-to-right swipe brought up the Delete button for the row; for instance, Apple's Mail application that ships with iOS takes this approach. Just adding the following method back into *CGViewController.m* will reimplement this functionality:

```
- (void) tableView:(UITableView *)tv
  commitEditingStyle:(UITableViewCellEditingStyle) editing
    forRowAtIndexPath:(NSIndexPath *)indexPath {
    if( editing == UITableViewCellEditingStyleDelete ) {
        [cities removeObjectAtIndex:indexPath.row];
        [tv deleteRowsAtIndexPaths:[NSArray arrayWithObject:indexPath]
          withRowAnimation:UITableViewRowAnimationLeft];
    }
}
```

The Image Picker View Controller

As promised in Chapter 5, I'm going to talk about the image picker view controller. This view controller manages Apple-supplied interfaces for choosing images and movies, and on supported devices, it takes new images or movies with the camera. As this class handles all of the required interaction with the user, it is very simple to use. All you need to do is tell it to start, and then dismiss it after the user selects an image or movie.

Adding the Image Picker to the City Guide Application

In this section, we'll continue to build on our City Guide application. Either of the two versions of the application we now have will do, as all of the changes we're going to make will be confined to the AddCityController class. In the preceding section, we made only relatively minor changes in this class that won't affect our additions here.

However, if you want to follow along, I'm going to return to our original version and work on that. As we did in the preceding section, you should work on a copy of the project, so right-click or Control-click on the folder containing the project files and select Duplicate. A folder called *CityGuide copy* will be created containing a duplicate of our project. You should probably rename the folder to something more sensible. I suggest *CityGuide3*, and then after opening it in Xcode, rename the project as we did in the last section by clicking on the blue Project icon at the top of the Project navigator and hitting the Enter key (see Figure 6-26).

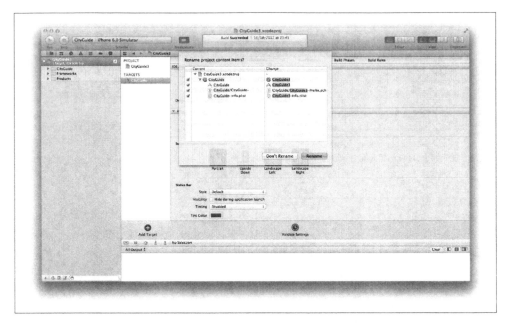

Figure 6-26. Renaming the duplicate project

The first thing we need to do is build an interface to allow the user to trigger the image picker. If you remember from Chapter 5, our Add City view was built out of two custom table view cells. The easiest way to add this ability is to add another table view cell.

Click on the *AddCityController.xib* file to open it in Interface Builder. Drag and drop a table view cell (UITableViewCell) from the Object Library into the Editor window; set the cell selection type from Blue to None in the Attributes Inspector.

We need to resize this cell so that it can hold a small thumbnail of our selected image, so go to the Size Inspector and change its height from the default 44 points to H = 83 points.

Go back to the new cell and grab a label (UILabel) from the Object Library and drop it onto the tableview cell. In the Attributes Inspector, change the label's text to "Add a picture:" and then position the label left-and-centered inside the cell.

Next, drop a round rect button (UIButton) onto the cell, and in the Attributes Inspector, change its type from Rounded Rect to Add Contact. The button should now appear as a blue circle enclosing a plus sign. Position it right-and-centered in the cell.

Finally, grab an image view (UIImageView) from the Object Library and drop it onto the cell, and resize it to be W = 83 and H = 63 using the Size Inspector. Then in the Attributes Inspector, set the Tag attribute to 777 (as this lets us easily refer to this subview from our code) and set the view mode to Aspect Fill.

After doing this, you should have something that looks a lot like Figure 6-27. Make sure you've saved your changes to the nib file, and then open the *AddCityController.h* and *AddCityController.m* files in Xcode.

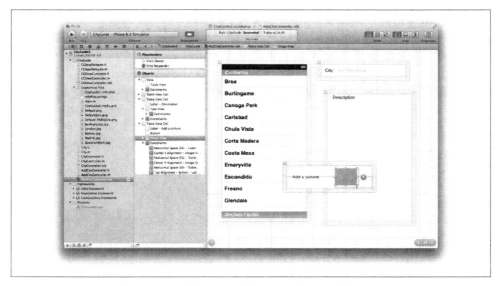

Figure 6-27. The Add Picture table view cell in Interface Builder

In the *AddCityController.h* interface file, the first thing we need to do is add an `IBOut let` to allow us to connect our code to the new table view cell inside Interface Builder. We must also add an instance variable of type `UIImage` called `cityPicture`, which we'll use to hold the image passed back to us from the image picker, along with an `addPic ture:` method that we'll connect to the `UIButton` in the cell, allowing us to start the image picker. Add the lines shown in bold to the file:

```
#import <UIKit/UIKit.h>

@interface AddCityController : UIViewController
  <UITableViewDataSource, UITableViewDelegate> {
    IBOutlet UITableView *tableView;
    IBOutlet UITableViewCell *nameCell;
    IBOutlet UITableViewCell *pictureCell;
    IBOutlet UITableViewCell *descriptionCell;

    UIImage *cityPicture;
}

- (IBAction)addPicture:(id)sender;

@end
```

Before implementing the code to go with this interface, we need to quickly go back into Interface Builder and make those two connections. Reopen the *AddCityController.xib* file and right-click and drag from the blue button in the new add picture table view cell to File's Owner to connect the button the `addPicture:` received action; see Figure 6-28.

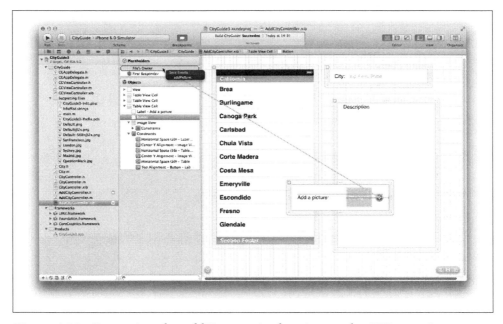

Figure 6-28. Connecting the addCity: received action to the UIButton in our new UITableViewCell to allow it to trigger the image picker

Then click and drag from File's Owner to the table view cell in the editor, as shown in Figure 6-29, and connect the `pictureCell` outlet to our newly created table view cell.

We now need to save this file, and then go back into Xcode to finish our implementation. In the *AddCityController.m* implementation file, first we have to provide a default image for the `UIImage` in the cell (otherwise, it will appear blank). We can do this inside the `viewDidLoad:` method by adding this line [you'll need an image called *QuestionMark.jpg* for this to work; see "Capturing the City Data" (page 119) in Chapter 5 for information on using this image in your project]:

```
cityPicture = [UIImage imageNamed:@"QuestionMark.jpg"];
```

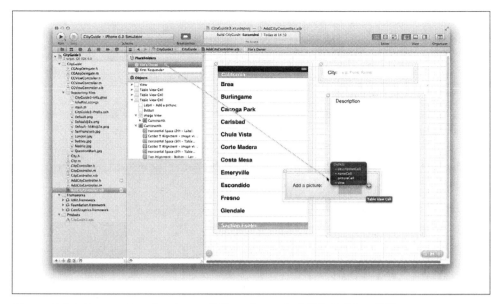

Figure 6-29. Connecting the pictureCell outlet to the UITableViewCell

We also have to make some changes to the table view delegate and data source methods (in the *AddCityController.m* implementation file) to take account of the new cell. First we need to change the number of rows returned by the `tableView:numberOfRowsIn` `Section:` method from two to three. Make the change shown in bold:

```
- (NSInteger)tableView:(UITableView *)tv
    numberOfRowsInSection:(NSInteger)section {
    return 3;
}
```

Now we need to modify the `tableView:cellForRowAtIndexPath:` method to return the extra cell in the correct position in our table view. Make the changes shown in bold:

```
- (UITableViewCell *)tableView:(UITableView *)tv
    cellForRowAtIndexPath:(NSIndexPath *)indexPath {
    UITableViewCell *cell = nil;
    if( indexPath.row == 0 ) { ❶
        cell = nameCell;
    } else if ( indexPath.row == 1 ) { ❷
        UIImageView *pictureView = (UIImageView *)[pictureCell viewWithTag:777];
        pictureView.image = cityPicture;
        cell = pictureCell;
    } else { ❸
        cell = descriptionCell;
    }
    return cell;
}
```

❶ In the first row of the table view, we return a `nameCell`, configured to allow the user to enter the city name.

❷ In the second row of the table view, we return the cell we just added. We first populate the `UIImageView` with the image held by the `cityPicture` variable that we initialized in the `viewDidLoad:` method earlier.

❸ Finally, we return the table view cell that we set up to allow the user to enter a description for the city.

We also need to change the `tableView:heightForRowAtIndexPath:` method to take account of the new cell. Make the changes shown in bold:

```
- (CGFloat)tableView:(UITableView *)tv
    heightForRowAtIndexPath:(NSIndexPath *)indexPath {
    CGFloat height;
    if( indexPath.row == 0 ) {
        height = 44;
    } else if( indexPath.row == 1 ) {
        height = 83;
    } else {
        height = 440;
    }
    return height;

}
```

Finally, we need to add a placeholder implementation for our `addPicture:` method, which we'll fill in later:

```
- (IBAction)addPicture:(id)sender {
    NSLog(@"addPicture: called.");
}
```

We're done, at least for now. Click the Run button in the Xcode toolbar to compile and run the application in iPhone Simulator. Once the application has started, tap the Edit button in the navigation bar and click Add New City (if you chose to modify the second version of the guide, click the Add button). Figure 6-30 shows the modified view.

Figure 6-30. The modified New City view

Now we have an interface to trigger the image picker for us, so let's implement the code to do that. First we need to add a UIImagePickerController variable to the *AddCity-Controller.h* interface file. We also need to declare the class to be a delegate. Make the changes shown in bold:

```
@interface AddCityController : UIViewController
  <UITableViewDataSource, UITableViewDelegate,
  UIImagePickerControllerDelegate, UINavigationControllerDelegate> { ①

    IBOutlet UITableView *tableView;
    IBOutlet UITableViewCell *nameCell;
    IBOutlet UITableViewCell *pictureCell;
    IBOutlet UITableViewCell *descriptionCell;

    UIImage *cityPicture;
    UIImagePickerController *pickerController;
```

```
    }

    - (IBAction)addPicture:(id)sender;

    @end
```

❶   We need to declare the class as both a `UIImagePickerControllerDelegate` and
       a `UINavigationControllerDelegate`. Both declarations are necessary for the
       class to interact with the `UIImagePickerController`.

In the *AddCityController.m* implementation file, we need to modify the `viewDid`
`Load:` method to initialize our `UIImagePickerController`. Make the changes shown in
bold:

```
    - (void)viewDidLoad {
        self.title = @"New City";
        self.navigationItem.rightBarButtonItem = [[UIBarButtonItem alloc]
          initWithBarButtonSystemItem:UIBarButtonSystemItemSave
          target:self action:@selector(saveCity:)];
        cityPicture = [UIImage imageNamed:@"QuestionMark.jpg"];

        pickerController = [[UIImagePickerController alloc] init]; ❶
        pickerController.allowsEditing = NO; ❷
        pickerController.delegate = self; ❸
        pickerController.sourceType =
            UIImagePickerControllerSourceTypeSavedPhotosAlbum; ❹

    }
```

❶   We allocate and initialize the `UIImagePickerController` (this means we're
       responsible for it and we must release it inside our `dealloc:` method).

❷   When using the image picker, the user may be allowed to edit the selected image
       before it is passed to our code. This disables that option here.

❸   We set the delegate class to be this class.

❹   Finally, we select the image source. There are three: `UIImagePickerController`
       `SourceTypeCamera`, `UIImagePickerControllerSourceTypePhotoLibrary`, and
       `UIImagePickerControllerSourceTypeSavedPhotosAlbum`.   Each   presents
       different views to the user, allowing her to take an image with the camera, pick
       it from the image library, or choose something from her photo album.

We also need to implement the `addPicture:` method, the method called when we tap
the button in our interface. This method simply starts the image picker interface, presenting it as a modal view controller. Replace the placeholder `addPicture:` method you
added to the *AddCityController.m* file as part of the instance methods pragma section
with the following:

```
- (IBAction)addPicture:(id)sender {
  [self presentViewController:pickerController animated:YES completion:nil];
}
```

Next, we need to implement the delegate method that will tell our code the user has finished with the picker interface—the imagePickerController:didFinishPicking MediaWithInfo: method. Add the following to *AddCityController.m*:

```
- (void)imagePickerController:(UIImagePickerController *)picker
    didFinishPickingMediaWithInfo:(NSDictionary *)info
{
    [[self dismissViewControllerAnimated:YES completion:nil]; ❶
    cityPicture = [info objectForKey:@"UIImagePickerControllerOriginalImage"]; ❷

    UIImageView *pictureView = (UIImageView *)[pictureCell viewWithTag:777]; ❸
    pictureView.image = cityPicture;
    [tableView reloadData];

}
```

❶   We dismiss the image picker interface; we don't need to add a completion block at this time so we just pass nil.

❷   We grab the UIImage selected by the user from the NSDictionary returned by the image picker and set the cityPicture variable.

❸   We grab a reference to the thumbnail UIImageView, populate it with the chosen image, and reload the table view so that the displayed image is updated.

Finally, in the saveCity: method, we need to add a line just before we add the new City to the cities array. Add the line shown in bold:

```
newCity.cityPicture = nil;
newCity.cityPicture = cityPicture;
[cities addObject:newCity];
```

This will take our new picture and serialize it into the data model for our application.

It's time to test our application. Make sure you've saved your changes and click on the Run button.

If you test the application in iPhone Simulator, you'll notice that there are no images in the Saved Photos folder. There is a way around this problem. In the simulator, tap the Safari icon and drag and drop a picture from your computer (you can drag it from the Finder or iPhoto) into the browser. You'll notice that the URL bar displays the file path to the image. Click and hold down the cursor over the image and a dialog will appear allowing you to save the image to the Saved Photos folder.

Once the application has started, tap the Edit button in the navigation bar and go to the New City view. Tapping the blue button will open the image picker, as shown in Figure 6-31, and allow you to select an image. Once you've done that, the image picker will be dismissed, and you'll return to the New City interface.

Figure 6-31. Adding a new image

Is everything working? Not exactly; depending on how you tested the interface you may have noticed the problem. Currently, if you enter text in the City field and then click on the "Add a picture" button before clicking on the Description field, the text in the City field will be lost when you return from the image picker. However, if you enter text in the City field and *then* enter text in (or just click on) the Description field, the text will still be there when you return from the image picker. Any text entered in the Description field will remain in any case.

This is actually quite a subtle bug and is a result of the different ways in which a UIText Field and UITextView interact as first responders. We're going to talk about the *responder chain* in Chapter 8 when we deal with data handling in more detail. However, to explain this without getting into too much detail, the first responder is the object in the application that is the current recipient of any UI events (such as a touch). The UIWindow class sends events to the registered first responder, giving it the first chance to handle the event. If it fails to do so, the event will be passed to the next object.

By default, the `UITextField` doesn't commit any changes to its text until it is no longer the first responder, which is where the problem comes from. While we could change this behavior through the `UITextFieldDelegate` protocol, there is a simpler fix. Add the lines shown in bold to the `addPicture:` method:

```
- (IBAction)addPicture:(id)sender {
    UITextField *nameEntry = (UITextField *)[nameCell viewWithTag:777];
    [nameEntry resignFirstResponder];

    [self presentModalViewController:pickerController animated:YES];
}
```

With this change, we force the `UITextField` to resign as first responder before we open the image picker. This means that when the image picker is dismissed, the text we entered before opening it will remain when we are done.

Save your changes, and then click on the Run button in the Xcode toolbar. When the application starts up, return to the New City view and confirm that this simple change fixes the bug.

We're done with the City Guide application for a while. However, we'll be back in Chapter 8, where I'll fix the last remaining problem with the application and talk about data storage. Until then, cities you add will not be saved when you exit the application, so don't enter all your favorite cities just yet.

Master-Detail Applications

Up until now we've been building examples for the iPhone. There is no particular reason for that—the code we've looked at so far is going to function identically on the iPad, and in fact, a good exercise at this point would be to go back and rebuild one of our previous applications for the iPad. You'll find it easy going.

I've been using applications targeted to the iPhone first because of exactly that point—that the code would be identical between the two platforms—but mostly because more people have an iPhone, or an iPod touch, than have an iPad.

However, sometimes the code isn't the same, and this is the case of the Xcode Master-Detail Application template. On the iPhone it is implemented using a `UINavigation Controller`; however, on the iPad, it is implemented using a `UISplitView Controller`. This is a container view controller that manages two panes of information, and is *iPad only*; there is no equivalent controller for the iPhone.

Creating a Universal Application

Open up Xcode and create a new project and choose the Master-Detail template from the drop-down, as shown in Figure 6-32.

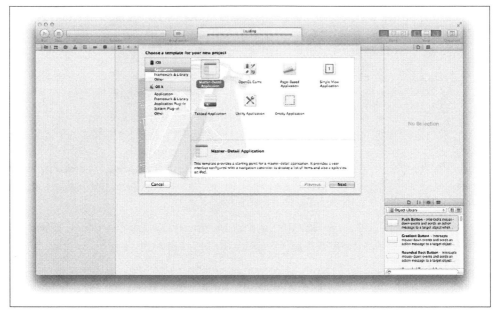

Figure 6-32. Picking the Master-Detail Application template

When prompted, name the project **MDExample** and ensure that the ARC checkbox is ticked; however, for the first time, set the Device Family to Universal rather than iPhone (or iPad for that matter), as shown in Figure 6-33.

This will create a *universal application*, which will run on both the iPhone and the iPad. You may have come across these in iTunes; they're marked with the small plus symbol on the application's icon.

A universal application will generally have separate nib files for iPhone and iPad (see Figure 6-34) along with application logic to handle that. Essentially, if we think about things using the MVC pattern, the views (nib files) and controllers (view controllers) are separate, while the model (the backend representation of our data) is shared.

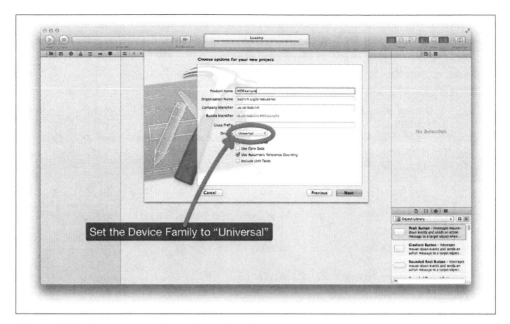

Figure 6-33. Creating a universal application

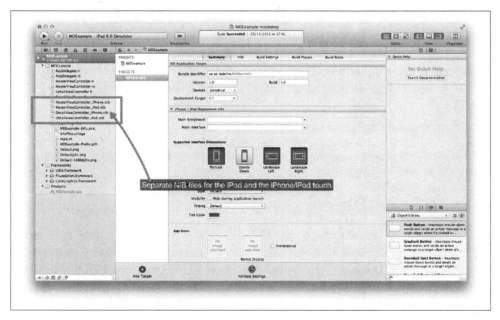

Figure 6-34. Separate nib files for the iPad and the iPhone/iPod touch

Let's look at the application delegate. Click on the *AppDelegate.m* file to open it in the Standard Editor. If you look at the `application:didFinishLaunchingWithOptions:` method, you'll see that it the application launches and does very different things depending on whether it is running on an iPhone or an iPad.

```
- (BOOL)application:(UIApplication *)application
           didFinishLaunchingWithOptions:(NSDictionary *)launchOptions {
    self.window =
        [[UIWindow alloc] initWithFrame:[[UIScreen mainScreen] bounds]];❶
    if ([[UIDevice currentDevice] userInterfaceIdiom] ==
        UIUserInterfaceIdiomPhone) {

        // The application is running on an iPhone or iPod touch

    } else {

        // The application is running on an iPad
    }
    [self.window makeKeyAndVisible];❷
    return YES;
}
```

❶ Programmatically create the application's main window.

❷ Make this window visible to the user.

It does this by checking the `userInterfaceIdiom` in the shared `UIDevice` class:

```
[[UIDevice currentDevice] userInterfaceIdiom]
```

Currently, this can either be `UIUserInterfaceIdiomPhone` or `UIUserInterfaceIdiom Pad`. If the application detects that it is running on an iPhone, it runs the following code block:

```
        MasterViewController *masterViewController =
          [[MasterViewController alloc] initWithNibName:
          @"MasterViewController_iPhone" bundle:nil];❶
          self.navigationController =
  [[UINavigationController alloc] initWithRootViewController:
     masterViewController];❷
          self.window.rootViewController = self.navigationController;❸
```

❶ The `MasterViewController` is a `UITableViewController`; up until now we've built our table views by hand using `UIViewControllers`. However, a `UITable ViewController` is an Apple-provided convenience class that handles some of the heavy lifting involved in managing a table view. It provides default connections to the table view's data source and delegate and does some behind-the-scenes management. However, it's not magic, it's just a subclass of `UIView Controller`.

❷ We set the root view of our `UINavigationController` to be our table view.

❸   We set the root view controller of our applications window to be the navigation controller.

Apart from the appearance of the UITableViewController, the Apple-provided convenience class for handling table views, this is all pretty standard stuff and shouldn't be new to you. However, something very different happens if the application is running on an iPad. Here, three distinct things happen. First, the master view controller is created and assigned as the root view of a navigation controller:

```
MasterViewController *masterViewController =
  [[MasterViewController alloc] initWithNibName:@"MasterViewController_iPad"
                                         bundle:nil];
UINavigationController *masterNavigationController =
  [[UINavigationController alloc] initWithRootViewController:
    masterViewController];
```

Then we create a separate detail view alongside the master view, and assign it as the root view of a separate navigation controller:

```
DetailViewController *detailViewController =
[[DetailViewController alloc] initWithNibName:@"DetailViewController_iPad"
                                       bundle:nil];
UINavigationController *detailNavigationController =
  [[UINavigationController alloc]
     initWithRootViewController:detailViewController];
```

Finally, a UISplitViewController is created, the detail view controller is set as the delegate class, and the two managing navigation controllers are passed as an array to the split view controller:

```
self.splitViewController = [[UISplitViewController alloc] init];
self.splitViewController.delegate = detailViewController;
self.splitViewController.viewControllers =
  [NSArray arrayWithObjects:masterNavigationController,
           detailNavigationController,
           nil];

self.window.rootViewController = self.splitViewController;❶
```

❶   We set the root view controller of our application's window to be the split view controller.

 If you're finding the code in the universal application a bit overwhelming, you might want to create two separate applications based on the Master-Detail Application template; one targeted for the iPhone, the other for the iPad. Then open both projects in Xcode and compare the now split code base.

You can take a look at the difference this makes by running the template application in the iPhone and iPad Simulators and seeing how the application behaves in both cases. To do so, you should change the Scheme in the drop-down menu in the Xcode toolbar (see Figure 6-35), in exactly the same way you choose to target the simulator or the device for a normal build, and then click the Run button to build and deploy your application into the relevant simulator (or onto your device for that matter).

Figure 6-35. Changing the target of your build, the iPad Simulator

Running the application on both simulators should hopefully make clear the difference between the two user interfaces (see Figure 6-36).

The iPhone interface is a standard table view interface, much like the interfaces we're talked about up until now, while the iPad interface is different. You'll have come across this view controller in the Mail application that ships with the iPad.

You might notice that, at least by default, in portrait orientation the split view controller shows only the larger (detail) panel and provides a toolbar button for displaying the first panel (the table view) using another view that slides in from the left. However, if you rotate the iPad or the iPad Simulator using the Hardware→Rotate Right (or Rotate Left) menu item, you'll see that this view changes and the master view is inset to the left of the detail view.

Figure 6-36. The Master-Detail Application in the iPad (left) using a UISplitView-Controller and the iPhone (right) using a standard UINavigationController

If this is not the behavior you want—for instance, the Settings application that ships with the iPad displays the master controller to the left of the detail controller in both landscape and portrait orientations—you can change it. In the application delegate, we set the detail view controller as the UISplitViewControllerDelegate and we can use this delegate protocol to tell the split view controller how to display the two controllers.

Add the following code to the *DetailViewController.m* implementation:

```
- (BOOL)splitViewController: (UISplitViewController*)svc
  shouldHideViewController:(UIViewController *)vc
          inOrientation:(UIInterfaceOrientation)orientation {
    return NO;
}
```

and then click the Run button to rebuild the application and run it in the iPad Simulator. You should see the interface has now changed to place the two controllers next to each other.

Because the two panes (master and detail) are destined to contain application-specific content, there isn't any default interaction between the two controllers; it's up to us to provide and manage those in code.

If you take a look at the *DetailViewController.[h,m]* interface and implementation files, you should notice that the class provides two properties: a `detailItem` and a `detail DescriptionLabel`. The `setDetailItem:` method provided by the template, which overrides the default method generated by synthesizing the `detailItem` property, calls a further `configureView` method, which in turn takes the `description` of the object passed to the controller and provides that as the text in the associated `UILabel` in the `DetailViewController` nib file.

If you tap the "+" button a couple of times to add a few items to the table view in the master controller, and then go ahead and tap on one of these in turn, you'll see that the description in the detail view pane changes to be the same as the item you selected.

 When building universal applications, you should always remember that an iPad is not just a "big" iPod touch and that the user interface for an iPad application should not necessarily be a direct replica of the iPhone.

Popover Controllers

I mentioned earlier in the chapter that we were going to take a more detailed look at popover controllers. Although not actually a view controller itself, the class manages the presentation of view controllers.

 Before the arrival of iOS 6 the `UISplitViewController` used a Popover Controller to present the master view when the iPad was in portrait mode rather than sliding a separate view in from the left. Like the `UISplitViewController` we looked at in the last section, the popover controller is only available on the iPad. There is no equivalent on the iPhone.

You can associate a popover controller with any piece of your UI—for instance, allowing you to present detailed information about a specific piece of your user interface, or a submenu of controls. We can create a `UIPopoverController` very simply, for instance in a button callback:

```
- (IBAction)itemTapped:(id)sender {
    UIViewController* content = [[UIViewController alloc] init];
    UIPopoverController* popover = [[UIPopoverController alloc]
        initWithContentViewController:content];
    popover.delegate = self;

    self.popoverController = popover;
    [self.popoverController presentPopoverFromBarButtonItem:sender
        permittedArrowDirections:UIPopoverArrowDirectionAny animated:YES];
}
```

Popovers are dismissed automatically when the user taps outside the popover view. Taps within the popover do not cause it to be automatically dismissed. When a popover is dismissed due to user taps outside the popover view, the popover automatically notifies its delegate of the action.

It's not necessary to tie the presentation of the popup to a button; you can also attach the popover to a rectangular area in your main view. Depending on where it is positioned, it may appear at any side of the "hot spot." The code for attaching it this way is almost identical to the first:

```
[self.popoverController
    presentPopoverFromRect:CGRectMake(10.0f, 10.0f, 10.0f, 10.0f)
    inView:self.view
    permittedArrowDirections:UIPopoverArrowDirectionAny animated:YES];
```

Here, instead of attaching it to a button, we are attaching it to an arbitrary rectangle inside our view constructed using the CGRectMake method call (where the parameters of CGRectMake are **x**, **y**, **width**, and **height**). You can get the CGRect of an arbitrary UIView, such as a button or other user interface element, by calling:

```
CGRect frame = view.frame;
```

CHAPTER 7

Connecting to the Network

The iOS platform is designed with always-on connectivity in mind. Developers have taken advantage of this to create some innovative third-party applications. Most iOS applications will make a network connection at some point, and many are so fundamentally tied to web services that they need a network connection to function.

Detecting Network Status

Before your application attempts to make a network connection, you need to know whether you have a network available, and depending on what you want to do, you might also want to know whether the device is connected to a WiFi or cellular network.

 One of the more common reasons for Apple to reject an application submitted for review is that the application doesn't correctly notify the user when the application fails to access the network. Apple requires that you detect the state of the network connection and report it to the user when the connection is unavailable, or otherwise handle it in a graceful manner.

Apple's Reachability Class

Helpfully, Apple has provided some sample code to deal with detecting current network status. The Reachability code is available in the iOS Developer Library (*http://develop er.apple.com/library/ios/samplecode/Reachability/*).

Two different versions of the Apple Reachability code are in general circulation. The earlier version, which appears in many web tutorials and has been widely distributed, dates from the pre-2.0 SDK. The newer version, released in August 2009, and then updated with the release of iOS 4, is much improved and supports asynchronous connection monitoring. However, the interface offered by the two versions is very different, so to avoid confusion, you need to be aware which version of the Reachability code you're using.

Download the *Reachability.zip* file from Apple, and unzip it.

Reusing the Reachability class

We're more interested in reusing the *Reachability.[h,m]* class files in our own projects than Apple's Reachability example. Open the *Reachability/Classes* directory in the Finder and grab the *Reachability.h* and *Reachability.m* files from the Xcode project and copy them onto your desktop (or any convenient location). This is the actual `Reachability` class that we want to reuse in our projects.

To use the `Reachability` class in a project, you must do the following after you create a new project in Xcode:

1. Drag and drop both the header and implementation files into the main group in your project, and be sure to tick the "Copy items into destination group's folder (if needed)" checkbox in the pop-up dialog that appears when you drop the files into Xcode (see Figure 7-1).

2. Click on the Project icon at the top of the Project pane in Xcode, then click on the main Target for the project, and then on the Build Phases tab. Finally, click on the Link Binary with Libraries item to open up the list of linked frameworks, and click the + symbol to add a new framework. Select the System Configuration framework (*SystemConfiguration.framework*) from the drop-down list and click the Add button (see Figure 7-2).

When adding files to your project, make sure the "Add to target" checkbox is ticked; otherwise, the files won't be linked to your application's binary.

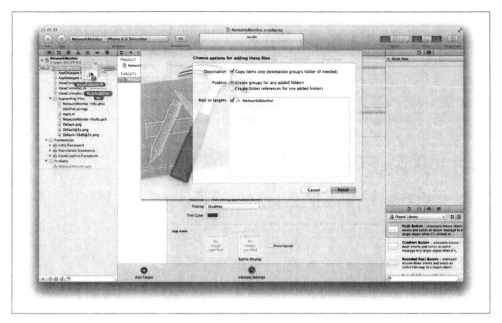

Figure 7-1. Adding the Reachability class files to the project

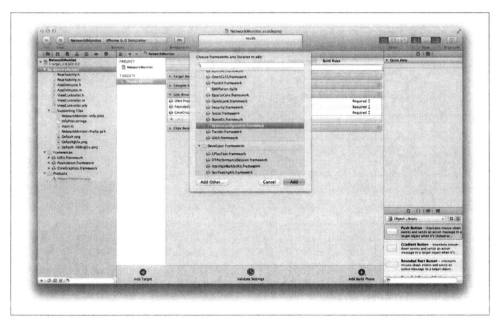

Figure 7-2. Adding the System Configuration framework to the project

There are two ways to make use of Apple's Reachability code: synchronously or asynchronously.

Synchronous Reachability

The synchronous case is the simpler of the two approaches; here we import the *Reachability.h* header file into our code and then carry out a "spot-check" as to whether the network is reachable, and whether we have a wireless or WWAN connection:

```
#import "Reachability.h"
... some code omitted ...

Reachability *reach = [Reachability reachabilityForInternetConnection];
NetworkStatus status = [reach currentReachabilityStatus];
```

or alternatively, whether a specific host is reachable:

```
Reachability *reach = [Reachability reachabilityWithHostName: @"www.apple.com"];
NetworkStatus status = [reach currentReachabilityStatus];
```

We can then use a simple `switch` statement to decode the network status. The following code turns the `status` flag into an `NSString`, perhaps to update a `UILabel` in the application interface. You can trigger any action you need to (disabling parts of your user interface, perhaps?) depending on the current network status:

```
- (NSString *)stringFromStatus:(NetworkStatus) status {

    NSString *string;
    switch(status) {
        case NotReachable:
            string = @"Not Reachable";
            break;
        case ReachableViaWiFi:
            string = @"Reachable via WiFi";
            break;
        case ReachableViaWWAN:
            string = @"Reachable via WWAN";
            break;
        default:
            string = @"Unknown";
            break;
    }
    return string;
}
```

We can easily put together a quick application to illustrate use of the Reachability code. Open Xcode and start a new project, choose a Single View Application targeted at the iPhone, and when prompted, name it **NetworkMonitor**.

Import the Reachability code and then add the *SystemConfiguration.framework* into the project, as we discussed previously. Then open the *AppDelegate.h* interface file in the

Xcode Editor, import the Reachability interface file, and declare the `stringFromSta` tus: method as shown in the following code:

```objectivec
#import <UIKit/UIKit.h>
#import "Reachability.h"

@class ViewController;

@interface AppDelegate : UIResponder <UIApplicationDelegate>

@property (strong, nonatomic) UIWindow *window;
@property (strong, nonatomic) ViewController *viewController;

- (NSString *)stringFromStatus:(NetworkStatus )status;

@end
```

Save your changes, and open the *AppDelegate.m* implementation file in the editor and modify the `applicationDidFinishLaunchingWithOptions:` method:

```objectivec
-   (BOOL)application:(UIApplication *)application
        didFinishLaunchingWithOptions:(NSDictionary *)launchOptions {
    self.window = [[UIWindow alloc] initWithFrame:[[UIScreen mainScreen] bounds]];

    self.viewController =
        [[ViewController alloc] initWithNibName:@"ViewController" bundle:nil];
    self.window.rootViewController = self.viewController;
    [self.window makeKeyAndVisible];

    Reachability *reach = [Reachability reachabilityForInternetConnection];
    NetworkStatus status = [reach currentReachabilityStatus];
    UIAlertView *alert = [[UIAlertView alloc] initWithTitle:@"Reachability"
        message:[self stringFromStatus:status] delegate:nil
        cancelButtonTitle:@"OK" otherButtonTitles:nil];
    [alert show];

    return YES;
}
```

The final step is to add the `stringWithStatus:` method I showed earlier to *AppDelegate.m*. Save your changes and click the Run button on the Xcode toolbar to compile your code and deploy it into iPhone Simulator. You should see something similar to Figure 7-3.

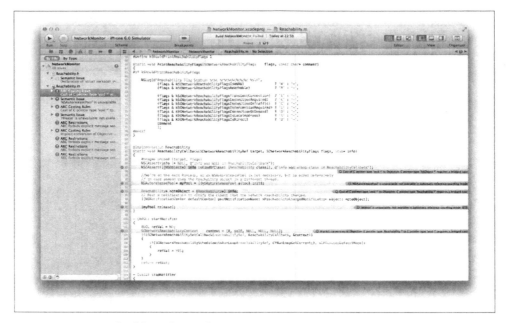

Figure 7-3. Errors building the application

Something has gone horribly wrong! If you look at errors thrown by the compiler, you'll see that all of the issues are semantic problems having to do with Automatic Reference Counting (ARC). Unfortunately, while our code uses ARC, the Reachability class, which was originally written for iOS 3 and updated for iOS 4, doesn't.

Don't worry, there are a several ways around this. We can either rewrite the Reachability class to be ARC-compatible by hand, by making use of Xcode's automated tools, or we can mark the *Reachability.[h,m]* files as not using ARC.

Since we're only dealing with a single class, let's first try turning off ARC for the Reachability class. Click on the Project icon at the top of the Project pane in Xcode, then click on the NetworkMonitor Target for the project, and then on the Build Phases tab. Finally, click on the Compile Sources tab to expand the list of sources. Double-click on *Reachability.m*, and in the drop-down box, type **-fno-objc-arc**. (see Figure 7-4).

After doing this, click the Run button once again to compile the application. The errors thrown by the previous build should disappear, and you should see something very much like Figure 7-5 in the iPhone Simulator.

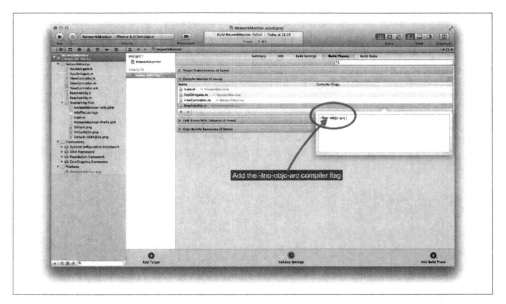

Figure 7-4. Adding compiler flags to individual files

Figure 7-5. The NetworkMonitor application running in the iPhone Simulator

Just turning off ARC for the Reachability class files, while leaving it on for the rest of our project, has allowed us to reuse the code.

 During the transition period around the introduction of ARC, and possibly for several years afterward, until ARC is more widely adopted, you'll be running into problems with Objective-C code written for iOS that doesn't make use of ARC. Despite this, there is no good reason to start new projects without enabling ARC. I'll briefly talk about how to refactor existing projects to use ARC later in the chapter.

Asynchronous reachability

The asynchronous approach is (only slightly) more complicated, but using the Reachability class in this way means your application can be notified of changes in the current network status. You must first import the *Reachability.h* header file into your code. After that, you need to register the class that must monitor the network as an observer for the kReachabilityChangedNotification event:

```
[[NSNotificationCenter defaultCenter] addObserver: self
  selector: @selector(reachabilityChanged:)
  name: kReachabilityChangedNotification
  object: nil];
```

Then you need to create a Reachability instance and start event notification:

```
Reachability *reach =
  [[Reachability reachabilityWithHostName: @"www.apple.com"] retain];
[reach startNotifier];
```

When the network reachability status changes, the Reachability instance will notify your code by calling the reachabilityChanged: method. What you do in that method of course very much depends on *why* you're monitoring the network status in the first place; however, the stub of such a method would look like this:

```
- (void) reachabilityChanged: (NSNotification *)notification {
    Reachability *reach = [notification object];
    if( [reach isKindOfClass: [Reachability class]]) { ❶
        NetworkStatus status = [reach currentReachabilityStatus];
        // Insert your code here
    }
}
```

❶ The isKindOfClass: method returns a Boolean that indicates whether the receiver is an instance of a given class. Here we check whether the Reachability object passed as part of the notification is indeed of type Reachability.

Using Reachability directly

The Apple `Reachability` class is just a friendly wrapper around the `SCNetworkReacha bility` programming interface, which is part of *SystemConfiguration.framework*. While I recommend using Apple's sample code if possible, you can use the interfaces directly if you need to do something out of the ordinary.

 If you are interested in alternative approaches to checking for network reachability, I recommend looking at the `UIDevice-Reachability` extensions provided by Erica Sadun in *The iOS 6 Developer's Cookbook* (Addison-Wesley). The Reachability code is available for download from the GitHub source repository that accompanies the book (*https://github.com/erica/iOS-6-Cookbook*). The code is located in the *C13/01 - Reachability/* folder in the repository.

Updating the Reachability project

Apple's Reachability example project was originally written for iOS 3, or iPhone OS 3, as it was called back then, so the code is laid out somewhat differently than you might expect.

If you want to run the example project directly it's advisable to update it. Click on the Issue navigator in the Navigator panel, and you'll see there is a validation issue with the *Reachbility.xcodeproj* project file itself (rather than with the code in the project). If you click on this issue, a drop-down panel will appear, asking you whether you want to update the project settings (see Figure 7-6).

Click the Perform Changes button to update the project, and most of the warnings will disappear. What will be left is that there is no Retina 4 Support. if you click on this issue, another drop-down panel will appear, asking you if you want to add a `Default-568h@2x.png` launch image [Figure 7-7; see also "Adding a Launch Image" (page 390)].

After resolving these two problems you should be able to compile the example project and run it on the iPhone Simulator under iOS 6 without any problems.

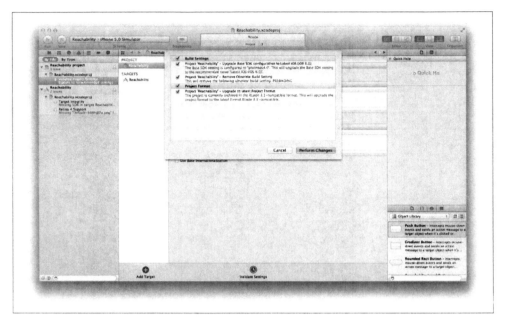

Figure 7-6. Updating the project

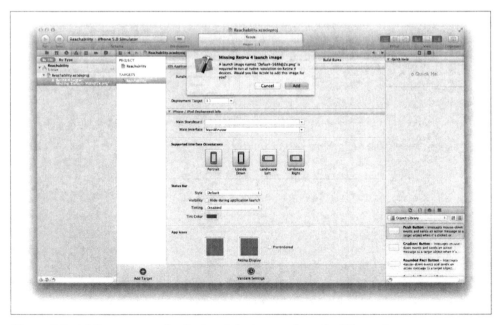

Figure 7-7. Adding support for Retina 4 devices, such as the iPhone 5

You'll be left with a single warning, "Declaration of 'struct sockaddr_in' will not be visible outside of this function." You can safely ignore this warning for now.

 You should be aware that at this point in the conversation, the Reachability example still uses manual memory management rather than Automatic Reference Counting (ARC). Additionally, while the project will run on the iPhone 5, the UI has not been updated for the increased display size.

We now need to update the project to use ARC. Click Edit→Refactor→Convert to Objective-C ARC in the Xcode menu to start the refactor; you should see something much like Figure 7-8.

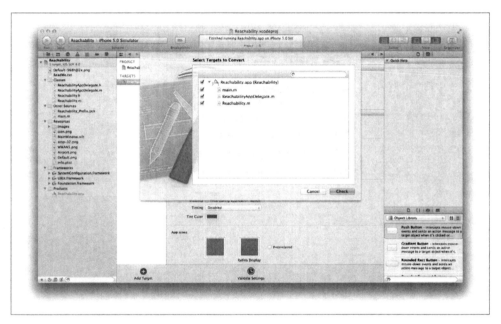

Figure 7-8. Converting the project to ARC

Make sure the checkbox next to *Reachability.app* is ticked and click on the Check and Close button. Unfortunately, things won't go as smoothly as we'd like, and you should see something like Figure 7-9.

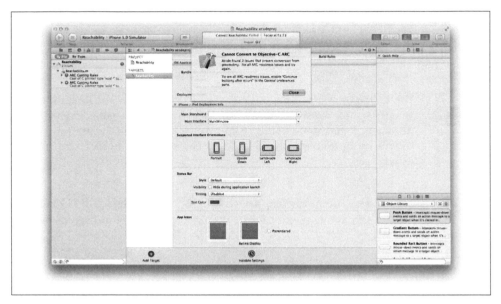

Figure 7-9. Automatic conversion to ARC has failed

There are two outstanding issues that Xcode can't deal with automatically, as shown in Figure 7-10.

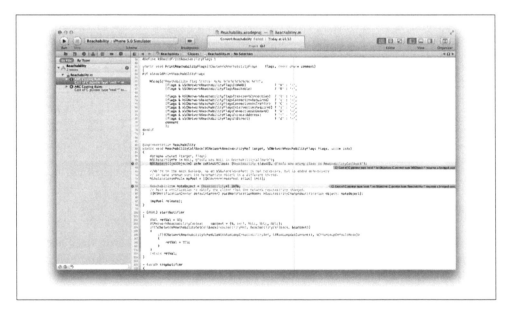

Figure 7-10. Two issues that must be dealt with manually before automatic conversion of the project is possible for Xcode

If we look at the code, both issues are in the `ReachabilityCallback( ... )` method:

```
static void ReachabilityCallback(SCNetworkReachabilityRef target,
                                 SCNetworkReachabilityFlags flags,
                                 void* info) {
    #pragma unused (target, flags)
    NSCAssert(info != NULL, @"info was NULL in ReachabilityCallback");
    NSCAssert([(NSObject*) info isKindOfClass: [Reachability class]],
        @"info was wrong class in ReachabilityCallback");

    NSAutoreleasePool* myPool = [[NSAutoreleasePool alloc] init];
    Reachability* noteObject = (Reachability*) info;
    [[NSNotificationCenter defaultCenter]
        postNotificationName: kReachabilityChangedNotification object:
        noteObject];
    [myPool release];
}
```

Refactor this routine as follows:

```
static void ReachabilityCallback(SCNetworkReachabilityRef target,
                                 SCNetworkReachabilityFlags flags,
                                 void* info) {
    #pragma unused (target, flags)
    NSCAssert(info != NULL, @"info was NULL in ReachabilityCallback");
    NSCAssert([(__bridge NSObject*) info isKindOfClass: [Reachability class]],
        @"info was wrong class in ReachabilityCallback");❶

    @autoreleasepool {❷

        Reachability* noteObject = (__bridge Reachability*) info;❸
        [[NSNotificationCenter defaultCenter] postNotificationName:
            kReachabilityChangedNotification object: noteObject];

    }
}
```

❶ Since we're casting between an Objective-C and a Core Foundation object, we need to tell the compiler about the object's ownership so it can properly clean it up. Here we're using the simplest case, a __bridge cast, for which ARC will not do any extra work, as it assumes you handle the object's memory yourself.

❷ ARC does not make use of the `NSAutoReleasePool` objects, providing `@autore leasepool` blocks instead. These have an advantage of being more efficient than `NSAutoreleasePool` but essentially serve the same function. So here we're replacing the creation and release of an autorelease object with an autorelease block.

❸ We again make use of a __bridge cast as we're casting between an Objective-C and a Core Foundation object.

After making the changes, go back and click Edit→Refactor→Convert to Objective-C ARC in the Xcode menu to start the refactor again. This time, things should go more smoothly and you should see something like Figure 7-11.

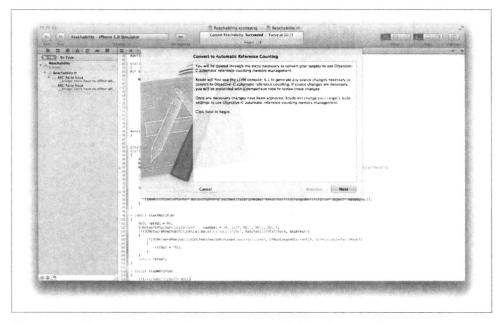

Figure 7-11. Trying to convert the project to use ARC for the second time

Click the Next button and you should be presented with another drop-down, as in Figure 7-12.

You might want to take a look at the changes that Xcode is suggesting at this point, but in any case, you should accept them by clicking the Save button. The project has now successfully been converted from manual memory management to use ARC.

Click the Run button in the Xcode toolbar to build and deploy the application into the iPhone Simulator. You should see something much like Figure 7-13.

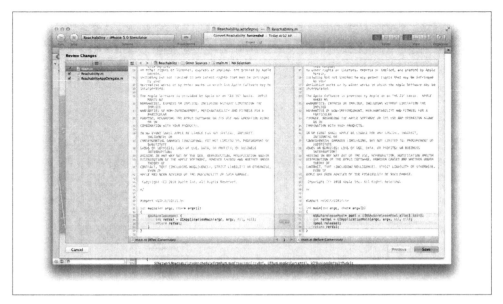

Figure 7-12. Refactoring the project

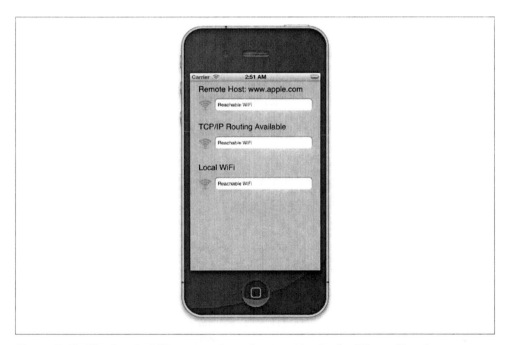

Figure 7-13. The Reachability example project running in the iPhone Simulator

For more background on what we did in this section, you should take a look at the guide to moving to ARC (*http://bit.ly/UHY2UB*), which is part of Apple's developer documentation.

Embedding a Web Browser in Your App

The `UIWebView` class allows you to embed web content inside your application. This class is the simplest but least flexible way of getting network content into your application. A `UIWebView` is best used to display content. If you want to manipulate the content programmatically, you should skip ahead a couple of sections and look at the discussion of the `NSURLConnection` class. However, there are a few tricks you can play to retrieve the displayed content from the `UIWebView` once it has been downloaded, and I'll talk about them later in the section.

A Simple Web View Controller

There are a number of cases where you might want to load a URL and display a web page, but keep users inside your application rather than closing it and opening Safari. If this is what you need to do, you should be using a `UIWebView`.

So, let's build some code that you'll be able to reuse in your own applications later. The specification for this code is a view controller that we can display modally, which will display a `UIWebView` with a specified web page, and can then be dismissed, returning us to our application.

I'm going to prototype the code here, hanging it off a simple view with a button that will pull up the modal view. However, the view controller class is reusable without modification; just drag and drop the code out of this project and into another. So this is a good exercise in writing reusable code.

Open Xcode and start a new project, choose a Single View Application for iOS, and when prompted, name it **Prototype**. Ensure that the Device Family is set to iPhone and the checkbox for ARC is ticked, but the boxes for storyboard and unit tests are not ticked, as we don't require them for this project.

The first thing we want to do is set up our main view; this is going to consist of a single button that we'll click to bring up the web view. Click on the *ViewController.xib* nib file to open it in Interface Builder, and drag and drop a round rect button (`UIButton`) into the view. Double-click on the button and change the text to **Go**. Switch to the Assistant Editor and then Control-click and drag from the button to the *ViewController.h* interface file and create a `goButton` property as an `IBOutlet`, then Control-click and drag once again to create a `pushedGo:` method as an `IBAction` (see Figure 7-14).

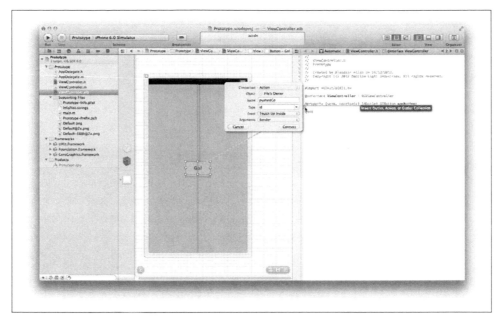

Figure 7-14. Connecting outlets and actions in Interface Builder

After making the connections, your interface file should now look something like this:

```
#import <UIKit/UIKit.h>;

@interface ViewController : UIViewController

@property (weak, nonatomic) IBOutlet UIButton *goButton;

- (IBAction)pushedGo:(id)sender;

@end
```

While in the associated implementation file, you should see that a stub for our push edGo: method has been created. You'll notice the filled gray circle next to the method; if you click on this, you'll get a pop-up that shows the UI element that this action is connected to (see Figure 7-15).

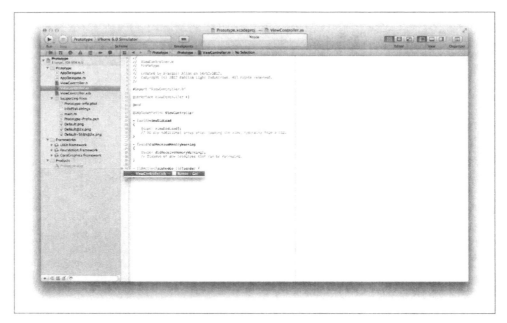

Figure 7-15. The pushedGo: method

We're done in Interface Builder for now.

Next, we need to add a new view controller class to the project. This is the class we're going to use to manage our `UIWebView`.

Right-click on the Prototype group in the Project Navigator window and select New File, then choose the `UIViewController` subclass template. When prompted, name the new class **WebViewController**, remembering to make sure that the "With XIB for user interface" checkbox is ticked.

Three files will be created: the interface file *WebViewController.h*, the implementation file *WebViewController.m*, and the view nib file *WebViewController.xib*.

Now we need to build our web view. Click on *WebViewController.xib* to open the nib file in Interface Builder. Drag and drop a navigation bar (`UINavigationBar`) from Object Library, and position it at the top of the view.

Then drag a web view (`UIWebView`) from the Object Library into the view and resize it to fill the remaining portion of the View window. Check the box marked Scales Page to Fit in the Attributes Inspector tab of the Utilities panel.

Finally, drag a bar button item (`UIBarButton`) onto the navigation bar, and again in the Attributes Inspector tab of the Utilities panel, change its identifier from Custom to Done. Once you've done this, your view will look similar to Figure 7-16.

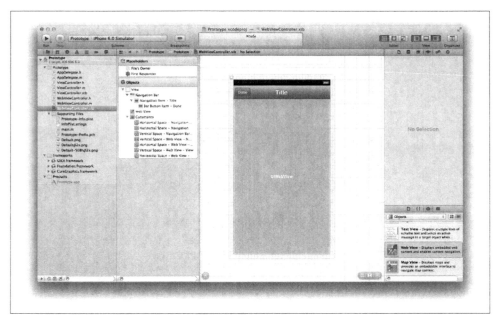

Figure 7-16. Creating our web view in Interface Builder

Save your changes to the *WebViewController.xib* file, and open the *WebViewController.h* interface file. We want to make this class self-contained so that we can reuse it without any modifications. Therefore, we're going to override the `init:` function to pass in the URL when instantiating the object. Make the following changes to the file (notice that I've added `<UIWebViewDelegate>` to the interface declaration):

```
#import <UIKit/UIKit.h>

@interface WebViewController : UIViewController <UIWebViewDelegate> {
    NSURL *theURL;
    NSString *theTitle;
    IBOutlet UIWebView *webView;
    IBOutlet UINavigationItem *webTitle;

}

- (id)initWithURL:(NSURL *)url;
- (id)initWithURL:(NSURL *)url andTitle:(NSString *)string;
- (IBAction) done:(id)sender;

@end
```

You'll notice that unfilled circles appear next to the two IBOutlet declarations and the IBAction declaration, which indicates that, unlike when we create them directly from inside Interface Builder, we have yet to connect these outlets and action to a user interface element.

In fact, to give a bit more flexibility to the class, I provided two different init: functions: initWithURL: and initWithURL:andTitle:. There's also a done: method flagged as an IBAction that we can connect to our Done UIBarButtonItem when we go back into Interface Builder.

We've declared an NSURL and an NSString to store the URL and view title passed to our init methods, along with a UIWebView and a UINavigationItem flagged as IBOutlet to connect to the UI elements we created previously in Interface Builder.

Navigation Bars and Interface Builder

If you add the UINavigationBar to your modal view inside Interface Builder, as we have done here, it is not managed by a UINavigationController. This means you cannot set the title of the navigation bar inside your view controller using the self.title or the self.NavigationItem.title property.

There are several ways around this problem, but one of the easier ways is to declare a UINavigationItem IBOutlet in the view controller's interface file, and then in Interface Builder, connect this outlet to the UINavigationItem that contains the title (you'll need to switch the *WebView.xib* window into list mode with Option-⌘-2 and expand the navigation bar).

Once this is done, you can set the title in the navigation bar from the viewDidLoad: or viewDidAppear: method using the title property of the instance variable pointing to your UINavigationItem IBOutlet variable that you declared.

Now, open the *WebViewController.m* implementation file. We'll start by implementing the two initWith methods. Add the following code to the file:

```
- (id)initWithURL:(NSURL *)url andTitle:(NSString *)string {
    if( self = [super init] ) {
        theURL = url;
        theTitle = string;
    }
    return self;
}

-(id)initWithURL:(NSURL *)url {
```

```
        return [self initWithURL:url andTitle:nil]; ❶
}
```

❶ We implemented the initWithURL: method by calling the initWithURL:andTi
   tle: method with an empty (nil) title. Doing it this way means that if we need
   to change the implementation of the initialization method later, we have to do so
   in only one place.

Next, we have to load the URL into the view, and we'll do that in the viewDidLoad:
method. Go ahead and add the lines shown in bold:

```
- (void)viewDidLoad {
    [super viewDidLoad];
    webTitle.title = theTitle; ❶
    NSURLRequest *requestObject = [NSURLRequest requestWithURL:theURL]; ❷
    [webView loadRequest:requestObject]; ❸
}
```

❶ We set the title property of the NSNavigationBarItem to the title string we
   passed earlier in the initWithURL:andTitle: method.

❷ We *marshal* (gather together along with the other necessary data) the URL we
   passed in the initWithURL:andTitle: method to form an NSURLRequest object.

❸ Here, we load the requested URL into the UIWebView.

Now we have to deal with what happens when the user dismisses the view by tapping
the Done button. Add the following to the file:

```
- (IBAction) done:(id)sender {
    [self dismissViewControllerAnimated:YES completion:nil]; ❶
}

- (void)viewWillDisappear:(BOOL)animated {
    [super viewWillDisappear:animated];
    webView.delegate = nil; ❷
    [webView stopLoading]; ❸
}
```

❶ In the done: method, we dismiss the modal view, which will trigger the view
   Will Disappear:animated: method.

❷ In the viewWillDisappear:animated: method, we have to set the delegate class
   for our UIWebView to nil. We're about to deallocate our object, or rather, the code
   generated by Xcode using ARC is, and if we don't set the delegate property to
   nil before this happens, messages sent to the nonexistent object by the UIWeb
   ViewDelegate protocol will cause our application to crash.

❸ We also have to stop loading from our URL because the events generated as the
   web page continues to load will cause the application to crash.

We're not quite done yet. Back in the *ViewController.m* file, we still need to implement the pushedGo: method. Since we're about to make use of the new WebViewController class, we need to import the *WebViewController.h* header file into the View Controller class. So go to the top of *ViewController.m* and add this line:

```
#import "WebViewController.h"
```

Then in the pushedGo: method, add the code shown in bold:

```
-(IBAction) pushedGo:(id)sender {
    NSURL *url = [NSURL URLWithString:@"http://www.apple.com/"];
    WebViewController *webViewController =
      [[WebViewController alloc] initWithURL:url andTitle:@"Apple"]; ❶
    [self presentViewController:webViewController animated:YES completion:nil]; ❷
}
```

❶   We create an instance of our WebViewController using initWithURL:andTi
     tle:.

❷   We present the new controller modally.

Now we have to go back into Interface Builder and connect the web view to our controller code. Click on the *WebViewController.xib* file to open it in Interface Builder. Then right-click on the File's Owner icon (yellow wire-frame cube) in the dock to open the Outlets pop-up, and click and drag from the webTitle outlet to the Title item (UINavigation Item) in the navigation bar (see Figure 7-17); the webView outlet to the main UIWeb View; and finally the done: received action to the Done button in the navigation bar.

After doing so, close the pop-up and then right-click and drag from the UIWebView to the File's Owner icon and connect the delegate back to File's Owner, and in doing so, specify that the File's Owner (in this case, the WebViewController class) will be the UIWebViewDelegate.

At this stage, we should be able to click on the Run button in the Xcode toolbar to build and deploy our application into the iPhone Simulator, as shown in Figure 7-18. Tap the Go button and the Apple website should load in your view. Remember that you're making a network connection here, so you might have to be a bit patient depending on the speed of your connection.

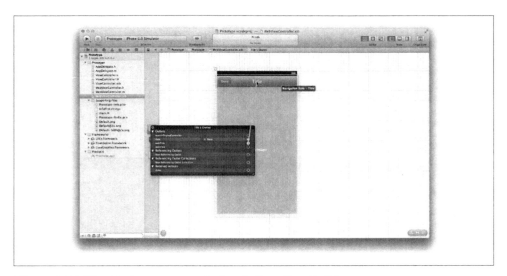

Figure 7-17. The Outlets pop-up window in Interface Builder

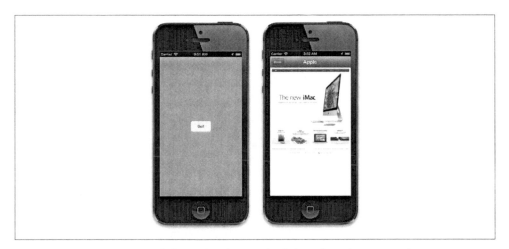

Figure 7-18. The harness (left) and web view (right) in the iPhone Simulator

Of course, users don't like to be patient, and we currently don't have a way to indicate to them that our application is doing something they need to be patient about. This is where the `UIWebViewDelegate` protocol comes in; we declared `WebViewController` as a web view delegate, but so far we haven't taken advantage of that.

The delegate protocol offers two methods: `webViewDidStartLoad:` and `webViewDidFi nishLoad:`. We can use these to start and stop the network activity indicator in the iPhone's toolbar to indicate that we're transferring data and the user should be patient. Add these two methods to *WebViewController.m*:

```
- (void)webViewDidStartLoad:(UIWebView *)wv {
    [UIApplication sharedApplication].networkActivityIndicatorVisible = YES;
}

- (void)webViewDidFinishLoad:(UIWebView *)wv {
    [UIApplication sharedApplication].networkActivityIndicatorVisible = NO;
}
```

But what happens if our URL fails to load? Even if we checked reachability before creating the view controller, what if we lose the network connection while the page itself is loading? The delegate protocol also provides the webView:didFailLoadWithError: method to inform us that something has gone wrong. Add the following to *WebView-Controller.m*:

```
- (void)webView:(UIWebView *)wv didFailLoadWithError:(NSError *)error {
    [UIApplication sharedApplication].networkActivityIndicatorVisible = NO;

    NSString *errorString = [error localizedDescription];
    NSString *errorTitle = [NSString stringWithFormat:@"Error (%d)", error.code];
    UIAlertView *errorView =
        [[UIAlertView alloc] initWithTitle:errorTitle
            message:errorString delegate:self cancelButtonTitle:nil
            otherButtonTitles:@"OK", nil];  ❶
    [errorView show];
}
```

❶   Here we grab the error description and open an alert view to display the error. We declare our view controller class to be the alert's delegate.

Since we said our view controller class is now the UIAlertView delegate, we also have to declare the class as a UIAlertViewDelegate in the *WebViewController.h* interface file:

```
@interface WebViewController :
  UIViewController <UIWebViewDelegate, UIAlertViewDelegate> {

... no changes to the code inside the declaration ...

}
```

With this change made, we can make use of the UIAlertViewDelegate protocol back in our implementation to dismiss the Web View pane when an error is received loading our URL. Add the following to *WebViewController.m*:

```
- (void)didPresentAlertView:(UIAlertView *)alertView {
    [self dismissViewControllerAnimated:YES completion:nil];
}
```

We're done. With these changes, the application can tell the user that it is doing something, and can handle any errors that occur when loading the URL.

Click the Run button in the Xcode toolbar to build and start the application in iPhone Simulator. Tap the Go button, and you should see the activity indicator spinning in the toolbar next to the WiFi signal strength icon as the application loads Apple's web page. When it finishes, the spinner should stop.

Click Done, and then either turn Airport off or unplug your Ethernet cable. Now try again, and you should get something that looks like Figure 7-19, informing you that you no longer have an Internet connection.

Figure 7-19. The webView:didFailLoadWithError: method creates a UIAlertView and dismisses the web view when we fail to load the URL we passed to it

At this point, you have a reusable `WebViewController` class and associated nib file that you can copy and drop directly into your own projects. You might also want to think about improvements if you do that, of course. For instance, the only error checking we do occurs after we attempt to load the view. Perhaps you could make use of the `Reach ability` class we looked at earlier in the chapter inside the `viewWillAppear:` method, before the web view is even displayed, to check the network connection. Then you can pop up an alert view if you are unable to reach `theURL` (which we passed to the view controller as part of the `initWithURL:` or `initWithURL:andTitle:` method) before the view is displayed to the user rather than afterward.

Displaying Static HTML Files

We can use the UIWebView class to display HTML files bundled into our project. In fact, we can add HTML documents to our project in the same way we dragged and dropped the images into the City Guide application; see "Adding Images to Your Projects" (page 84) in Chapter 5.

Suppose we're going to use a web view to display a help document for our application. We could do so as follows:

```
NSString *filePath =
    [[NSBundle mainBundle] pathForResource:@"HelpDocument" ofType:@"html"];
NSData *htmlData = [NSData dataWithContentsOfFile:filePath];

if (htmlData) {
  [webView loadData:htmlData MIMEType:@"text/html" textEncodingName:@"UTF-8"
          baseURL:[NSURL URLWithString:@"http://www.babilim.co.uk"]];
}
```

We grab the file path to our bundled resource, create an NSData object, and pass this to our web view.

Embedding Images in the Application Bundle

Since we can specify the base URL of our web view, we can use a trick to embed small images directly into our application bundle by setting this base URL for our HTML document correctly. For instance, if we have an HTML document in the NSString variable htmlDocument, we could add this snippet:

```
NSString *filePath = [[NSBundle mainBundle] bundlePath];
NSURL *baseURL = [NSURL fileURLWithPath:filePath];
[webView loadHTMLString:htmlDocument baseURL:baseURL];
```

This will load the HTML document into our UIWebView. However, it will also set the base URL to the root of the application bundle and allow us to add images (or other content) into our application and refer to them directly in our document (or an associated CSS file):

```
<img src="image.png">;
```

You should note that even if you store your images inside a folder in your Xcode project, they will be at the root of the application bundle file when you build and deploy your application.

Getting Data Out of a UIWebView

A `UIWebView` is primarily intended to display a URL, but if need be, you can retrieve the content that has been loaded into the view using the `stringByEvaluatingJavaScript FromString:` method:

```
NSString *content =
  [webView stringByEvaluatingJavaScriptFromString:@"document.body.outerHTML"]; ❶
```

❶   Here we retrieve the contents of the HTML <body> ... </body> tag.

Sending Email

The `MFMailComposeViewController` class provides access to the same interface used by the Mail client to edit and send an email. The most common way to present this interface is to do so modally using the `presentViewController:animated:completion:` method, just as we did in the preceding section to create a reusable web view class.

We can therefore reuse our Prototype application code from the preceding section to demonstrate how the mail composer works; we'll just drop in a class that displays the mail interface instead of the web interface.

Open the Finder and navigate to the location where you saved the *Prototype* project. Right-click or Control-click on the folder containing the project files and select Duplicate. A folder called *Prototype copy* will be created containing a duplicate of our project. You should probably rename it to something more sensible. I suggest *Prototype2*. Now open the new version of the project in Xcode and mouse over the blue Project icon at the top of the Project navigator and hit the Enter key, which will make the project name editable. Enter **Prototype2** as the new project name, and a drop-down will appear prompting you to approve the changes to the project. Click on Rename when prompted to do so to rename the project.

Next, prune back the code:

1. Open the copy of the project in Xcode and delete the *WebViewController.h*, *WebViewController.m*, and *WebViewController.xib* files by right-clicking on each file in the Project Navigator panel and selecting Delete from the pop-up menu (rather than Remove References Only).

2. Now click on the *ViewController.m* file to open it in the editor. Delete the line where you import the *WebViewController.h* file and delete all the code in the `pushedGo:` method, but not the method itself.

At this point, we have just the stub of the application, with that Go button and associated `pushedGo:` method we can use to trigger the display of our mail composer view. So, let's write the code to do that now.

The first thing we need to do is add the *MessageUI.framework* framework to the project. Click the Project icon at the top of the Project pane in Xcode, then click on the main Target for the project, and then on the Build Phases tab. Finally, click on the Link Binary with Libraries item to open up the list of linked frameworks, and click the + symbol to add a new framework. Select the System Configuration framework (*MessageUI.framework*) from the drop-down list and click the Add button.

Unlike the web view we implemented earlier in the chapter, the mail composer view won't dismiss itself when the user clicks the Send or Cancel button. We need to know when it is dismissed by the user; for that to happen, we must implement the MFMail ComposeViewControllerDelegate protocol.

We therefore need to import the framework headers into the *ViewController.h* interface file, which we do by importing the *MessageUI.h* header file:

```
#import <MessageUI/MessageUI.h>
```

We also have to declare our ViewController as a delegate class for the mail view by changing the declaration in *ViewController.h*, as shown here:

```
@interface ViewController : UIViewController
  <MFMailComposeViewControllerDelegate>
  ... no changes to the code in here ...
```

We're going to present our mail composer view when the Go button is clicked using our pushedGo: method. However, before we do, we need to see if the device is even configured to send email, using the canSendMail: class method. If it isn't, we need to inform the user that the device isn't able to send mail. When writing a real application that relies on email being available, you might want to do this check when the application starts inside your application delegate, and then either inform the user that there is a problem or disable the parts of your application that depend on it being able to send mail. Add the following code to the pushedGo: method in *ViewController.m* file:

```
-(IBAction) pushedGo:(id)sender {

    if (![MFMailComposeViewController canSendMail]) { ❶
        NSString *errorTitle = @"Error";
        NSString *errorString = @"This device is not configured to send email.";
        UIAlertView *errorView =
            [[UIAlertView alloc] initWithTitle:errorTitle
            message:errorString delegate:self cancelButtonTitle:nil
            otherButtonTitles:@"OK", nil];
        [errorView show];
    } else {
        MFMailComposeViewController *mailView =
        [[MFMailComposeViewController alloc] init]; ❷
        mailView.mailComposeDelegate = self; ❸
        [mailView setSubject:@"Test"];
        [mailView setMessageBody:@"This is a test message" isHTML:NO];
        [self presentViewController:mailView animated:YES completion:nil]; ❹
```

```
        }

    }
```

❶   Here we check to see if the device is capable of sending mail. If it isn't, we present a UIAlertView to inform the user.

❷   We allocate and initialize an instance of the mail composer view controller.

❸   We set the delegate for the controller to be this class, which implies that we have to implement the delegate protocol for the mail composer view controller.

❹   After setting the subject and the message body, we present the view controller modally.

The mail controller delegate protocol implements only one method, which dismisses the view controller and handles any errors: the mailComposeController:didFinishWithResult:error: method. Let's implement that now as part of our ViewController class. Add the following method to *ViewController.m*:

```
-(void)mailComposeController:(MFMailComposeViewController *)controller
 didFinishWithResult:(MFMailComposeResult)result error:(NSError *)error {
    if (error) { ❶
        NSString *errorTitle = @"Mail Error";
        NSString *errorDescription = [error localizedDescription];
        UIAlertView *errorView = [[UIAlertView alloc]
          initWithTitle:errorTitle
          message:errorDescription
          delegate:self
          cancelButtonTitle:nil
          otherButtonTitles:@"OK", nil];
        [errorView show];

    } else { ❷
        // Add code here to handle the MFMailComposeResult
    }

    [controller dismissViewControllerAnimated:YES completion:nil];❸
}
```

❶   If the controller returns an error, we use a UIAlertView to inform the user.

❷   If no error is returned, we should handle the MFMailComposeResult instead.

❸   In either case, we need to dismiss the controller's view and release the controller.

Before we discuss how to handle the MFMailComposeResult, let's test our code. Click the Run button on the Xcode toolbar to compile and start the application in iPhone Simulator. Once the application opens, click the Go button. If all goes well, you should see something very similar to Figure 7-20.

Figure 7-20. The MFMailMailComposeViewController view

Now that the application is working, let's handle that MFMailComposeResult. The simplest way to illustrate how to handle the result is to add a label to the ViewController nib file, and display the result returned by the mail composer view there.

The first thing you need to do is to add a UILabel property to the *ViewController.h* interface file and declare it as an IBOutlet. Add the line shown in bold:

```
#import <UIKit/UIKit.h>
#import <MessageUI/MessageUI.h>

@interface ViewController :
    UIViewController <MFMailComposeViewControllerDelegate>

@property (weak, nonatomic) IBOutlet UIButton *goButton;
@property (weak, nonatomic) IBOutlet UILabel *resultLabel;
```

```
- (IBAction)pushedGo:(id)sender;

@end
```

We now need to open the *ViewController.xib* file in Interface Builder and add the label. Open the nib file and then drag and drop a label (UILabel) from the Object Library panel onto the view. Now right-click on File's Owner and connect the resultLabel outlet to the new UILabel, as in Figure 7-21.

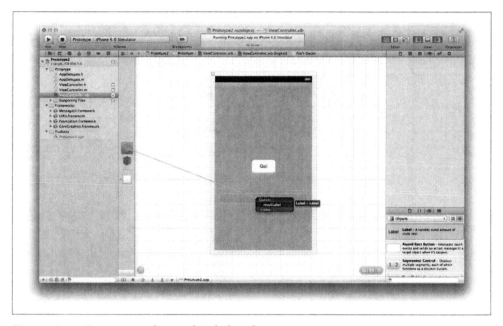

Figure 7-21. Connecting the resultLabel outlet

Now we can use the label to display the results. Inside the mail composer delegate method, replace the line that reads // Add code here to handle the MFMailCompo seResult with the following code:

```
NSString *string;
switch (result) {
    case MFMailComposeResultSent:
        string = @"Mail sent.";
        break;
    case MFMailComposeResultSaved:
        string = @"Mail saved.";
        break;
    case MFMailComposeResultCancelled:
        string = @"Mail cancelled.";
        break;
    case MFMailComposeResultFailed:
```

```
        string = @"Mail failed.";
        break;
    default:
        string = @"Unknown";
        break;
}
self.resultLabel.text = string;
```

The switch statement we just added enumerates the possible results and then sets the label string to a human-readable result. We're done. If you build the application again and send an email from the composer view, you should see something very much like Figure 7-22.

Figure 7-22. We successfully sent the mail message

Attaching an Image to a Mail Message

You can attach an image to your mail message by using the addAttachmentData:mime
Type:Filename: method. This should be called before displaying the mail composer
interface, directly after the call to the setMessageBody:isHTML: method. You should
not call this method after displaying the composer interface to the user.

If necessary, you can change the image type using the UIImageJPEGRepresentation()
or UIImagePNGRepresentation() UIKit function, as shown here:

```
UIImage *image = [UIImage imageNamed:@"Attachment.png"];
NSData *data = UIImageJPEGRepresentation(image, 1.0);
[mailView addAttachmentData:data mimeType:@"image/jpeg"
  fileName:@"Picture.jpeg"];
```

This example will look for *Attachment.png* at the root of the application bundle (to put
a file there, drag it into the top level of the Project Navigator), convert it to a JPEG, and
attach it under the filename *Picture.jpeg*.

Getting Data from the Internet

If you want to retrieve data from the Internet and process it programmatically, rather
than just display it in a view, you should use the NSURLConnection class. While it's more
complicated than the UIWebView we looked at earlier in the chapter, it's inherently more
flexible.

The NSURLConnection class can make both synchronous and asynchronous requests to
download the contents of a URL, and the associated delegate methods provide feedback
and control for asynchronous requests.

Synchronous Requests

The easiest, but not the best, way to use the NSURLConnection class is to make a synchronous request for data:

```
NSString *url = @"http://www.apple.com";
NSURLRequest *request =
  [NSURLRequest requestWithURL:[NSURL URLWithString:url]];

NSURLResponse *response = nil;
NSError *error = nil;
NSData *content = [NSURLConnection sendSynchronousRequest:request
  returningResponse:&response error:&error];

NSString *string = [[NSString alloc] initWithData:content
```

```
      encoding:NSUTF8StringEncoding];
    NSLog(@"response: %@", string);
```

sendSynchronousRequest: is a convenience method built on top of the asynchronous request code. It's important to note that if you use this method, the calling thread will block until the data is loaded or the request times out. If the calling thread is the main thread of your application, your application will freeze while the request is being made. This is generally considered not a good thing from a UI perspective; I strongly encourage you to use the asynchronous connection and associated delegate methods.

Asynchronous Requests

Most of the time when you use the NSURLConnection class, you'll make asynchronous requests this way:

```
NSString *string = [NSString stringWithFormat:@"http://www.apple.com/];
NSURL *url = [[NSURL URLWithString:string] retain];
NSURLRequest *request = [NSURLRequest requestWithURL:url];
[[NSURLConnection alloc]
  initWithRequest:request delegate:self]; ❶
```

❶ Here we make the asynchronous call and set the delegate class to be self.

For this to work, you need to implement the following methods at a minimum. We'll take a closer look at NSURLConnection next:

```
- (NSURLRequest *)connection:(NSURLConnection *)connection
  willSendRequest:(NSURLRequest *)request
  redirectResponse:(NSURLResponse *)redirectResponse {
    return request;
}

- (void)connection:(NSURLConnection *)connection
  didReceiveResponse:(NSURLResponse *)response {
    [responseData setLength:0]; ❶
}

- (void)connection:(NSURLConnection *)connection
  didReceiveData:(NSData *)data {
    [responseData appendData:data]; ❷
}

- (void)connection:(NSURLConnection *)
  connection didFailWithError:(NSError *)error {
  ... implementation code would go here ...
} ❸

- (void)connectionDidFinishLoading:(NSURLConnection *)connection {
  ... implementation code would go here ...
} ❹
```

❶ You need to declare an NSMutableData variable (responseData in this example) in the interface file of your delegate class to hold the response data. As a stylistic choice, you may prefer to alloc and init your NSMutableData object, rather than calling the setLength: method as we have done here.

❷ This appends the data as it is received to the response data variable. There may be multiple calls to this delegate method as data comes in from the response.

❸ This method is called if an error occurs during the connection.

❹ This method is called if the connection completes successfully.

Using Web Services

With the (re)emergence of REpresentational State Transfer (REST) as the dominant paradigm for modern web service architectures, chiefly championed by emerging Web 2.0 companies and platforms, the number of available services has grown significantly over the past few years.

> If you are interested in learning more about RESTful web services, I recommend the book *RESTful Web Services* by Leonard Richardson and Sam Ruby (O'Reilly).

The Weather Underground service

To illustrate the NSURLConnection class, we're going to look at one of these RESTful services offered by Weather Underground. The are a number of services offered by the Weather Underground. However, a request of the form http://api.wunder ground.com/api/*YOUR_API_KEY*/conditions/q/*COUNTRY*/*CITY_NAME*.xml outside the United States, or http://api.wunderground.com/api/*YOUR_API_KEY*/conditions/q/ *STATE_SHORT_CODE*/*CITY_NAME*.xml inside the United States, will return the current conditions for that city.

> To make use of the Weather Underground service you must first sign up for an API key which is used as part of each request to the service. You can sign up for a key through the Weather Underground website (*http://bit.ly/YypYGk*).
>
> If you're interested in the forecast rather than the current conditions, you can substitute *forecast* for *conditions* in the HTTP call to return a three-day forecast.

So, for instance, if we made a request of the Weather Underground API for the current conditions and forecast in London, the request would look like http://api.wunder

ground.com/api/*YOUR_API_KEY*/conditions/q/UK/London.xml. If we do that, the service will return an XML document containing the current and forecasted conditions:

```xml
<?xml version="1.0"?>
<response>
    <version>0.1</version>
    <termsofService>
        http://www.wunderground.com/weather/api/d/terms.html
    </termsofService>
    <features>
        <feature>conditions</feature>
    </features>
    <current_observation>
        <image>
            <url>
                http://icons-ak.wxug.com/graphics/wu2/logo_130x80.png
            </url>
            <title>Weather Underground</title>
            <link>http://www.wunderground.com</link>
        </image>
        <display_location>
            <full>London, United Kingdom</full>
            <city>London</city>
            <state/>
            <state_name>United Kingdom</state_name>
            <country>UK</country>
            <country_iso3166>GB</country_iso3166>
            <zip>00000</zip>
            <latitude>51.47999954</latitude>
            <longitude>-0.44999999</longitude>
            <elevation>24.00000000</elevation>
        </display_location>
        <observation_location>
            <full>London,</full>
            <city>London</city>
            <state/>
            <country>UK</country>
            <country_iso3166>GB</country_iso3166>
            <latitude>51.47999954</latitude>
            <longitude>-0.44999999</longitude>
            <elevation>79 ft</elevation>
        </observation_location>
        <estimated/>
        <station_id>EGLL</station_id>
        <observation_time>Last Updated on December 14, 7:50 PM GMT
        </observation_time>
        <observation_time_rfc822>Fri, 14 Dec 2012 19:50:00 +0000
        </observation_time_rfc822>
        <observation_epoch>1355514600</observation_epoch>
        <local_time_rfc822>Fri, 14 Dec 2012 19:57:12 +0000</local_time_rfc822>
        <local_epoch>1355515032</local_epoch>
        <local_tz_short>GMT</local_tz_short>
```

```
<local_tz_long>Europe/London</local_tz_long>
<local_tz_offset>+0000</local_tz_offset>
<weather>Partly Cloudy</weather>
<temperature_string>48 F (9 C)</temperature_string>
<temp_f>48</temp_f>
<temp_c>9</temp_c>
<relative_humidity>71%</relative_humidity>
<wind_string>From the SW at 17 MPH</wind_string>
<wind_dir>SW</wind_dir>
<wind_degrees>220</wind_degrees>
<wind_mph>17</wind_mph>
<wind_gust_mph>0</wind_gust_mph>
<wind_kph>28</wind_kph>
<wind_gust_kph>0</wind_gust_kph>
<pressure_mb>980</pressure_mb>
<pressure_in>28.94</pressure_in>
<pressure_trend>+</pressure_trend>
<dewpoint_string>39 F (4 C)</dewpoint_string>
<dewpoint_f>39</dewpoint_f>
<dewpoint_c>4</dewpoint_c>
<heat_index_string>NA</heat_index_string>
<heat_index_f>NA</heat_index_f>
<heat_index_c>NA</heat_index_c>
<windchill_string>NA</windchill_string>
<windchill_f>NA</windchill_f>
<windchill_c>NA</windchill_c>
<feelslike_string>48 F (9 C)</feelslike_string>
<feelslike_f>48</feelslike_f>
<feelslike_c>9</feelslike_c>
<visibility_mi>6.2</visibility_mi>
<visibility_km>10.0</visibility_km>
<solarradiation/>
<UV>0</UV>
<precip_1hr_string>-9999.00 in (-9999.00 mm)</precip_1hr_string>
<precip_1hr_in>-9999.00</precip_1hr_in>
<precip_1hr_metric>-9999.00</precip_1hr_metric>
<precip_today_string>0.00 in (0.0 mm)</precip_today_string>
<precip_today_in>0.00</precip_today_in>
<precip_today_metric>0.0</precip_today_metric>
<icon>partlycloudy</icon>
<icon_url>http://icons-ak.wxug.com/i/c/k/nt_partlycloudy.gif</icon_url>
<forecast_url>
    http://www.wunderground.com/global/stations/03772.html
</forecast_url>
<history_url>
    http://www.wunderground.com/history/airport/EGLL/2012/12/14/↵
DailyHistory.html
</history_url>
<ob_url>
    http://www.wunderground.com/cgi-bin/findweather/getForecast?↵
query=51.47999954,-0.44999999
</ob_url>
```

```
        </current_observation>
    </response>
```

Building an application

Much like Apple's own Weather application, the application we're going to wrap around the Weather Underground service will be a utility application. Open Xcode and start a new project. Select the Utility Application template from the iOS OS category, and name the project **Weather** when prompted for a filename. Remember to make sure the checkbox to use ARC is ticked.

 I could easily have implemented the Weather application as a table view; in fact, programmatically, this is probably the easiest way, but it's not the prettiest.

Pretty is important, both to people developing applications for Apple products and to the typical customer. If you intend to sell your application on the App Store, you should think seriously about how your application looks. First impressions are important, and with so many applications available, both the UI and the application's icon are tools you can use to make your application stand out from the others.

While we're going to be spending some time putting together the interface for the application, that isn't the main focus of this chapter. However, most of the time you'll be using the NSURLConnection class asynchronously, so it's important for you to pay attention to the way it fits into the UI and your application's overall structure.

First we need to add a number of IBOutlets to our *MainViewController.h* interface file. We're going to populate our GUI by querying the Weather Underground service and then parsing the XML we get back. If you compare the following to the XML file shown earlier, you should see we're only using a few of the many XML elements to populate our UI elements:

```
#import "FlipsideViewController.h"

@interface MainViewController : UIViewController
    <FlipsideViewControllerDelegate> {

    IBOutlet UIActivityIndicatorView *loadingActivityIndicator;

    IBOutlet UILabel *cityLabel;

    IBOutlet UIImageView *weatherImage;
    IBOutlet UILabel *weatherLabel;

    IBOutlet UILabel *centigradeLabel;
    IBOutlet UILabel *fahrenheitLabel;
```

```
        IBOutlet UILabel *humidityLabel;
        IBOutlet UILabel *windLabel;

        IBOutlet UIButton *refreshButton;

}

- (IBAction)showInfo;
- (IBAction)refreshView:(id) sender; ❶
- (void)updateView; ❷

@end
```

❶   This method is called when the user taps the Refresh button. It starts the loading activity indicator spinning, and makes the call to query the Weather Underground service.

❷   We're going to use this function as a callback when we have successfully retrieved the XML document from the Weather Underground service. It will update the current view.

Now let's open *MainViewController.xib* in Interface Builder and put together the UI. I'm not going to walk you through the steps for building the interface this time. You've built enough UIs by this point that you should be familiar with how to go about it. Look at Figure 7-23 to see my final interface.

Figure 7-23. Building the UI for the main view

Remember: to change the font color, minimum size, and other settings, use the Attribute Inspector in the Utilities panel. You can change the attributes of several elements at once by dragging to select them and then using the Attribute Inspector.

There are a few points to note:

- The UIImage element must be resized to 50×50 pixels, the size of the weather icon provided by the Weather Underground service.

- I set the style of the UIActivityIndicatorViewer to Large White in the Attributes Inspector and ticked the Hide When Stopped checkbox. We'll use this indicator to show network or other activity.

- I added a custom PNG icon for the Refresh button to the project, setting the UI Button type to Custom and the image to point at my Refresh icon (you will need to drag your icon into your Xcode project before it will be available as a custom image). I resized the Refresh button to be the same size as the Info button provided by the template, setting the View Mode to Scale to Fill in the Attributes tab of the Inspector window.

- When connecting each UIButton to the received actions—for example, when dragging the refreshView: action to the Refresh button—choose Touch Up Inside (the default event) from the drop-down menu of events when you make the connection.

After laying out the user interface, go ahead and connect each IBOutlet to the appropriate interface element, as in Figure 7-24. Afterwards, you should see something much like Figure 7-25.

For this application, I wrote the interface code first and then connected these outlets to the user interface in Interface Builder. However, as we've done before on several other occasions, we could have done this the other way around; we could have built the user interface and then dragged and dropped using the Assistant Editor to create properties (and the associated outlets) in our code. However, since I didn't see any point in making each of these outlets a property, I instead chose to make them instance variables and do things this way. If you want to do things the other way, that's just fine—it'll work just as well.

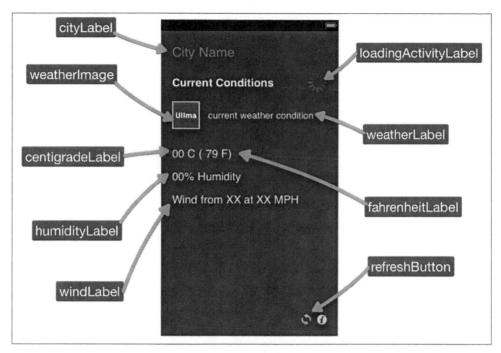

Figure 7-24. Associating names and variables with individual UI elements

Figure 7-25. All the user interface elements associated inside Interface Builder

Although we've now written the interface for the view controller and built and connected our view to the interface, we haven't implemented it yet. Let's hold off on that until we've built our data model.

Our model class needs to query the weather service, parse the response, and populate the data model. Right-click the Weather group in the Project Navigator panel in Xcode and click New File, then select the Objective-C class from the drop-down window. Name the new class WeatherForecast when prompted and select NSObject from the "Subclass of" drop-down menu.

Click the newly created *WeatherForecast.h* interface file to open in the Standard Editor. Like our UI, the interface file reflects the structure of the XML document we retrieved from the Weather Underground service. Add the lines shown in bold to the file:

```
#import <Foundation/Foundation.h>

@class MainViewController;

@interface WeatherForecast : NSObject {

    // Parent View Controller ❶
    MainViewController *viewController;

    // Weather Underground Service ❷
    NSString *apiKey;
    NSMutableData *responseData;
    NSURL *theURL;
}

// Information
@property (weak, nonatomic) NSString *location;

// Current Conditions
@property (weak, nonatomic) NSString *icon;
@property (weak, nonatomic) NSString *condition;

@property (weak, nonatomic) NSString *centigrade;
@property (weak, nonatomic) NSString *fahrenheit;
@property (weak, nonatomic) NSString *humidity;
@property (weak, nonatomic) NSString *wind;

- (void)queryServiceWithState:(NSString *)state
                      andCity:(NSString *)city
                   withParent:(UIViewController *)controller; ❸

@end
```

❶ This is the variable used to hold the parent view controller. We're going to pass this in to the Forecast object when we call the queryService:withParent method.

❷   These are the variables used by the `NSURLConnection` class during its asynchronous request.

❸   This is the method we'll use to trigger the asynchronous `NSURLConnection` request. We pass as arguments the name of the city we're interested in and the parent view controller. This allows us to substitute the city name into a partially formed REST request to the Weather Underground service.

Now open the implementation file (*WeatherForecast.m*) in the Xcode Editor. Here we need to add our `queryService:withParent:` method that will start the asynchronous `NSURLConnection` process. Add the lines shown in bold to this file, remembering to insert your own API key where prompted to do so:

```
#import "WeatherForecast.h"
#import "MainViewController.h"

@implementation WeatherForecast

- (void)queryServiceWithState:(NSString *)state
                      andCity:(NSString *)city
                   withParent:(UIViewController *)controller {
    viewController = (MainViewController *)controller;
    responseData = [NSMutableData data];
    apiKey = @"YOUR WEATHER UNDERGROUND API KEY";

    NSString *url =
      [NSString stringWithFormat:
        @"http://api.wunderground.com/api/%@/conditions/q/%@/%@.xml",
        apiKey, state, city]; ❶

    theURL = [NSURL URLWithString:url];
    NSURLRequest *request = [NSURLRequest requestWithURL:theURL]; ❷
    [[NSURLConnection alloc] initWithRequest:request delegate:self]; ❸

}

@end
```

❶   This builds the URL from the base URL and the city string that was passed to the `queryService:withParent:` method.

❷   This builds the `NSURLRequest` from the URL string.

❸   This makes the call to the Weather Underground service using an asynchronous call to `NSURLConnection`.

We just declared our `WeatherForecast` class as the delegate for the `NSURLConnection` class. Now we need to add the necessary delegate methods. For now, let's just implement the delegate methods; we'll get around to parsing the response later. Add the following lines to *WeatherForecast.m* just before the @end directive:

```
#pragma mark NSURLConnection Delegate Methods

- (NSURLRequest *)connection:(NSURLConnection *)connection
            willSendRequest:(NSURLRequest *)request
            redirectResponse:(NSURLResponse *)redirectResponse {
    @autoreleasepool {
        theURL = [request URL];
    }
    return request;
}

- (void)connection:(NSURLConnection *)connection
didReceiveResponse:(NSURLResponse *)response {
    [responseData setLength:0];
}

- (void)connection:(NSURLConnection *)connection
        didReceiveData:(NSData *)data {
    [responseData appendData:data];
}

- (void)connection:(NSURLConnection *)connection didFailWithError:
    (NSError *)error {
    NSLog( @"Error = %@", error );
}

- (void)connectionDidFinishLoading:(NSURLConnection *)connection {
    NSString *content =
      [[NSString alloc] initWithBytes:[responseData bytes]
                               length:[responseData length]
                             encoding:NSUTF8StringEncoding];
    NSLog( @"Data = %@", content );

    //    ...Insert code to parse the content here...

    [viewController updateView];
}
```

We're going to use the application delegate to create the WeatherForecast object and pass it to our MainViewController object. Add the lines shown in bold to *Weather-AppDelegate.m*:

```
- (BOOL)application:(UIApplication *)application
        didFinishLaunchingWithOptions:(NSDictionary *)launchOptions {
    self.window = [[UIWindow alloc] initWithFrame:[[UIScreen mainScreen] bounds]];
    self.mainViewController = [[MainViewController alloc]
        initWithNibName:@"MainViewController" bundle:nil];

    WeatherForecast *forecast = [[WeatherForecast alloc] init]; ❶
```

```
    self.mainViewController.forecast = forecast; ❷

    self.window.rootViewController = self.mainViewController;
    [self.window makeKeyAndVisible];
    return YES;
}
```

❶ We're creating an instance of this class, which we will store inside the main view
    controller. You'll need to also add `#import "WeatherForecast.h"` to the top of
    WeatherAppDelegate.m.

❷ We pass the `forecast` object to the view controller and then release it in the app
    delegate. There is no need to store an instance here, as we won't be using it from
    the delegate. Don't worry that the `MainViewController` doesn't yet have a forecast
    property; we're going to add one in a moment.

We have the view, model, and interface for the view controller. Now we know how the
model works and how we're going to push it into the view controller. So, let's implement
the controller and tie up those loose ends. Open up *MainViewController.m* and modify
the `viewDidLoad` method as follows:

```
- (void)viewDidLoad { ❶
    [super viewDidLoad];
    [self refreshView:self];
}
```

❶ This is called when the view loads. This calls the `viewDidLoad:` method in the
    superclass and then calls the `refreshView:` method.

Then add the following code:

```
- (IBAction)refreshView:(id)sender { ❶
    [loadingActivityIndicator startAnimating];
    [self.forecast queryServiceWithState:@"UK" andCity:@"London"
        withParent:self];

}

- (void)updateView { ❷

    ...Add code to update view here...

    [loadingActivityIndicator stopAnimating];

}
```

❶ This method is called when the Refresh button is tapped, and also from the `viewDidLoad:` method. This starts the `UIActivityViewIndicator` spinning and then calls the `queryService:withParent:` method in the `WeatherForecast` object.

❷ This method is called from the `WeatherForecast` object when it finishes loading the XML from the remote service. This method will contain the code to update the view using the newly populated `WeatherForecast` object. For now, all it does is stop the `UIActivityView` from spinning and hides it.

Additionally, we need to make sure we do the following inside *MainViewController.h*:

1. Import the *WeatherForecast.h* interface file.
2. Declare the forecast property.

To do this, add the following line to the top of *MainViewController.h*:

```
#import "WeatherForecast.h"
```

Next, add the following property declaration the end of *MainViewController.h* just before the @end statement,

```
@property (strong, nonatomic) WeatherForecast *forecast;
```

This is a good point to pause, take stock, and test the application. Click the Run button in the Xcode toolbar to build and deploy the application into the iPhone Simulator. When the application opens you should see the `UIActivityIndicator` briefly appear in the top lefthand corner of the view, and then disappear when the `WeatherForecast` object finishes loading the XML document from the Weather Underground service.

If it doesn't automatically open when the application starts in the simulator, open the Debug area by clicking on the middle button of the three in the View segmented control in the Xcode toolbar. You should see something very much like Figure 7-26. This is the XML document retrieved from the weather service.

At this point, all that is left to implement is the XML parsing code inside the `Weather Forecast`'s `connectionDidFinishLoading:` method, and the code to take the data model from the `forecast` object and display it in the view inside the `MainView Controller`'s `updateView:` method.

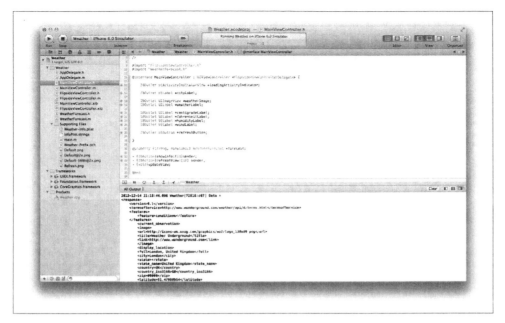

Figure 7-26. The Debug area panel showing the XML retrieved from the Weather Underground service

Parsing the XML document

We're going to talk in detail about parsing data in the next chapter. This chapter is about networking, so I'm not going to discuss in depth how to parse the returned XML document here. If you're familiar with DOM-based XML parsers, the following should be familiar. If not, hang on until the next chapter.

 Making use of the NSXMLDocument class is the normal method for tree-based parsing of XML files on the Mac. However, despite being available in iOS Simulator, this class is not available on the device itself.

However, for simple files, such as those returned by the Weather Underground service, I've never been a big fan of event-driven parsing. Since the NSXMLDocument class is not available under iOS, I generally use the *libxml2* library directly, via Matt Gallagher's excellent XPath wrappers for the library.

For more information about the XPath wrappers for the *libxml2* library, see Matt's original blog post (*http://bit.ly/ZJc3Ai*).

Using the XPath Wrappers

Download the wrappers (*http://bit.ly/Z7gaFp*). Next, unzip the file and drag the *XPath-Query.h* and *XPathQuery.m* files into your project, remembering to tick the "Copy items into destination group's folder" checkbox. This will add the interface and implementation files for the wrappers to the project.

To use these wrappers, you need to add the *libxml2.dylib* library to the project. However, adding the *libxml2* library underlying these wrappers is slightly more involved than adding a normal framework:

1. As we've done before to add frameworks, click on the Weather Project icon in the Project Navigator panel in Xcode and go to the Build Phases tab of the Project Info window. Click the Link Binaries with Libraries and click + to add the *libxml2.dylib* library.

2. Now click the Build Settings tab and then click the All button in the tool ribbon to show all the settings (if it's not already checked).

3. Go to the Search Paths subsection in this window, and in the Header Search Paths field, double-click on the entry field.

4. Click the + button and add `${SDKROOT}/usr/include/libxml2` to the paths, then click OK.

5. Then in the Linking subsection of this window, double-click the Other Linker Flags field and click +. Add `-lxml2` to the flags, and then click OK.

Once we've done that, we can open the *WeatherForecast.m* implementation file and import the *XPathQuery.h* interface file. Add the following line to the top of *Weather-Forecast.m*:

```
#import "XPathQuery.h"
```

After importing the interface file, we now have everything in place to write our `connec tionDidFinishLoading:` method, using the XPath query language and *libxml2* to parse the XML document returned by the Weather Service. My intention here is not to teach you XPath, as several good books are available on that topic. However, if you examine the `xpathQueryString` variables in each XPath query, you will see how the data model maps onto the original XML document returned by the Weather Service. Here is the new `connectionDidFinishLoading:` method along with two methods (`fetchCon tent:` and `populateArray:fromNodes:`) to take care of some repetitive tasks:

```
// Retrieves the content of an XML node, such as the temperature, wind,
// or humidity in the weather report.
//
- (NSString *)fetchContent:(NSArray *)nodes {
    NSString *result = @"";
    for ( NSDictionary *node in nodes ) {
        for ( id key in node ) {
            if( [key isEqualToString:@"nodeContent"] ) {
                result = [node objectForKey:key];
            }
        }
    }
    return result;
}


// For nodes that contain more than one value we are interested in,
// this method fills an NSMutableArray with the values it finds.
// For example, the forecast returns four days, so there will be
// an array with four day names, an array with four forecast icons,
// and so forth.
//
- (void) populateArray:(NSMutableArray *)array fromNodes:(NSArray*)nodes {
    for ( NSDictionary *node in nodes ) {
        for ( id key in node ) {
            if( [key isEqualToString:@"nodeContent"] ) {
                [array addObject:[node objectForKey:key]];
            }
        }
    }
}


- (void)connectionDidFinishLoading:(NSURLConnection *)connection {

    NSString *xpathQueryString;
    NSArray *nodes;

    xpathQueryString = @"//response/current_observation/display_location/full";
    nodes = PerformXMLXPathQuery(responseData, xpathQueryString);
    self.location = [self fetchContent:nodes];
    NSLog(@"location = %@", self.location);

    xpathQueryString = @"//response/current_observation/icon_url";
    nodes = PerformXMLXPathQuery(responseData, xpathQueryString);
    self.icon = [self fetchContent:nodes];
    NSLog(@"icon = %@", self.icon);

    xpathQueryString = @"//response/current_observation/weather";
    nodes = PerformXMLXPathQuery(responseData, xpathQueryString);
    self.condition = [self fetchContent:nodes];
    NSLog(@"condition = %@", self.condition);

    xpathQueryString = @"//response/current_observation/temp_c";
```

```
      nodes = PerformXMLXPathQuery(responseData, xpathQueryString);
      self.centigrade = [self fetchContent:nodes];
      NSLog(@"condition = %@", self.centigrade);

      xpathQueryString = @"//response/current_observation/temp_f";
      nodes = PerformXMLXPathQuery(responseData, xpathQueryString);
      self.fahrenheit = [self fetchContent:nodes];
      NSLog(@"condition = %@", self.fahrenheit);

      xpathQueryString = @"//response/current_observation/relative_humidity";
      nodes = PerformXMLXPathQuery(responseData, xpathQueryString);
      self.humidity = [self fetchContent:nodes];
      NSLog(@"condition = %@", self.humidity);

      xpathQueryString = @"//response/current_observation/wind_string";
      nodes = PerformXMLXPathQuery(responseData, xpathQueryString);
      self.wind = [self fetchContent:nodes];
      NSLog(@"condition = %@", self.wind);

      [viewController updateView];
  }
```

Populating the UI

Now that we've populated the data model, let's create the `updateView:` method in our
view controller. This is where we take the data that we just parsed from the XML and
push it into the current view. Replace the `updateView:` method in *MainView-
Controller.m* with the following:

```
- (void)updateView {
    cityLabel.text = self.forecast.location;

    NSURL *url = [NSURL URLWithString:(NSString *)self.forecast.icon];
    NSData *data = [NSData dataWithContentsOfURL:url];
    weatherImage.image = [[UIImage alloc] initWithData:data];

    weatherLabel.text = self.forecast.condition;

    centigradeLabel.text =
      [NSString stringWithFormat:@"%@ C", self.forecast.centigrade];
    fahrenheitLabel.text =
      [NSString stringWithFormat:@"(%@ F)", self.forecast.fahrenheit];
    humidityLabel.text =
      [NSString stringWithFormat:@"%@ humidity",self.forecast.humidity];
    windLabel.text = self.forecast.wind;

    [loadingActivityIndicator stopAnimating];
}
```

We're done. Click the Run button on the Xcode toolbar to build and deploy the application in iPhone Simulator. Once the application starts up, and if all goes well, you

should get something that looks similar to Figure 7-27. There is, after all, almost always a chance of rain in London.

Figure 7-27. The Weather application running in iPhone Simulator

Tidying up

There are several things you can do to tidy up this bare-bones application. First you should clean up the UI, as it's pretty untidy when the application opens. The easiest way to do this is to have all your labels start as blank, and then populate the text when the view finishes loading the information from the Weather Underground Service.

You might also want to add reachability checks when the application opens, and add some error handling in the `connection:didFailWithError:` delegate method inside the `WeatherForecast` class. You should also allow the user to choose which city to use by adding a text entry box on the flipside view, or perhaps even a map view.

We'll come back to this example when we discuss using device sensors. Most people are usually more concerned with the weather where they are now than the weather somewhere else, so we'll use the Core Location framework and the iPhone's GPS to locate users and provide them with a weather forecast for their current location.

CHAPTER 8

Handling Data

Most applications on the iOS platform will make a network connection to retrieve data at some point. This data will usually be formatted so that it can be easily parsed, either as XML or, more frequently these days, as JSON.

In this chapter, we're going to look at how to get data directly from the user via the UI, and then how to parse data we've retrieved from the network. Finally, we'll look at how to store that data on the device.

Data Entry

The Cocoa Touch framework (and the iOS SDK) offers a number of UI elements, ranging from text entry fields to switches and segmented controls. Any of these can be used for data entry, but often when we talk about data entry, we're talking about getting textual information into an application.

The two main UI elements that allow you to enter text are the UITextField and UIText View classes. While they may sound similar, they are actually quite different. The most noticeable difference between the two is that the UITextView allows you to enter (and display) a multiline text field, while UITextField doesn't.

The most annoying difference between the two is the issue of *resigning first responder*. When tapped, both display a keyboard to allow the user to enter text. However, while the UITextField class allows the user to dismiss the keyboard (at which time the text field resigns as first responder) when the user taps the Done button, the UITextView class does not. Though there are multiple ways around this problem, as we'll find later on, it's still one of the more annoying quirks in the Cocoa Touch framework.

UITextField and Its Delegate

In Chapter 5, we used a UITextField as part of our AddCityController view. However, we didn't really exploit the full power of this class. We were simply polling the text field to see if the user had entered any text when the Save button was tapped, and perhaps more important, we weren't dismissing the keyboard when the user pressed the Return key. Here's the saveCity:sender method from that example:

```
- (void)saveCity:(id)sender {

    CGAppDelegate *delegate =
        (CGAppDelegate *)[[UIApplication sharedApplication] delegate];
    NSMutableArray *cities = delegate.cities;

    UITextField *nameEntry = (UITextField *)[nameCell viewWithTag:777];
    UITextView *descriptionEntry =
    (UITextView *)[descriptionCell viewWithTag:777];

    if ( nameEntry.text.length > 0 ) {
        City *newCity = [[City alloc] init];
        newCity.cityName = nameEntry.text;
        newCity.cityDescription = descriptionEntry.text;
        newCity.cityPicture = nil;
        [cities addObject:newCity];

        CGViewController *viewController = delegate.viewController;
        [viewController.tableView reloadData];
    }
    [delegate.navController popViewControllerAnimated:YES];

}
```

However, the UITextFieldDelegate protocol offers a rich set of delegate methods. To use them, you must declare your class as implementing that delegate protocol (lines with changes are shown in bold):

```
@interface AddCityController : UIViewController
    <UITableViewDataSource, UITableViewDelegate, UITextFieldDelegate> {

    UITextField *activeTextField; ❶

    ... remainder of example code not shown ...
}
```

❶ If your application has more than one text field in the view, it's useful to keep track of which is currently the active field by using an instance variable.

After implementing the delegate protocol, open the nib that contains the UITextField (that would be the *AddCityController.xib* in the case of CityGuide). Then click and Control-drag from the UITextField to the File's Owner icon and select delegates from the pop-up that appears to make the connection. Save the nib when you're done.

When the user taps the text field, the textFieldShouldBeginEditing: method is called in the delegate to ascertain whether the text field should enter edit mode and become the first responder. To implement this, you'd add the following to your controller's implementation (such as *AddCityController.m*):

```
- (BOOL)textFieldShouldBeginEditing:(UITextField *)textField {
    activeTextField = textField; ❶
    return YES;
}
```

❶ If your application has more than one text field in the view, here's where you'd set the currently active field.

If this method returns NO, the text field will not become editable. Only if this method returns YES will the text field enter edit mode. At this point, the keyboard will be presented to the user; the text field will become the first responder; and the textFieldDid BeginEditing: delegate method will be called.

The easiest way to hide the keyboard is to implement the textFieldShouldReturn: delegate method and explicitly resign as the first responder. This method is called in the delegate when the Return key on the keyboard is pressed. To dismiss the text field when you tapped on the Return button, you'd add the following to your controller's implementation:

```
- (BOOL)textFieldShouldReturn:(UITextField *)textField {
    activeTextField = nil; ❶
    [textField resignFirstResponder];
    return YES;
}
```

❶ If your application is keeping track of the currently active text field, this is where you should set the active field to nil before it resigns as first responder.

This method is usually used to make the text field resign as first responder, at which point the delegate methods textFieldShouldEndEditing: and textFieldDidEndEdit ing: will be triggered.

These methods can be used to update the data model with new content if required, or after parsing the input, to make other appropriate changes to the UI such as adding or removing additional elements.

UITextView and Its Delegate

As with the `UITextField` we used as part of our `AddCityController` view in Chapter 5, we didn't exploit the full power of the `UITextView` class in that example. Like the `UITextField`, the `UITextView` class has an associated delegate protocol that opens up its many capabilities.

Dismissing the UITextView

The `UITextViewDelegate` protocol lacks the equivalent to the `textFieldShouldReturn:` method, presumably since we shouldn't expect the Return key to be a signal that the user wishes to stop editing the text in a multiline text entry dialog (after all, the user may want to insert line breaks by pressing Return).

However, there are several ways around the inability of the `UITextView` to resign as first responder using the keyboard. The usual method is to place a Done button in the navigation bar when the `UITextView` presents the pop-up keyboard. When tapped, this button asks the text view to resign as first responder, which will then dismiss the keyboard.

However, depending on how you've planned out your interface, you might want the `UITextView` to resign when the user taps outside the `UITextView` itself.

To do this, you'd subclass `UIView` to accept touches, and then instruct the text view to resign when the user taps outside the view itself. Right-click on the main group in the Project Navigator panel, select New File from the menu, and choose to create an Objective-C Class. Then choose `UIView` from the "Subclass of" menu and name the class **CustomView**.

In the interface (*CustomView.h*), add an IBOutlet for a UITextView:

```
#import <UIKit/UIKit.h>

@interface CustomView : UIView {
    IBOutlet UITextView *textView;
}

@end
```

Then, in the implementation (*CustomView.m*), implement the `touchesEnded:withEvent:` method and ask the `UITextView` to resign as first responder. Here's what the implementation should look like (added lines are shown in bold):

```
#import "CustomView.h"

@implementation CustomView

- (id)initWithFrame:(CGRect)frame {
    if (self = [super initWithFrame:frame]) {
```

```
        // Initialization code
    }
    return self;
}

- (void) awakeFromNib {
    self.multipleTouchEnabled = YES;
}

- (void)touchesEnded:(NSSet *)touches withEvent:(UIEvent *)event {
    NSLog(@"touches began count %d, %@", [touches count], touches);

    [textView resignFirstResponder];
    [self.nextResponder touchesEnded:touches withEvent:event];
}

@end
```

Once you've added the class, you need to save all your changes, then go into Interface Builder and click on your view. Open the Identity Inspector in the Utilities panel and change the type of the view in your nib file to be your CustomView rather than the default UIView class. Then in the Connections Inspector, drag the textView outlet to the UITextView. After doing so, and once you rebuild your application, touches outside the active UI elements will now dismiss the keyboard.

 If the UIView you are subclassing is "behind" other UI elements, these elements will intercept the touches before they reach the UIView layer.

For instance, in the case of the *CityGuide3* application from Chapter 6 and its Add City interface, you would have to declare your custom view to be a subclass of the UITableViewCell class rather than a UI View. You would then need to change the class of the three table view cells in the *AddCityController.xib* main window to be CustomView rather than the default UITableViewCell (don't change the class of the view).

You'd then need to connect the textView outlet of all three table view cells to the UITextView in the table view cell used to enter the long description.

While this solution is elegant, it can be used in only some situations. In many cases, you'll have to resort to the brute-force method of adding a Done button to the navigation bar to dismiss the keyboard.

Parsing XML

The two widely used methods for parsing an XML document are SAX and DOM. A SAX (Simple API for XML) parser is event-driven. It reads the XML document incrementally and calls a delegate method whenever it recognizes a token. Events are generated at the beginning and end of the document, and the beginning and end of each element. A DOM (Document Object Model) parser reads the entire document and forms a tree-like corresponding structure in memory. You can then use the XPath query language to select individual nodes of the XML document using a variety of criteria.

Most programmers find the DOM method more familiar and easier to use; however, SAX-based applications are generally more efficient, run faster, and use less memory. So, unless you are constrained by system requirements, the only real factor when deciding to use SAX or DOM parsers comes down to preference.

If you want to know more about XML, I recommend *Learning XML, Second Edition* by Erik T. Ray (O'Reilly) as a good place to start.

Parsing XML with libxml2

We met the *libxml2* parser and Matt Gallagher's XPath wrappers in the preceding chapter, and my advice is to use these wrappers if you want to do DOM-based parsing of XML on the iPhone or iPod touch.

See the sidebar "Using the XPath Wrappers" (page 232) in Chapter 7 for instructions on adding the XPathQuery wrappers to your project.

The wrappers offer two methods. The only difference between the two is that one expects an HTML document and is therefore less strict about what constitutes a "proper" document than the other, which expects a valid XML document:

```
NSArray *PerformHTMLXPathQuery(NSData *document, NSString *query);
NSArray *PerformXMLXPathQuery(NSData *document, NSString *query);
```

If you want to return the entire document as a single data structure, the following will do that. Be warned that except for the simplest of XML documents, this will normally generate a heavily nested structure of array and dictionary elements, which isn't particularly useful:

```
NSString *xpathQueryString;
NSArray *nodes;

xpathQueryString = @"/*";
nodes = PerformXMLXPathQuery(responseData, xpathQueryString);
NSLog(@"nodes = %@", nodes );
```

Let's take a quick look at a simple XML document snippet with a nested structure:

```
<forecast_conditions>
    ...
    <icon data="/ig/images/weather/chance_of_rain.gif">
</forecast_conditions>
<forecast_conditions>
    ...
    <icon data="/ig/images/weather/chance_of_rain.gif">
</forecast_conditions>
<forecast_conditions>
    ...
    <icon data="/ig/images/weather/chance_of_rain.gif">
</forecast_conditions>
<forecast_conditions>
    ...
    <icon data="/ig/images/weather/chance_of_rain.gif">
</forecast_conditions>
```

To extract the URL of the icons, we can carry out an XPath query:

```
xpathQueryString = @"//forecast_conditions/icon/@data"; ❶
nodes = PerformXMLXPathQuery(responseData, xpathQueryString);
```

❶ Here, we're looking for the data attributes as part of an `<icon>` element, nested
   inside a `<forecast_conditions>` element. An array of all such occurrences will
   be returned.

The `nodes` array returned by the `PerformXMLXPathQuery` method will look like this:

```
(   {
            nodeContent = "/ig/images/weather/mostly_sunny.gif";
            nodeName = data;
    },
        {
            nodeContent = "/ig/images/weather/chance_of_rain.gif";
            nodeName = data;
    },
        {
            nodeContent = "/ig/images/weather/mostly_sunny.gif";
            nodeName = data;
    },
        {
            nodeContent = "/ig/images/weather/mostly_sunny.gif";
            nodeName = data;
    }
)
```

This structure is an `NSArray` of `NSDictionary` objects, and we can parse this by iterating
through each array entry and extracting the dictionary value for the key `nodeContent`,
adding each occurrence to the `icons` array:

```
for ( NSDictionary *node in nodes ) {
    for ( id key in node ) {
        if( [key isEqualToString:@"nodeContent"] ) {
            [icons addObject: [node objectForKey:key]];
        }
    }
}
```

Parsing XML with NSXMLParser

The official way to parse XML on the iPhone is to use the SAX-based NSXMLParser class. However, the parser is strict and cannot take HTML documents:

```
NSString *url = @"http://feeds.feedburner.com/oreilly/news";
NSURL *theURL = [[NSURL URLWithString:url] retain];

NSXMLParser *parser = [[NSXMLParser alloc] initWithContentsOfURL:theURL];
[parser setDelegate:self];
[parser setShouldResolveExternalEntities:YES];
BOOL success = [parser parse];
NSLog(@"Success = %d", success);
```

We use the parser by passing it an XML document and then implementing its delegate methods. The NSXMLParser class offers the following delegate methods:

```
parserDidStartDocument:
parserDidEndDocument:
parser:didStartElement:namespaceURI:qualifiedName:attributes:
parser:didEndElement:namespaceURI:qualifiedName:
parser:didStartMappingPrefix:toURI:
parser:didEndMappingPrefix:
parser:resolveExternalEntityName:systemID:
parser:parseErrorOccurred:
parser:validationErrorOccurred:
parser:foundCharacters:
parser:foundIgnorableWhitespace:
parser:foundProcessingInstructionWithTarget:data:
parser:foundComment:
parser:foundCDATA:
```

The most heavily used delegate methods out of all of those available methods are the parser:didStartElement:namespaceURI:qualifiedName:attributes: method and the parser:didEndElement:namespaceURI:qualifiedName: method. These two methods, along with the parser:foundCharacters: method, will allow you to detect the start and end of a selected element and retrieve its contents. When the NSXMLParser object traverses an element in an XML document, it sends three separate messages to its delegate, in the following order:

```
parser:didStartElement:namespaceURI:qualifiedName:attributes:
parser:foundCharacters:
parser:didEndElement:namespaceURI:qualifiedName:
```

Returning to our weather application, if we wanted to move away from our existing DOM model to use SAX, we would remove the NSURLConnection call from the existing queryServiceWithState:andCity:withParent: method. Then, we would go ahead and delete the NSURLConnection delegate methods, instead relying on the NSXMLParser delegate methods to handle parsing the XML file.

Unless you're familiar with SAX-based parsers, I suggest that XPath and DOM are conceptually easier to deal with than the event-driven model of SAX. This is especially true if you're dealing with HTML, as an HTML document would have to be cleaned up before being passed to the NSXMLParser class.

Parsing JSON

JSON (*http://www.json.org/*) is a lightweight data-interchange format, which is more or less human-readable but still easily machine-parsable. While XML is document-oriented, JSON is data-oriented. If you need to transmit a highly structured piece of data, you should probably render it in XML. However, if your data exchange needs are somewhat less demanding, JSON might be a good option.

The obvious advantage JSON has over XML is that since it is data-oriented and (almost) parsable as a hash map, there is no requirement for heavyweight parsing libraries. Additionally, JSON documents are much smaller than the equivalent XML documents. In bandwidth-limited situations, such as you might find on the iPhone, this can be important. JSON documents normally consume around half the bandwidth of an equivalent XML document for transferring the same data.

NSJSONSerialization

Until the arrival of iOS 5, there was no native support for parsing JSON. However, the SDK now includes the NSJSONSerialization class supporting the conversion between JSON documents and Foundation objects and between Foundation objects and JSON documents.

 Use of the NSJSONSerialization class is limited to devices running iOS 5. However, and perhaps somewhat unfortunately, calling these class methods on devices running an older version of the operating system will not cause the application to crash; instead, calls will fail silently.

Parsing JSON documents

While it also supports parsing data from a stream using an NSInputStream, the most common way to use NSJSONSerialization class is to pass it a JSON document as an NSData object using the JSONObjectWithData:options:error: static class method:

```
NSError *error = nil;
id object = nil;
NSData *json = [NSData dataWithContentsOfFile:path];❶
object = [NSJSONSerialization JSONObjectWithData:json options:0 error:&error];

if( error ) {

    ... code to handle error conditions ...

}
```

❶   Would retrieve a JSON document from a file.

Notice that an object of class id is returned by the NSJSONSerialization class method; this object will (in the normal course of events) either be an NSArray or an NSDiction ary depending on the structure of the original JSON document. The above example returns a generic object; however, if you are sure which Foundation object will be created, you can explicitly cast the returned object to an NSArray or an NSDictionary.

 You can pass various options when creating Foundation objects from JSON data, including:

NSJSONReadingMutableContainers
Specifies that arrays and dictionaries are created as mutable objects.

NSJSONReadingMutableLeaves
Specifies that leaf strings in the JSON object graph are created as instances of NSMutableString.

NSJSONReadingAllowFragments
Specifies that the parser should allow top-level objects that are not an instance of NSArray or NSDictionary.

Multiple arguments can be passed by concatenating them with a logical operator, e.g. NSJSONReadingMutableContainers|NSJSONReadingAl lowFragments.

Creating JSON documents

A Foundation object that may be converted to JSON has to have the following properties:

- The top-level Foundation object must be either an NSArray or NSDictionary.
- All objects are instances of NSString, NSNumber, NSArray, NSDictionary, or NULL.
- All dictionary keys are instances of NSString.
- Numbers are not NaN or infinity.

If your object meets these criteria, you can serialize it to JSON as follows:

```
NSError *error = nil;
NSData *json = nil;

if( [NSJSONSerialization isValidJSONObject:object] ) {❶
    json = [NSJSONSerialization dataWithJSONObject:object options:0
        error:&error];
} else {

    ... handle non-valid objects ...
}

if( error ) {

    ... code to handle error conditions ...

}
```

❶ Here, we test to see if the object we pass is a valid object for serialization. Calling the isValidJSONObject: method or attempting a conversion are the only definitive ways to tell if a given object can be converted to JSON data.

The JSON Framework

Stig Brautaset's *json-framework* library implements both a JSON parser and a generator and can be integrated into your project fairly simply. If you need backwards compatibility in your iOS application so that it works on devices not running iOS 5 or above, you might well want to consider making use of the *json-framework* library.

You can download the disk image with the latest version of the *json-framework* library from this GitHub page (*https://github.com/stig/json-framework/*). Open the disk image and drag and drop the JSON folder into the Classes group in the Project Navigator panel of your project. Remember to tick the "Copy items into destination group's folder" checkbox before adding the files. This will add the JSON source files to your project; you will still need to import the *JSON.h* file into your class to use it.

Linking to the JSON Framework

Since dynamic linking to third-party embedded frameworks is not allowed on the iOS platform, copying the JSON source files into your project is probably the simplest way to make the parser available to your application. However, there is a slightly more elegant approach if you don't want to add the entire JSON source tree to every project where you use it.

Open the Finder and create an *SDKs* subfolder inside your home directory's *Library* folder, and copy the *JSON* folder located inside the *SDKs* folder in the disk image into the newly created *~/Library/SDKs* directory.

Back in Xcode, open your project and double-click on the Project icon at the top of the Project Navigator to open the Project Info drop-down. Click on the Project icon in the drop-down (not the target icon) and switch to the Build Settings panel.

In the Architectures subsection in the Build tab, double-click on the Additional SDKs field and add *$HOME/Library/SDKs/JSON/${PLATFORM_NAME}.sdk* to the list of additional SDKs in the pop-up window. Now go to the Linking subsection of the Build tab, double-click on the Other Linker Flags field, and add `-ObjC -all_load -ljson` to the flags using the pop-up window.

Now you just have to add the following inside your source file:

```
#import <JSON/JSON.h>;
```

Note the use of angle brackets rather than double quotes around the imported header file, denoting that it is located in the standard include path rather than in your project.

Retrieving Twitter Trends

To let you get familiar with JSON, we're going to implement a bare-bones application to retrieve the trending topics on Twitter by making use of the Twitter API and the native Twitter framework and then use the `NSJSONSerialization` class to parse the returned results.

 If you're interested in the Twitter API, you should definitely look at Twitter's documentation (*https://dev.twitter.com/*) for more details regarding the available methods.

Making a request to the Twitter Search API (*https://api.twitter.com/1/trends/1.json*) will return a JSON document containing the top 10 topics that are currently trending on Twitter. The response includes the time of the request, the name of each trend, and the URL to the Twitter Search results page for that topic:

```
[
    {"trends":[
        {"name":"#MyLifeIn5Words",
         "events":null,
         "url":"http://twitter.com/search?q=%23MyLifeIn5Words",
         "promoted_content":null,
         "query":"%23MyLifeIn5Words"},
        {"name":"#ThankYouForBelieveAcoustic",
         "events":null,
         "url":"http://twitter.com/search?q=%23ThankYouForBelieveAcoustic",
         "promoted_content":null,
         "query":"%23ThankYouForBelieveAcoustic"},
        {"name":"#NoConfíoEn",
         "events":null,
         "url":"http://twitter.com/search?q=%23NoConf%C3%ADoEn",
         "promoted_content":null,
         "query":"%23NoConf%C3%ADoEn"},
        {"name":"#1DAilesiTakipleşiyor",
         "events":null,
         "url":"http://twitter.com/search?q=%231DAilesiTakiple%C5%9Fiyor",
         "promoted_content":null,
         "query":"%231DAilesiTakiple%C5%9Fiyor"},
        {"name":"#MentionADateYoullNeverForget",
         "events":null,
         "url":"http://twitter.com/search?q=%23MentionADateYoullNeverForget",
         "promoted_content":null,
         "query":"%23MentionADateYoullNeverForget"},
        {"name":"Believe Acoustic Deserves A Grammy",
         "events":null,
         "url":"http://twitter.com/search?q=
                %22Believe%20Acoustic%20Deserves%20A%20Grammy%22",
         "promoted_content":null,
         "query":"%22Believe%20Acoustic%20Deserves%20A%20Grammy%22"},
        {"name":"Irmã Zuleide",
         "events":null,
         "url":"http://twitter.com/search?q=%22Irm%C3%A3%20Zuleide%22",
         "promoted_content":null,
         "query":"%22Irm%C3%A3%20Zuleide%22"},
        {"name":"Office 2013",
         "events":null,
         "url":"http://twitter.com/search?q=%22Office%202013%22",
         "promoted_content":null,
         "query":"%22Office%202013%22"},
        {"name":"Vote for Directioners For Favorite",
         "events":null,
         "url":"http://twitter.com/search?q=
                %22Vote%20for%20Directioners%20For%20Favorite%22",
         "promoted_content":null,
         "query":"%22Vote%20for%20Directioners%20For%20Favorite%22"},
        {"name":"D-League",
         "events":null,
         "url":"http://twitter.com/search?q=D-League",
```

```
      "promoted_content":null,
      "query":"D-League"}],
  "as_of":"2013-01-29T15:33:51Z",
  "created_at":"2013-01-29T15:30:02Z",
  "locations":[
     {"name":"Worldwide",
      "woeid":1}]}]
```

Using the Social Framework

Since the arrival of iOS 5 the SDK now provides native support for sending Twitter API requests, as well as for composing and sending tweets.

In iOS 6 the Social framework handles the user authentication part of any Twitter API requests for you and provides a template for creating the HTTP portion of the request. You can retrieve Twitter credentials manually using the Accounts framework, and we'll be looking at that in Chapter 11, where we talk about integrating your application into iOS.

In iOS 5 the Twitter framework was used to make requests to the Twitter API. However with the introduction of native Facebook and Weibo (a Chinese social network), support for this was deprecated in favor of the new Social framework, which handles all such requests.

To make use of the Social framework, you'll have to import it into your project in the same fashion we've done before, and then import the interface file into your code. After doing so, you should be able to retrieve the currently trending topics from the Social API as follows:

```
SLRequest *request = [SLRequest
   requestForServiceType:SLServiceTypeTwitter
   requestMethod:SLRequestMethodGET
   URL:[NSURL URLWithString:@"https://api.twitter.com/1/trends/1.json"]
   parameters:nil];

[request performRequestWithHandler:^(NSData *responseData,
       NSHTTPURLResponse *urlResponse, NSError *error) {❶
   if ([urlResponse statusCode] == 200) {
      NSError *error;
      id obj = [NSJSONSerialization JSONObjectWithData:responseData
          options:0 error:&error];
      NSLog(@"Response: %@", obj);
   }
   else {
      NSLog(@"Error: HTTP code %i", [urlResponse statusCode]);
```

```
    }
  }];
```

❶ Here we make the request and provide a block, which is simply an anonymous method, called as a handler function when the results are returned. In this case, the method takes three arguments: the response data, the response object, and an error object.

The Twitter Trends Application

We've got enough to start building our application at this point. Open Xcode and start a new iOS application targeted to the iPhone. Select the Single View application template and name the project **TwitterTrends** when prompted for a filename.

We're going to use the native NSJSONSerialization class to parse the JSON document returned by the Twitter API, and since that document provides a URL, we're also going to reuse the WebViewController class we wrote in Chapter 7. Open the *Prototype* project from Chapter 7, and drag and drop the *WebViewController.m*, *WebViewController.h*, and *WebViewController.xib* files from there into your new project.

 Remember to select the "Copy items into destination group's folder" checkbox in the pop-up window when copying the files in both cases, and ensure that the "Add to Target" checkbox is checked.

Retrieving the trends

Let's start by retrieving the trending topics, and by writing a class to retrieve the trends using the Twitter API using the TWRequest class. Right-click on the Project Navigator panel, click on New File, and choose to make a new Objective-C class, a subclass of NSObject (rather than being a sub-class of UIView, which is the default). Name the new class **TwitterTrends** when prompted.

We'll be using the Twitter framework, so we'll need to import it into our project. Click on the Project icon at the top of the Project pane in Xcode, then click on the main Target for the project, and then on the Build Phases tab. Finally click on the Link Binary with Libraries item to open up the list of linked frameworks, and click on the + symbol to add a new framework. Select the Twitter framework (*Twitter.framework*) from the drop-down list and click the Add button.

Next open the *TwitterTrends.h* interface file in the Xcode Editor. We're going to need a method to allow us to make the request to the Search Service. We're going to trigger the request from the ViewController class. We'll need a reference back to the view controller so that we can update the view, so we'll pass that in as an argument. Add the lines shown in bold:

```
#import <Foundation/Foundation.h>

@class ViewController;

@interface TwitterTrends : NSObject {
    ViewController *viewController;
}

- (void)queryServiceWithParent:(UIViewController *)controller;

@end
```

Now open the *TwitterTrends.m* implementation file in the Xcode Editor and add the
following code:

```
#import "TwitterTrends.h"
#import "ViewController.h"

#import <Social/Social.h>

@implementation TwitterTrends

- (void)queryServiceWithParent:(UIViewController *)controller {
    viewController = (ViewController *)controller;

    SLRequest *request  = [SLRequest
      requestForServiceType:SLServiceTypeTwitter
      requestMethod:SLRequestMethodGET
      URL:[NSURL URLWithString:@"https://api.twitter.com/1/trends/1.json"]
      parameters:nil];

    [request performRequestWithHandler:^(NSData *responseData,
            NSHTTPURLResponse *urlResponse, NSError *error) {
        if ([urlResponse statusCode] == 200) {
            NSError *error;
            id obj = [NSJSONSerialization JSONObjectWithData:responseData
                options:0 error:&error];
            NSLog(@"Response: %@", obj);
        }
        else {
            NSLog(@"Error: HTTP code %i", [urlResponse statusCode]);
        }
    }];

}

@end
```

Now that we have a class that can query the trends endpoint, let's use it. Click on the *ViewController.m* implementation file and import the *TwitterTrends.h* header file:

```
#import "TwitterTrends.h"
```

Inside the `viewDidLoad:` method, add the following two lines of code:

```
TwitterTrends *trends = [[TwitterTrends alloc] init];
[trends queryServiceWithParent:self];
```

This is a good point to check our code. Make sure you've saved your changes and click the Run button in the Xcode toolbar to build and deploy your application into iPhone Simulator. We started the asynchronous query of the Search service from the `viewDid Load:` method, printing the results to the console log when the query completes. So, once the application has started and you see the gray screen of the default view, open the Debug Area (the middle button in the View segmented control in the Xcode toolbar).

After the asynchronous network call completes and returns, you should see something very similar to Figure 8-1. You've successfully retrieved the JSON trends file from the Twitter trends endpoint.

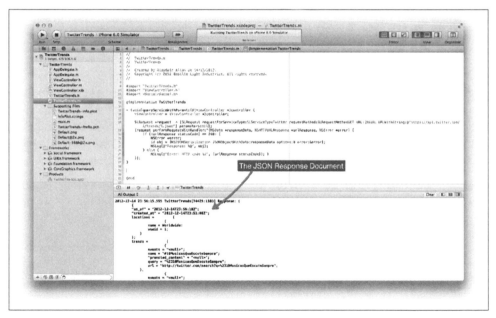

Figure 8-1. The console log showing the retrieved JSON document

Building a UI

Now that we've managed to successfully retrieve the trends data, let's build a UI for the application. Looking at the JSON file, the obvious UI to implement here is a `UITable View`. The text in each cell will be the trend name, and when the user clicks on the cell, we can open the associated Search Service URL using our `WebControllerView`.

Let's start by modifying the `ViewController` class; since this is a simple bare-bones application, we're going to use the view controller class to both control our view and hold our data model. Open the *ViewController.h* interface file in the Xcode Editor and add the code shown in bold:

```
#import <UIKit/UIKit.h>

@interface ViewController : UIViewController
    <UITableViewDataSource, UITableViewDelegate> {

}

@property (weak, nonatomic) IBOutlet UITableView *serviceView;
@property (strong, nonatomic) NSMutableArray *names;
@property (strong, nonatomic) NSMutableArray *urls;

@end
```

Click on the *ViewController.xib* file to open it in Interface Builder. You'll initially be presented with a blank view. Drag and drop a navigation bar (`UINavigationBar`) from the Object Library window into the View window and position it at the top of the view. Double-click on the title and change it from Title to Twitter Trends. Now drag and drop a table view (`UITableView`) into the View window, and resize it to fill the remaining part of the view.

Right-click and drag from the File's Owner icon to the table view and connect it to the `serviceView` outlet, then right-click and drag from the table view to File's Owner and connect both the `dataSource` and `delegate` outlets.

That's it; you're done in Interface Builder, and you should be looking at something similar to Figure 8-2.

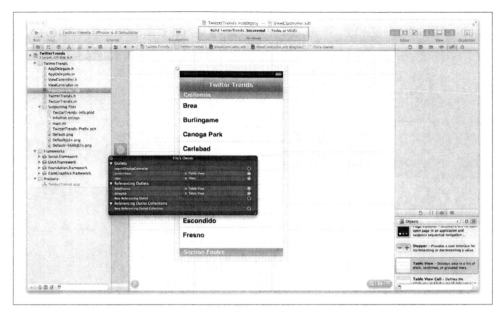

Figure 8-2. The ViewController.xib file in Interface Builder

Open the *ViewController.m* implementation file in the Xcode Editor, and modify the
`viewDidLoad` method as follows:

```
- (void)viewDidLoad {
    [super viewDidLoad];

    self.names = [[NSMutableArray alloc] init]; ❶
    self.urls = [[NSMutableArray alloc] init];

    [UIApplication
        sharedApplication].networkActivityIndicatorVisible = YES; ❷
    TwitterTrends *trends = [[TwitterTrends alloc] init];
    [trends queryServiceWithParent:self]; ❸
}
```

❶   Here we initialize the `names` and `urls` arrays we declared in the interface file.
     These will be populated by the `TwitterTrends` class.

❷   This is where we start the network activity indicator spinning in the iPhone status
     bar.

❸   Here is where we start the asynchronous query to the trends API endpoint.

Now we need to implement the `UITableViewDelegate` methods; we need to implement
only three of the delegate methods. Add the following methods to *ViewController.m*:

```
- (NSInteger)tableView:(UITableView *)tableView
        numberOfRowsInSection:(NSInteger)section {
    return self.names.count; ❶
}

- (UITableViewCell *)tableView:(UITableView *)tableView
        cellForRowAtIndexPath:(NSIndexPath *)indexPath {
    static NSString *CellIdentifier = @"Cell";
    UITableViewCell *cell =
    [tableView dequeueReusableCellWithIdentifier:CellIdentifier];
    if (cell == nil) {
        cell = [[UITableViewCell alloc]
initWithStyle:UITableViewCellStyleDefault reuseIdentifier:CellIdentifier];
    }

    cell.textLabel.text = [self.names objectAtIndex:indexPath.row]; ❷
    return cell;
}


- (void)tableView:(UITableView *)tableView
        didSelectRowAtIndexPath:(NSIndexPath *)indexPath {
    // Add code to handle selection here.

    [tableView deselectRowAtIndexPath:indexPath animated:YES];
}
```

❶   We're going to display a number of cells (equal to names.count) to the user. The names array will be filled from the TwitterTrends instance we created in the viewDidLoad: method.

❷   This is where we set the cell label text to be the name of the trending topic.

Click the Run button to build and deploy your application to the iPhone Simulator to test your code. If all goes well, you should still get the JSON document in the console, but now your view should be a blank table view. Why is it blank? Well, we haven't parsed the JSON and populated our data model yet. Let's do that now.

 You may also have noticed that the activity indicator keeps spinning. We'll take care of that, too.

Parsing the JSON document

We need to modify the handler block in the queryServiceWithParent: method to populate the view controller's data model, and then request it to reload the table view with the new data:

```objc
- (void)queryServiceWithParent:(UIViewController *)controller {
    viewController = (ViewController *)controller;

    SLRequest *request = [SLRequest
      requestForServiceType:SLServiceTypeTwitter
      requestMethod:SLRequestMethodGET
      URL:[NSURL URLWithString:@"https://api.twitter.com/1/trends/1.json"]
      parameters:nil];

    [request performRequestWithHandler:^(NSData *responseData,
            NSHTTPURLResponse *urlResponse, NSError *error) {
        if ([urlResponse statusCode] == 200) {
            NSError *error;
            NSArray *json = [NSJSONSerialization
                JSONObjectWithData:responseData options:0 error:&error];

            NSArray *trends = [[[json objectAtIndex:0] objectForKey:@"trends"];

            for (NSDictionary *trend in trends) {
                [viewController.names addObject:[trend objectForKey:@"name"]];
                NSLog(@"name = %@", [trend objectForKey:@"name"]);
                [viewController.urls addObject:[trend objectForKey:@"url"]];
                NSLog(@"url = %@", [trend objectForKey:@"url"]);
            }
            [UIApplication  sharedApplication].networkActivityIndicatorVisible =
                NO;
            dispatch_async( dispatch_get_main_queue(), ^{
                [viewController.serviceView reloadData];
            });❶
        }
        else {
            NSLog(@"Error: HTTP code %i", [urlResponse statusCode]);
        }
    }];

}
```

❶ The handler block is put into the global dispatch queue and executed asynchronously, and since we want to update the user interface, we have to create a separate block that is then put into a dispatch queue on the main thread to do that. This is a FIFO queue, and tasks are run at event time (i.e., inside the run loop).

If you rebuild your application in Xcode and run it, you should get something similar to Figure 8-3. The table view is now populated with the current trending topics on Twitter.

Figure 8-3. The Twitter Trends application running in iPhone Simulator

However, clicking on individual cells doesn't do anything yet, so we need to modify the `tableView:didSelectRowAtIndexPath:` method to use our `WebViewController` class.

Import the *WebViewController.h* interface file into the view controller by adding the following to the top of *ViewController.m*:

```
#import "WebViewController.h"
```

Then replace the `tableView:didSelectRowAtIndexPath:` method in *View-Controller.m* with the following:

```
- (void)tableView:(UITableView *)tableView
      didSelectRowAtIndexPath:(NSIndexPath *)indexPath {
  NSString *title = [self.names objectAtIndex:indexPath.row];
  NSURL *url = [NSURL URLWithString:[self.urls objectAtIndex:indexPath.row]];
  WebViewController *webViewController =
    [[WebViewController alloc] initWithURL:url andTitle:title];
  [self presentModalViewController:webViewController animated:YES];
```

```
    [tableView deselectRowAtIndexPath:indexPath animated:YES];
}
```

If you rebuild the application again and click on one of the trending topics, the web view should open modally and you should see something similar to Figure 8-4.

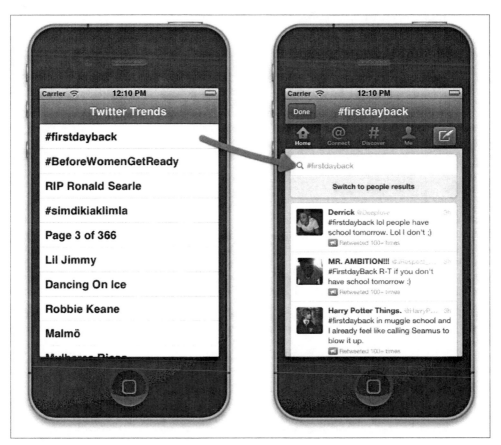

Figure 8-4. The Twitter Trends web view

Tidying up

There are a few bits and pieces that I haven't added to this application but that you really should add if you are going to release it. Most of it has to do with error handling; for instance, you should do a reachability check before trying to retrieve the JSON document. However, what this example should have illustrated is that retrieving and parsing JSON documents is a relatively simple task.

Regular Expressions

Regular expressions, commonly known as *regexes*, are a pattern-matching standard for text processing, and are a powerful tool when dealing with strings. With regular expressions, an expression serves as a pattern to compare with the text being searched. You can use regular expressions to search for patterns in a string, replace text, and extract substrings from the original string.

Introduction to Regular Expressions

In its simplest form, you can use a regular expression to match a literal string; for example, the regular expression "string" will match the string "this is a *string*." Each character in the expression will match itself, unless it is one of the special characters +, ?, ., *, \^, $, (,), \[, {, |, or \. The special meaning of these characters can be *escaped* by prepending a backslash character, \.

We can also tie our expression to the start of a string (^string) or the end of a string (string$). For the string "this is a string" \^string will not match the string, while string$ will.

We can also use quantified patterns. Here, * matches *zero or more* times, ? matches *zero or one* time, and + matches *one or more* times. So, the regular expression 23*4 would match 1245, 12345, and 123345, but the expression 23?4 would match 1245 and also 12345. Finally, the expression 23+4 would match 12345 and 123345 but not 1245.

Unless told otherwise, regular expressions are always greedy; they will normally match the longest string possible.

While a backslash escapes the meaning of the special characters in an expression, it turns most alphanumeric characters into special characters. Many special characters are available; however, the main ones are:

\d

    Matches a numeric character

\D

    Matches a nonnumeric character

\s

    Matches a whitespace character

\S

    Matches a nonwhitespace character

`\w`

Matches an alphanumeric (or the underscore) character

`\W`

Matches the inverse of `\w`

All of these special character expressions can be modified by the quantifier modifiers.

Many other bits of more complicated and advanced syntax are available. If you find yourself making heavy use of regexes, I recommend the books *Regular Expressions Cookbook* by Jan Goyvaerts and Steven Levithan and *Mastering Regular Expressions, Third Edition* by Jeffrey E. F. Friedl (both from O'Reilly).

NSRegularExpression

Native regular expression support was added to the SDK with the arrival of iOS 4 and the addition of the `NSRegularExpression` class.

The following snippet will use a regular expression to match an arbitrary URL in a `NSString` and return the URL as another `NSString`:

```
NSError *error = nil;

NSString *regexString =
    @"(?i)\\b((?:[a-z][\\w-]+:(?:/{1,3}|[a-z0-9%])|www\\d{0,3}[.]|"
    @"[a-z0-9.\\-]+[.][a-z]{2,4}/)(?:[^\\s()<>]+|\\(([^\\s()<>]+|("
    @"\\(([^\\s()<>]+\\)))*\\))+(?:\\(([^\\s()<>]+|(\\(([^\\s()<>]+\\"
    @")))*\\)|[^\\s`!()\\[\\]{};:'\".,<>?«»""'']))"; ❶

NSString *aString =
    @"This is a sentence with a random URL"
    @"http://apple.com embedded in the sentence.";

NSRegularExpression *regex = [NSRegularExpression
                regularExpressionWithPattern:regexString
                                     options:NSRegularExpressionCaseInsensitive
                                       error:&error];

NSString *match =
    [aString substringWithRange:[regex rangeOfFirstMatchInString:aString
    options:NSMatchingCompleted range:NSMakeRange(0, [aString length])]];

NSLog(@"Matched string: %@", match);
```

❶ This is a boilerplate regular expression for matching URLs created by John Gruber (*http://daringfireball.net/2010/07/improved_regex_for_matching_urls*).

Regular expressions use the backslash (\) character to escape characters that have special meaning inside the regular expression. However, since the backslash character is the C escape character, these in turn have to escape any uses of this character inside your regular expression by prepending it with another backslash character. For example, to match a literal ampersand (&) character, you must first prepend it with a backslash to escape it for the regular expression engine, and then prepend it with another backslash to escape this in turn for the compiler—that is, \&. To match a single literal backslash (\) character with a regular expression therefore requires four backslashes: \\\\.

In addition to matching patterns, we can create new strings by replacing characters matching a regular expression pattern with a template pattern:

```
NSError *error = nil;
NSRegularExpression *regex =
    [NSRegularExpression
regularExpressionWithPattern:@"\\s"
                    options:NSRegularExpressionCaseInsensitive error:&error];
NSString *newString =
    [regex stringByReplacingMatchesInString:originalString
    options:0 range:NSMakeRange(0, [originalString length])
        withTemplate:@"%20"];

NSLog(@"New string: %@",newString);
```

Here we find any whitespace characters in the `orginalString` and replace them with the URL encoding for whitespace, `%20`, and return a `newString`.

RegexKitLite

The RegexKit_Lite_ library adds regular expression support to the base `NSString` class. While there is now native support for regular expressions in iOS, a lot of legacy code will make use of this library, so it's important to understand how it works. See the RegexKitLite page (*http://regexkit.sourceforge.net/RegexKitLite/*) for more details.

Adding RegexKitLite to Your Own Project

To add RegexKit_Lite_ to your own project, download the *RegexKitLite-<X.X>.tar.bz2* compressed tarball (*X.X* will be the current version, such as 4.0), and uncompress and double-click it to extract it. Open the directory and drag and drop the two files, *RegexKitLite.h* and *RegexKitLite.m*, into your project. Remember to select the "Copy items into destination group's folder" checkbox before adding the files.

We're not done yet; we still need to add the *libicucore.dylib* library to our project. Click the Project icon in the Project Navigator panel in Xcode and go to the Build Phases tab

---

of the Project Info window. Click on the Link Binaries with Libraries and click + to add the *libicucore.dylib* library. Now click the Build Settings tab and then click the All button in the tool ribbon to show all of the settings, if it's not already checked. Go to the Linking subsection of this window, double-click the Other Linker Flags field, and click +. Add -licucore to the flags.

You'll want to use regular expressions to perform three main tasks: matching strings, replacing strings, and extracting strings. RegexKitLite allows you to do all of these, but remember that when you want to use it, you need to import the *RegexKitLite.h* file into your class.

As was the case for Apple's Reachability code we discussed in Chapter 7, the RegexKitLite code has not been updated for ARC. You'll need to go ahead and turn off ARC for the RegexKitLite code in the same way you did for Reachability before you compile your project.

The RegexKit_Lite_ library operates by extending the NSString class via an Objective-C category extension mechanism, making it very easy to use. If you want to match a string, you simply operate directly on the string you want to match.

```
NSString *string = @"This is a string";
NSString *match = [string stringByMatching:@"a string$" capture:0]; ❶
NSLog(@"%@", match);
```

❶   This will return the first occurrence of the matched string.

If the match fails, the match variable will be set to nil, and if you want to replace a string, it's almost as easy:

```
NSString *string2 = @"This is a string";
NSString *regexString = @"a string$";
NSString *replacementString = @"another string";

NSString *newString = nil;
newString = [string2 stringByReplacingOccurrencesOfRegex:regexString
                                        withString:replacementString];
NSLog(@"%@", newString);
```

This will match "a string" in the variable string2, replacing it and creating the string "This is another string" in the variable newString.

The RegexKit_Lite_ library provides many other methods on top of those I've covered here, so if you need to perform regular expression tasks I haven't talked about, you might want to look at the documentation (*http://regexkit.sourceforge.net/RegexKitLite/*).

RegexKit_Lite_ uses the regular expression engine provided by the ICU library. Before the release of iOS 3.2, Apple did not officially support linking directly to the *libicucore.dylib* library. Despite that, many applications were available on the App Store that made use of this library, and as of iOS 3.2, use of the regular expression functionality included in the library was officially permitted.

However, you should be aware that while the ICU library also contains a lot of functionality for dealing with internationalization and localization, permission has not been granted to use that additional functionality. Only use of the regular expression methods was approved for applications submitted to the App Store.

Faking regex support with the built-in NSPredicate

As well as NSRegularExpression, Core Data provides the NSPredicate class, which allows you to carry out some operations that would normally be done via regular expressions. For those familiar with SQL, the NSPredicate class operates in a very similar manner to the SQL WHERE statement.

Let's assume we have an NSArray of NSDictionary objects, structured like this:

```
NSArray *arrayOfDictionaries = [NSArray arrayWithObjects:
  [NSDictionary dictionaryWithObjectsAndKeys:
    @"Learning iPhone Programming", @"title", @"2010", @"year", nil],
  [NSDictionary dictionaryWithObjectsAndKeys:
    @"Arduino Orbital Lasers", @"title", @"2012", @"year", nil],
  nil];
```

We can test whether a given object in the array matches the criteria foo = "bar" AND baz = "qux" as follows:

```
NSPredicate *predicate =
  [NSPredicate predicateWithFormat:@"year = '2012'"];
for (NSDictionary *dictionary in arrayOfDictionaries) {
  BOOL match = [predicate evaluateWithObject:dictionary];
  if (match) {
    NSLog(@"Found a match!");
  }
}
```

Alternatively, we can extract all entries in the array that match the predicate:

```
NSPredicate *predicate2 =
  [NSPredicate predicateWithFormat:@"year = '2012'"];
NSArray *matches =
  [arrayOfDictionaries filteredArrayUsingPredicate:predicate2];
for (NSDictionary *dictionary in matches) {
  NSLog(@"%@", [dictionary objectForKey: @"title"]);
}
```

However, we can also use predicates to test strings against regular expressions. For instance, the following code will test the email string against the regex we provided, returning YES if it is a valid email address:

```
NSString *email = @"alasdair@babilim.co.uk";
NSString *regex = @"^\\b[a-zA-Z0-9._%+-]+@[a-zA-Z0-9.-]+\\.[a-zA-Z]{2,4}\\b$";
NSPredicate *predicate3 =
    [NSPredicate predicateWithFormat:@"SELF MATCHES %@", regex];
BOOL match = [predicate3 evaluateWithObject:email];
if (match) {
    NSLog(@"Found a match!");
}
```

While the NSPredicate class is actually defined as part of the Foundation framework, it is intended (and used extensively) as part of the Core Data framework. We're not going to cover Core Data in this book. If you're interested in this framework, I recommend you look at *Core Data: Apple's API for Persisting Data on Mac OS X* by Marcus S. Zarra (Pragmatic Programmers).

Storing Data

If the user creates data while running your application, you may need a place to store the data so that it's there the next time the user runs it. You'll also want to store user preferences, passwords, and many other forms of data. You can store data online somewhere, but then your application won't function unless it's online. An iOS device can store data in lots of ways.

Using Flat Files

So-called *flat files* are files that contain data, but are typically not backed by the power of a full-featured database system. They are useful for storing small bits of text data, but they lack the performance and organizational advantages that a database provides.

Applications running on an iOS device are *sandboxed*; you can access only a limited subset of the filesystem from your application. If you want to save files from your application, you should save them into the application's *Document* directory.

Here's the code you need to locate the application's *Document* directory:

```
NSArray *arrayPaths = NSSearchPathForDirectoriesInDomains(
    NSDocumentDirectory,   NSUserDomainMask, YES);
NSString *docDirectory = [arrayPaths objectAtIndex:0]; ❶
```

❶   The first entry in the array will contain the file path to the application's *Document* directory.

Reading and writing text content

The NSFileManager methods generally deal with NSData objects.

For writing to a file, you can use the writeToFile:atomically:encoding:error: method:

```
NSString *string = @"Hello, World";
NSString *filePath = [docDirectory stringByAppendingString:@"/File.txt"];
[string writeToFile:filePath
        atomically:YES
        encoding:NSUTF8StringEncoding
        error:nil];
```

If you want to simply read a plain-text file, you can use the NSString class method stringWithContentsOfFile:encoding:error: to read from the file:

```
NSString *fileContents = [NSString stringWithContentsOfFile:filePath
                           encoding:NSUTF8StringEncoding error:nil];
NSLog(@"%@", fileContents);
```

Creating temporary files

To obtain the path to the default location to store temporary files, you can use the NSTemporaryDirectory method:

```
NSString *tempDir = NSTemporaryDirectory();
```

Other file manipulation

The NSFileManager class can be used for moving, copying, creating, and deleting files.

Storing Information in a SQL Database

The public domain SQLite library (*http://www.sqlite.org*) is a lightweight transactional database. The library is included in the iOS SDK and will probably do most of the heavy lifting you need for your application to store data. The SQLite engine powers several large applications on Mac OS X, including the Apple Mail application, and is extensively used by the latest generation of browsers to support HTML5 database features. Despite the "Lite" name, the library should not be underestimated.

Interestingly, unlike most SQL database engines, the SQLite engine makes use of dynamic typing. Most other SQL databases implement static typing: the column in which a value is stored determines the type of a value. Using SQLite the column type specifies only the type affinity (the recommended type) for the data stored in that column. However, any column may still store data of any type.

Each value stored in a SQLite database has one of the storage types shown in Table 8-1.

Table 8-1. SQLite storage types

Storage type	Description
NULL	The value is a NULL value.
INTEGER	The value is a signed integer.
REAL	The value is a floating-point value.
TEXT	The value is a text string.
BLOB	The value is a blob of data, stored exactly as it was input.

If you're not familiar with SQL, I recommend you read *Learning SQL, Second Edition*] by Alan Beaulieu (O'Reilly). If you want more information about SQLite specifically, I also recommend *SQLite* by Chris Newman (Sams).

Adding a database to your project

Let's create a database for the City Guide application. Open the *CityGuide* project in Xcode and take a look at the application delegate implementation where we added four starter cities to the application's data model. Each city has three bits of interesting information associated with it: its name, description, and an associated image. We need to put this information into a database table.

 If you don't want to create the database for the City Guide application yourself, you can download a prebuilt copy containing the starter cities from this book's website (*http://learningiphoneprogramming.com/ pages/samplecode.html*).

Open a Terminal window, and at the command prompt, type the code shown in bold:

```
$ sqlite3 cities.sqlite
```

This will create a cities database and start SQLite in interactive mode. At the SQL prompt, we need to create our database tables to store our information. Type the code shown in bold (sqlite> and ...> are the SQLite command prompts):

```
SQLite version 3.4.0
Enter ".help" for instructions
sqlite> CREATE TABLE cities(id INTEGER PRIMARY KEY AUTOINCREMENT,
    ...> name TEXT, description TEXT, image BLOB);
sqlite> .quit
```

At this stage, we have an empty database and associated table. We need to add image data to the table as BLOB (*binary large object*) data; the easiest way to do this is to use Mike Chirico's *eatblob.c* program available online (*http://souptonuts.sourceforge.net/ code/eatblob.c.html*).

The *eatblob.c* code should compile out of the box on OS X Mountain Lion. However, it makes use of the getdelim and getline functions. Both of these are GNU-specific and may not be available on previous versions of OS X. However, you can download the necessary source code from this website (*http://learningiphoneprogramming.com/pages/samplecode.html*).

Once you have downloaded the *eatblob.c* source file, you can compile the *eatblob* program from the command line:

```
gcc -o eatblob eatblob.c -lsqlite3
```

So, for each of our four original cities defined inside the app delegate, we need to run the *eatblob* code:

```
./eatblob cities.sqlite ./London.jpg "INSERT INTO cities (id, name,
description, image) VALUES (NULL, 'London', 'London is the capital of the
United Kingdom and England.', ?)"
```

to populate the database file with our "starter cities."

It's arguable whether including the images inside the database using a BLOB is a good idea, except in the case of small images. It's normal practice to include images as a file and include only metadata inside the database itself; for example, the path to the included image. However, if you want to bundle a single file (with starter data) into your application, it's a good trick.

We're now going to add the cities database to the City Guide application. However, you might want to make a copy of the City Guide application before modifying it. Open the Finder and navigate to the location where you saved the *CityGuide* project; right-click or Control-click on the folder containing the project files and select Duplicate. A folder called *CityGuide copy* will be created containing a duplicate of our project. You should probably rename it to something more sensible. I suggest *CityGuide4*. Now open the new version of the project in Xcode and mouse over the blue Project icon at the top of the Project navigator and hit the Enter key, which will make the project name editable.

Enter **CityGuide4** as the new project name, and a drop-down will appear prompting you to approve the changes to the project. Click on Rename when prompted to do so to rename the project.

After you've done this, open the Finder again and navigate to the directory where you created the *cities.sqlite* database file. Open the *CityGuide4* project in Xcode, then drag and drop it into the *Supporting Files* folder of the *CityGuide4* project in Xcode. Remember to check the box to indicate that Xcode should "Copy items into destination group's folder."

To use the SQLite library, you'll need to add it to your project. Click on the Project icon in the Project Navigator panel in Xcode and go to the Build Phases tab of the Project Info window. Click the Link Binaries with Libraries and click + to add the `libsq lite3.dylib` library. Now click on the Build Settings tab and then click on the All button in the tool ribbon to show all of the settings (if it's not already checked). Go to the Linking subsection of this window, double-click the Other Linker Flags field, and click +. Add `-lsqlite3` to the flags and then click OK.

Data persistence for the City Guide application

We've now copied our database into our project, so let's add some data persistence to the City Guide application.

Since our images are now inside the database, you can delete the images from the Supporting Files group in the Project Navigator panel in Xcode. Remember not to delete the *QuestionMark.jpg* file, because our add city view controller will need that file.

 SQLite runs much slower on an iOS device than it does in simulator. Queries that run instantly on the simulator may take several seconds to run on the iPhone, especially on older models. You need to take this into account in your testing.

If you're just going to be querying the database, you can leave *cities.sqlite* in place and refer to it via the application bundle's resource path. However, files in the bundle are read-only. If you intend to modify the contents of the database as we do, your application must copy the database file to the application's document folder and modify it from there. One advantage to this approach is that the contents of this folder are preserved when the application is updated, and therefore cities that users add to your database are also preserved across application updates.

We're going to add two methods to the application delegate (*CGAppDelegate.m*). The first copies the database we included inside our application bundle to the application's *Document* directory, which allows us to write to it. If the file already exists in that location, it won't overwrite it. If you need to replace the database file for any reason, the easiest way is to delete your application from the simulator and then redeploy it using Xcode.

You'll need to import the *sqlite3.h* header file into the implementation, so add this line to the top of *CityGuideDelegate.m*:

```
#include <sqlite3.h>
```

Then add the following method to *CGAppDelegate.m*:

```
- (NSString *)copyDatabaseToDocuments {
    NSFileManager *fileManager = [NSFileManager defaultManager];
```

```
        NSArray *paths =
          NSSearchPathForDirectoriesInDomains(NSDocumentDirectory,
                                              NSUserDomainMask, YES);
        NSString *documentsPath = [paths objectAtIndex:0];
        NSString *filePath = [documentsPath
                              stringByAppendingPathComponent:@"cities.sqlite"];

        if ( ![fileManager fileExistsAtPath:filePath] ) {
            NSString *bundlePath = [[[NSBundle mainBundle] resourcePath]
                stringByAppendingPathComponent:@"cities.sqlite"];
            [fileManager copyItemAtPath:bundlePath toPath:filePath error:nil];
        }
        return filePath;
    }
```

The second method will take the path to the database passed back by the previous
method and populate the cities array. Add this method to *GAppDelegate.m*:

```
    -(void) readCitiesFromDatabaseWithPath:(NSString *)filePath {

        sqlite3 *database;

        if(sqlite3_open([filePath UTF8String], &database) == SQLITE_OK) {
            const char *sqlStatement = "select * from cities";
            sqlite3_stmt *compiledStatement;
            if(sqlite3_prepare_v2(database, sqlStatement,
                                  -1, &compiledStatement, NULL) == SQLITE_OK) {
                while(sqlite3_step(compiledStatement) == SQLITE_ROW) {

                    NSString *cityName =
                      [NSString stringWithUTF8String:(char *)
                      sqlite3_column_text(compiledStatement, 1)];
                    NSString *cityDescription =
                      [NSString stringWithUTF8String:(char *)
                      sqlite3_column_text(compiledStatement, 2)];

                    NSData *cityData = [[NSData alloc]
                      initWithBytes:sqlite3_column_blob(compiledStatement, 3)
                      length: sqlite3_column_bytes(compiledStatement, 3)];
                    UIImage *cityImage = [UIImage imageWithData:cityData];

                    City *newCity = [[City alloc] init];
                    newCity.cityName = cityName;
                    newCity.cityDescription = cityDescription;
                    newCity.cityPicture = (UIImage *)cityImage;
                    [self.cities addObject:newCity];
                }
            }
            sqlite3_finalize(compiledStatement);
        }
        sqlite3_close(database);
    }
```

You'll also have to declare the methods in *CityGuideDelegate.m*'s interface file, so add the following lines to *CityGuideDelegate.h* just before the @end directive:

```
-(NSString *)copyDatabaseToDocuments;
-(void) readCitiesFromDatabaseWithPath:(NSString *)filePath;
```

After we add these routines to the delegate, we must modify the applicationDidFi nishLaunching: method, removing our hardcoded cities and instead populating the cities array using our database.

Replace the applicationDidFinishLaunching:withOptions: method in *CGAppDelegate.m* with the following. The highlighted lines are where we add our cities directly from the database:

```
- (BOOL)application:(UIApplication *)application
        didFinishLaunchingWithOptions:(NSDictionary *)launchOptions {

    self.window = [[UIWindow alloc] initWithFrame:[[UIScreen mainScreen] bounds]];

    self.cities = [[NSMutableArray alloc] init];
    NSString *filePath = [self copyDatabaseToDocuments];
    [self readCitiesFromDatabaseWithPath:filePath];

    self.viewController = [[CGViewController alloc]
        initWithNibName:@"CGViewController" bundle:nil];
    self.navController = [[UINavigationController alloc]
        initWithRootViewController:self.viewController];
    self.window.rootViewController = self.navController;
    [self.window makeKeyAndVisible];
    return YES;
}
```

We've reached a good point to take a break. Make sure you've saved your changes, and click the Run button on the Xcode toolbar. If all goes well, when your application starts, it shouldn't look different from the City Guide application at the end of Chapter 5.

OK, we've read in our data in the application delegate. However, we still don't save newly created cities; we need to insert the new cities into the database when the user adds them from the AddCityController view.

Declare the following method in the *AddCityController.h* interface:

```
#import <UIKit/UIKit.h>

@class City;

@interface AddCityController : UIViewController
        <UITableViewDataSource, UITableViewDelegate,
        UIImagePickerControllerDelegate, UINavigationControllerDelegate> {
    IBOutlet UITableView *tableView;
    IBOutlet UITableViewCell *nameCell;
    IBOutlet UITableViewCell *pictureCell;
```

```
        IBOutlet UITableViewCell *descriptionCell;

    UIImage *cityPicture;
    UIImagePickerController *pickerController;
}

- (IBAction)addPicture:(id)sender;
- (void) addCityToDatabase:(City *)newCity;

@end
```

and then add the implementation to the view controller (*AddCityController.m*):

```
-(void) addCityToDatabase:(City *)newCity {
    NSArray *paths =
        NSSearchPathForDirectoriesInDomains(NSDocumentDirectory,
                                            NSUserDomainMask, YES);
    NSString *documentsPath = [paths objectAtIndex:0];
    NSString *filePath =
        [documentsPath stringByAppendingPathComponent:@"cities.sqlite"];

    sqlite3 *database;

    if(sqlite3_open([filePath UTF8String], &database) == SQLITE_OK) {
        const char *sqlStatement =
            "insert into cities (name, description, image) VALUES (?, ?, ?)";
        sqlite3_stmt *compiledStatement;
        if(sqlite3_prepare_v2(database, sqlStatement,
                              -1, &compiledStatement, NULL) == SQLITE_OK)
        {
            sqlite3_bind_text(compiledStatement, 1,
                              [newCity.cityName UTF8String], -1,
                              SQLITE_TRANSIENT);
            sqlite3_bind_text(compiledStatement, 2,
                              [newCity.cityDescription UTF8String], -1,
                              SQLITE_TRANSIENT);
            NSData *dataForPicture =
                UIImagePNGRepresentation(newCity.cityPicture);
            sqlite3_bind_blob(compiledStatement, 3,
                              [dataForPicture bytes],
                              [dataForPicture length],
                              SQLITE_TRANSIENT);

        }
        if(sqlite3_step(compiledStatement) == SQLITE_DONE) {
            sqlite3_finalize(compiledStatement);
        }
    }
    sqlite3_close(database);
}
```

We also need to import the *sqlite3.h* header file; add this line to the top of *AddCityController.m*:

```
#include <sqlite3.h>
```

Then insert the call into the `saveCity:` method, directly after the line where you added the `newCity` to the `cities` array. The added line is shown in bold:

```
if ( nameEntry.text.length > 0 ) {
    City *newCity = [[City alloc] init];
    newCity.cityName = nameEntry.text;
    newCity.cityDescription = descriptionEntry.text;
    newCity.cityPicture = nil;
    newCity.cityPicture = cityPicture;
    [cities addObject:newCity];
    [self addCityToDatabase:newCity];

    CGViewController *viewController = delegate.viewController;
    [viewController.tableView reloadData];
}
```

We're done. Build and deploy the application by clicking the Run button in the Xcode toolbar. When the application opens, tap the Edit button and add a new city. Make sure you tap on Save, then leave edit mode.

Then tap the Home button in iPhone Simulator to quit the City Guide application. Tap the application again to restart it, and you should see that your new city is still in the list.

Congratulations, the City Guide application can now save its data.

Refactoring and rethinking

If we were going to add more functionality to the City Guide application, we should probably pause at this point and refactor. There are, of course, other ways we could have built this application, and you've probably already noticed that the database (our data model) is now exposed to the `AddCityViewController` class as well as the `CGAppDelegate` class.

First, we'd change things so that the `cities` array is only accessed through the accessor methods in the application delegate, and then move all of the database routines into the delegate and wrap them inside those accessor methods. This would isolate our data model from our view controller. We could even do away with the `cities` array and keep the data model "on disk" and access it directly from the SQL database rather than preloading a separate in-memory array.

Although we could do this refactoring now, we won't do so in this chapter.

Core Data

Sitting above SQLite, and several other possible low-level data representations, is Core Data. The Core Data framework is an abstraction layer above the underlying data representation. Technically, Core Data is an object-graph management and persistence framework. Essentially, this means that Core Data organizes your application's model layer, keeping track of changes to objects. It allows you to reverse those changes on demand—for instance, if the user performs an undo command—and then allows you to serialize (archive) the application's data model directly into a persistent store.

Core Data is an ideal framework for building the model part of an MVC-based application, and if used correctly, it is an extremely powerful tool. I'm not going to cover Core Data in this book, but if you're interested in exploring the Core Data framework, I've provided some pointers to further reading in Chapter 14.

CHAPTER 9

Using Sensors

Mobile phones aren't just for making phone calls anymore. The iPhone, like a lot of high-end smartphones these days, comes with a number of sensors: camera, accelerometer, GPS module, and digital compass. We're entering a period of change: more and more users expect these sensors to be integrated into the "application experience." If your application can make use of them, it probably should.

Hardware Support

Unique among modern mobile platforms, Apple has gone to great lengths to ensure that your code will run on all of the current iOS-based devices. Yet despite this, there is still some variation in hardware between the various models (see Table 9-1).

Table 9-1. Hardware support in various iPhone, iPod touch, and iPad models

Hardware features	iPhone				iPod touch					iPad		iPad 2		New iPad		iPad Mini	
	3G	3GS	4 and 4S	5	1st gen	2nd gen	3rd gen	4th gen	5th gen	WiFi	3G	WiFi	3G	WiFi	3G	WiFi	3G
Cellular	✓	✓	✓	✓	✗	✗	✗	✗	✗	✗	✓	✗	✓	✗	✓	✗	✓
WiFi	✓	✓	✓	✓	✓	✓	✓	✓	✓	✓	✓	✓	✓	✓	✓	✓	✓
Bluetooth	✓	✓	✓	✓	✗	✓	✓	✓	✓	✓	✓	✓	✓	✓	✓	✓	✓
Speaker	✓	✓	✓	✓	✗	✓	✓	✓	✓	✓	✓	✓	✓	✓	✓	✓	✓
Audio In	✓	✓	✓	✓	✗	✓	✓	✓	✓	✓	✓	✓	✓	✓	✓	✓	✓
Accelerometer	✓	✓	✓	✓	✓	✓	✓	✓	✓	✓	✓	✓	✓	✓	✓	✓	✓
Magnetometer	✗	✓	✓	✓	✗	✗	✗	✗	✓	✗	✓	✓	✓	✓	✓	✓	✓
Gyroscope	✗	✗	✓	✓	✗	✗	✗	✓	✓	✗	✗	✓	✓	✓	✓	✓	✓
GPS	✓	✓	✓	✓	✗	✗	✗	✗	✗	✗	✓	✗	✓	✗	✓	✗	✓
Proximity Sensor	✓	✓	✓	✓	✗	✗	✗	✗	✗	✗	✗	✗	✗	✗	✗	✗	✗
Camera	✓	✓	✓	✓	✗	✗	✗	✓	✓	✗	✗	✓	✓	✓	✓	✓	✓
Video	✗	✓	✓	✓	✗	✗	✗	✓	✓	✗	✗	✓	✓	✓	✓	✓	✓
Vibration	✓	✓	✓	✓	✗	✗	✗	✗	✗	✗	✗	✗	✗	✗	✗	✗	✗
Retina Display	✗	✗	✓	✓	✗	✗	✗	✓	✓	✗	✗	✗	✗	✓	✓	✗	✗

Network Availability

We covered Apple's Reachability code in detail in "Apple's Reachability Class" (page 185) in Chapter 7. We can easily determine whether the network is reachable, and whether we are using the wireless or WWAN interface:

```
Reachability *reach = [Reachability reachabilityForInternetConnection];
NetworkStatus status = [reach currentReachabilityStatus]; ❶
```

❶   This call will return a network status: NotReachable, ReachableViaWiFi, or Reach ableViaWWAN.

Camera Availability

We cover the camera in detail later in this chapter. However, it is simple to determine whether a camera is present in the device:

```
BOOL available = [UIImagePickerController
    isSourceTypeAvailable:UIImagePickerControllerSourceTypeCamera];
```

Once you have determined that a camera is present, you can inquire whether it supports video by making a call to determine the available media types the camera supports:

```
NSArray *media = [UIImagePickerController availableMediaTypesForSourceType:
                    UIImagePickerControllerSourceTypeCamera];
```

If the kUTTypeMovie media type is returned as part of the array, the camera will support video recording.

Audio Input Availability

You can poll whether audio input is available using the AVAudioSession singleton class by checking the inputAvailable class property:

```
AVAudioSession *audioSession = [AVAudioSession sharedInstance];
BOOL audioAvailable = audioSession.inputAvailable;
```

 The AVAudioSession class is part of the *AVFoundation.Framework*. You'll also need to import the header:

```
#import <AVFoundation/AVFoundation.h>
```

You can also be notified of any changes in the availability of audio input (e.g., a second-generation iPod touch user has plugged in headphones with microphone capabilities). First, nominate your class as a delegate:

```
audioSession.delegate = self;
```

Declare it as implementing the `AVAudioSessionDelegate` protocol in the declaration:

```
@interface YourAppDelegate : NSObject <UIApplicationDelegate,
    AVAudioSessionDelegate>
```

Then implement `inputIsAvailableChanged:` in the implementation:

```
- (void)inputIsAvailableChanged:(BOOL)audioAvailable {
    NSLog(@"Audio availability has changed");
}
```

GPS Availability

I'm going to cover the Core Location framework, and the GPS, in the next chapter. However, the short answer to a fairly commonly asked question is that, unfortunately, the Core Location framework does not provide any way to get direct information about the availability of specific hardware such as the GPS at application runtime, although you can check whether location services are enabled:

```
BOOL locationAvailable = [CLLocationManager locationServicesEnabled];
```

However, while you cannot check for the availability of GPS using Core Location from your application, you can require the presence of GPS hardware for your application to load.

> The `CLLocationManager` class is part of the *CoreLocation.Framework*. You'll also need to import the header:
>
> ```
> #import <CoreLocation/CoreLocation.h>
> ```

Magnetometer Availability

Core Location allows you to check for the presence of the magnetometer (digital compass) fairly simply:

```
BOOL magnetometerAvailable = [CLLocationManager headingAvailable];
```

Setting Required Hardware Capabilities

If your application requires specific hardware features in order to run, you can add a list of required capabilities to your application's *Info.plist* file. Your application will not start unless those capabilities are present on the device.

When updating an app that has already been submitted to the iTunes Store, you cannot add new restrictions to the Required Device Capabilities. You only get one chance to set these restrictions. It's worth noting, however, that lowering the required device capabilities is possible, you can become less restrictive in the hardware your app will run on.

Later in the chapter, we'll modify the Weather application to make use of the Core Location framework to determine current position, so let's modify it now to make sure this capability is available.

You may want to make a copy of the Weather application before modifying, as we have done previously. Navigate to where you saved the project and make a copy of the project folder, and then rename it. Then open the new (duplicate) project inside Xcode and click on the Project icon at the top of the Project navigator to rename the project itself.

Open the Weather application in Xcode, then go ahead and open the *Weather-Info.plist* file in the editor. These days and in most cases there will already be a entry for "Required device capabilities" (the UIRequiredDeviceCapabilities key) requiring armv7 support for your application. However if there isn't, right-click on the bottommost entry to bring up a menu. Click on Add Row to add a new row to the table; then scroll down the list of possible options and select "Required device capabilities" (the UIRequiredDeviceCapabilities key) as shown Figure 9-1. This will add an (empty) array to the *.plist* file.

If there wasn't a "Required device capabilities" entry in the *plist* file add "location-services" (see Figure 9-2) as Item 0, otherwise to add another entry to the array, select Item 0 and click the plus button to the right side of the table and go ahead and add the "location-services" restriction.

After doing so, your application will no longer start if such services are unavailable.

The allowed values for the keys are telephony, sms, still-camera, auto-focus-camera, video-camera, wifi, accelerometer, location-services, gps, magnetometer, microphone, opengles-1, opengles-2, armv6, armv7, and peer-peer. A full description of the possible keys is available in the Device Support section of the iOS Application Programming Guide available from the iOS Dev Center.

Figure 9-1. Setting the "Required device capabilities" key

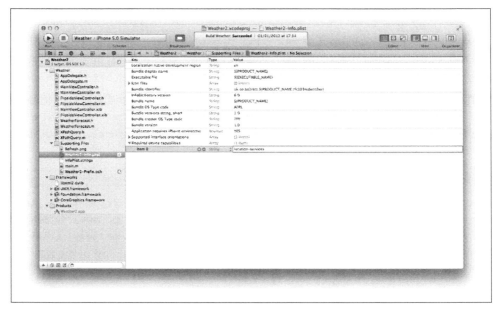

Figure 9-2. Adding the location-services item to "Required device capabilities"

Persistent WiFi

Additionally, if your application requires a persistent WiFi connection, you can set the Boolean `UIRequiresPersistentWiFi` key in the Application's *Info.plist* file to ensure that this is the case. If set to `YES`, the operating system will open a WiFi connection when your application is launched and keep it open while the application is running. If this key is not present, or is set to `NO`, then the operating system will close the active WiFi connection after 30 minutes.

Background Modes

Setting the `UIBackgroundModes` key in the application's *Info.plist* file notifies the operating systems that the application should continue to run in the background after the user closes it, since it provides specific background services.

 Apple has this to say about background modes: "These keys should be used sparingly and only by applications providing the indicated services. Where alternatives for running in the background exist, those alternatives should be used instead. For example, applications can use the significant location change interface to receive location events instead of registering as a background location application."

There are three possible key values: `audio`, `location`, and `voip`. The `audio` key indicates that after closing, the application will continue to play audible content; the `location` key indicates that the application provides location-based information for the user using the standard Core Location services, rather than the newer significant location change service. Finally, the `voip` key indicates that the application provides Voice-over-IP services. Applications marked with this key are automatically launched after system boot so that the application can attempt to reestablish VoIP services.

Differences Between iPhone and iPad

The most striking, and obvious, difference between the iPhone and the iPad is screen size. The earlier iPhone models had screens with 480×320 pixel resolution at 163 pixels per inch, the iPhone 4, 4S, and iPod touch with Retina displays have 960×640 pixel resolution at 326 pixels per inch, the iPhone 5 has 1136×640 pixel resolution at 326 pixels per inch.

However the iPad, iPad 2 and iPad mini screen have 1024×768 pixels at 132 pixels per inch and the iPad 3 has 2048×1536 pixel resolution at 264 pixels per inch. This difference will be the single most fundamental thing to affect the way you design your user interface on the two platforms. Attempting to treat the iPad as simply a rather oversized iPod touch or iPhone will lead to badly designed applications.

The increased screen size of the device means that you can develop desktop-sized applications, not just phone-sized applications, for the iPad platform. Although in doing so, a rethink of the user interface to adapt to multitouch is needed. What works for the iPhone or the desktop won't automatically work on an iPad. For example, Apple totally redesigned the user interface of the iWork suite when they moved it to the iPad. If you're intending to port a Mac OS X desktop application to the iPad, you should do something similar.

 Interestingly, there is now an option for iOS developers to port their iPhone and iPad projects directly to Mac OS X. The Chameleon Project (*http://chameleonproject.org/*) is a drop-in replacement for UI Kit that runs on Mac OS X, allowing iOS applications to be run on the desktop with little—or in some cases, no—modification.

Due to its size and function, the iPad is immediately associated in our minds with other more familiar objects like a legal pad or a book. Holding the device triggers powerful associations with these items, and we're mentally willing to accept the iPad as a successor to these objects. This was simply not true for the iPhone; the device was physically too small.

Using the Camera

We looked at the image picker view controller in Chapter 6, where we used it to add pictures to our City Guide application using our AddCityController class. We have to change only one line in our code from Chapter 6 to make our City Guide application use the camera instead of the saved photo album.

If you open the *CityGuide3* project in Xcode and look at the viewDidLoad: method in the AddCityController class, you'll see that we set the source of the image picker controller to be the photo album:

```
pickerController.sourceType =
    UIImagePickerControllerSourceTypeSavedPhotosAlbum;
```

Changing the source to UIImagePickerControllerSourceTypeCamera will mean that when you call presentModalViewController:, which presents the UIImagePicker Controller, the camera interface rather than the photo album will be presented to the user, allowing him to take a new picture.

If you want to enable video, you need to add the relevant media type to the array indicating the media types to be accessed by the picker. By default, this array contains only the `image` media type. The following code should determine whether your device supports a camera, and if it does, it will add all of the available media types (including video on the iPhone 3GS) to the media types array. If there is no camera present, the source will be set to the photo album as before:

```
if ([UIImagePickerController
      isSourceTypeAvailable:UIImagePickerControllerSourceTypeCamera]) {
    pickerController.sourceType = UIImagePickerControllerSourceTypeCamera;
    NSArray* mediaTypes =
      [UIImagePickerController availableMediaTypesForSourceType:
                               UIImagePickerControllerSourceTypeCamera];
    pickerController.mediaTypes = mediaTypes;
} else {
    pickerController.sourceType =
      UIImagePickerControllerSourceTypeSavedPhotosAlbum;
    pickerController.allowsEditing = YES;
}
```

The Core Motion Framework

The Core Motion framework allows your application to receive motion data from the accelerometer, magnetometer, and (on the some devices) the gyroscope.

 There is no support for Core Motion in the iOS Simulator; therefore, all testing of your Core Motion–related code must be done on the device.

Making use of the `CMMotionManager` class, you can start receiving accelerometer, gyroscope, and combined device-motion events at a regular interval or you can poll for them periodically. While the class offers both the raw accelerometer and gyroscope data separately, in addition it offers access to a combined `CMDeviceMotion` object that encapsulates the processed device-motion data from both the accelerometer and the gyroscope (if present). With this combined motion measurement, Core Motion provides highly accurate measurements of device attitude, the (unbiased) rotation rate of a device, the direction of gravity on a device, and the acceleration that the user is giving to a device.

 The rotation rate reported by the `CMDeviceMotion` object is different than that reported directly by the gyroscope. Even if the device is sitting flat on the table, the gyro will not read zero. It will read some nonzero value that differs from device to device, and over time due to changes in things like device temperature. Core Motion actively tracks and removes this bias from the gyro data.

We can check whether device motion is available as follows:

```
CMMotionManager *motionManager = [[CMMotionManager alloc] init];
if (!motionManager.isDeviceMotionAvailable) {
        ... add code here ...
}
```

Pulling Motion Data

The CMMotionManager class offers two approaches to obtaining motion data. The simplest way is to pull the motion data. Your application will start an instance of the manager class and periodically ask for measurements of the combined device motion:

```
[motionManager startDeviceMotionUpdates];
CMDeviceMotion *motion = motionManager.deviceMotion;
```

This is the most efficient method of obtaining motion data. However, if there isn't a natural timer in your application, such as a periodic update of your main view, then you may need an additional timer to trigger your update requests. Remember to stop the updates and release the motion manager after you're done with them:

```
[motionManager stopDeviceMotionUpdates];
```

 Your application should create only a single instance of the CMMotion Manager class. Multiple instances of this class can affect the rate at which an application receives data from the accelerometer and gyroscope.

Pushing Motion Data

In addition to this simple pull methodology, you can alternatively specify an update interval and implement a block for handling the motion data; the manager class can then be asked to deliver updates to that block using the NSOperationsQueue, allowing it to push the measurements to your application, e.g.:

```
motionManager.deviceMotionUpdateInterval = 1.0/60.0;
[motionManager startDeviceMotionUpdatesToQueue: queue withHandler: handler];
```

While with this second methodology you'll get a continuous stream of motion data, there is a large increased overhead associated with implementing it (see Table 9-2), and your application may not be able to keep up with the associated data rate, especially if the device is in rapid motion.

Table 9-2. Example CPU usage for Core Motion push updates at 100 and 20Hz[a]

	At 100Hz		At 20Hz	
	Total	Application	Total	Application
DeviceMotion	65%	20%	65%	10%
Accelerometer	50%	15%	46%	5%
Accel + Gyro	51%	10%	50%	5%

[a] Figures for an application running on an iPhone 4 (Credit: Jeffrey Powers, Occipital)

Additionally, while Core Motion's CMDeviceMotion combines both the raw accelerometer and the gyroscope readings into a single simplified object, this does not come "free." See Table 9-2 again. Using Core Motion's combined CMDeviceMotion object, as opposed to accessing the raw CMAccelerometer or CMGyroData objects, consumes roughly 15% more total CPU regardless of the update rate. The good news is that is not because of the gyroscope itself; reading both the accelerometer and gyroscope directly is not noticeably slower than reading the accelerometer on its own.

Because of this associated CPU overhead, this second method making use of NSOpera tionsQueue and blocks is really only recommended for data collection applications where the point of the application is to obtain the motion data itself.

However, if your application does need to be rapidly updated as to device motion, we can do so easily, as follows:

```
CMMotionManager *motionManager = [[CMMotionManager alloc] init];
motionManager.deviceMotionUpdateInterval = 1.0/60.0;

if (motionManager.deviceMotionAvailable ) {
    queue = [[NSOperationQueue currentQueue] retain];
    [motionManager startDeviceMotionUpdatesToQueue:queue
        withHandler:^ (CMDeviceMotion *motionData, NSError *error) {
            CMAttitude *attitude = motionData.attitude;
            CMAcceleration gravity = motionData.gravity;
            CMAcceleration userAcceleration = motionData.userAcceleration;
            CMRotationRate rotate = motionData.rotationRate;
            CMCalibratedMagneticField field = motionData.magneticField;

            ...handle data here......
        }];
}
```

The Accelerometer

An accelerometer measures the linear acceleration of the device so that it can report its roll and pitch, but not its yaw.

Yaw, pitch, and *roll* refer to the rotation of the device in three axes. If you think about an aircraft in the sky, pushing the nose down or pulling it up modifies the pitch angle of the aircraft. However, if you keep the nose straight ahead, you can also modify the roll of the aircraft using the flaps; one wing will come up, the other will go down. Finally, keeping the wings level, you can use the tail flap to change the heading (or yaw) of the aircraft (rotating it in a 2D plane).

If you are dealing with an iPhone that has a magnetometer (digital compass), you can combine the accelerometer and magnetometer readings to have roll, pitch, and yaw measurements [see "The Magnetometer" (page 294) for details on how to access the magnetometer].

The accelerometer reports three figures: X, Y, and Z (see Figure 9-3). Acceleration values for each axis are reported directly by the hardware as G-force values. Therefore, a value of 1.0 represents a load of approximately 1-gravity (Earth's gravity). X corresponds to roll, Y to pitch, and Z to whether the device is front-side-up or front-side-down, with a value of 0.0 being reported when the iPhone is edge-on.

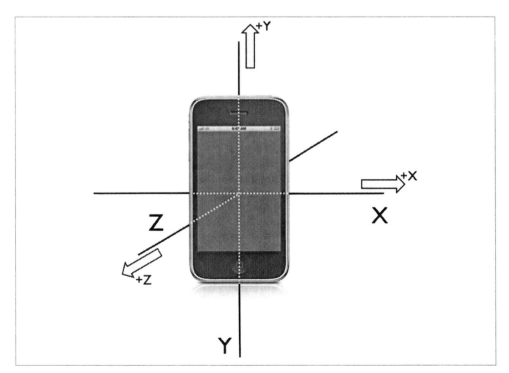

Figure 9-3. The iPhone accelerometer axes

When dealing with acceleration measurements, you must keep in mind that the accelerometer is measuring just that: the linear acceleration of the device. When at rest (in whatever orientation), the figures represent the force of gravity acting on the device, and correspond to the roll and pitch of the device (in the X and Y directions at least). But while in motion, the figures represent the acceleration due to gravity, plus the acceleration of the device itself relative to its rest frame.

Using the accelerometer directly

Let's implement a simple view-based application to illustrate how to approach the accelerometer. Open Xcode and start a new iPhone project, select a Single View–based Application template, and name the project **Accelerometer** when prompted for a name.

 Until iOS 4, the accelerometer was accessed using the UIAccelerometer class, but this was replaced with the Core Motion framework, which also allows access to the gyroscope (if one is included in the device). The UIAccelerometer class and Core Motion framework existed in parallel until the arrival of iOS 5, when the UIAccelerometer class was deprecated. You should now use the Core Motion framework to access the accelerometer.

Since we'll be making use of the Core Motion framework, the first thing we need to do is add it to our new project. Click on the project file at the top of the Project Navigator window on the right in Xcode, select the Target and click on the Build Phases tab, click on the Link Binary with Libraries drop-down, and click on the + button to open the file pop-up window. Select *CoreMotion.framework* from the list of available frameworks and click the Add button.

Click on the *ViewController.xib* nib file to open it in Interface Builder. We'll want to report the raw figures from the accelerometer and also display them using a progress bar, so drag and drop three Progress Views (UIProgressView) controls from the Object Library into the View window. Then add two label (UILabel) elements for each progress bar: one to hold the X, Y, or Z label and the other to hold the accelerometer measurements. After you do that, the view should look a lot like Figure 9-4.

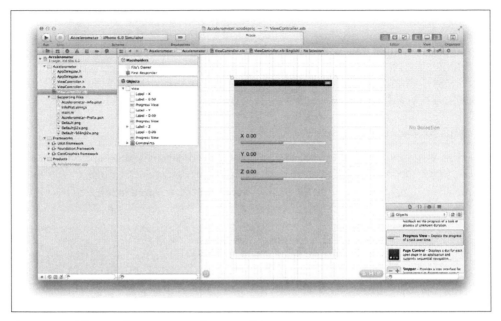

Figure 9-4. The Accelerometer application UI

Close the Utilities panel and click to open the Assistant Editor; the *AcclerometerView-Controller.h* header file should be displayed in the Assistant Editor on the righthand side of the Xcode interface. Then Control-click and drag the three `UIProgressView` elements, and the three `UILabel` elements we're going to use to hold the accelerometer values, to the header file (see Figure 9-5) to create a property for each of the user interface elements.

Afterward, your interface file should look something like this:

```
#import <UIKit/UIKit.h>

@interface ViewController : UIViewController

@property (weak, nonatomic) IBOutlet UILabel *xLabel;
@property (weak, nonatomic) IBOutlet UILabel *yLabel;
@property (weak, nonatomic) IBOutlet UILabel *zLabel;

@property (weak, nonatomic) IBOutlet UIProgressView *xBar;
@property (weak, nonatomic) IBOutlet UIProgressView *yBar;
@property (weak, nonatomic) IBOutlet UIProgressView *zBar;

@end
```

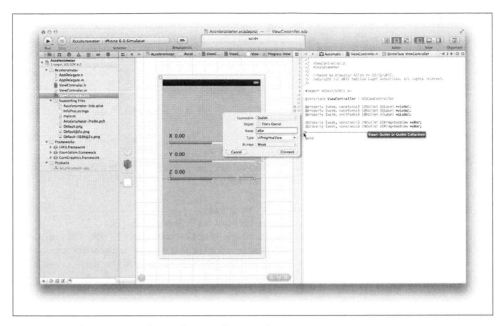

Figure 9-5. Connecting the outlets to the interface

Close the Assistant Editor and return to the Standard Editor and click on the *View-Controller.h* interface file. Import the Core Motion header file, and declare `CMMotion Manager` and `NSOperationQueue` instance variables. Here's how the code should look when you are done:

```
#import <UIKit/UIKit.h>
#import <CoreMotion/CoreMotion.h>

@interface ViewController : UIViewController {

    CMMotionManager *motionManager;
    NSOperationQueue *queue;
}


@property (weak, nonatomic) IBOutlet UILabel *xLabel;
@property (weak, nonatomic) IBOutlet UILabel *yLabel;
@property (weak, nonatomic) IBOutlet UILabel *zLabel;

@property (weak, nonatomic) IBOutlet UIProgressView *xBar;
@property (weak, nonatomic) IBOutlet UIProgressView *yBar;
@property (weak, nonatomic) IBOutlet UIProgressView *zBar;

@end
```

Make sure you've saved your changes and click on the corresponding *View-Controller.m* implementation file to open it in the Xcode Editor. We don't actually have to do very much here, as Interface Builder handled most of the heavy lifting with respect to the UI; we just need to go ahead an implement the guts of the application to monitor the gyroscope updates in the viewDidLoad: method:

```
- (void)viewDidLoad {
    [super viewDidLoad];

    motionManager = [[CMMotionManager alloc] init];
    motionManager.accelerometerUpdateInterval = 1.0/10.0; // Update at 10Hz
    if (motionManager.accelerometerAvailable) {
        NSLog(@"Accelerometer avaliable");
        queue = [NSOperationQueue currentQueue];
        [motionManager startAccelerometerUpdatesToQueue:queue
          withHandler:^(CMAccelerometerData *accelerometerData, NSError *error) {
            CMAcceleration acceleration = accelerometerData.acceleration;
            self.xLabel.text = [NSString stringWithFormat:@"%f", acceleration.x];
            self.xBar.progress = ABS(acceleration.x);

            self.yLabel.text = [NSString stringWithFormat:@"%f", acceleration.y];
            self.yBar.progress = ABS(acceleration.y);

            self.zLabel.text = [NSString stringWithFormat:@"%f", acceleration.z];
            self.zBar.progress = ABS(acceleration.z);
        }];

    }
}
```

Let's test that. Click on the Run button in the Xcode toolbar to build and deploy your application onto your device (remember: you can't test this code in the iOS Simulator for obvious reasons). If all goes well, you should see something much like Figure 9-6 as you roll the device around the y-axis.

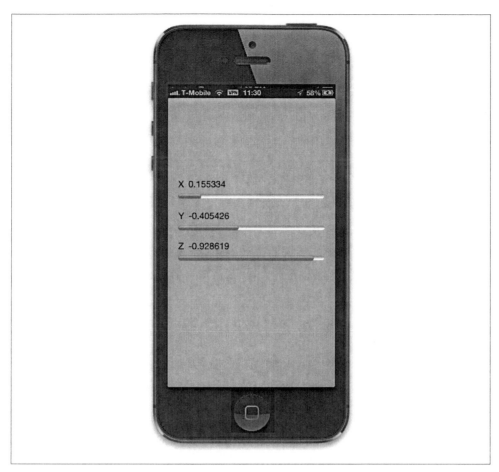

Figure 9-6. The Accelerometer application running on an iPhone 4S sitting face-up on my desk, measuring a 1-gravity acceleration straight down

The Gyroscope

While an accelerometer provides measurement of forces in the x-, y-, and z-axes, it cannot measure rotations. On the other hand, a gyroscope is a rate-of-change device; as the phone rotates around an axis, it allows you to measure the change in such rotations. By using both sensors in combination, you can measure the movement of the device in a six degrees-of-freedom inertial system, allowing you to use dead reckoning to find the physical location (and orientation of the device) relative to an initial starting position.

All inertial systems have an inherent drift, so dead reckoning should not be regarded as being stable over the long term.

Using the gyroscope directly

We can easily modify our Accelerometer application to report data from the gyroscope.

Open the Finder and navigate to the location where you saved the *Accelerometer* project. Right-click or Control-click on the folder containing the project files and select Duplicate. A folder called *Accelerometer copy* will be created containing a duplicate of our project. You should rename it **Gyroscope**. Now open the new version of the project in Xcode and mouse over the blue Project icon at the top of the Project Navigator and hit the Enter key, which will make the project name editable. Enter **Gyroscope** as the new project name, and a drop-down will appear prompting you to approve the changes to the project. Click on Rename when prompted to do so to rename the project.

Go into the *ViewController.m* implementation file and modify the viewDidLoad: method:

```
- (void)viewDidLoad {
    [super viewDidLoad];

    motionManager = [[CMMotionManager alloc] init];
    motionManager.gyroUpdateInterval = 1.0/2.0; // Update every 1/2 second.

    if (motionManager.gyroAvailable) {
        queue = [NSOperationQueue currentQueue];
        [motionManager startGyroUpdatesToQueue:queue
                withHandler: ^ (CMGyroData *gyroData, NSError *error) {
            CMRotationRate rotate = gyroData.rotationRate;
            xLabel.text = [NSString stringWithFormat:@"%f", rotate.x];
            xBar.progress = ABS(rotate.x);

            yLabel.text = [NSString stringWithFormat:@"%f", rotate.y];
            yBar.progress = ABS(rotate.y);

            zLabel.text = [NSString stringWithFormat:@"%f", rotate.z];
            zBar.progress = ABS(rotate.z);

        }];

    }
}
```

The CMRotationRate passed to our block is a simple structure, which breaks the rotation down into rotations (in units of radians per second) around x-, y-, and z-axes (see the documentation in the iOS Developer Library (*http://bit.ly/ZgJYjJ*)). When inspecting the structure, remember the righthand rule to determine the direction of positive rotation. The direction your fingers curl will give the positive rotation direction around that axis. For example, if you wrap your right hand around the x-axis such that the tip of the thumb points toward positive x, a positive rotation is one toward the tips of the other fingers (see Figure 9-7). A negative rotation goes away from the tips of those fingers.

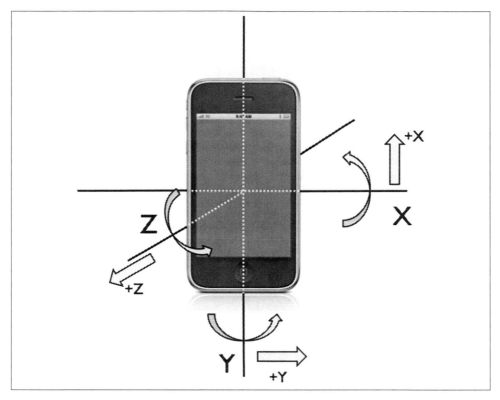

Figure 9-7. The iPhone gyroscope axes

Let's test that. Click on the Run button in the Xcode toolbar to build and deploy your application onto your device (remember: you can't test this code in the iOS Simulator for obvious reasons). If all goes well, you should see something much like Figure 9-8 as you roll the device around the y-axis.

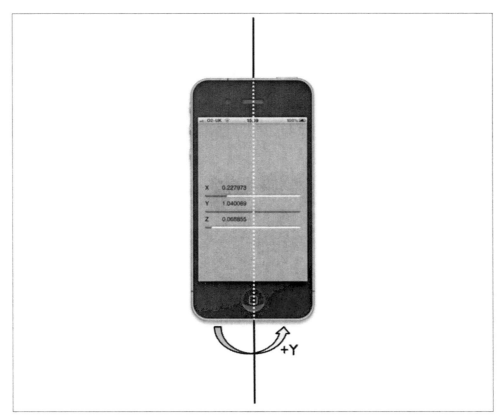

Figure 9-8. Measuring rotation on the iPhone 4 while rolling it around the y-axis

As mentioned before, the measurement of rotation rate encapsulated by a CMGyroData object is biased by various factors. You can obtain a much more accurate (unbiased) measurement by accessing the rotationRate (*http://bit.ly/V6qf7B*) property of CMDeviceMotion (*http://bit.ly/XEnhE2*) if that is needed by your application.

The Magnetometer

You can use the magnetometer as a digital compass. However, much like using the gyroscope in conjunction with the accelerometer, combining the heading (yaw) information (see Figure 9-9) returned by this sensor with the roll and pitch information returned by the accelerometer will let you determine the true orientation of the iPhone in real time.

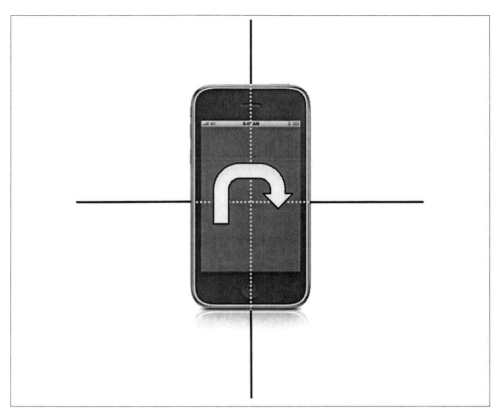

Figure 9-9. Using the magnetometer (a.k.a. the digital compass), you can determine the heading (yaw) of the device

You should be aware that the magnetometer is measuring the strength of the magnetic field surrounding the device. In the absence of any strong local fields, these measurements will be of Earth's ambient magnetic field, allowing the device to determine its "heading" with respect to the geomagnetic North Pole. The geomagnetic heading and true heading, relative to the geographical North Pole, can vary widely (by several tens of degrees depending on your location).

Using the magnetometer directly

Like the accelerometer and gyroscope, you can use the CMMotionManager class to obtain readings from the magnetometer. The values returned are in microtesla (µT) and represent the total magnetic field observed by the device: the Earth's geomagnetic field plus bias introduced from the device itself and its surroundings.

This is the "raw" magnetic field value, unlike the calibrated value returned as a CMCalibratedMagneticField object from the magneticField property of CMDevice

`Motion`, which filters out the bias introduced by the device and, in some cases, its surrounding fields.

 Originally introduced solely to serve as a digital compass, until iOS 5, magnetometer readings could only be obtained from the Core Location rather than the Core Motion framework. These methods to get the device heading still exist in the Core Location framework, and we'll look at them in the next chapter.

We can easily modify either our Accelerometer or Gyroscope applications to report data from the magnetometer. Open the Finder and navigate to the location where you saved the *Accelerometer* project and duplicate it as we did in the last section for the Gyroscope project, but this time, rename the project `Magnetometer`.

Open the *ViewController.h* interface file and delete the three `UIProgressBar` outlet definitions, then go into the corresponding *ViewController.m* implementation and remove any mention of them from the file. If you correctly deleted the definitions in the interface file first, they'll be helpfully flagged with a red error icon next to each line you'll need to remove.

Click on the *ViewController.xib* nib file to open it in Interface Builder and add one more set of labels for the Total field (as in Figure 9-10).

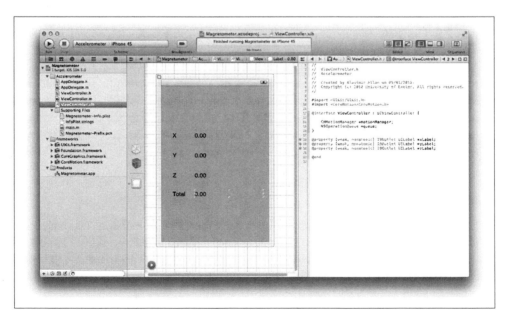

Figure 9-10. Adding another set of labels to the interface

Afterward, switch to the Assistant Editor and Control-click and drag from the fourth value label to our interface file and create another property. Your interface file should now look something like this:

```
#import <UIKit/UIKit.h>
#import <CoreMotion/CoreMotion.h>

@interface ViewController : UIViewController {

    CMMotionManager *motionManager;
    NSOperationQueue *queue;
}

@property (weak, nonatomic) IBOutlet UILabel *xLabel;
@property (weak, nonatomic) IBOutlet UILabel *yLabel;
@property (weak, nonatomic) IBOutlet UILabel *zLabel;
@property (weak, nonatomic) IBOutlet UILabel *totalLabel;

@end
```

Then switch to the *viewController.m* implementation file and modify the viewDid Load: method as follows:

```
- (void)viewDidLoad {
    [super viewDidLoad];
    motionManager = [[CMMotionManager alloc] init];
    motionManager.magnetometerUpdateInterval = 1.0/10.0; // Update at 10Hz
    if (motionManager.magnetometerAvailable) {
        queue = [NSOperationQueue currentQueue];
        [motionManager startMagnetometerUpdatesToQueue:queue
            withHandler:
                ^(CMMagnetometerData *magnetometerData, NSError *error) {
            CMMagneticField field = magnetometerData.magneticField;
            self.xLabel.text = [NSString stringWithFormat:@"%f", field.x];
            self.yLabel.text = [NSString stringWithFormat:@"%f", field.y];
            self.zLabel.text = [NSString stringWithFormat:@"%f", field.z];
            self.totalLabel.text = [NSString stringWithFormat:@"%f",
                sqrt(field.x*field.x + field.y*field.y + field.z*field.z)];
        }];
    }
}
```

Save your changes and click the Run button in the Xcode toolbar to deploy your application onto your device; you should see something like Figure 9-11.

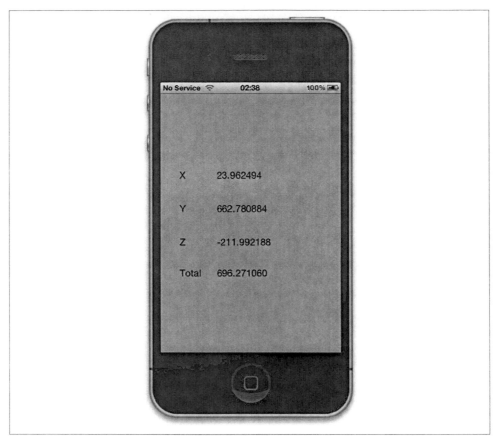

Figure 9-11. The raw magnetic field readings

Accessing the Proximity Sensor

The proximity and ambient light sensors are two separate sensors. The ambient light sensor is used to change the brightness level of the device's screen automatically; the proximity sensor is used by the device to turn the screen off when you put the phone to your ear to make a call. Although it does have an ambient light sensor, the iPod touch does not have a proximity sensor.

Unfortunately, there is no way to access the ambient light sensor in the official SDK. However, developers can access the proximity sensor via the `UIDevice` class. This sensor is an infrared LED emitter/detector pair positioned near the earpiece, as shown in Figure 9-12. It measures the return reflection of the transmitted infrared beam to detect (large) objects near the phone.

Figure 9-12. The IR LED of the proximity sensor is located near the earpiece

You can enable the sensor in your application by toggling the proximityMonitoringEn abled Boolean\:

```
UIDevice *device = [UIDevice currentDevice];
device.proximityMonitoringEnabled = YES;
```

You can query whether the proximity sensor is close to the user:

```
BOOL state = device.proximityState;
```

If proximity monitoring is enabled, a UIDeviceProximityStateDidChangeNotifica tion notification will be posted by the UIDevice when the state of the proximity sensor changes; you can ask that your application is notified when this occurs by registering your class as an observer with the notification center:

```
[[NSNotificationCenter defaultCenter]
    addObserver:self selector:@selector(proximityChanged:)
    name:@"UIDeviceProximityStateDidChangeNotification" object:nil];
```

Notifications would then get received by the `proximityChanged:` method:

```
- (void) proximityChanged: (NSNotification *)note {
    UIDevice *device = [note object];
    NSLog(@"In proximity: %i", device.proximityState);
}
```

Using Vibration

 The motor that controls vibration is not a sensor; technically, it's an actuator. Because sensors and actuators generally go hand in hand, we'll look at the capability here.

Making the iPhone vibrate is a simple system call. You first need to add the Audio-Toolbox framework to your project, and then import the AudioToolbox headers into the class where you intend to trigger the vibration:

```
#import <AudioToolbox/AudioToolbox.h>
```

At this point, you can make the device produce a short buzz by calling the following method:

```
AudioServicesPlaySystemSound(kSystemSoundID_Vibrate);
```

Unfortunately, despite the fact that the underlying (private) Telephony framework offers relatively subtle levels of control over the vibration pattern, the official support in the SDK is limited to this single call.

 You need to be careful about using the vibration feature. Using continuous vibration, or using a timer to maintain the vibration, is a reason for rejection during the App Store review process.

CHAPTER 10

Geolocation and Mapping

The Core Location API is one of the great things about the iOS platforms, but until the arrival of the MapKit Framework in the 3.0 SDK, it was actually quite hard to take that location-aware goodness and display it on a map. The arrival of the MapKit framework has simplified this enormously.

Let's look at the Core Location framework first and then work through a few example applications using MapKit to get you familiar with how the two frameworks interact.

The Core Location Framework

The Core Location framework is an abstraction layer in front of several different methods to find the user's location (and, by extrapolation, her speed and course). It can provide the latitude, longitude, and altitude of the device (along with the level of accuracy to which this is known). There are three levels of accuracy:

- The least accurate level uses the cell network to locate the user (the process is similar to triangulation, but more complex). This can quickly provide a position to around 12 km accuracy, which can be reduced to 1–3 km after some time depending on the tower density at your current location.

- The next accuracy level is obtained by utilizing a WiFi-based positioning system. This is much more precise, giving a position to approximately 100 m. However, it depends on the user being in range of a known wireless hotspot.

- The highest level of accuracy is obtained by using GPS hardware, which should provide a position to less than 40 m.

On the iPod touch and non-3G enabled iPads, the user's location is derived solely from WiFi positioning. The original iPhone will use WiFi and cell tower triangulation, however, all later iPhone models and 3G-enabled iPads can also make use of the built-in GPS hardware.

The actual method used to determine the user's location is abstracted away from both the user and the developer. The only control the developer has over the chosen method is by requesting a certain level of accuracy, although the actual accuracy achieved is not guaranteed. Further, the battery power consumed and the time to calculate the position increase with increasing accuracy.

 Some users may choose to explicitly disable reporting of their position. You should therefore always check to see whether location services are enabled before attempting to turn on these services. This will avoid unnecessary prompting from your application.

The Core Location framework is implemented using the `CLLocationManager` class. The following code will create an instance of this class, and from then on will send location update messages to the designated delegate class:

```
self.locationManager = [[CLLocationManager alloc] init];
self.locationManager.delegate = self;
if( [CLLocationManager locationServicesEnabled] ) {
    [self.locationManager startUpdatingLocation];
} else {
    NSLog(@"Location services not enabled.");
}
```

To use this code, you will need to:

1. Import `CoreLocation` in your declaration with the following code:

   ```
   #import <CoreLocation/CoreLocation.h>
   ```

2. Declare a `CLLocationManager` property named `locationManager` in your class declaration:

   ```
   @property (nonatomic, strong) CLLocationManager *locationManager;
   ```

3. Add the Core Location framework to your target.

4. Declare your class, e.g. your view controller class, as implementing the `CLLocation ManagerDelegate` protocol.

We can filter these location update messages based on a distance filter. Changes in position of less than this amount will not generate an update message to the delegate:

```
self.locationManager.distanceFilter = 100;  // 100 m
```

We can also set a desired level of accuracy; this will determine the location method(s) used by the Core Location framework to determine the user's location:

```
self.locationManager.desiredAccuracy = kCLLocationAccuracyKilometer;
```

 You should set these filters before calling startUpdatingLocation on your location manager.

The CLLocationManagerDelegate protocol offers two methods. The first is called when a location update occurs:

```
- (void)locationManager:(CLLocationManager *)manager
  didUpdateToLocation:(CLLocation *)newLocation
  fromLocation:(CLLocation *)oldLocation {
    NSLog(@"Moved from %@ to %@", oldLocation, newLocation);
}
```

The second is called when an error occurs:

```
- (void)locationManager:(CLLocationManager *)manager
  didFailWithError:(NSError *)error {
    NSLog(@"Received Core Location error %@", error);
    [manager stopUpdatingLocation];
}
```

If the location manager is not able to ascertain the user's location immediately, it reports a kCLErrorLocationUnknown error and keeps trying. In most cases, you can choose to ignore the error and wait for a new event. However, if the user denies your application access to the location service, the manager will report a kCLErrorDenied error. Upon receiving such an error, you should stop the location manager.

 As well as Standard location service, iOS also offers a Significant Change service that relies on the availability of cellular radio hardware on your iOS device as it functions using cell positioning. This offers large power savings and the ability to receive location updates even if your application is not running and has been backgrounded. This service is available only in iOS 4.0 and later.

Device Heading

As well as reporting the current location, the CLLocationManager class can, in the case where the device's hardware supports it with the presence of a magnetometer, report the current heading of the device. The following code will create an instance of the class, and will send both location and heading update messages to the designated delegate class:

```
self.locationManager = [[CLLocationManager alloc] init];
self.locationManager.delegate = self;
if( [CLLocationManager locationServicesEnabled]
    && [CLLocationManager headingAvailable] ) { ❶
  [self.locationManager startUpdatingLocation];
  [self.locationManager startUpdatingHeading];
}
```

❶ It's even more important to check whether heading information is available than it is to check whether location services are available, as fewer devices have the necessary hardware (see the preceding chapter).

We can filter these update messages based on an angular filter. Changes in heading of less than this amount will not generate an update message to the delegate:

```
self.locationManager.headingFilter = 5;  // 5 degrees
```

The default value of this property is kCLHeadingFilterNone. Use this value if you want to be notified of all heading updates.

The CLLocationManagerDelegate protocol offers a method that is called when the heading is updated:

```
- (void)locationManager:(CLLocationManager*)manager
        didUpdateHeading:(CLHeading*)newHeading {

  // If the accuracy is valid, process the event.
  if (newHeading.headingAccuracy > 0) {
    CLLocationDirection theHeading = newHeading.magneticHeading;

    NSLog(@"New heading is %@", theHeading);

  }
}
```

If location updates are also enabled, the location manager returns both true heading and magnetic heading values. If location updates are not enabled, the location manager returns only the magnetic heading value:

```
CLLocationDirection trueHeading = newHeading.trueHeading;
```

As mentioned previously, the magnetometer readings will be affected by local magnetic fields, so the `CLLocationManager` will attempt to calibrate its heading readings (if needed) by displaying a heading Calibration panel before it starts to issue update messages. However, before it does so, it will call the `locationManagerShouldDisplayHeadingCalibration:` delegate method:

```
- (BOOL)locationManagerShouldDisplayHeadingCalibration:
    (CLLocationManager *)manager {
  return YES;
}
```

If you return `YES` from this method, the `CLLocationManager` will proceed to display the device Calibration panel on top of the current window. The Calibration panel prompts the user to move the device in a figure-eight pattern so that Core Location can distinguish between Earth's magnetic field and any local magnetic fields. The panel will remain visible until calibration is complete or until you dismiss it manually by calling the `dismissHeadingCalibrationDisplay:` method in the `CLLocationManager` class.

Location-Dependent Weather

In Chapter 7, we built a simple Weather application, but it would be much better if the application gave us weather information for our current location. We can use the Core Location framework to retrieve the user's latitude and longitude. Unfortunately the Weather Underground service, which we used to back our Weather application, takes only city names, not latitude or longitude arguments.

There are several ways around this problem. If you were developing on a platform that didn't support geocoding, you'd need to make use of one of the many web services that provide geocoding (see sidebar for one such service); however, since iOS 5, Apple has provided native support for both forward and reverse geocoding.

 Although reverse geocoding was provided in the MapKit framework by the now deprecated `MKReverseGeocoder` class, until the arrival of iOS 5, there was no forward geocoding capabilities offered natively by the SDK. With the introduction of the `CLGeocoder` class, part of the Core Location framework, both capabilities are now natively provided. The `CLGeocoder` class should be used for all new application development.

Both forward and reverse geocoding requests make a network connection back to web services hosted by Apple. The calls will fail without a network connection.

Using the GeoNames Reverse Geocoding Service

There are many third-party web services that provide reverse geocoding. One of these is offered by GeoNames.org (*www.geonames.org/*), and it will return an XML or JSON document listing the nearest populated place using reverse geocoding. If you want an XML document returned, requests to the service take the form *http://ws.geonames.org/ findNearbyPlaceName?lat=***XX.X**&*lng=***XX.X**, or *http://ws.geonames.org/findNearby- PlaceNameJSON?lat=***XX.X**&*lng=***XX.X** if you prefer a JSON document. There are several optional parameters: `radius` (in km), `max` (maximum number of rows returned), and `style` (SHORT, MEDIUM, LONG, and FULL).

Passing the longitude and latitude of Cupertino, California, the JSON service would return the following JSON document:

```
{
    "geonames":[
        {
            "countryName":"United States",
            "adminCode1":"CA",
            "fclName":"city, village,...",
            "countryCode":"US",
            "lng":-122.0321823,
            "fcodeName":"populated place",
            "distance":"0.9749",
            "fcl":"P",
            "name":"Cupertino",
            "fcode":"PPL",
            "geonameId":5341145,
            "lat":37.3229978,
            "population":50934,
            "adminName1":"California"
        }
    ]
}
```

Reverse Geocoding

Reverse geocoding is the process of converting coordinates (latitude and longitude) into place name information. From iOS 5, you should use the CLGeocoder class to make reverse-geocoding requests by passing it a CLLocation object:

```
CLLocation *location =
    [[CLLocation alloc] initWithLatitude:37.323 longitude:-122.031];
CLGeocoder *geocoder = [[CLGeocoder alloc] init];

[geocoder reverseGeocodeLocation: location
    completionHandler: ^(NSArray *placemarks, NSError *error) {❶

        for (CLPlacemark *placemark in placemarks) {

            NSLog(@"Placemark is %@", placemark);

        }
    }];
```

❶ The completion handler block is called when the reverse geocoding request returns.

Forward Geocoding

Forward geocoding is the process of converting place names into coordinates (latitude and longitude). From iOS 5, you can use the CLGeocoder class to make forward-geocoding requests using either a dictionary of address book information (see Chapter 11) or an NSString. There is no designated format for string-based requests; delimiter characters are welcome, but not required, and the geocoder service treats the string as case-insensitive.

```
NSString *address = @"1 Infinite Loop, CA, USA";
CLGeocoder *geocoder = [[CLGeocoder alloc] init];

[geocoder geocodeAddressString:address
    completionHandler:^(NSArray* placemarks, NSError* error){ ❶

        for (CLPlacemark *placemark in placemarks) {

            NSLog(@"Placemark is %@", placemark);

        }
    }];
```

❶ The completion handler block is called when the reverse geocoding request returns.

CLPlacemark Objects

Both forward and reverse geocoding requests return CLPlacemark objects, which store information for a given latitude and longitude. The data includes information such as the country, state, city, and street address associated with the specified coordinate, although it can also include points of interest and geographically related data nearby.

Modifying the Weather Application

Let's modify our Weather application to make use of Core Location and (optionally) give us the weather where we are, rather than just for a hardwired single location. Open the Weather project in Xcode.

We'll need to add the Core Location framework to our project. Click on the Project icon at the top of the Project Navigator pane in Xcode, then click on the main Target for the project, and then on the Build Phases tab. Finally, click on the Link Binary with Libraries item to open up the list of linked frameworks, and click the + symbol to add a new framework. Select the Core Location framework (*CoreLocation.framework*) from the drop-down list and click the Add button.

We're going to use the application delegate to manage the CLLocationManager. I've highlighted the changes you need to make to the *AppDelegate.h* interface file in bold:

```
#import <CoreLocation/CoreLocation.h>

@class MainViewController;

@interface AppDelegate :UIResponder
  <UIApplicationDelegate, CLLocationManagerDelegate> ❶

@property (strong, nonatomic) IBOutlet UIWindow *window;
@property (strong, nonatomic) MainViewController *mainViewController;
@property (nonatomic) BOOL updateLocation; ❷
@property (strong, nonatomic) CLLocationManager *locationManager; ❸

@end
```

❶   We declare that the application delegate is a CLLocationManagerDelegate as well as a UIApplicationDelegate.

❷   We declare a Boolean variable that we'll use to indicate whether we're currently supposed to be monitoring the device's location.

❸   We declare an instance of the CLLocationManager as a property.

In the corresponding implementation file (*AppDelegate.m*) add the code shown in bold to the application:didFinishLaunchingWithOptions: method. This creates an instance of the CLLocationManager class and sets the delegate for the class to be the current class (the application delegate):

```
- (BOOL) application:(UIApplication *)application
    didFinishLaunchingWithOptions:(NSDictionary *)launchOptions {

    self.window = [[UIWindow alloc] initWithFrame:[[UIScreen mainScreen] bounds]];
    self.mainViewController =
      [[MainViewController alloc] initWithNibName:
        @"MainViewController" bundle:nil];
```

```
        self.locationManager = [[CLLocationManager alloc] init]; ❶
        self.locationManager.delegate = self; ❷

        WeatherForecast *forecast = [[WeatherForecast alloc] init];
        self.mainViewController.forecast = forecast;

        self.window.rootViewController = self.mainViewController;
        [self.window makeKeyAndVisible];

        return YES;
    }
```

❶   This creates the CLLocationManager instance.

❷   This sets the delegate for the instance to the current class.

Finally, we have to implement the two CLLocationManagerDelegate methods we're
going to need. Make the changes shown in bold:

```
    #pragma mark CLLocationManager Methods

    - (void)locationManager:(CLLocationManager *)manager
        didUpdateToLocation:(CLLocation *)newLocation
             fromLocation:(CLLocation *)oldLocation { ❶

        NSLog(@"Location: %@", [newLocation description]);
        if ( newLocation != oldLocation ) {

            // Placeholder for code we'll write later

        }
    }

    - (void)locationManager:(CLLocationManager *)manager
          didFailWithError:(NSError *)error { ❷
        NSLog(@"Error: %@", [error description]);
    }
```

❶   This is the delegate method to handle changes in location.

❷   This is the delegate method to handle any errors that occur.

We're going to modify the (currently unused) flipside of the Weather application and
add a switch (UISwitch), similar to our Battery Monitor application from Chapter 6.
This will toggle whether our application should be updating its location. However, let's
modify the FlipsideViewController interface file before we go to the nib file, adding
both a switch and a switchThrown: interface builder action that we'll connect to the
switch. Make the changes shown in bold to *FlipsideViewController.h*:

```
#import <UIKit/UIKit.h>

@class FlipsideViewController;

@protocol FlipsideViewControllerDelegate
- (void)flipsideViewControllerDidFinish:(FlipsideViewController *)controller;
@end

@interface FlipsideViewController : UIViewController {
    IBOutlet UISwitch *toggleSwitch;

}

@property (weak, nonatomic) IBOutlet id <FlipsideViewControllerDelegate>
    delegate;

- (IBAction)done:(id)sender;
- (IBAction)switchThrown;

@end
```

In the corresponding implementation (*FlipsideViewController.m*), import both the Core Location framework and the application delegate interface file:

```
#import <CoreLocation/CoreLocation.h>
#import "AppDelegate.h"
```

Then in the viewDidLoad: method, we need to populate the reference to the application delegate and use the value of the updateLocation Boolean declared earlier to set the state of the UISwitch. Add the lines shown in bold:

```
- (void)viewDidLoad {
    [super viewDidLoad];
    AppDelegate * appDelegate =
     (AppDelegate *)[[UIApplication sharedApplication] delegate];
    toggleSwitch.on = appDelegate.updateLocation;

}
```

Next, provide an implementation of the switchThrown: method that you'll attach to the UISwitch in Interface Builder:

```
-(IBAction)switchThrown {
    NSLog(@"Switch thrown");
    AppDelegate * appDelegate =
      (AppDelegate *)[[UIApplication sharedApplication] delegate];
    appDelegate.updateLocation = toggleSwitch.on;❶
    if ( toggleSwitch.on ) {
        appDelegate.locationManager.distanceFilter = 100;
        [appDelegate.locationManager startUpdatingLocation];
    } else {
        [appDelegate.locationManager stopUpdatingLocation];
```

```
            }
    }
```

❶   We must set the same `updateLocation` Boolean variable in the application delegate to be that of the state of the switch. We do this before starting location updates, as calls to the `didUpdateToLocation:fromLocation:` method will trigger a call of the `refreshView` method, which will check the state of the `updateLocation` Boolean. If we haven't already set this variable, it's possible that we'll end up with a race condition.

Now let's add that switch to the flipside view. Make sure you've saved all your changes and then click on the *FlipsideView.xib* file to open it in Interface Builder. Drag and drop a label (`UILabel`) and a switch (`UISwitch`) element from the Object Library window into the Flipside View window and use the Attributes Inspector to set the default position of the switch to `Off`. Position them and adjust the attributes of the label so that your layout looks like Figure 10-1. While you're here, double-click on the navigation bar title and change the text to **Preferences**. Save your changes; we're done here.

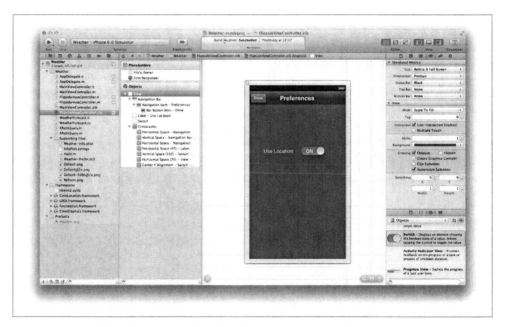

Figure 10-1. Adding the UISwitch to the FlipsideView controller

Right-click and drag from File's Owner to connect the `toggleSwitch` outlet to the `UISwitch`. Then right-click and drag back from the switch to File's Owner to connect the `switchThrown:` action (see Figure 10-2).

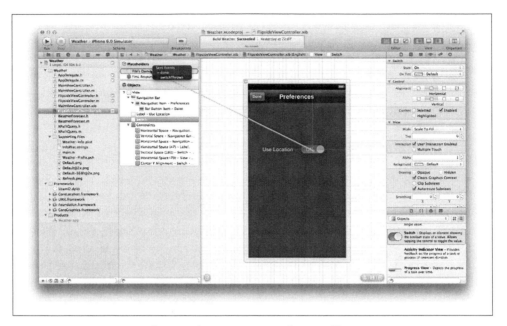

Figure 10-2. Connecting the switch action in Interface Builder

We've reached a natural point to take a break and test the application. Save *Flipside-View.xib* and click the Run button in the Xcode toolbar to build and deploy the Weather application into the simulator. Once it's running, click the Info button to go to the flip side of the application and toggle the switch. The Simulator will prompt you and ask whether you're happy for it to use your current location. Tap the OK button to allow it (see Figure 10-3).

If you look at the Debug area, you should (after a short time) see something that looks a lot like Figure 10-4.

Figure 10-3. The flipside of the Weather application running in the iPhone Simulator with location services turned off (left), the permissions Alert window (middle), and with location services turned on (right)

Figure 10-4. The Weather application reporting the simulated location (of iPhone Simulator) in the Debug area when the flipside switch is thrown

In the past, the iPhone Simulator reported its location as being at Lat. +37.33168900, Long. −122.03073100, corresponding to 1 Infinite Loop, Cupertino, CA. With the arrival of Xcode 4.2, the Simulator can now report your actual position (based on the WiFi position of your development machine).

Alternatively, you can use the Debug→Location menu item in the iOS Simulator to choose to use a different custom location or to choose a simulated run, bike ride, or freeway car journey.

Quit the simulator. Back in Xcode, click on the *MainViewController.h* interface file to open it in the Standard Editor. Since we're now going to have multiple locations, we need somewhere to store the name of the location that we'll get back from the reverse geocoder. We'll also need to take out UIActivityIndicator instance variable and make it a property.

Delete the instance variable:

```
IBOutlet UIActivityIndicatorView *loadingActivityIndicator;
```

and add the following properties:

```
@property (strong, nonatomic) NSString *locationState;
@property (strong, nonatomic) NSString *locationCity;
@property (strong, nonatomic)
   IBOutlet UIActivityIndicatorView *loadingActivityIndicator;
```

You should notice that the circle next to the newly created IBOutlet property initially starts as unfilled, but after a few moments becomes a filled circle. This indicates that the outlet is properly connected to the activity indicator in the nib file. If the circle doesn't fill, you'll need to go back into Interface Builder and connect the activity indicator back up to File's Owner.

At this point, you need to fix all the occurrences of loadingActivityIndicator to be self.loadingActivityIndicator. There are two: one at the start of the refresh View: method, and the other at the very end of the updateView method.

Then in the viewDidLoad: method, initialize the location strings:

```
- (void)viewDidLoad {
    [super viewDidLoad];
    self.locationState = [[NSString alloc] init];
    self.locationCity = [[NSString alloc] init];
    [self refreshView:self];
}
```

We'll need access to the application delegate, so the next thing we need to do is import it at the top of the MainViewController implementation. Add this line to the top of the file:

```
#import "AppDelegate.h"
```

Next, in the `refreshView:` method, check whether the app is monitoring the device's location so that you know whether to query the Weather Underground service with the app's default location (London, UK) or with the current location:

```
- (IBAction)refreshView:(id)sender {
    [self.loadingActivityIndicator startAnimating];

    AppDelegate *appDelegate =
      (AppDelegate *)[[UIApplication sharedApplication] delegate];
    if( appDelegate.updateLocation ) {
        NSLog( @ "updating for location = %@, %@ ",
              self.locationCity, self.locationState );
        NSString *encodedState = [self.locationState
              stringByAddingPercentEscapesUsingEncoding:NSUTF8StringEncoding];
        NSString *encodedCity  = [self.locationCity
              stringByAddingPercentEscapesUsingEncoding:NSUTF8StringEncoding];
        [self.forecast queryServiceWithState:encodedState
                                     andCity:encodedCity
                                  withParent:self];

    } else {
        [self.forecast queryServiceWithState:@"UK"
            andCity:@"London" withParent:self];
    }

}
```

Now we're ready to do our reverse geocoding. Open up the *AppDelegate.m* implementation, and in the `didUpdateToLocation:` method, add the code shown in bold:

```
- (void)locationManager:(CLLocationManager *)manager
    didUpdateToLocation:(CLLocation *)newLocation
           fromLocation:(CLLocation *)oldLocation {

    NSLog(@"Location: %@", [newLocation description]);

    if ( newLocation != oldLocation ) {
        CLGeocoder *geocoder = [[CLGeocoder alloc] init];
        [geocoder reverseGeocodeLocation:newLocation
               completionHandler: ^(NSArray *placemarks, NSError *error) {
            CLPlacemark *placemark = [placemarks objectAtIndex:0];
            NSLog(@"%@",[NSString stringWithFormat:@"%@,%@",
                placemark.locality, placemark.administrativeArea] );
            dispatch_async( dispatch_get_main_queue(), ^{
                self.mainViewController.locationState =
                    placemark.administrativeArea;
                self.mainViewController.locationCity = placemark.locality;
                [self.mainViewController refreshView:self];
            });
```

```
        }];
    }
}
```

Here we simply retrieve the latitude and longitude from the `CLLocation` object, and we pass them to the `CLGeocode` class to resolve. There the handler block takes care of updating the main view controller.

We're done. Save your changes and click the Run button in the Xcode toolbar to deploy the application in iPhone Simulator. Once it's running, click the Info button to go to the flip side of the application and toggle the switch. Click the Done button and return to the main view. After a little while, the activity indicator in the top-righthand corner should start spinning, and the weather information should change from London to that of your nearest town (see Figure 10-5).

Figure 10-5. The weather in Cupertino, CA

User Location and MapKit

Let's build a simple application to answer the question: "Where am I?" Start a new project in Xcode, select a Single View Application template, choose the iPhone as a device family, and name the project **WhereAmI** when prompted.

Add the MapKit and Core Location frameworks to your new project's target. You do not need the Core Location framework to work with MapKit, but we're going to use it later in the chapter, so we may as well add it now.

To do that, click on the Project icon at the top of the Project pane in Xcode, then click on the main Target for the project, and then on the Build Phases tab. Finally, click on the Link Binary with Libraries item to open up the list of linked frameworks, and click on the + symbol to add a new framework. Select the Core Location framework (*CoreLocation.framework*) from the drop-down list and click the Add button. Do this a second time, this time for the MapKit framework (*MapKit.framework*).

Once that's done, click on the *ViewController.h* interface file to open it in the Standard Editor and add a map view instance to the class, and import both the Core Location and MapKit framework header files:

```
#import <UIKit/UIKit.h>
#import <MapKit/MapKit.h>
#import <CoreLocation/CoreLocation.h>

@interface ViewController : UIViewController

@property (strong, nonatomic) IBOutlet MKMapView *mapView;

@end
```

Save your changes and click on the *ViewController.xib* file to open it in Interface Builder. Drag and drop a map view (MKMapView) from the Object Library window into the View window. Then right-click and drag from the File's Owner icon to connect the mapView outlet to the MKMapView, as shown in Figure 10-6.

This is a good place to check our code. Save your changes to the nib file, and click the Run button in the Xcode toolbar to build and deploy your application in iPhone Simulator. You should see something similar to Figure 10-7.

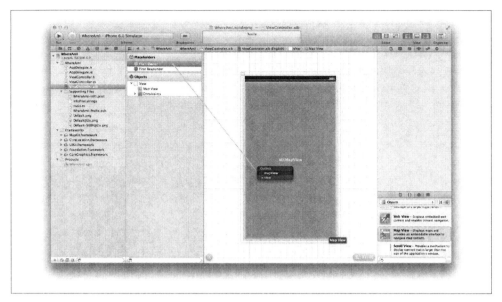

Figure 10-6. Connecting the mapView outlet to the MKMapView

Figure 10-7. The default map view in iPhone Simulator

It's not amazingly interesting so far, so let's use Core Location to change that.

While MapKit knows the current user location and can mark it on the map (you'll see the property that enables this, showsUserLocation, in the didUpdateToLocation:from Location: method shortly), there is no way to monitor it or update the current map view when the location changes. So, we're going to implement an application that uses Core Location to determine and zoom to the current location and then display the standard user location marker using MapKit.

Click on the *AppDelegate.h* interface file to open it in the Xcode Editor. We're going to declare that the application delegate also implement the CLLocationManager Delegate protocol, and add a locationManager property to the class declaration. Make the changes shown in bold to this interface file:

```
#import <UIKit/UIKit.h>
#import <CoreLocation/CoreLocation.h>

@class ViewController;

@interface AppDelegate : UIResponder <UIApplicationDelegate,
                                      CLLocationManagerDelegate>

@property (strong, nonatomic) UIWindow *window;
@property (strong, nonatomic) ViewController *viewController;
@property (strong, nonatomic) CLLocationManager *locationManager;

@end
```

In the implementation file (*AppDelegate.m*), we need to create an instance of the location manager and start updating our location (see earlier in the chapter for an overview of the location manager):

```
#import "AppDelegate.h"
#import "ViewController.h"

@implementation AppDelegate

- (BOOL)                 application:(UIApplication *)application
    didFinishLaunchingWithOptions:(NSDictionary *)launchOptions {

    self.window =
        [[UIWindow alloc] initWithFrame:[[UIScreen mainScreen] bounds]];

    self.locationManager = [[CLLocationManager alloc] init];
    if ( [CLLocationManager locationServicesEnabled] ) {
        self.locationManager.delegate = self;
        self.locationManager.distanceFilter = 1000;
        [self.locationManager startUpdatingLocation];
    }

    self.viewController =
```

```
    [[ViewController alloc] initWithNibName:@"ViewController" bundle:nil];
    self.window.rootViewController = self.viewController;
    [self.window makeKeyAndVisible];
    return YES;
}

// ... rest of the methods not shown...

@end
```

Now we must implement the `locationManager:didUpdateToLocation:fromLoca`
`tion:` delegate method. Add the following to *AppDelegate.m*:

```
- (void)locationManager:(CLLocationManager *)manager
    didUpdateToLocation:(CLLocation *)newLocation
        fromLocation:(CLLocation *)oldLocation {

    double miles = 12.0;
    double scalingFactor =
      ABS( cos(2 * M_PI * newLocation.coordinate.latitude /360.0) );

    MKCoordinateSpan span;
    span.latitudeDelta = miles/69.0;
    span.longitudeDelta = miles/( scalingFactor*69.0 );

    MKCoordinateRegion region;
    region.span = span;
    region.center = newLocation.coordinate;

    [self.viewController.mapView setRegion:region animated:YES];
    self.viewController.mapView.showsUserLocation = YES;
}
```

Here we set the map region to be 12 miles square, centered on the current location. Then
we zoom in and display the current user location.

 The number of miles spanned by a degree of longitude range varies
based on the current latitude. For example, one degree of longitude
spans a distance of approximately 69 miles at the equator but shrinks
to 0 at the poles. However, unlike longitudinal distances, which vary
based on the latitude, one degree of latitude is always around 69 miles
(ignoring variations due to the slightly ellipsoidal shape of Earth).

Length of 1 degree of Longitude (miles) = cosine (latitude) × 69 (miles).

Click the Run button on the Xcode toolbar to build and deploy your application in
iPhone Simulator. You should see something like Figure 10-8.

Figure 10-8. Asking user permission for the current location (left) and afterward, the map view showing the current user location (right)

If your current location changes, the user location will be automatically updated on the map.

Before leaving this example, let's add one more feature to display the current latitude and longitude on top of the map. Open the *ViewController.h* interface file and add two outlets to UILabel for the latitude and longitude values:

```
#import <UIKit/UIKit.h>
#import <MapKit/MapKit.h>
#import <CoreLocation/CoreLocation.h>

@interface ViewController : UIViewController
```

```
@property (strong, nonatomic) IBOutlet MKMapView *mapView;
@property (strong, nonatomic) IBOutlet UILabel *latitude;
@property (strong, nonatomic) IBOutlet UILabel *longitude;

@end
```

Make sure you've saved those changes, and click on the *ViewController.xib* nib file to open it in Interface Builder. Drag and drop a round rect button (UIButton) onto the view form the Object Library, resizing it roughly to the size shown in Figure 10-9, and remembering to remove the default text.

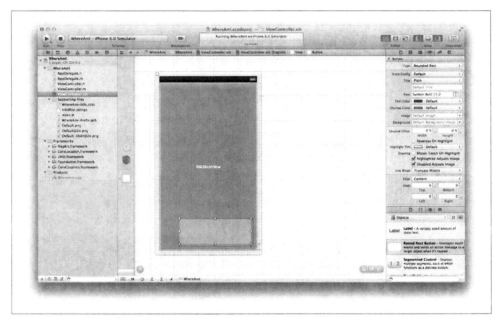

Figure 10-9. Resizing the UIButton we'll be using as a backdrop for our labels

We're going to use the button as a backdrop for latitude and longitude labels. It's actually a fairly common trick to do this, as it gives a nice box with rounded corners, but you must uncheck the User Interaction Enabled box in the View section of the Attributes Inspector tab in the Utilities panel. This will disable the user's ability to select the button. If you're uncomfortable doing this, you could equally well use a UIImage as a backdrop, or simply set the UILabel background to white or another appropriate color.

Next, drag and drop two labels from the Library on top of the button in the View window and change the label contents to be **Latitude** and **Longitude**. Finally, drag and drop two more labels onto the button and position them next to the previous two and set the contents to be **0.00**.

Now right-click and drag from File's Owner and connect the longitude and latitude outlets to the two labels we're intending to use, as shown in Figure 10-10.

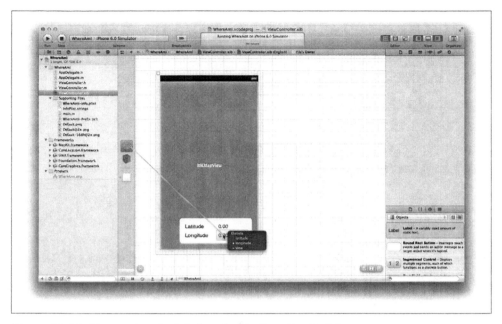

Figure 10-10. Connecting the label outlets in Interface Builder

Save your changes to the nib file and click on the *AppDelegate.m* file to open it in the Standard Editor. All we have to do at this point is populate the two labels we just added. In the `locationManager:didUpdateToLocation:fromLocation:` method, add the lines shown in bold:

```
- (void)locationManager:(CLLocationManager *)manager
    didUpdateToLocation:(CLLocation *)newLocation
           fromLocation:(CLLocation *)oldLocation {

    double miles = 12.0;
    double scalingFactor =
      ABS( cos(2 * M_PI * newLocation.coordinate.latitude /360.0) );

    MKCoordinateSpan span;
    span.latitudeDelta = miles/69.0;
    span.longitudeDelta = miles/( scalingFactor*69.0 );

    MKCoordinateRegion region;
    region.span = span;
    region.center = newLocation.coordinate;

    [self.viewController.mapView setRegion:region animated:YES];
```

```
self.viewController.mapView.showsUserLocation = YES;

self.viewController.latitude.text =
  [NSString stringWithFormat:@"%f", newLocation.coordinate.latitude];
self.viewController.longitude.text =
  [NSString stringWithFormat:@"%f", newLocation.coordinate.longitude];

}
```

Make sure you've saved your changes and click the Run button in the Xcode toolbar. If all goes well, you should be presented with a view that looks similar to Figure 10-11.

Figure 10-11. The current user location

Annotating Maps

Just as we did for the UIWebView in Chapter 7, we're going to build some code that you'll be able to reuse in your own applications later. We're going to build a view controller that we can display modally, and which will display an MKMapView annotated with a marker pin that can then be dismissed, returning us to our application.

We can reuse the Prototype application code we built back in Chapter 7 as a stub to hang our view controller from. Open the Finder and navigate to the location where you saved the *Prototype* project. Right-click on the folder containing the project files and select Duplicate; a folder called *Prototype copy* will be created containing a duplicate of our project. Rename the folder *Prototype3*.

Now open the new version of the project in Xcode and mouse over the blue Project icon at the top of the Project navigator and hit the Enter key, which will make the project name editable. Enter **Prototype3** as the new project name, and a drop-down will appear prompting you to approve the changes to the project. Click Rename when prompted to rename the project.

Then, just as we did when we rebuilt the Prototype application to demonstrate the mail composer, prune the application down to the stub with the Go button and associated pushedGo: method we can use to trigger the display of our map view [see the section "Sending Email" (page 211) in Chapter 7 for details].

Now, right-click on the Prototype group in the Project Navigator panel and click on New File from the menu. Under Cocoa Touch, select a UIViewController subclass, and name it **MapViewController**. Ensure that the "With XIB for user interface" checkbox is ticked.

You'll need to add both the MapKit and the Core Location frameworks to your project, just as you did in the last section.

We're going to be using the Core Location and MapKit frameworks throughout this project; instead of having to include them every time we need them, we can use the *Prototype_prefix.pch* header file to import them into all the source files in the project. Open this file (it's in the Supporting Files group) and change it to read as follows:

```
#ifdef __OBJC__
    #import <UIKit/UIKit.h>
    #import <Foundation/Foundation.h>
    #import <CoreLocation/CoreLocation.h>
    #import <MapKit/MapKit.h>
#endif
```

This file is called a *prefix file* because it is prefixed to all of your source files. However, the compiler precompiles it separately; this means it does not have to reparse the file on each compile run, which can dramatically speed up your compile times on larger projects.

Let's start by creating the UI for the new map view. Click on the *MapViewController.xib* file to open the nib file in Interface Builder. Drag and drop a navigation bar (UINavigationBar) from Object Library, and position it at the top of the view. Then drag a map view (MKMapView) into the view and resize it to fill the remaining portion of the View window. Finally, drag a bar button item (UIBarButton) onto the navigation bar, and again in the Attributes Inspector tab of the Utilities panel, changing its identifier from Custom to Done. Once you've done this, your view will look similar to what's shown in Figure 10-12.

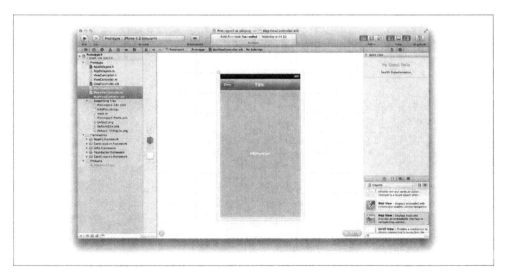

Figure 10-12. Creating our map view in Interface Builder

After saving the changes to the *MapViewController.xib* file, open the *MapViewController.h* interface file. Just as we did for the web view, we want to make this class self-contained so that we can reuse it without any modifications. We're therefore going to override the `init:` function again to pass the information you need when instantiating the object:

```
#import <UIKit/UIKit.h>

@interface MapViewController : UIViewController <MKMapViewDelegate> {
    CLLocationCoordinate2D theCoords;
    NSString *theTitle;
    NSString *theSubTitle;
    IBOutlet MKMapView *mapView;
    IBOutlet UINavigationItem *mapTitle;
}

- (id) initWithCoordinates:(CLLocationCoordinate2D)coordinates;
- (id) initWithCoordinates:(CLLocationCoordinate2D)coordinates
                  andTitle:(NSString *)title;
- (id) initWithCoordinates:(CLLocationCoordinate2D)coordinates
                  andTitle:(NSString *)title
               andSubTitle:(NSString *)subtitle;
- (IBAction) done:(id)sender;

@end
```

I've actually provided three independent `init` methods; which one you use depends on how much metadata you want to pass to the `MapViewController` class. If you look at the corresponding implementation in the *MapViewController.m* file, you'll notice that I've really only coded one of them. The other two are simply convenience methods that are chained to the first:

```
#import "MapViewController.h"

@implementation MapViewController

- (id)initWithNibName:(NSString *)nibNameOrNil bundle:
    (NSBundle *)nibBundleOrNil {
    self = [super initWithNibName:nibNameOrNil bundle:nibBundleOrNil];
    if (self) {
        // Custom initialization
    }
    return self;
}

- (id) initWithCoordinates:(CLLocationCoordinate2D)coordinates
                  andTitle:(NSString *)title
               andSubTitle:(NSString *)subtitle {
    if ( self = [super init] ) {
        theTitle = title;
        theSubTitle = subtitle;
```

```
        theCoords = coordinates;
    }
    return self;
}

- (id) initWithCoordinates:(CLLocationCoordinate2D)coordinates
               andTitle:(NSString *)title {
    return [self initWithCoordinates:coordinates andTitle:title andSubTitle:nil];
}

- (id) initWithCoordinates:(CLLocationCoordinate2D)coordinates {
    return [self initWithCoordinates:coordinates andTitle:nil andSubTitle:nil];
}

- (IBAction) done:(id)sender {
    [self dismissViewControllerAnimated:YES completion:nil];
}

- (void)viewDidLoad {
    [super viewDidLoad];
    mapTitle.title = theTitle;

    // ... code to add annotations goes here later ...

}

- (void)didReceiveMemoryWarning {
    [super didReceiveMemoryWarning];
}

@end
```

Save your changes and click on the *MapViewController.xib* nib file to open it in Interface Builder. Right-click and drag from File's Owner to the title item in the navigation bar and connect it to the mapTitle outlet, and then right-click and drag from File's Owner to the map view to connect it to the mapView outlet. Finally, right-click and drag from the Done button to File's Owner and connect it to the done: received action (see Figure 10-13) and from the map view to File's Owner to connect it as a delegate.

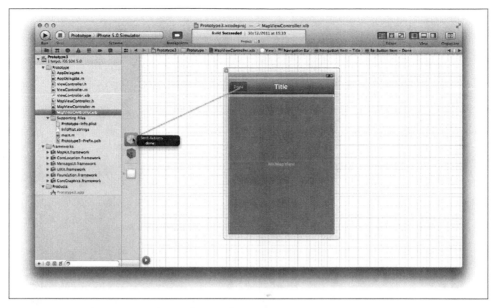

Figure 10-13. Connecting the outlets and actions

Save your changes to the nib file and switch to the *ViewController.m* implementation file, then import the MapViewController class:

```
#import "MapViewController.h"
```

Next, replace the pushedGo: method with the following:

```
-(IBAction) pushedGo:(id)sender {
    CLLocationCoordinate2D coord = {37.331689, -122.030731};
    MapViewController *mapView =
      [[MapViewController alloc] initWithCoordinates:coord
                                            andTitle:@"Apple"
                                         andSubTitle:@"1 Infinite Loop"];
    [self presentViewController:mapView animated:YES completion:nil];

}
```

It's time to stop and test our application. Save the file and click the Run button to compile and start the application in iPhone Simulator. Tap the Go button and the map view should load. Right now, we haven't specified any annotations, or a region, so you should just see a default world map (see Figure 10-14).

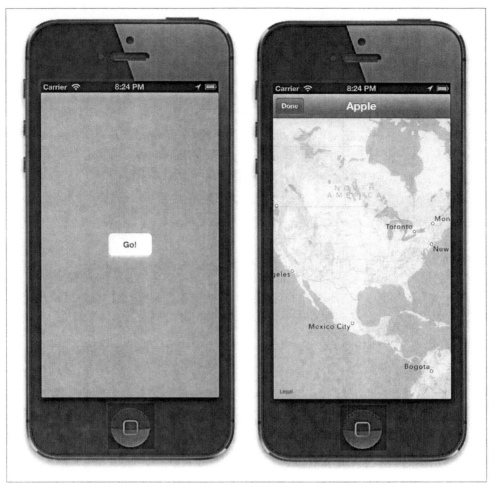

Figure 10-14. The initial main view (left) and the web view (right)

Let's change that. The first thing we need to do is create a class that implements the MKAnnotation protocol. Right-click on the Prototype group in the Project Navigator panel and click on New File from the menu. Select an Objective-C class, a subclass of NSObject, and name it **SimpleAnnotation** when prompted.

Open the *SimpleAnnotation.h* interface file Xcode has just created in the editor and modify it as follows:

```
#import <Foundation/Foundation.h>

@interface SimpleAnnotation : NSObject <MKAnnotation>

@property (nonatomic) CLLocationCoordinate2D coordinate;
@property (copy, nonatomic) NSString *title;
```

```
@property (copy, nonatomic) NSString *subtitle;

+ (id)annotationWithCoordinate:(CLLocationCoordinate2D)coord;
- (id)initWithCoordinate:(CLLocationCoordinate2D)coord;

@end
```

Open the corresponding *SimpleAnnotation.m* implementation file, and make the changes shown here:

```
#import "SimpleAnnotation.h"

@implementation SimpleAnnotation

+ (id)annotationWithCoordinate:(CLLocationCoordinate2D)coord {
    return [[[self class] alloc] initWithCoordinate:coord];
}

- (id)initWithCoordinate:(CLLocationCoordinate2D)coord {
    if ( self = [super init] ) {
        self.coordinate = coord;
    }
    return self;
}

@end
```

The `SimpleAnnotation` class is just a container; it implements the `MKAnnotation` protocol to allow it to hold the coordinates and title (with subtitle) of our annotation.

Save your changes and click on the *MapViewController.m* implementation file to open it in the Xcode Editor. Import the `SimpleAnnotation` class:

```
#import "SimpleAnnotation.h"
```

Edit the `viewDidLoad:` method to add the annotation using `theCoords`, `theTitle`, and `theSubTitle` passed to the `MapViewController` when it was initialized:

```
- (void)viewDidLoad {
    [super viewDidLoad];
    mapTitle.title = theTitle;

    SimpleAnnotation *annotation =
      [[SimpleAnnotation alloc] initWithCoordinate:theCoords];
    annotation.title = theTitle;
    annotation.subtitle = theSubTitle;

    MKCoordinateRegion region = { theCoords, {0.2, 0.2} };
    [mapView setRegion:region animated:NO];
    [mapView addAnnotation: annotation];
}
```

We're done. Make sure all your changes are saved, and click the Run button in the Xcode toolbar to build and deploy your application in iPhone Simulator. If all goes well, clicking on the Go button should give you a view that looks like Figure 10-15.

Figure 10-15. The finished MapViewController

At this point, you have reusable `MapViewController` and `SimpleAnnotation` classes, along with an associated nib file that you can drag and drop directly into your own projects.

You might want to think about some improvements if you do that, of course. For instance, you could easily expand the class to handle multiple annotations. While the annotations themselves can provide a much richer interface than a simple pushpin, look at the documentation for the `MKAnnotationView` class for some inspiration.

CHAPTER 11

Introduction to iCloud

Cloud computing has been heavily hyped, but at least in the consumer marketplace, uptake has been slow or nonexistent. Not many people have understood the advantages. iCloud has the potential to change that. This is cloud storage for the mass consumer market, and Apple has gone to great lengths to make things as seamless as possible for the user. However, that means there is an increased burden on the developer.

How Can I Use iCloud?

There are two main mechanisms to iCloud-enable your application. If you want to share small amounts of configuration data between instances of your application, you can make use of iCloud's key-value storage. However, the space available to use key-value stores is limited to just 64 KB. For larger amounts of data, you should use iCloud's document storage.

Adopting iCloud for storage will require changes in the data model and how it tracks and manages files, especially when it comes to detecting and dealing with conflicts between file versions. Resolving conflicts is the job of your application and, except in the case of key-value storage where last value set for the key is always regarded as the current value, this needs to be done manually by you.

Depending on your application, this might mean that you must also make changes to your user interface.

 The iCloud framework is aimed at file management. At least at the present time, there are no standard user interface elements, like those available for the camera roll and other standard view controllers we've talked about earlier chapters.

iCloud Backup

Everything in your application's *Documents* directory is automatically backed up into iCloud daily. Since the arrival of iOS 5 and iCloud backups, Apple has started to discourage developers from storing large amounts of data in the *Documents* directory. Only documents and other data that is user-generated, that cannot be recreated by your application, should be stored in the Application's *Documents* directory.

Other data, which can be regenerated or downloaded again, should be stored in the Application's *Library/Caches* directory, while temporarily data should be stored in the Application's *tmp* directory.

However, both the *Library/Caches* and *tmp* directories aren't backed up, but are "cleaned" out when the device is low on space. So if you have data that doesn't need to be backed up but needs to remain on the device even in low-storage situations because your application will make use of them offline, you can use the "do not back up" attribute for specifying files that should remain on your device:

```
#include <sys/xattr.h>

- (BOOL)addSkipBackupAttributeToItemAtURL:(NSURL *)URL {
    const char* filePath = [[URL path] fileSystemRepresentation];

    const char* attrName = "com.apple.MobileBackup";
    u_int8_t attrValue = 1;

    int result =
        setxattr(filePath, attrName, &attrValue, sizeof(attrValue), 0, 0);
    return result == 0;
}
```

This attribute works on marked files regardless of what directory they are in, including the *Documents* directory. These files will not be purged and will not be included in the user's iCloud or iTunes backup. Your application is responsible for monitoring and purging these files periodically.

 The "do not back up" attribute was only introduced with iOS 5.0.1; it is not respected by previous versions of the operating system.

Provisioning Your Application for iCloud

Access to iCloud is controlled using entitlements. If these entitlements are not present, your app is prevented from accessing files and data in iCloud. To enable an application to use iCloud, you must first enable the App ID [see the section "Creating an App ID" (page 20) in Chapter 2] for iCloud access.

Open a browser and go to the iOS Developer Center (*http://developer.apple.com/ios*). Look for the iOS Provisioning Portal link on the right. After clicking on App IDs in the menu, you should see something like Figure 11-1.

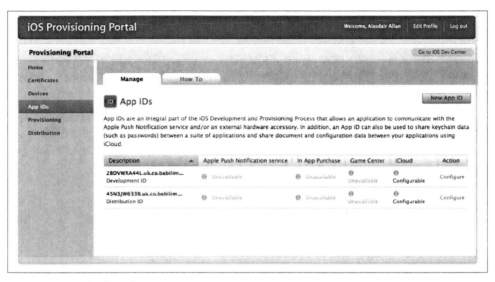

Figure 11-1. The list of App IDs

Since we used a wildcard Bundle ID rather than an application-specific ID, we cannot enable Push Notifications, In-App Purchase, or Game Center. However, we can configure iCloud access. Click on the Configure link to the right of our Development ID, and you'll be presented with a page that looks like Figure 11-2.

Click on the checkbox to Enable for iCloud, you'll see a pop-up advisory window (Figure 11-3).

This is telling us that we have to regenerate our provisioning profile. Click OK, and then the Done button to return to the list of App IDs. iCloud should now be enabled. Now let's go and regenerate our provisioning profile. Go to the Provisioning section of the Provisioning Portal, select the Development tab, and click the Edit link next to our Development Provisioning Profile, and then Modify in the drop-down menu.

Make sure the correct App ID is selected and click on the Submit button in the lower right. You'll be returned to the list of provisioning profiles. The profile you've just changed will be marked as Pending. Click the Refresh button in your browser toolbar until this changes to Active. Then click on the Download button to download a copy of the regenerated profile. Drag and drop it into Xcode.

The Xcode Organizer window should open automatically. If it doesn't, you can open it manually by going to Window→Organizer in the Xcode menu bar. You should see two copies of the Developer Profile; one will have a current timestamp, the other (the one we generated back in Chapter 2 and have been using throughout the book), an older timestamp (see Figure 11-4).

Right-click on the older of the two profiles and select Delete Profile from the drop-down menu.

Figure 11-2. Enabling iCloud for the App ID

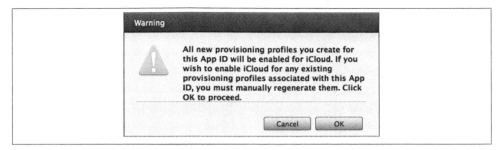

Figure 11-3. The pop-up advisory window

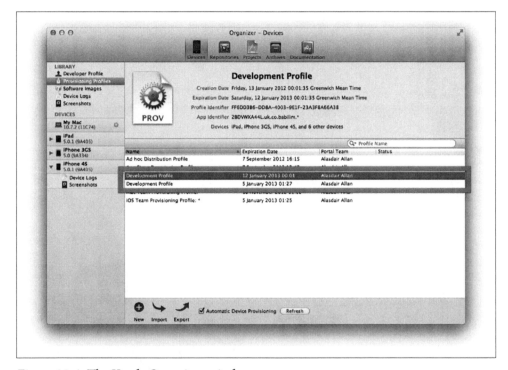

Figure 11-4. The Xcode Organizer window

Using Key-Value Storage

Let's build a simple application that shares a number across devices using the Key-Value Storage option. Open Xcode and create a new Single View Application, name the project **iCloudDemo** when prompted, and make sure that ARC is enabled and that it is targeted for the iPhone.

Once the project has opened in Xcode, select the (blue) Project icon at the top of the Project Navigator and then select the target. Select the Summary tab, and scroll all the way down to the Entitlements section (see Figure 11-5).

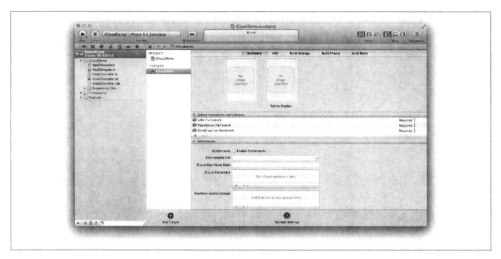

Figure 11-5. The Entitlements section of the Project Summary

Click the Enable Entitlements checkbox; it will autopopulate the other fields based on the App ID (see Figure 11-6), and an *iCloudDemo.entitlements* file will appear in the Project Navigator.

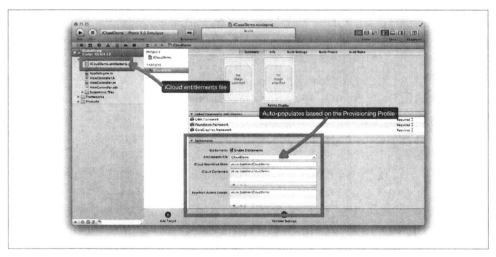

Figure 11-6. The Entitlements are autopopulated based on the App ID

When building an application that makes use of iCloud, you should check for the availability of iCloud as soon as your application starts. Although iCloud is available on all iOS 5 devices, it may not be configured.

Click the *AppDelegate.m* file and in the `application:didFinishLaunchingWithOp tions:` method, add the following code:

```
- (BOOL)application:(UIApplication *)application
      didFinishLaunchingWithOptions:(NSDictionary *)launchOptions {
    self.window =
        [[UIWindow alloc] initWithFrame:[[UIScreen mainScreen] bounds]];

    NSURL *ubiq = [[NSFileManager defaultManager]
        URLForUbiquityContainerIdentifier:nil];
    if (ubiq) {
        NSLog(@"iCloud at %@", ubiq);

    } else {
        NSLog(@"No iCloud access");
    }

    self.viewController =
        [[ViewController alloc] initWithNibName:@"ViewController" bundle:nil];
    self.window.rootViewController = self.viewController;
    [self.window makeKeyAndVisible];
    return YES;
}
```

Plug your iOS device into your Mac and set the scheme to target the device rather than the simulator, then click on the Run button in the Xcode toolbar to build and deploy the application onto your device.

You must test iCloud-enabled applications directly on your device rather than in the iPhone Simulator, as there is no iCloud support in the simulator.

If all goes well, you should see something much like Figure 11-7, showing a *file://* URL that points to the iCloud container for our application.

Figure 11-7. The Debug area shows that our device has connected to its iCloud container

Now that we have iCloud up and working, let's build the very simple user interface for our demonstration application. Click on *ViewController.xib* nib file to open it in Interface Builder and drag and drop a text field and a label into our view. You might want to add some placeholder text to the text field using the Attribute Inspector in the Utilities panel—I added "Enter a number"—and then change the default text of the label to be something sensible like "No number." Finally, you should change the keypad of the text field from Default to Numbers and Punctuation (see Figure 11-8) and the Return key from Default to Send.

Switch to the Assistant Editor and Control-click and drag from the text field and label to the *ViewController.h* interface file (which should be displayed on the second pane of the Assistant Editor) to create two properties called `numberEntry` and `numberLabel`, respectively (see Figure 11-9).

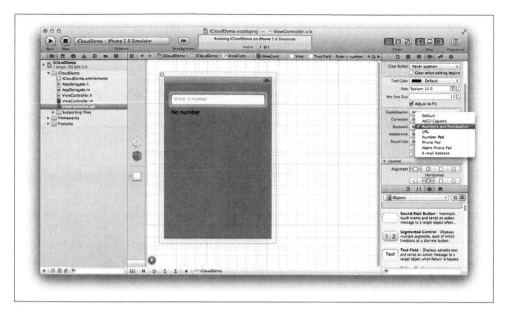

Figure 11-8. Configuring the user interface elements

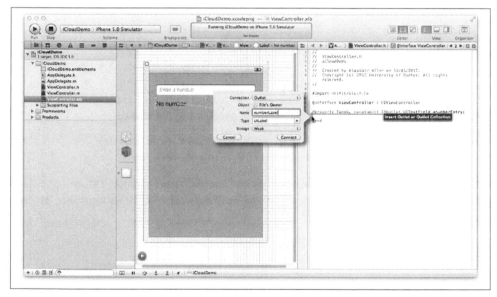

Figure 11-9. Connecting the outlets in Interface Builder

Now right-click and drag from the text field to the File's Owner icon in the dock and make it the text field's delegate. Once you've done that, you should declare the View Controller the delegate in the Assistant Editor. After you've done that, your *View-Controller.h* file should look something like this:

```
#import <UIKit/UIKit.h>

@interface ViewController : UIViewController <UITextFieldDelegate>

@property (weak, nonatomic) IBOutlet UITextField *numberEntry;
@property (weak, nonatomic) IBOutlet UILabel *numberLabel;

@end
```

Switch back to the Standard Editor and open up the *ViewController.m* implementation, add the following delegate methods:

```
- (BOOL)textFieldShouldReturn:(UITextField *)textField {
    [textField resignFirstResponder];
    return YES;
}

- (void)textFieldDidEndEditing:(UITextField *)textField {

    NSLog(@"Number is %@", self.numberEntry.text);
    self.numberLabel.text = self.numberEntry.text;

}
```

If you click the Run button in the Xcode toolbar to build and deploy the application into the simulator (or onto your device, although we aren't making use of iCloud at the moment, so that's not necessary quite yet), you should see the label change when you enter a number in the text field and tap on Send (see Figure 11-10).

Now that we have our user interface in place, let's send the number to iCloud when the user enters it and store it using the iCloud key-value store.

To write data to the key-value data store, we use the `NSUbiquitousKeyValueStore` class. This class allows you to save and retrieve simple data types such as numbers, strings, dates, and arrays.

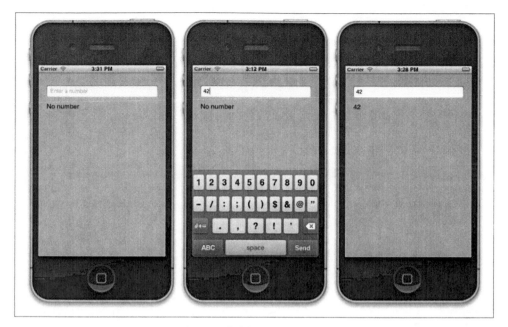

Figure 11-10. Entering text in the text field

Click on the *ViewController.m* file and add the following code to the viewDidLoad method:

```
- (void)viewDidLoad {
    [super viewDidLoad];
    NSUbiquitousKeyValueStore* store = [NSUbiquitousKeyValueStore defaultStore];
    [[NSNotificationCenter defaultCenter]
        addObserver:self selector:@selector(updateNumber:)
        name:NSUbiquitousKeyValueStoreDidChangeExternallyNotification
        object:store]; ❶
    [store synchronize];
}
```

❶ Here we're registering a method called updateNumber: in self as the callback when a notification is received that a key-value has changed in iCloud.

Then click on the corresponding *ViewController.h* interface file and declare our callback:

```
- (void)updateNumber:(NSNotification*)notification;
```

Once that's done, we can switch back to the implementation file and update our text FieldDidEndEditing: method to store the entered text into the iCloud key-value store.

```
- (void)textFieldDidEndEditing:(UITextField *)textField {
```

```
        NSLog(@"Number is %@", textField.text);

        NSUbiquitousKeyValueStore* store = [NSUbiquitousKeyValueStore defaultStore];
        [store setObject:textField.text forKey:@"text"];
        [store synchronize];

        self.numberLabel.text = textField.text;

    }
```

Finally, we can add the updateNumber: implementation:

```
    - (void)updateNumber:(NSNotification*)notification {

        NSDictionary* userInfo = [notification userInfo];
        NSNumber* reasonForChange =
            [userInfo objectForKey:NSUbiquitousKeyValueStoreChangeReasonKey];

        NSInteger reason = -1;
        reason = [reasonForChange integerValue];
        if ((reason == NSUbiquitousKeyValueStoreServerChange) ||
            (reason == NSUbiquitousKeyValueStoreInitialSyncChange)) {❶

            NSUbiquitousKeyValueStore* store =
                [NSUbiquitousKeyValueStore defaultStore];
            NSArray* changedKeys =
                [userInfo objectForKey:NSUbiquitousKeyValueStoreChangedKeysKey];
            for (NSString* key in changedKeys) {
                if ( [key isEqualToString:@"text"] ) {
                    NSLog(@"Update from iCloud: %@ = %@", key,
                        (NSString *)[store objectForKey:key]);
                    self.numberLabel.text = (NSString *)[store objectForKey:key];
                }
            }
        }
    }
```

❶ The NSUbiquitousKeyValueStoreServerChange reason for change indicates that the key-value store has changed in the cloud, most likely because another device has sent a new value; whereas the NSUbiquitousKeyValueStoreInitial SyncChange reason for change occurs the first time the application runs and during its initial sync with iCloud.

The easiest way to test our application at this point is to build and deploy it onto two separate devices. Running the application on both devices simultaneously, we can type the number into one of them and watch it appear on the other.

If you don't have two iOS devices to test the application code, you should be able to test it by running the application, setting the number, and then deleting the application from the phone before reinstalling it. The application should pull the number from the key-value store on initial startup. If you have the device plugged into your Mac when you start the application, you should be able to see this happening in the Debug area in Xcode.

I had an iPhone 4S and an iPhone 3GS on hand, so I'm going to use those to test the application. Assuming you have a roughly similar setup, plug the first phone into your Mac and click the Run button in the Xcode toolbar to build and deploy the application to the device. Once the application is running, click the Stop button on the Xcode toolbar, and unplug the device. Then plug the second phone into your Mac and (once you've made sure Xcode is configured to use this second device) click the Run button again to build and deploy your application to the second device.

On the first device, restart the application. You should now have the application running on both phones. Bring up the Debug area so you can see any log statements, and in the phone that is not connected to your Mac, enter a number into the text field and tap Send.

After a few moments—and it can take a little while, so you'll need some patience—the notification will arrive from iCloud that a key-value pair has been updated and your updateNumber: method will trigger. You should see some evidence of this in your Debug area, but also rather crucially, the number in the numberLabel should be updated without you typing anything into the text field on that phone (see Figure 11-11).

 In practice, you will find that it can take anywhere from a few seconds to over a minute for changes to propagate between devices.

Congratulations, you just built your first application using iCloud.

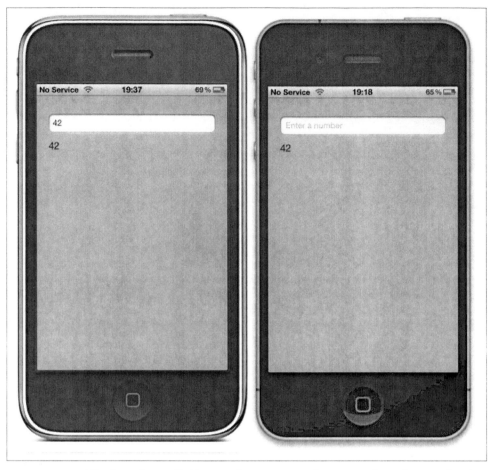

Figure 11-11. The first device (left), an iPhone 3GS in this case, where the number has been entered manually along with the second device (right), an iPhone 4S (which should be the one plugged into your Mac), showing the number automatically updated

Wrapping Up

I've only really scratched the surface in this chapter; dealing with iCloud is a book by itself. I've not talked about document storage, which is much more involved than the key-value store and deserves more space than I can dedicate to it here. Other issues include conflict resolution or how to keep your user interface synchronized with your data model. Both of these are absolutely crucial when dealing with iCloud-enabled applications. Fortunately, Apple has put a lot of information up online about iCloud; if you're interested in going further, the Apple Developer site (*http://developer.apple.com/icloud/*) is a good place to start.

Remember that if the user has enabled device backup to iCloud, your application's documents directory will be backed up. It really only makes sense to enable iCloud in your application if you're planning to use it as a synchronization tool between instances of your application (for instance, between the user's iPhone and iPad) or between platforms (an iOS and an OS X version of the application).

CHAPTER 12
Integrating Your Application

iOS devices offer standard view controllers for, among other things, taking pictures with the camera and sending email from within your own application. The software ecosystem surrounding your application is extremely rich with such built-in services and applications. You should take advantage of these as much as possible. In this chapter, we'll look at how you can do that.

Application Preferences

Users look for application preferences in two main settings: in the application itself, and in the standard iOS Settings application. For simple applications, applications with few preferences, and applications with preferences that need to be modified regularly, you should keep the preferences within the application itself. However, for more complicated applications, applications with complicated or numerous different preferences, and applications with preferences that the user will rarely have to modify, it's preferable to use the Settings application.

 Despite it being done in some applications currently for sale on the App Store, Apple advises that you should never split your preferences between the Settings application and a custom settings screen inside your own application. According to Apple, "If you have preferences, pick one solution and use it exclusively." This is good advice; having multiple places to change settings is confusing not just for the user, but also for you as a developer.

Adding a Preferences panel for your application to the main Settings application is easy. You do this by adding a special *Settings.bundle* file to your application and then configuring the *Root.plist* file contained inside the bundle in the Xcode Editor.

When the built-in Settings application launches, it checks each third-party application for the presence of a Settings Bundle. For each bundle it finds, it displays the application's name and icon on the main page. When the user taps the row belonging to the application, Settings loads the *Root.plist* Settings Page file and uses that file to display your application's main page of preferences.

Let's add a Settings Bundle to the Where Am I? application we wrote in Chapter 10.

 Open the Finder and navigate to the location where you saved the latest version of the *WhereAmI* project. Right-click on the folder containing the project files and select Duplicate. Rename the copy to *WhereA-mI2*. Now open the new version of the project in Xcode and mouse over the blue Project icon at the top of the Project navigator and hit the Enter key, which will make the project name editable. Enter `WhereAmI2` as the new project name, and a drop-down will appear, prompting you to approve the changes to the project. Click on Rename when prompted to do so to rename the project.

Open the *WhereAmI2* project in Xcode, right-click on the Supporting Files group in the Project Navigator panel, and select New File from the menu. In the template chooser window that appears, look at the lefthand panel and select the Resource category in the iOS section, and then select the Settings Bundle from the main panel and click the Next button (see Figure 12-1).

The settings bundle should appear inside the Supporting Files group. If you click the arrow beside it to expand the bundle, you'll see the *Root.plist* file that contains an XML description of the settings root page, and an *en.lproj* directory containing the localized string resource file (for English). You can add further localizations to your Settings Bundle if needed. Click the *Root.plist* file to open it in the editor and expand the Preference Items, and you should see something like Figure 12-2.

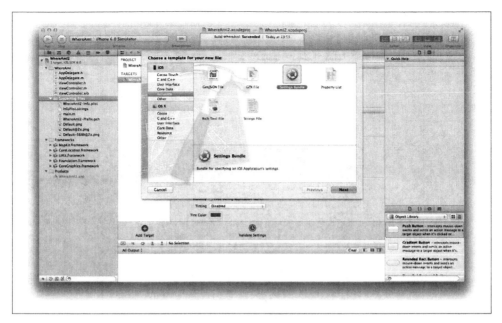

Figure 12-1. Adding a Settings Bundle to your application

Figure 12-2. The contents of the default Settings.bundle file

As you can see, the default Settings Bundle contains some example settings. Click the Run button in the Xcode toolbar to build and deploy the application into iPhone Simulator. Tap the simulator's Home button to quit the application, and then find the Settings application on the Home screen. Tap the Settings application to open it, and you should see something similar to Figure 12-3.

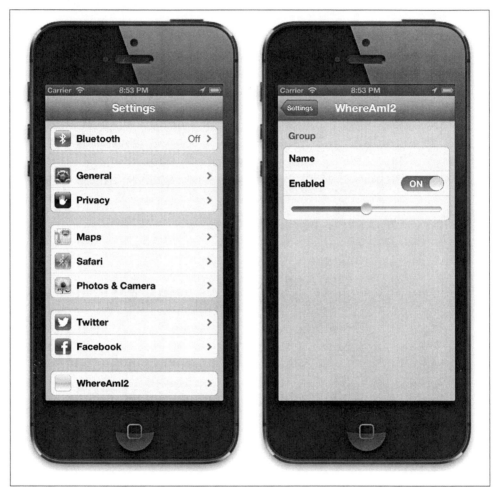

Figure 12-3. The simulator Settings application (left) with the default Settings Bundle we added to the Where Am I? application (right)

Since we haven't added an icon to the application [see the section on "Adding an Icon" (page 385) in the next chapter], the space to the left of the WhereAmI entry has a blank icon; if we had added an icon, it would be displayed next to our application name. If you now tap the WhereAmI entry, you'll be presented with the default Preferences pane generated from the Settings Bundle.

 If a file called *Icon-Settings.png* (a 29×29-pixel image) is located at the top level of your application's bundle directory (drag it into the top level of your project under Groups & Files and check the box to copy the item), that icon is used to identify your application preferences in the Settings application. If no such image is present, the Settings application uses a scaled-down version of your application's icon file instead. See the next chapter for more details about adding Icons to your project.

Returning to Xcode, click the *Root.plist* file inside *Settings.bundle* to open it in the Xcode Editor, and you'll see the property list description of the Settings page. Like any property list file, Xcode by default displays the *Root.plist* file as a key-value pair list. However, you can see the raw XML of the *Root.plist* property list by right-clicking on the Preference Items key and selecting Property List Type→None (see Figure 12-4).

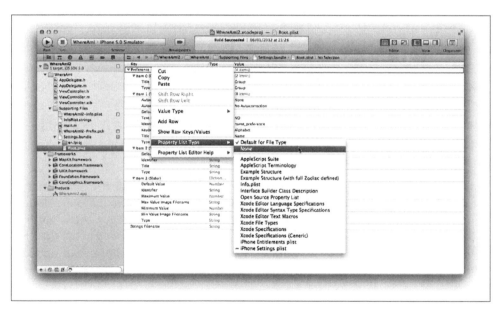

Figure 12-4. Changing the way the property list is displayed in the Xcode Editor

If you compare Figures 12-2 and 12-3, you can see how the property list file compares to the rendered user interface:

- Item 0 (`PSGroupSpecifier`) is a group label whose value is the string Group.
- Item 1 (`PSTextFieldSpecifier`) is a text label whose value is the string Name.

- Item 2 (`PSToggleSwitchSpecifier`) is a toggle switch labeled "Enabled" with a default value of YES.
- Item 3 (`PSSliderSpecifier`) is a slider bar with a minimum value of 0, a maximum value of 1, and a default value of 0.5.

Each interface element in the Settings panel is an item described in the Preference Items array. There are six possible property list keys:

- Group (`PSGroupSpecifier`)
- Title (`PSTitleValueSpecifier`)
- Text Field (`PSTextFieldSpecifier`)
- Toggle Switch (`PSToggleSwitchSpecifier`)
- Multi Value (`PSMultiValueSpecifier`)
- Slider (`PSSliderSpecifier`)

Additionally, although we won't go into it here, you can point to Child Preference panes (additional settings pages) using the Child Pane (`PSChildPaneSpecifier`) property list key.

But let's modify the default property key list provided by Xcode.

Click on Item 3 and press the Backspace key to delete it from the property list file, then do the same for Item 1. You should be left with a Group and a Toggle Switch.

Rename the Group: under Item 0, double-click on the Title property's value and enter **Latitude & Longitude**. Keep the Toggle Switch unmodified. After doing this, the *Root.plist* file should resemble Figure 12-5.

Make sure you've saved your changes to the *Root.plist* file and click the Run button in the Xcode toolbar. Once the application has started, tap the Home button and make your way to the Settings application. Tap the WhereAmI preference entry, and you should now see something closely resembling Figure 12-6. We're going to use the Preference pane to toggle whether we want the application to display the latitude and longitude on the screen when it displays our map.

Figure 12-5. The edited Property List pane in the editor

Figure 12-6. The edited Property List pane in the Settings application

When you run your application in Simulator, it stores preference values for your applications in your home directory. The preferences are saved in *~/Library/Application Support/iPhone Simulator/<VERSION>/ Applications/<APP_ID>/Library/Preferences*, where *<VERSION>* is the revision of the operating system the simulator is running (e.g., 5.0) and *<APP_ID>* is a randomly generated directory name. Each time Xcode performs a clean install of your application, any previous version of the application's preferences will be deleted.

Return to Xcode and click on the *AppDelegate.m* file to open it in the Xcode Editor. Now add the following class method, which initializes the default settings for the application:

```
+ (void)initialize {
    NSUserDefaults *defaults = [NSUserDefaults standardUserDefaults];
    NSDictionary *defaultsToRegister =
        [NSDictionary dictionaryWithObject:@"YES" forKey:@"enabled_preference"];
    [defaults registerDefaults:defaultsToRegister];
    [defaults synchronize];
}
```

If your user has already accessed the application's settings inside the Settings application before running the application, the default settings will already have been initialized. If this has not been done, the values will not exist and will be set to nil (or in the case of Booleans, to NO). As the application delegate is loaded, this method initializes the user defaults (the initialize: message is sent to each class before it receives any other messages).

Using this method to set the defaults has the unfortunate side effect that you have to specify your defaults in two places: in the *Root.plist* file, where they properly belong, and in your application delegate, where they don't.

The right way to deal with this problem is to read in the defaults from the *Settings.bundle* file, which is stored as part of your application. To do this, replace the initialize: method with the following:

```
+ (void)initialize {
    NSUserDefaults *defaults = [NSUserDefaults standardUserDefaults];
    NSString *settingsBundle =
        [[NSBundle mainBundle] pathForResource:@"Settings" ofType:@"bundle"];
    NSDictionary *settings =
        [NSDictionary dictionaryWithContentsOfFile:
            [settingsBundle stringByAppendingPathComponent:@"Root.plist"]];

    NSArray *preferences = [settings objectForKey:@"PreferenceSpecifiers"];
    NSMutableDictionary *defaultsToRegister =
        [[NSMutableDictionary alloc] initWithCapacity:[preferences count]];
```

```
    [defaults registerDefaults:defaultsToRegister];
    [defaults synchronize];

}
```

If your application preferences don't exist when your application is launched, you can therefore read the values directly from the *Settings.bundle* file rather than having to store the defaults in two places.

You can check that your preference bundle is working correctly by adding the following into the application delegate's `applicationDidFinishLaunching:withOptions` method and looking in the Debug area after the application launches. Add the lines shown in bold:

```
- (BOOL)application:(UIApplication *)application
    didFinishLaunchingWithOptions:(NSDictionary *)launchOptions {

    self.window =
        [[UIWindow alloc] initWithFrame:[[UIScreen mainScreen] bounds]];

    NSUserDefaults *defaults = [NSUserDefaults standardUserDefaults];
    BOOL enabled = [defaults boolForKey:@"enabled_preference"];
    NSLog(@"enabled = %d", enabled);

    self.locationManager = [[CLLocationManager alloc] init];
    if ( [CLLocationManager locationServicesEnabled] ) {
        self.locationManager.delegate = self;
        self.locationManager.distanceFilter = 1000;
        [self.locationManager startUpdatingLocation];
    }

    self.viewController = [[ViewController alloc] initWithNibName:
        @"ViewController" bundle:nil];
    self.window.rootViewController = self.viewController;
    [self.window makeKeyAndVisible];
    return YES;
}
```

We may have working preferences, but they don't do anything yet. Let's change that right now. Click on the *ViewController.h* interface file to open it in the Xcode Editor, and add the following outlets (shown in bold) to the declaration (inside the curly braces of the `@interface` block):

```
#import <UIKit/UIKit.h>
#import <MapKit/MapKit.h>
#import <CoreLocation/CoreLocation.h>

@interface ViewController : UIViewController {
    IBOutlet UIButton *backgroundButton;
    IBOutlet UILabel *latLabel;
    IBOutlet UILabel *longLabel;
}
```

```
@property (strong, nonatomic) IBOutlet MKMapView *mapView;
@property (strong, nonatomic) IBOutlet UILabel *latitude;
@property (strong, nonatomic) IBOutlet UILabel *longitude;

@end
```

There is no need to make them properties.

Click the *ViewController.xib* nib file to open it in Interface Builder. Right-click and drag
from File's Owner to connect the backgroundButton outlet to the UIButton we used as
a background for the labels, as shown in Figure 12-7; then connect the latLabel and
longLabel outlets to the "Latitude" and "Longitude" UILabel elements, respectively.

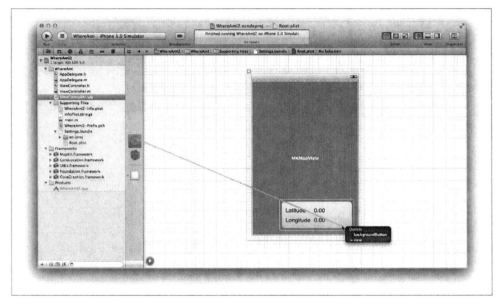

Figure 12-7. Connecting the new outlets to File's Owner

Save your changes to the nib file and return to Xcode. Then click on the *View-
Controller.h* interface file to open it in the editor, and add the following method
declaration:

```
#import <UIKit/UIKit.h>
#import <MapKit/MapKit.h>
#import <CoreLocation/CoreLocation.h>

@interface ViewController : UIViewController {
    IBOutlet UIButton *backgroundButton;
    IBOutlet UILabel *latLabel;
    IBOutlet UILabel *longLabel;
}
```

```
@property (strong, nonatomic) IBOutlet MKMapView *mapView;
@property (strong, nonatomic) IBOutlet UILabel *latitude;
@property (strong, nonatomic) IBOutlet UILabel *longitude;

- (void)updateFromDefaults;

@end
```

Then in the corresponding *ViewController.m* file, to open it in the Xcode Editor, add the implementation:

```
- (void)updateFromDefaults {
    NSUserDefaults *defaults = [NSUserDefaults standardUserDefaults];
    [defaults synchronize];

    if ( [defaults boolForKey:@"enabled_preference"] ) {
        backgroundButton.hidden = NO;
        latLabel.text = @"Latitude";
        longLabel.text = @"Longitude";
    } else {
        backgroundButton.hidden = YES;
        latLabel.text = @"";
        longLabel.text = @"";
    }
}
```

and add a viewWillAppear: method:

```
- (void)viewWillAppear:(BOOL)animated {
    [self updateFromDefaults];
    [super viewWillAppear:animated];
}
```

This method checks the application preferences to see if Latitude & Longitude are enabled. If they are, we set the text of the labels appropriately and make sure the button is visible. Correspondingly, if Latitude & Longitude are disabled, we hide the button and empty both strings.

The viewWillAppear: method will be called before our view is made visible to the user; however, if the user goes off and takes a phone call, or makes a change to the application's settings, and then switches back to your application, this method will not be called again. As far as the application is concerned, this view was always visible and has never disappeared. We therefore also must call the updateFromDefaults method from our application delegate in the applicationWillEnterForeground: method.

Open the *AppDelegate.m* file and add the following call:

```
- (void)applicationWillEnterForeground:(UIApplication *)application {
    [self.viewController updateFromDefaults];
}
```

We also need to make a small change to the `locationManager:didUpdateToLoca tion:fromLocation:` method. Here we have to stop the application from printing the current latitude and longitude to the screen if Latitude & Longitude are disabled via preferences. Add the lines shown in bold (wrapping the two existing assignments):

```
- (void)locationManager:(CLLocationManager *)manager
    didUpdateToLocation:(CLLocation *)newLocation
          fromLocation:(CLLocation *)oldLocation {

    double miles = 12.0;
    double scalingFactor =
      ABS( cos(2 * M_PI * newLocation.coordinate.latitude /360.0) );

    MKCoordinateSpan span;
    span.latitudeDelta = miles/69.0;
    span.longitudeDelta = miles/( scalingFactor*69.0 );

    MKCoordinateRegion region;
    region.span = span;
    region.center = newLocation.coordinate;

    [self.viewController.mapView setRegion:region animated:YES];
    self.viewController.mapView.showsUserLocation = YES;

    NSUserDefaults *defaults = [NSUserDefaults standardUserDefaults];
    [defaults synchronize];

    if ( [defaults boolForKey:@"enabled_preference"] ) {
        self.viewController.latitude.text =
          [NSString stringWithFormat:@"%f", newLocation.coordinate.latitude];
        self.viewController.longitude.text =
          [NSString stringWithFormat:@"%f", newLocation.coordinate.longitude];
    } else {
        self.viewController.latitude.text = @"";
        self.viewController.longitude.text = @"";
    }
}
```

This brackets the lines that set the text of the `UILabel` elements with an `if()` block; we set the text of the labels only if Latitude & Longitude are enabled in the preferences.

We're done here. Make sure all of your changes have been saved, and click the Run button in the Xcode toolbar to compile and deploy your application into iPhone Simulator.

By default, the Latitude & Longitude display is enabled, so everything should appear as before. However, if you disable Latitude & Longitude in Settings and relaunch the Where Am I? application, you'll see that Latitude & Longitude has disappeared, as shown in Figure 12-8.

Figure 12-8. With Latitude & Longitude enabled in the preferences (left) and disabled (right)

The Accounts Framework

The Accounts framework (*Accounts.framework*) provides a single sign-on model for user accounts. Originally the framework only supported Twitter accounts; however, it is generic, and was built so that Apple can easily add additional account types at a later date without affecting existing code. They duly did so with the arrival of iOS6 and the addition of support for Facebook and Weibo accounts.

The Accounts framework was introduced with the arrival of iOS 5, hand in hand with the now deprecated Twitter framework.

Single sign-on improves the user experience, because applications no longer need to prompt a user separately for login information related to an account. It also simplifies development for sign-on to manage the account authorization process for your application. You can use this framework in conjunction with the Twitter framework to access a user's Twitter account, and you no longer have to include code to handle OAuth or xAuth in your own application.

We can query and store accounts in the account database using the ACAccountStore class, which is part of the Accounts framework.

 To use the Accounts and Social frameworks, we need to add them to the project. Click the Project icon at the top of the Project Navigator panel in Xcode, then click the main Target for the project, and then on the Build Phases tab. Finally, click the Link Binary with Libraries item to open up the list of linked frameworks, and click the + symbol to add the frameworks.

Calling the requestAccessToAccountsWithType:withCompletionHandler: method on the store will present a dialog to the user confirming whether the application should have access to the accounts of this type. If granted, the application has access to protected properties of and operations on all accounts of the type specified.

```
ACAccountStore  *account = [[ACAccountStore alloc] init];
ACAccountType *accountType = [account accountTypeWithAccountTypeIdentifier:
    ACAccountTypeIdentifierTwitter];

[account requestAccessToAccountsWithType:accountType
                withCompletionHandler:^(BOOL granted, NSError *error) {

    if (granted == YES){
       NSArray *array = [account accountsWithAccountType:accountType];
       NSLog(@"%@",array);
    }
}];
```

If there are no registered accounts of the requested type in the accounts database, then the returned accounts array will be nil. You can add accounts to the database using the Twitter and Facebook panels in the Settings application (see Figure 12-9).

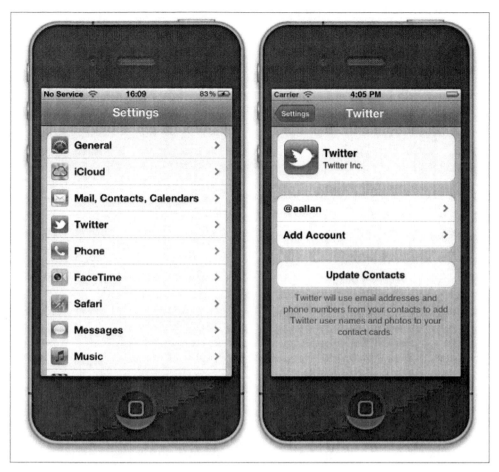

Figure 12-9. The Twitter panel of the iOS Settings application

The Social Framework

We've already looked at the Social framework earlier in the book where we built a simple table view-based application to retrieve the list of trending topics on Twitter (see Chapter 8). As I mentioned there, that's not the only thing the Social framework can do; much as the standard view controller can send email, the standard modal view controller allows you to send tweets and post to Facebook.

Sending Tweets

Let's recycle our Prototype application one more time.

Right-click or Control-click on the folder containing the project files and select Duplicate. Rename the copied folder to *Prototype4*. Now open the new version of the project in Xcode and mouse over the blue Project icon at the top of the Project navigator and hit the Enter key, which will make the project name editable. Enter **Prototype4** as the new project name, and a drop-down will appear prompting you to approve the changes to the project. Click Rename when prompted to rename the project.

Next, prune back the code:

1. Open the copy of the project in Xcode and delete the *WebViewController.h*, *Web-ViewController.m*, and *WebViewController.xib* files by right-clicking on each file in the Project Navigator panel and selecting Delete from the pop-up menu (rather than Remove References Only).

2. Now click the *ViewController.m* file to open it in the editor. Delete the line where you import the *WebViewController.h* file and delete all the code in the pushedGo: method, but not the method itself.

3. At this point, we have just the stub of the application, with that Go button and associated pushedGo: method we can use to trigger the display of our tweet composer view.

Add the Social framework to the project. Then click on the *ViewController.m* implementation file to import the framework into the class:

```
#import <Social/Social.h>
```

and add the following code to the pushedGo: method:

```
- (IBAction)pushedGo:(id)sender {

    SLComposeViewController *socialComposer;
    if ( [SLComposeViewController isAvailableForServiceType:
        SLServiceTypeTwitter] ) {
        socialComposer =
          [SLComposeViewController
            composeViewControllerForServiceType:SLServiceTypeTwitter];
        [socialComposer addImage:[UIImage imageNamed:@"oreilly_logo.gif"]];
        [socialComposer
          addURL:[NSURL URLWithString:@"http://learningiphoneprogramming.com/"]];
        [socialComposer
          setInitialText:@"A tweet from an iOS app and the Twitter framework."];

    }
    socialComposer.completionHandler = ^(SLComposeViewControllerResult result){
        NSString *msg;
        if (result == SLComposeViewControllerResultCancelled) {
            msg = @"Tweet compostion was canceled.";
        } else if (result == SLComposeViewControllerResultDone) {
            msg = @"Tweet composition completed.";
        }
        UIAlertView* alertView =
          [[UIAlertView alloc] initWithTitle:@"Tweet Status"
```

```
                        message:msg
                        delegate:nil
                cancelButtonTitle:@"Okay"
                otherButtonTitles:nil];
        [alertView show];
        [self dismissViewControllerAnimated:YES completion:nil];
    };
    [self presentViewController:socialComposer animated:YES completion:nil];

}
```

Before running the code, you'll need to configure a Twitter account (see Figure 12-9 again). If you skip this step, you'll see the dialog (on the left) in Figure 12-10; otherwise, you'll see the standard tweet view controller (right).

Figure 12-10. The warning message generated when there are no configured accounts (left) and the standard tweet composition view (right)

Making Posts to Facebook

Changing our code to make posts to Facebook is as simple as changing the account type from `SLServiceTypeTwitter` to `SLServiceTypeFacebook` and restarting our application.

Custom URL Schemes

One of the more interesting features provided by the SDK is the ability for your application to use custom URL schemes to launch other applications, and in turn, to register custom URL schemes of its own. These schemes can be used to launch your application, either from the browser or from another application on the device. Additionally, such schemes are not just limited to launching the application; you can pass additional information to your application via the URL.

Using Custom Schemes

Most of the built-in applications Apple provides respond to custom URL schemes; for example, the Maps, Mail, YouTube, iTunes, and App Store applications will all open in response to custom URLs. However, there are also many established third-party applications with published URL schemes that you can use in your own application.

 At the time of this writing, a fairly extensive list of URL schemes for third-party iPhone applications was available at handleOpenURL (*http://handleopenurl.com/*).

Making a telephone call

You can easily trigger a telephone call from your application by using the `tel:` URL scheme:

```
NSString *string = @"tel:+19995551234"; ❶
NSURL *url = [NSURL URLWithString:string];
[[UIApplication sharedApplication] openURL:url];
```

❶ The phone number must not contain spaces or square brackets, although it can contain dashes and a leading + sign indicating that the international call prefix should be prepended.

Opening the Settings application

With the arrival of iOS 5, the Settings application acquired a custom URL scheme. Before this, it wasn't possible to open the Settings application at a specific page:

```
NSString *string = @"prefs:root=AIRPLANE_MODE";
NSURL *url = [NSURL URLWithString:string];
[[UIApplication sharedApplication] openURL:url];
```

If the Settings page you want to open has subpages, you can use strings of the form
`prefs:root=General&path=Bluetooth` to access them.

Registering Custom Schemes

Regardless of what you intend to do after a custom URL launches your application, you
must first register your custom scheme using your application's *CityGuide-Info.plist* file.
Let's do that for our City Guide application.

> You can choose any of the versions of the City Guide application we've
> worked on so far for this addition. I'm going to be using the version
> from Chapter 8, which was backed by a SQLite database.

Open the project in Xcode and click on its *CityGuide-Info.plist* file to open it in the
Standard Editor. Right-click the top row's Information Property List and select Add
Row (see Figure 12-11).

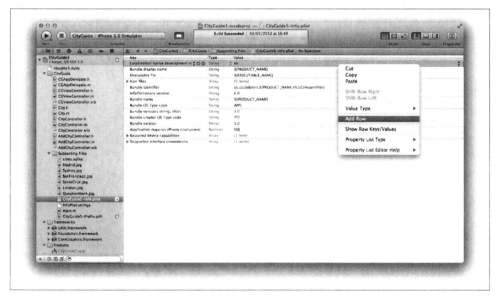

Figure 12-11. Adding a row to the plist file

A row will be added and you'll be prompted to select a key from a drop-down menu.
Scroll to the bottom and select "URL types" (see Figure 12-12).

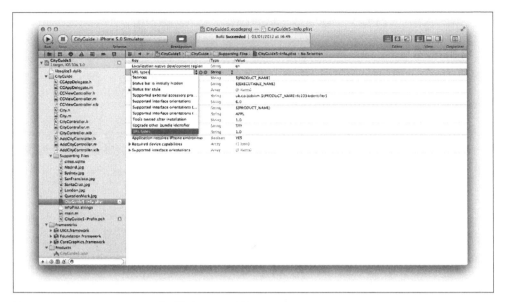

Figure 12-12. Registering the "URL types" key item

This will create an array key item, so click the disclosure triangle next to "URL types" to expand it.

Click on Item 0 to expand it to show the URL identifier line. The value for this can actually be anything, but it's normal to use the Bundle Identifier, so double-click the Bundle Identifier value to select it and then copy the identifier string. Then double-click the field to the right of the URL identifier and paste it into the box.

Now right-click on Item 0, and select Add Row. You'll be presented with a shorter drop-down of possible values; this time select URL Schemes. This will create an array key item. Expand it, double-click the value box for its Item 0, and enter **cityguide**.

If you've followed the procedure correctly, your *Info.plist* file should now look like mine does in Figure 12-13. We're done; adding a custom URL scheme to your application really is that easy.

Of course, now that we've added the custom URL scheme, we need to modify our application code so that it knows what to do with it. We're going to modify the City Guide application to take URLs of the form *cityguide://<City Name>* and open the relevant city page (e.g., the London page for *cityguide://London*).

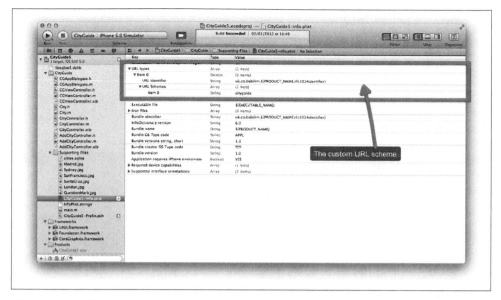

Figure 12-13. The custom scheme

If two different applications register with the same URL scheme, the most recently installed application will be the one that responds to custom URLs conforming to the URL scheme.

If you have separate (i.e., non-universal) applications for the iPhone and the iPad, you should not use the same URL scheme for both applications. If both are installed on the same iOS device, deleting the second application registered against the scheme means that the first application will also no longer be recognized as a responder and the first application will not be registered against it.

To be clear, there is no real way to work around this problem, except by picking a unique URL scheme name and hoping other app developers don't pick the same one as you.

We really need to make only a few changes to the City Guide application to implement handling custom URL schemes.

If your application is not running when another application requests it to open a custom URL, then an `application:didFinishLaunchingWithOptions:` message is sent, which includes a `UIApplicationLaunchOptionsURLKey` key in the launch options. If the application is already running, and backgrounded by the operating system, then the `application:openURL:sourceApplication:annotation:` method is invoked in the application delegate. If this method is not implemented, then the deprecated `application:handleOpenURL:` method is called.

Click the *CGAppDelegate.m* implementation file to open it in the Xcode Editor, and add the following methods:

```
- (BOOL)application:(UIApplication *)application
            openURL:(NSURL *)url
  sourceApplication:(NSString *)sourceApplication annotation:(id)annotation {

    return [self application:application handleOpenURL:url];
}

- (BOOL)application:(UIApplication *)application handleOpenURL:(NSURL *)url {
    [self.viewController displayCityNamed:[url host]];❶
    return YES;
}
```

❶   We'll implement the `displayCityNamed:` in the `CGViewController` class to handle displaying the relevant city.

Additionally, you should add the following code to the `application:didFinishLaunch ing WithOptions:` method:

```
- (BOOL)application:(UIApplication *)application
    didFinishLaunchingWithOptions:(NSDictionary *)launchOptions {

    self.window = [[UIWindow alloc] initWithFrame:[[UIScreen mainScreen] bounds]];

    self.cities = [[NSMutableArray alloc] init];
    NSString *filePath = [self copyDatabaseToDocuments];
    [self readCitiesFromDatabaseWithPath:filePath];

    self.viewController =
      [[CGViewController alloc] initWithNibName:@"CGViewController" bundle:nil];
    self.navController = [[UINavigationController alloc]
    initWithRootViewController:self.viewController];
    self.window.rootViewController = self.navController;
    [self.window makeKeyAndVisible];

    // If the UIApplicationLaunchOptionsURLKey is present,
    // we have been launched with a URL
    if ( [launchOptions objectForKey:UIApplicationLaunchOptionsURLKey] != nil ) {
        NSURL *url =
          (NSURL *)[launchOptions valueForKey:UIApplicationLaunchOptionsURLKey];
        if([[[UIDevice currentDevice] systemVersion] hasPrefix:@"3.2"]) {
            [self application:application handleOpenURL:url];
        }
    }

    return YES;
}
```

Save your changes and then click the *CGViewController.h* interface file. Here, we need to declare the `displayCityNamed:` method:

```
- (void)displayCityNamed:(NSString *)name;
```

Then, in the corresponding *CGViewController.m* implementation file, add the method:

```
- (void)displayCityNamed:(NSString *)host {

    NSIndexPath *indexPath;
    for( int i = 0; i < cities.count; i++ ) {
        City *thisCity = [cities objectAtIndex:i];
        if( [thisCity.cityName isEqualToString:host] ) {
            indexPath = [NSIndexPath indexPathForRow:i inSection:0];
        }
    }

    // Begin debugging code ❶
    UIAlertView *alert =
                [[UIAlertView alloc]
                    initWithTitle:host
                    message:[NSString stringWithFormat:
                        @"indexPath = %@", indexPath]
                    delegate:nil
                    cancelButtonTitle:nil
                    otherButtonTitles:@"OK", nil];
    [alert show];
    // End debugging code

    CityController *city = [[CityController alloc] initWithIndexPath:indexPath];

    CGAppDelegate *delegate =
    (CGAppDelegate *)[[UIApplication sharedApplication] delegate];
    [delegate.navController pushViewController:city animated:NO];
}
```

❶ Displaying the `UIAlertView` is purely for debugging purposes to give some feedback. We're using it because the Debugger console is unavailable, since the application is started by clicking a URL rather than by running under Xcode. It's not integral to handling the custom URL scheme, and once you understand what's going on, you can delete this section of the code.

We're done. Click the Run button to compile and deploy the application into iPhone Simulator. Once the application is launched, quit the application by clicking the Home button and navigate to Safari. Click on the address bar, enter **cityguide://London**, and click the Go button (or tap the Return key).

If all goes well, Safari should background and the City Guide application will launch. Soon afterward, you should see something similar to Figure 12-14.

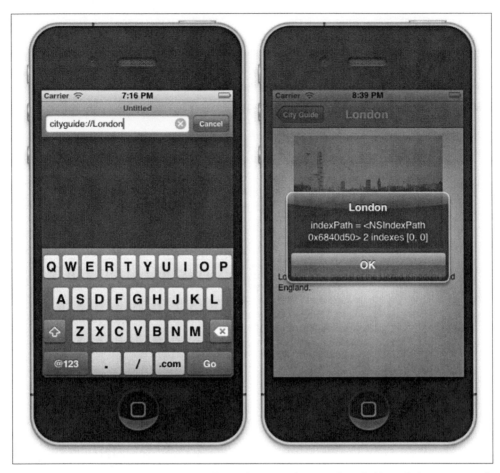

Figure 12-14. Opening the City Guide application from Safari (left) and the City Guide after it opens with the debug UIAlertView visible (right)

This doesn't work only in Safari; we can now open the City Guide application from other applications using the following snippet of code:

```
NSString *string = @"cityguide://London"; ❶
NSURL *url = [NSURL URLWithString:string];
[[UIApplication sharedApplication] openURL:url];
```

❶   This will open the London city guide in the City Guide application.

Media Playback

In much the same way as the standard view controllers for picking images and sending email and tweets, Apple has provided a standard way to select and play back iPod media inside your own application.

The `MPMediaPickerController` and associated classes make use of the iPod library; this is not present in iPhone Simulator and will work correctly only on the device itself.

However, things are a little bit more complicated than the other cases we've looked at; here, we use an `MPMediaPickerController` that, via the `MPMediaPickerController Delegate` protocol, returns an `MPMediaItemCollection` object containing the media items the user has selected, and that can be played using an `MPMusicPlayer Controller` object.

These picker classes are provided by the Media Player framework; if you want to use them, you must add the Media Player framework to your project in the normal way.

Let's reuse the Prototype application. Open the Finder and navigate to the location where you saved the *Prototype* project. Right-click the folder containing the project files and select Duplicate; a folder called *Prototype copy* will be created containing a duplicate of the project. Rename the folder *PrototypePlayer*, and just as we did in Chapter 7, prune the application down to the stub with the Go button and associated `pushedGo:` method that we'll use to trigger the display of our media player.

To prune the Prototype application down to the stub, you will need to:

1. Delete the *WebViewController.h*, *WebViewController.m*, and *WebView.xib* files from your project.

2. Remove the `#import "WebViewController.h"` line from *View-Controller.m*.

3. Delete the current body of the `pushedGo:` method.

Next, open the *ViewController.h* interface file, import the Media Player framework into the interface (.*h*) files, and declare your class as an `MPMediaPickerControllerDelegate`:

```
#import <UIKit/UIKit.h>
#import <MediaPlayer/MediaPlayer.h>
```

```
@interface ViewController : UIViewController <MPMediaPickerControllerDelegate>

@property (weak, nonatomic) IBOutlet UIButton *goButton;

- (IBAction)pushedGo:(id)sender;

@end
```

Save your changes, and open the *ViewController.m* implementation file. In the push
edGo: method, instantiate an MPMediaPickerController object and present its view
modally to the user:

```
-(IBAction) pushedGo:(id)sender {
  MPMediaPickerController *mediaPicker =
    [[MPMediaPickerController alloc]
      initWithMediaTypes: MPMediaTypeAnyAudio];
  mediaPicker.delegate = self;
  mediaPicker.allowsPickingMultipleItems = YES;
  [self presentViewController:mediaPicker animated:YES completion:nil];
}
```

Now implement the following two delegate methods:

```
- (void) mediaPicker:(MPMediaPickerController *) mediaPicker
  didPickMediaItems:(MPMediaItemCollection *) userMediaItemCollection
{
    [self dismissViewControllerAnimated:YES completion: nil];

    MPMusicPlayerController *musicPlayer =
      [MPMusicPlayerController applicationMusicPlayer];
    [musicPlayer setQueueWithItemCollection: userMediaItemCollection];
    [musicPlayer play]; ❶
}

- (void) mediaPickerDidCancel: (MPMediaPickerController *) mediaPicker {
    [self dismissModalViewControllerAnimated: YES];
}
```

❶   The MPMusicPlayerController responds to all the messages you might expect
     (e.g., play, pause, stop, volume). You can link these directly to buttons in your
     user interface if you want to give users direct control over these functions.

Like the UIImagePickerControllerDelegate methods we met earlier in the book, these
two methods are used to dismiss the view controller and handle the returned items.

Save your changes, and click on the Run button in the Xcode toolbar to build and deploy your code. Remember that you'll need to configure your project [see the section "Putting the Application on Your iPhone" (page 51) in Chapter 3] to allow you to deploy the application onto your iPhone or iPod touch so that you can test the application on your device.

Once your application loads, tap the Go button to bring up the MPMediaPicker Controller, select some songs, and tap the Done button in the navigation bar (see Figure 12-15). Your music should start playing.

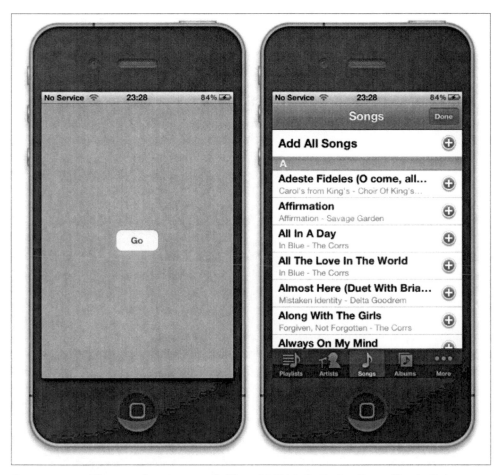

Figure 12-15. The initial main view (left) and MPMediaPickerController (right)

Once playback has begun, you need to keep track of the currently playing item and display that to the user, or at the very least provide some way for the user to pause (or stop) playback, or perhaps to change her selection. The MPMusicPlayerController class provides two methods: the beginGeneratingPlaybackNotifications: method and a corresponding endGeneratingPlaybackNotifications: method.

Add this line to the didPickMediaItems: method:

```
- (void) mediaPicker:(MPMediaPickerController *) mediaPicker
  didPickMediaItems:(MPMediaItemCollection *) userMediaItemCollection {
    [self dismissModalViewControllerAnimated: YES];

    MPMusicPlayerController *musicPlayer =
      [MPMusicPlayerController applicationMusicPlayer];
    [musicPlayer setQueueWithItemCollection: userMediaItemCollection];
    [musicPlayer beginGeneratingPlaybackNotifications];
    [musicPlayer play];
}
```

When the begin method is invoked, the class will start to generate notifications of when the player state changes and when the current playback item changes, which your application can register to handle by adding itself as an observer using the NSNotification Center class:

```
- (void) mediaPicker:(MPMediaPickerController *) mediaPicker
  didPickMediaItems:(MPMediaItemCollection *) userMediaItemCollection {
    [self dismissModalViewControllerAnimated: YES];

    MPMusicPlayerController *musicPlayer =
    [MPMusicPlayerController applicationMusicPlayer];
    [musicPlayer setQueueWithItemCollection: userMediaItemCollection];
    [musicPlayer beginGeneratingPlaybackNotifications];

    NSNotificationCenter *notificationCenter =
        [NSNotificationCenter defaultCenter];
    [notificationCenter
      addObserver:self
        selector:@selector(handleNowPlayingItemChanged:)
            name:@"MPMusicPlayerControllerNowPlayingItemDidChangeNotification"
          object:musicPlayer];

    [notificationCenter
      addObserver:self
        selector:@selector(handlePlaybackStateChanged:)
            name:@"MPMusicPlayerControllerPlaybackStateDidChangeNotification"
          object:musicPlayer];

    [musicPlayer play];

}
```

This will invoke the selector methods in our class when the appropriate notification arrives. (You could, for example, use the first to update a UILabel in your view telling the user the name of the currently playing song.)

However, for now let's just implement these methods to print messages to the console log. In the *ViewController.h* interface file, declare the selector methods:

```
@interface ViewController : UIViewController <MPMediaPickerControllerDelegate>

@property (weak, nonatomic) IBOutlet UIButton *goButton;

- (IBAction)pushedGo:(id)sender;
- (void)handleNowPlayingItemChanged:(id)notification;
- (void)handlePlaybackStateChanged:(id)notification;

@end
```

Then, in the *ViewController.m* implementation file, add the following method. This will be called when the current item being played changes:

```
- (void)handleNowPlayingItemChanged:(id)notification {
    MPMusicPlayerController *musicPlayer =
        [MPMusicPlayerController applicationMusicPlayer];
    MPMediaItem *currentItem = [musicPlayer nowPlayingItem]; ❶
    NSLog(@"%@", currentItem);
}
```

❶ Unusually, the MPMediaItem class has only one instance method: valueForProp erty:. This is because the class can wrap a number of media types, and each type can have a fairly wide range of metadata associated with it. You can find a full list of possible keys in the MPMediaItem class reference, but keys include MPMedia ItemPropertyTitle and MPMediaItemPropertyArtwork, among others.

While the second method handles changes in state, we can use this to update our user interface (e.g., changing the state of the Play and Stop buttons when the music ends):

```
- (void)handlePlaybackStateChanged:(id)notification {
    MPMusicPlayerController *musicPlayer =
        [MPMusicPlayerController applicationMusicPlayer];
    MPMusicPlaybackState playbackState = [musicPlayer playbackState];
    if (playbackState == MPMusicPlaybackStatePaused) {
        NSLog(@"Paused");

    } else if (playbackState == MPMusicPlaybackStatePlaying) {
        NSLog(@"Playing");

    } else if (playbackState == MPMusicPlaybackStateStopped) {
        NSLog(@"Stopped");

    }
}
```

Save your changes, and click the Run button in the Xcode toolbar to build and deploy your code onto your device. Once your application loads, tap the Go button to bring up the `MPMediaPickerController` again, select some songs, and tap the Done button in the navigation bar. Your music should start playing, and you should see log messages in the Debug area.

Using the Address Book

Just like the `MPMediaPickerController` class in the preceding section and the other classes we met earlier in the book, Apple has provided an `ABPeoplePickerNavigation Controller` and associated delegate protocol to allow you to both prompt the user for contact information and display contact information to the user. However, in this case, the framework it provides also allows your application to interact with person and group records directly.

 Once you reach the lower levels of the Address Book framework—for instance, dealing with individual person records—the interface presented by the framework is in C rather than Objective-C. This is especially obvious when dealing with the address book programmatically rather than interactively using the navigation controller.

Interactive People Picking

To illustrate how to use the `ABPeoplePickerNavigationController`, we're going to reuse the Prototype application code yet again. So, open the Finder and navigate to the location where you saved the *Prototype* project. Right-click on the folder containing the project files and select Duplicate; a folder called *Prototype copy* will be created containing a duplicate of the project. Rename the folder **Prototype5**, and just as we did before, prune the application down to the stub with the Go button and associated `pushedGo:` method that we'll use to trigger the display of our address book picker.

After you've done that, add the AddressBook and AddressBookUI frameworks into the project. Then click on the *ViewController.h* interface file to open it in the Xcode Editor. We need to declare the class as both an `ABPeoplePickerNavigationControllerDele gate` and a `UINavigationControllerDelegate`. Both declarations are necessary for the class to interact with the `ABPeoplePickerNavigationController`:

```
#import <UIKit/UIKit.h>
#import <AddressBook/AddressBook.h>
#import <AddressBookUI/AddressBookUI.h>

@interface ViewController : UIViewController
  <UINavigationControllerDelegate,ABPeoplePickerNavigationControllerDelegate>
```

```
@property (weak, nonatomic) IBOutlet UIButton *goButton;

-(IBAction) pushedGo:(id)sender;

@end
```

Now modify the pushedGo: method in the corresponding *ViewController.m* implementation file:

```
-(IBAction) pushedGo:(id)sender {
    ABPeoplePickerNavigationController *peoplePicker =
    [[ABPeoplePickerNavigationController alloc] init];
    peoplePicker.peoplePickerDelegate = self; ❶
    [self presentModalViewController:peoplePicker animated:YES];
}
```

❶   Unlike most Objective-C classes, the ABPeoplePickerNavigationController
     uses the peoplePickerDelegate property to specify its delegate rather than the
     more common delegate property.

Next, add the three mandatory ABPeoplePickerNavigationControllerDelegate
methods specified by the delegate protocol:

```
- (BOOL)peoplePickerNavigationController:
  (ABPeoplePickerNavigationController *)picker
  shouldContinueAfterSelectingPerson:(ABRecordRef)person ❶
{
    [self dismissModalViewControllerAnimated:YES];
    return NO;
}

- (BOOL)peoplePickerNavigationController:
  (ABPeoplePickerNavigationController *)picker
  shouldContinueAfterSelectingPerson:(ABRecordRef)person
  property:(ABPropertyID)property
  identifier:(ABMultiValueIdentifier)identifier ❷
{
    return NO;
}

- (void)peoplePickerNavigationControllerDidCancel:
  (ABPeoplePickerNavigationController *)picker ❸
{
    [self dismissModalViewControllerAnimated:YES];
}
```

❶   If this method returns YES, the picker will continue after the user selects a name
     from the address book, displaying the person's details. If the method returns NO,
     the picker will not continue. If you intend to return NO, you should also dismiss
     the view controller.

❷   This method lets you decide whether the picker should continue after the user selects a name from the address book. The address record is then displayed to the user. If this method returns YES, the picker will continue after the user selects a property (e.g., a mobile phone number, fax number). If the method returns NO, the picker will not continue. If you intend to return NO, you should also dismiss the view controller.

❸   This method is called when the user taps the Cancel button in the navigation bar of the picker interface.

We've reached a point where you can compile and check the code, but remember that you should also add the AddressBook and AddressBookUI frameworks to the project before clicking the Run button in the Xcode toolbar.

When you do so, you should see the familiar gray screen with the Go button as shown in Figure 12-16; click it and you'll be presented with a view of the address book. Selecting a name in the address book will dismiss the picker view and return you directly to the main gray screen.

The picker is displayed, but even if the user selects a name from the list, we don't do anything with the returned record. Let's add some additional code to the peoplePick erNavigationController:shouldContinueAfterSelectingPerson: method to fix that omission:

```
- (BOOL)peoplePickerNavigationController:
    (ABPeoplePickerNavigationController *)pickershouldContinueAfterSelectingPerson:
    (ABRecordRef)person  {

    NSString* name =
      (__bridge_transfer NSString *)ABRecordCopyCompositeName(person); ❶

    ABMutableMultiValueRef phones =
      ABRecordCopyValue(person, kABPersonPhoneProperty);
    NSArray *numbers =
      (__bridge_transfer NSArray *)ABMultiValueCopyArrayOfAllValues(phones);

    ABMutableMultiValueRef emails =
        ABRecordCopyValue(person, kABPersonEmailProperty);
    NSString *addresses =
      (__bridge_transfer NSString *)ABMultiValueCopyArrayOfAllValues(emails);

    NSString *note =
      (__bridge_transfer NSString *)
      ABRecordCopyValue(person, kABPersonNoteProperty);

    NSLog( @"name = %@, numbers = %@, email = %@, note = %@",
          name, numbers, addresses, note );

    [self dismissModalViewControllerAnimated:YES];
```

```
        return NO;
    }
```

❶ The `ABRecordCopyCompositeName()` method returns a human-readable name
    for the record. The `__bridge_transfer` annotation moves the value into ARC
    and *transfers ownership*. It tells ARC that this object is already retained, and that
    ARC doesn't need to retain it again.

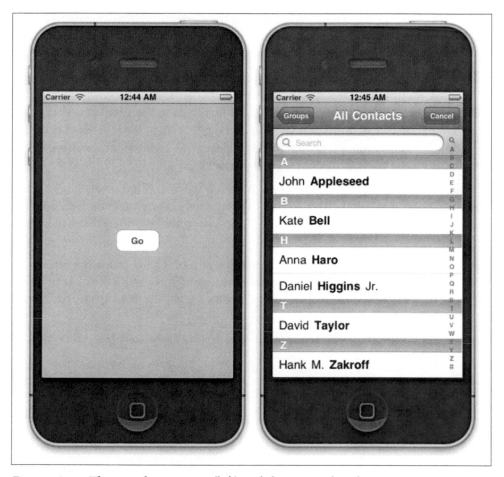

*Figure 12-16. The initial main view (left) and the ABPeoplePickerNavigationController
(right)*

There are two basic types of properties: single-value and multivalue. Single-value properties contain data that can have only a single value, such as a person's name. Multivalue
properties contain data that can have multiple values, such as a person's phone number.

You can see from the preceding code that single-value and multivalue properties are handled slightly differently.

 You can find a full list of the different properties available in an address book record in the ABPerson class documentation.

Make sure you've saved your changes and click the Run button in the Xcode toolbar to compile and deploy your application into iPhone Simulator. When the application launches, click the Go button and then select a name from the list. You should see the output in your Debug area.

What if we want to retrieve a specific phone number from the list? It's easier to let the user select the phone number they need, and that's where the peoplePickerNaviga tionController:shouldContinueAfterSelectingPerson:property:identifier: method would come into play (we returned NO from this earlier in this section, so this example does not allow the user to select a number).

A multivalue property is a list of values, but each value also has a text label and an identifier associated with it. This second delegate method provides you with both the property and the identifier for the value (i.e., a specific phone number) that is of interest to the user.

However, if you know which property value you're looking for inside the multivalue property, you can programmatically retrieve the identifier for that value. For example, here's how you'd select the mobile phone number from the list of returned phone numbers:

```
ABMultiValueRef phones = ABRecordCopyValue(person, kABPersonPhoneProperty);

ABMultiValueIdentifier identifier;
for( int i = 0; i < numbers.count; i++ ) {
    if( CFStringCompare( ABMultiValueCopyLabelAtIndex(phones, i),
        kABPersonPhoneMobileLabel, 1 ) == 0 ) {
        identifier = ABMultiValueGetIdentifierAtIndex(phones, i);
    }
}
```

You can then retrieve the mobile phone number at any time by using the identifier:

```
NSString *mobile =
  (__bridge_transfer NSString *)
  ABMultiValueCopyValueAtIndex(phones,
    ABMultiValueGetIndexForIdentifier(phones, identifier));
NSLog(@"Mobile = %@", mobile);
```

Programmatic People Picking

You do not have to use the `ABPeoplePickerNavigationController` to access the address book; you can access it directly, as shown here:

```
ABAddressBookRef addressBook = ABAddressBookCreate();
CFArrayRef allPeople = ABAddressBookCopyArrayOfAllPeople(addressBook);

for (int i = 0; i < ABAddressBookGetPersonCount(addressBook); i++) {
    ABRecordRef ref = CFArrayGetValueAtIndex(allPeople, i);
    NSString *contact =
        (__bridge_transfer NSString *)ABRecordCopyCompositeName(ref);
    NSLog( @"%@", contact );
}
```

The preceding code will instantiate a copy of the address book, retrieve references to all of the records, and then iterate through the array of records. Then, in the same way we dealt with records after interactively retrieving them with the picker controller, we print the full name of each contact to the Debug console.

Sending Text Messages

Analogously to the `MFMailComposeViewController` class we talked about in Chapter 7, the `MFMessageComposeViewController` from the MessageUI framework (you'll need to import *MessageUI/MessageUI.h* for this to work) allows you to compose and send text messages:

```
MFMessageComposeViewController *controller =
    [[MFMessageComposeViewController alloc] init];
if([MFMessageComposeViewController canSendText]) { ❶
    controller.body = @"Hello world";
    controller.recipients = [NSArray arrayWithObjects:@"12345678", nil];
    controller.messageComposeDelegate = self;
    [self presentModalViewController:controller animated:YES];
}
```

❶ Always call this method before attempting to present the message compose view controller.

In your header file, make your view controller an `MFMessageComposeViewController` `Delegate` and a `UINavigationControllerDelegate` and implement the following callback:

```
- (void)messageComposeViewController:(MFMessageComposeViewController *)controller
            didFinishWithResult:(MessageComposeResult)result {
    switch (result) {
        case MessageComposeResultCancelled:
            NSLog(@"Cancelled");
            break;
```

```
        case MessageComposeResultFailed:
            NSLog(@"Failed");
            break;
        case MessageComposeResultSent:
            break;
        default:
            break;
    }
    [self dismissViewControllerAnimated:YES completion:nil];
}
```

which we use to dismiss the modal view controller.

 The MFMessageComposeViewController does not currently support sending multimedia messages.

CHAPTER 13

Distributing Your Application

At this point, you have several applications that are almost ready to distribute, and perhaps you have ideas for your own applications and you want to start writing your first application and publish it to the App Store. However, before you can do that, you have to do some more housekeeping.

Adding Missing Features

Two things have been missing from your iOS applications, the first being the lack of a custom icon. This is crucial for the marketing of your application; you need to bring your application design together to present it to users. When a user scrolls through a long list of possible applications on the App Store, applications with strong icon design stand out. But remember that the user has to look at your application's icon every time he looks at the Home screen. The icon has to be distinctive to stand out, but it also has to be attractive so that the user is willing to keep your application around. I've uninstalled otherwise good applications because I couldn't put up with their icons, and I'm not alone.

Adding an Icon

The standard iPhone Home screen icon (*Icon.png*) used for your application is 57×57 pixel square in PNG format with no transparency or layers at 72 dpi. In addition to this, you can provide a 114×114 pixel high-resolution (*Icon@2x.png*) icon in the same format that will be used when the application is running hardware with a Retina display. If you write an application for the iPad, the Home screen icon (*Icon~ipad.png*) should be 72×72 pixels. If you are building a universal application intended to run on both the iPhone and the iPad, you should provide icons in all three sizes.

In general, applications should include two separate files for each image resource. One file provides a standard-resolution version of a given image, and the second provides a high-resolution version of the same image intended for Retina displays.

The naming conventions for each pair of image files is **<file><device_modifier>.<file_extension>** for standard resolution and **<file>@2x<device_modifier>.<file_extension>** for the high resolution version.

The **<file>** and **<file_extension>** portions of each name specify the usual name and extension for the file. The **<device_modifier>** portion is optional and contains either the string *~ipad* or \ *~iphone*. You include one of these modifiers when you want to specify different versions of an image for iPad and iPhone.

You also must provide Apple with a 512×512-pixel version of your application icon for display on the App Store (*iTunesArtwork* with no extension; you will need to provide this when you upload your app). This larger image must be in TIFF or JPEG format, and again it must have no transparency or layers.

It's sensible to design your icon in 512×512 pixels and scale it down to the 57×57-pixel version supplied inside your application's bundle. Doing things the other way around usually means that an unattractive and often pixelated icon is shown on the App Store.

You can also provide a small icon, such as a 29×29-pixel PNG file, in your application bundle called *Icon-Small.png* along with a corresponding 58×58-pixel high-resolution image called *Icon-Small@2x.png*. Spotlight will use this icon on the device when the application name matches a term in the search query. Additionally, if your application includes a Settings Bundle (see the previous chapter for more on Settings Bundles), this icon is displayed next to your application's name in the Settings application. If you do not provide this icon, your 57×57-pixel image is automatically scaled and used instead.

Table 13-1 details the different icon sizes that you may need to deal with when building an iOS application.

Table 13-1. Custom icons and images

Description	Status	Size (width×height pixels)		
		iPhone		iPad
		Standard	Retina	
Application icon	Required	57×57	114×114	72×72
App Store icon	Required	512×512		
Small icon	Recommended	29×29	58×58	50×50 (Spotlight)
				29×29 (Settings)
Document icon	Optional	22×29	44×58	64×64
				320×320
Toolbar and navigation bar icon	If needed	20×20	40×40	20×20
Tab bar icon	If needed	30×30	60×60	30×30
Newstand icon	Newstand Apps	At least 512 pixels on the longest edge		
Launch image	Required	320×480	640×960	768×1004 (portrait)
				1024×748 (landscape)

Both the iPhone and the iTunes Store will, by default, apply some visual effects to the icon you provide. They will round the corners, and add both drop shadows and reflected shine.

You can prevent iTunes from adding visual effects by setting the "Icon already includes glass and bevel effects" flag (UIPrerenderedIcon) inside the application's *Info.plist* file. To do so, open the *<ApplicationName>-Info.plist* file for your project in the editor. Open the "Icons (iOS 5)" group and expand the Primary Icon entry and select "Icon already includes gloss and bevel effects," as shown in Figure 13-1. Set this to YES to turn off the default visual effects added by both the App Store and the device.

Let's generate an icon for the City Guide application we built in Chapter 5. Figure 13-2 shows a sample image from the Tango Desktop Project, which was released into the public domain and is available from Wikimedia Commons (*http://commons.wikime dia.org*). You can find many public domain images at Wikimedia Commons. It's advisable for you to make modifications to the images you find there to avoid possible confusion—because the images are public domain, other people may use them in their own applications.

Figure 13-1. Adding the UIPrerenderedIcon flag to our application's Info.plist

Figure 13-2. A simple icon for our City Guide application

 You can download the icon shown in Figure 13-2 from Wikimedia Commons (*http://commons.wikimedia.org/wiki/File:Applications-internet.svg*) (either right-click or Control-click the link labeled *Applications-internet.svg* and choose Save Linked File). Open it in an image editor such as Adobe Illustrator or the free and open source Inkscape (*http://inkscape.org*).

Resize the file to 114×114 pixels and save it as a PNG file named *Icon@2x.png*. Then resize it again to 57×57 pixels and save it *Icon.png*. (If you are using Inkscape, you will need to use File→Export Bitmap, choose the Page option, and set the width and height to 57 before you click Export.)

Next, open the City Guide application in Xcode.

 You might want to make a copy of the CityGuide code, as we've done in the past, before modifying it.

Drag and drop the *Icon.png* file (and *Icon@2x.png* files) into App Icons placeholders by clicking on the Project icon (the blue icon at the top of the Project Navigator panel) and dragging and dropping the files into the App Icons section (see Figure 13-3).

Figure 13-3. Dragging and dropping the icon file into your project

If you deploy the application by clicking the Run button in the Xcode toolbar, the application will start inside iPhone Simulator. If you quit the application by clicking the Home button, you will see that it now has a shiny new icon, as shown in Figure 13-4.

Figure 13-4. The City Guide application with its new icon

Adding a Launch Image

One of the ways in which iOS devices cheat is by providing *launch images*. A launch image is immediately displayed on the screen when the application is started before the UI is displayed. Your application displays the launch image file while loading, which means there are no more blank screens while the application loads.

One change that occurred with the arrival of the iPhone 5, with a screen whose aspect ratio was different than previous iPhone models, was that the existence of an appropriate launch image was used to determine whether the application was "iPhone 5 Ready." As well as the normal *Default.png* and *Default@2x.png* images you should now add a *Default-568h@2x.png* image to your project.

Because of this change new projects created with recent Xcode revisions will have black launch images, whereas before this change projects were created without launch images.

Let's add one of these to the City Guide application. Build and deploy the City Guide application onto your iPhone or iPod touch. While your device is still connected and your application is still running, open the Organizer window by going to Window→Organizer in the Xcode menu bar. Go to the Devices tab of the Organizer window and you should see a glowing green dot next to your device. Select your device, and then the Screenshots item in the menu, and click the New Screenshot button. Xcode will take a screen capture from your application, as shown in Figure 13-5.

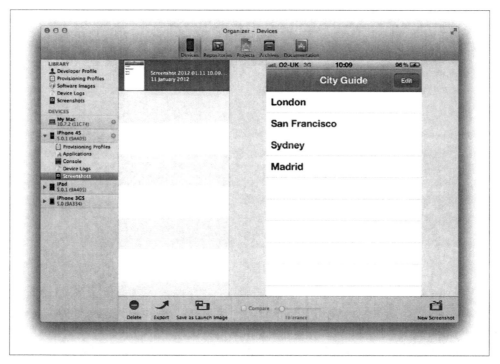

Figure 13-5. The Xcode Organizer window with a screen capture of the City Guide application's UI

Click the Save As Launch Image button, and you'll be presented with a drop-down asking you to save the image into your project (see Figure 13-6).

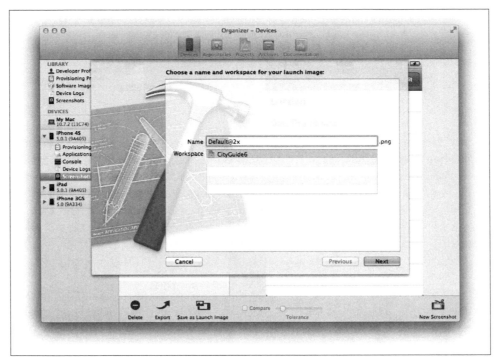

Figure 13-6. Saving the new Launch Image into the Xcode project

If you took the image on a standard-resolution iPhone, the image will be named *Default.png*, and on a high-resolution device, it'll be *Default@2x.png*. Finally, if you took the image on an 4-inch Retina device (e.g. iPhone 5) it'll be *Default-568h@2x.png*. Here, I took the screenshot using an iPhone 4S, so a high-resolution (640×960 pixel) image was generated.

If you now click on the Project icon at the top, you'll see it appears in the project summary, replacing the previous black launch image.

However, the other resolution version of the image isn't generated automatically from your initial version. You'll have to copy and resize your high-resolution image by hand.

To do this, right-click on the *Default@2x.png* image file in Xcode and select Show in Finder. This will open the Finder and highlight the image in your project folder. You can now open this image in your preferred image editor and make any changes you want. Remember, you need to save it as a single-layer PNG file without transparency; otherwise, your application will have problems loading the file at launch.

Once you've generated the lower resolution image (320×480 pixels), and an image for the 4-inch Retina device, you can drag and drop it into the project summary as we did for the icons earlier in the chapter.

If you rebuild the City Guide application at this point and redeploy it onto your device, the application will (at least apparently) now load instantly.

Although many developers have chosen to use the launch image as a splash screen, that's not how Apple intended for this image to be used. Instead, it is intended to improve the user experience. Its presence adds to the user's perception that your application is quick to load and immediately ready for use when it does load.

Because this is a mobile platform, users will switch between applications frequently. Even more than on the Web, where users' attention spans are notoriously short, on a mobile device, users will become frustrated with applications that take a long time to launch (or shut down). You need to work to keep the launch time of your application to a minimum, and use the launch image to make a subtle transition into your application.

The launch image should be identical to the first screen of your application. However, since this is an image, the content is static, so you should not include any interface elements that may change from launch to launch. Therefore, avoid displaying elements that might look different between the launch image and your first screen. For instance, the *Default.png* image file we generated for our City Guide application includes a list of cities, but what happens if the user adds more cities? The list will change. We can't update the list of cities in the launch image, so it's probably best to remove them, leaving only the table view. This also has the benefit of hinting to the user that she can't interact with the app just yet.

Most applications' launch images will be very plain; this is not a problem, as they are there solely to convince your users that your application is quick to load. If you interrupt the user experience with a splash screen, your users might ask themselves why you're wasting their time displaying such a screen, and why you don't just get on with it and load the application. If you make use of the launch image correctly, they'll know that you're doing your best to give them a seamless experience.

Changing the Display Name

The name displayed beneath your application icon on the iPhone Home screen is, by default, the name of your Xcode project. However, only a limited number of characters are displayed before an ellipsis is inserted and your application name is truncated. This is fairly messy, and generally users don't like it. Fortunately, you can change your application's display name by editing the "Bundle display name" field in the application's *Info.plist* file.

If you look at our City Guide application, you'll notice that the display name is the same as our project name: CityGuide. While the name is not long enough to be truncated when displayed on the iPhone's Home screen, we might want it to be displayed as City Guide instead. Let's make that change now.

Open the *CityGuide* project in Xcode and click on the *CityGuide-Info.plist* file to open it in the Xcode Editor. Double-click on the Value field in the "Bundle display name" field and change the ${PRODUCT_NAME} macro to City Guide, as shown in Figure 13-7.

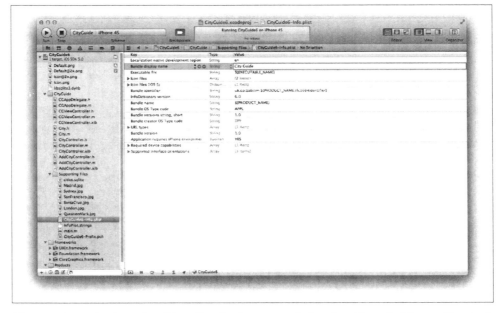

Figure 13-7. Setting the "Bundle display name" in the City Guide application's Info.plist file

If you rebuild the application and deploy it in iPhone Simulator, you'll notice that the name displayed below the City Guide application icon has changed from CityGuide6 to City Guide.

Enabling Rotation

Enabling and conversely disallowing rotations between Portrait and Landscape mode is actually amazingly easy. We can do it from the project summary page (see Figure 13-8). Editing this will automatically edit our *Info.plist* file to enable allowed orientations.

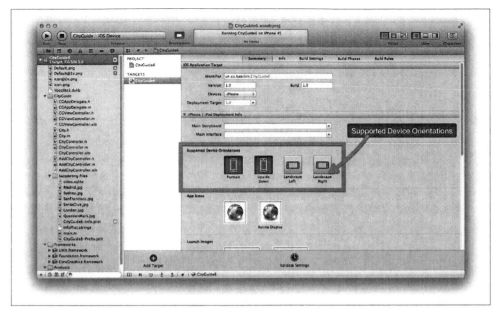

Figure 13-8. Setting allowed rotations

Additionally, in your view controller class, add the following method:

```
- (BOOL)shouldAutorotateToInterfaceOrientation:
    (UIInterfaceOrientation)interfaceOrientation {
    // Return YES for all supported orientations
    return YES;
}
```

 If you have multiple view controller classes, you should add this method to each of them.

If you allow rotations into landscape (left and right) and then rebuild your application and rotate your device, or if running in the Simulator if you select Hardware→Rotate Left or Hardware→Rotate from the menu, your UI will rotate into landscape mode.

 Although the shouldAutorotateToInterfaceOrientation: method is called in a timely fashion under some versions of the SDK, this is not always the case. To ensure that you are (reliably) notified of changes in the device orientation, you should register for notification of orientation change messages.

However, when the interface rotates, the UI elements will also squash and stretch into the new orientation. You need to make sure that the individual UI elements can cope with their new sizes elegantly. You can do that in one of two ways:

- Be careful when using the Size Inspector tab in the Utilities panel in Interface Builder to make sure they stretch in the correct fashion. The easiest way to do this is to make use of the Autosizing, Alignment, and Placement sections in the Size tab.

- Register for orientation change notifications and dynamically adapt your UI based on those events. For example, the built-in Calculator application has a different UI in portrait and landscape modes.

You can start generating orientation change notifications by calling this method of the `UIDevice` class (in the `viewDidLoad:` method of your view controller class):

```
[[UIDevice currentDevice] beginGeneratingDeviceOrientationNotifications];
```

When you are no longer concerned about orientation changes, you stop such notifications by calling this method:

```
[[UIDevice currentDevice] endGeneratingDeviceOrientationNotifications];
```

After starting notifications, you must also register your class to receive such messages using the `NSNotificationCenter` class:

```
NSNotificationCenter *notificationCenter = [NSNotificationCenter defaultCenter];
[notificationCenter addObserver:self
                    selector:@selector(handlerMethod:)
                    name:@"UIDeviceOrientationDidChangeNotification"
                    object:nil];
```

This would invoke the `handlerMethod:` selector (elsewhere in your view controller) in the current class when such a message was received:

```
-(void) handlerMethod:(NSNotification *)note {

    /* Deal with rotation of your UI here */
        NSLog(@"Rotating")
}
```

Building and Signing

The certificates we generated in Chapter 2 were intended only for development. If you want to distribute your application to end users, you'll need to return to the iOS Provisioning Portal, generate a different set of profiles, and rebuild your application, signing it this time with your new distribution profile rather than the development profile you have used thus far.

The different provisioning profiles are used for different purposes. The development profile you generated in Chapter 2 is intended for development and your own devices. The ad hoc distribution profile is for alpha and beta testing, while the App Store distribution profile is intended for distributing your final build to the iTunes App Store.

Ad Hoc Distribution

Ad hoc builds of your application are used to distribute your application outside your own development environment, and are intended to allow you to distribute your application to beta testers and for Enterprise distribution. In the same way you registered your iOS device for development, you must register all of the devices onto which you intend to distribute your application using an ad hoc build. You can register up to 100 devices per year in the iOS Provisioning Portal. This is a firm limit; deleting already registered devices will not allow you to add further devices.

Normally, when you distribute applications via the ad hoc method, no application artwork is displayed when the user looks at your application inside the iTunes interface. However, if you place a copy of the 512×512-pixel PNG of your icon in your application bundle and name it *iTunesArtwork* without any file extension, this will be used by iTunes.

To deploy your application to your users via the ad hoc method, you need to create a *distribution certificate*, register any devices you plan to use, and create an *ad hoc provisioning profile* in the iPhone Developer Program Portal.

Obtaining a distribution certificate

Just as in Chapter 2 when we dealt with development, the first thing you need is a distribution certificate, and to obtain that, you need to generate a certificate-signing request (CSR) using the Keychain Access application:

1. As you did for the CSR you generated for the development certificate [see "Creating a Development Certificate" (page 17) in Chapter 2], launch the Keychain Access application.

2. Select Keychain Access→Preferences from the menu. Go to the Certificates Preference pane to confirm that the Online Certificate Status Protocol (OCSP) and Certificate Revocation List (CRL) options are turned off.

3. Select Keychain Access→Certificate Assistant→Request a Certificate from a Certificate Authority from the Keychain Access menu, and enter the email address you selected as your Apple ID during the sign-up process and your name. Click the

"Saved to disk" radio button, check the "Let me specify key pair information" checkbox, and click Continue. You'll be prompted for a filename for your certificate request.

4. Accept the defaults (a key size of 2,048 bits using the RSA algorithm) and click Continue.

The application will proceed to generate a CSR file and save it to disk.

In the iOS Developer Center (sign in here (*http://developer.apple.com/ios*) and look for the iOS Provisioning Portal link on the right), click on the Certificates link in the left-hand menu and then in the Distribution tab, click Request Certificate (if you already have a certificate, this option will be unavailable as you need only one). Follow the instructions that appear, and upload your CSR to the portal when asked.

If you joined the development program as an individual, you need to approve the signing request (in the Distribution tab of the Certificates section of the portal) before proceeding to download the new certificate. If you are part of a team, the nominated development team administrator needs to do this. After the request is approved, you may need to click on the Distribution tab to refresh the page. When you see a Download button, click it to save the certificate to disk.

Once the certificate file has downloaded, double-click it to install it into your Mac OS X login keychain, as shown in Figure 13-9.

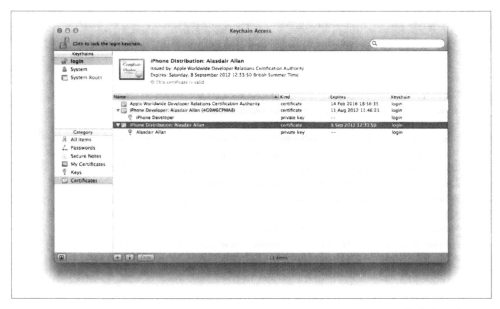

Figure 13-9. The Keychain Access application showing the newly installed distribution certificate needed by Xcode for ad hoc or App Store distribution

Registering devices

Before you create the provisioning profile, you'll need to register the devices you want the profile to support. To do this, you'll need the unique device identifier (UDID) of each of these devices. Once you have the device identifiers, you need to add your users' devices in the same way you added your own development device in "Getting the UDID of Your Development Device" (page 20) in Chapter 2.

In the iOS Provisioning Portal, click Devices, select the Manage tab, and click Add Devices. Enter a device name in the appropriate box and the UDID in the box labeled Device ID, and click the Submit button. (You can click the + button to add more rows so that you can add several devices at once.) You have now registered the device; you need to do this for all of the devices to which you intend to distribute ad hoc builds.

Creating a provisioning profile

Now you're ready to create a mobile provisioning profile. Go to the Provisioning section of the iOS Provisioning Portal, select the Distribution tab, and click New Profile.

Enter a profile name; you may be creating a number of ad hoc profiles, so naming your first distribution profile Ad-hoc Distribution Profile probably isn't a great idea. You may want to name it after the application you're distributing, so perhaps City Guide Beta Test Profile would be a good choice for distributing a beta of the City Guide application to testers.

Next, select the App ID you used for the application you're going to distribute (Chapter 2), and then select all of the devices for which this profile will be valid, as shown in Figure 13-10.

Click Submit to generate the new mobile provisioning profile that you'll use to distribute the application to your beta testers. The status will appear as pending; click the Distribution tab to reload it until it is no longer pending. When the profile is ready, click the Download button and download the provisioning profile to your Mac. Now drag the provisioning file onto the Xcode icon in the dock to make it available to the development environment.

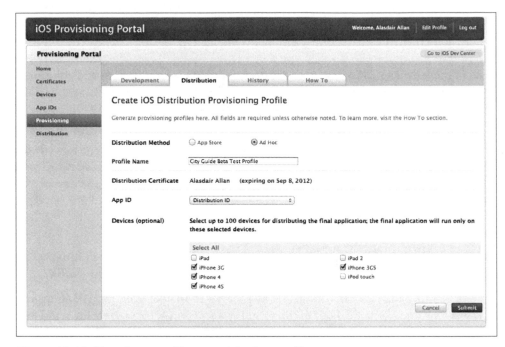

Figure 13-10. Creating an ad hoc provisioning profile

Building your application for ad hoc distribution

Let's make an ad hoc build of the City Guide application. Open your project in Xcode and make sure that "iOS Device" is selected as the Scheme in the Xcode toolbar; then, before building your application, open the *CityGuide-Info.plist* file and make sure the Bundle Identifier in your *Info.plist* file matches the one used to create the ad hoc mobile provisioning profile. See "Putting the Application on Your iPhone" (page 51) in Chapter 3 if you're unsure about this part. If you've been able to deploy your application onto your iPhone or iPod touch and you generated a wildcard app ID earlier, you shouldn't have to change anything.

Once you've checked that, select Product→Archive from the Xcode menu to build your application. The Organizer window should open automatically to the Archives tab (see Figure 13-11). If not, open it by selecting Window→Organizer (⇧⌘2) from the Xcode menu.

Click the Share button and you should see something like Figure 13-12.

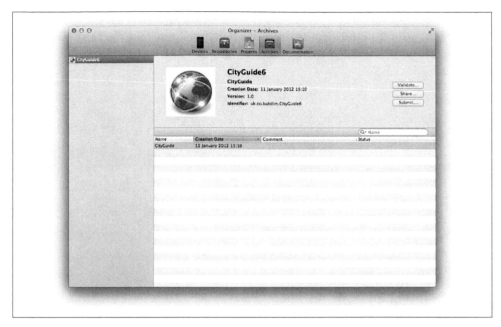

Figure 13-11. The Archive tab in the Xcode Organizer Window

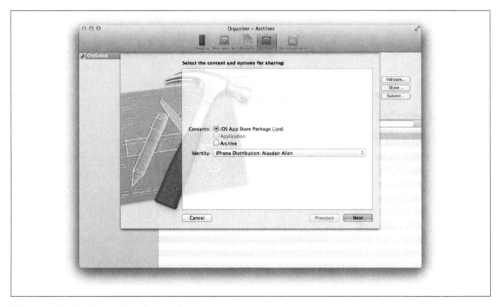

Figure 13-12. Creating the package

Make sure "iOS App Store Package (.ipa)" is selected and then choose your ad hoc provisioning profile in the Identity drop-down menu. Then click the Next button and save your store package on the Desktop (see Figure 13-13).

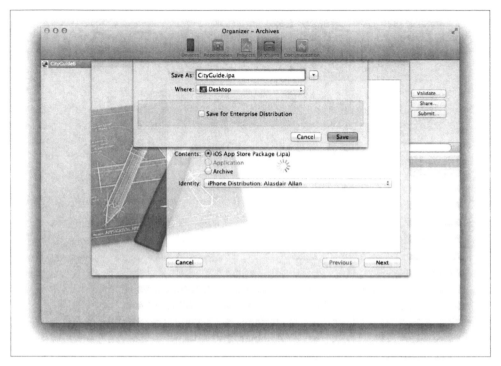

Figure 13-13. The Archive tab in the Xcode Organizer window

Distributing an ad hoc build

After you've saved your package file, drag and drop the package into iTunes and plug your device into your Mac. So long as the UDID of the device was specified as part of the ad hoc profile (see Figure 13-10), the app should sync to your iPhone or iPad like a normal application.

Similarly, to distribute the device to beta testers, ensure that their UDID is included in the profile and then drag and drop the *.ipa* file into an email.

There are more sophisticated ways to distribute ad hoc builds. For instance, you can do over-the-air beta distribution; while this has been available for some time, there are now off-the-shelf options for doing web distributions. Both open source projects such as BetaBuilder for iOS (*http://www.hanchorllc.com/betabuilder-for-ios/*), and commercial services such as TestFlight (*https://testflightapp.com/*), simplify the process.

Developer-to-Developer Distribution

Apple intended ad hoc distribution to be a way for you to distribute your software to beta testers. However, developers have used it extensively for other purposes, including bypassing the App Store entirely and selling directly to the consumer (a somewhat torturous process).

If your intended end user is another developer, you can vastly simplify the ad hoc distribution process. Just create a normal development build, as though you were going to deploy the code to your own device, and send a copy of the binary to your colleague. He can then re-sign the binary with his own developer certificate using the Xcode command line `codesign` utility:

```
#! /bin/bash
export CODESIGN_ALLOCATE=/usr/bin/codesign_allocate
codesign -f -s "iPhone Developer" $1.app
```

 Before running this script, if you have not already done so, you should install the Xcode Command Line Tools. To do so, open the Xcode preferences, and go to the Downloads tab, and click the Install button next to the tools in the Components panel. This will install copies of the core command-line tools and headers into the system folders.

 The way Xcode was distributed changed between version 4.2 and 4.3. If you have Xcode 4.2 installed, then the above snippet won't work for you, as the command-line tools will be installed into the */Developer* directory tree instead of into the system folders. Instead, use this snippet:

```
#! /bin/bash
export CODESIGN_ALLOCATE=/Developer/Platforms/iPhoneOS.platform\
/Developer/usr/bin/codesign_allocate
codesign -f -s "iPhone Developer" $1.app
```

Once he has re-signed the binary, he can use the Xcode Organizer window to install it onto his device. In the Applications section of the Summary tab, he should click the + symbol and select the binary. Xcode will then install it onto the appropriate iOS device.

App Store Distribution

Making a build of your application to submit to the App Store is similar to making an ad hoc build, and you'll use the same distribution certificate you created for the ad hoc build earlier in the chapter. However, you have to return to the iOS Provisioning Portal to generate a new distribution provisioning profile.

Open the iOS Provisioning Portal in a browser (start here (*http://developer.apple.com/ ios/*) and follow the links to the iOS Provisioning Portal), and in the Provisioning section, select the Distribution tab and click New Profile. Enter a profile name; you'll need only one App Store profile, so unlike the ad hoc profile, a good choice might be App Store Distribution Profile.

Finally, select the App ID you used for the application you're going to distribute; since this is an App Store provisioning profile, there is no need to select devices this time around.

 Most developers use one (wildcarded) App ID for all of their applications [see "Putting the Application on Your iPhone" (page 51) in Chapter 3]. The only reason you would need to use a separate profile for your application is if it makes use of In-App Purchase, Push Notifications, or Game Center.

Click Submit to generate the new mobile provisioning profile. The status will appear as pending; click the Distribution tab to reload it until it is no longer pending. When the profile is ready, click the Download button and download the provisioning profile to your Mac. Drag the provisioning file onto the Xcode icon in the dock to make it available to the development environment.

Submitting to the App Store

 While I'm going to walk you through building a version of the City Guide application that is ready to be submitted to the App Store, you should not actually submit it. The App Store might start to look a bit odd if every reader of this book did that.

Let's make an App Store build of our City Guide application. Before we build our application for distribution, we first have to create the application record in iTunes Connect.

Open iTunes Connect in a browser by going here (*https://itunesconnect.apple.com/*). You should see something like Figure 13-14.

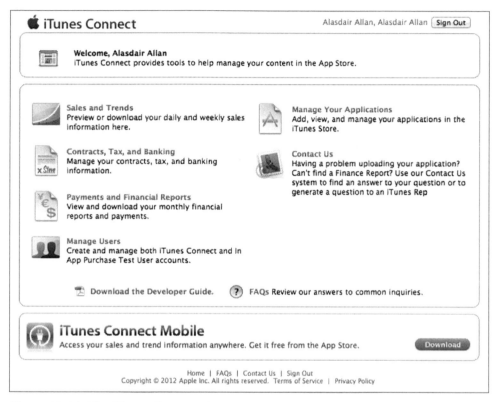

Figure 13-14. The iTunes Connect site

 If this is the first time you've submitted an application to iTunes Connect, you'll be asked what primary language you will be using to enter your applications to the store. You'll then be asked what company or developer name you want displayed on the App Store for all your applications. Both your primary language and your company name cannot be changed, so choose carefully. You won't be asked these questions again the next time you submit an application to the store.

Click through on the Manage Your Applications link, click on the blue Add New App button (top left), and select an iOS application. You'll be prompted for the application name, a SKU number, and to select the Bundle ID of your application along with suffix if you are using a wildcard ID (see Figure 13-15).

 The SKU (or stock-keeping unit) number must be a unique alphanumeric identifier that you choose for this product. Bear in mind that this SKU cannot be changed at any point in the future, even with the upload of a new binary (and version) of the application, so while you can choose just about anything, it should be fairly descriptive but not version-specific.

The application display name and description will appear as is on the iTunes App Store. You do not have to use the same name for the application as you used for your project binary or bundle display name. However, it should be related to the display name, or this might form grounds for rejection by the review team.

Figure 13-15. Adding a new app to iTunes Connect

Click Continue, and you will be asked to set the price tier (see Figure 13-16) and availability date for your application. Your application will be made available on the store on this date, or whenever it leaves the review process and is approved by the App Store review team, whichever is later.

The availability date, like all application metadata, applies to all versions of your application. If you later upload an update for your application and change the availability date to a date in the future, your current version will be removed from the App Store until that date arrives.

Figure 13-16. Selecting availability and pricing tier

Click Continue, and you'll be asked to describe your application (see Figure 13-17). Most of this is self-explanatory, but if you have any problems, click the question mark to the right of each entry and some explanatory text will be displayed in a pop-up.

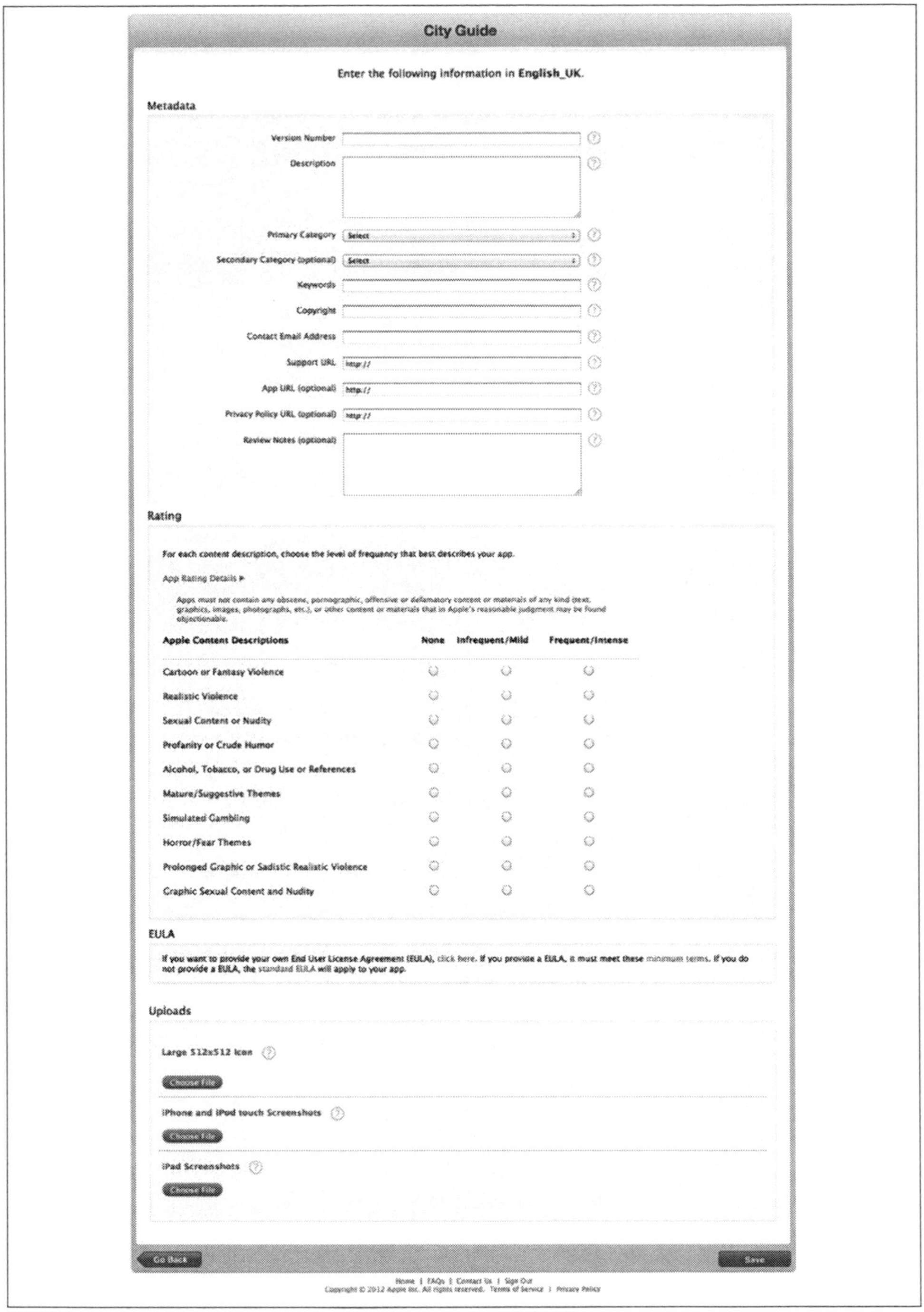

Figure 13-17. Describing the application

You should fill in all of the fields unless they are marked as being optional:

Version number
Provide the version number of the application. This must be 1.0 or above. Submitting apps to the store with a version number less than 1.0 is grounds for rejection.

Application description
You should try to keep your description fairly short so that your application screenshots will be "above the fold" (the part of the description the user will see without having to scroll) if the user is browsing the store from her mobile device.

Primary and secondary category
These are the App Store categories that best describe your application. You need only select the primary category.

Keywords
Application keywords are associated with the application binary and can be edited only when uploading a new binary, so think carefully about your choice of keywords for your application. Separate multiple keywords with commas, not spaces.

Contact email address
This is the email address that will be published to iTunes as the support address when your application is approved. It would be a sensible move to create a separate email address for each of your applications, rather than use a personal address. If your application becomes popular, you will receive a lot of email.

Support and Application URLs
Again, this is fairly self-explanatory. These are two URLs that can be identical; they link to support information about your application. Applications without associated URLs, or with URLs pointing to blank pages, will not be approved. Your support information should be in place before you upload your binary to iTunes Connect for review.

Review notes
If your application needs an account on an online service to be fully operative, supply an account name and password here. If you don't, the review team will summarily reject your application.

After entering this metadata, you'll be asked to rate your application under certain categories: Cartoon or Fantasy Violence; Realistic Violence; Sexual Content or Nudity; Profanity or Crude Humor; Alcohol, Tobacco, or Drug User or References; Mature/Suggestive Themes; Simulated Gambling; Horror/Fear Themes; Prolonged Graphic or Sadistic Realistic Violence; and Graphic Sexual Content and Nudity. This will generate your App Rating (4+, 9+, 12+, or 17+) that will allow users to filter your application using the parental controls inside iTunes. If you don't rate your application realistically, the review team may reject it during the review process.

Finally, you should upload the 512×512 pixel version of your icon intended for use in iTunes and, at the very least, one screenshot for use by the App Store. Click the Save button and you should be presented with something that looks a lot like Figure 13-18.

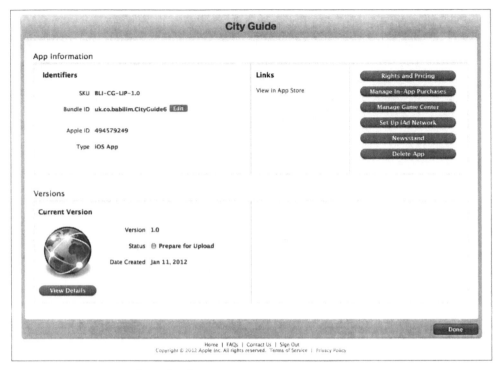

Figure 13-18. Prepare for upload

Click View Details to see the application summary screen. In the top right, you should see a bright blue Ready to Upload Binary button. Click on the button to tell iTunes Connect that you have a binary ready for upload.

You'll then be asked whether your application uses encryption (see Figure 13-19). If your application includes any encryption code, you may have to fill out some forms to comply with US commercial encryption export controls.

You'll then be returned to the summary screen; the Status of your application will now have changed from Prepare for Upload to Waiting for Upload. You should also receive an email notification, which is useful if you're working as part of a team (see Figure 13-20).

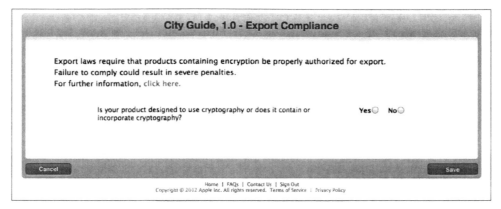

Figure 13-19. Prepare for upload

Figure 13-20. Email notification

We're ready to build our application and upload it to iTunes Connect.

Building Your Application for App Store Distribution

Open your project in Xcode and make sure that "iOS Device" is selected as the Scheme in the Xcode toolbar. Check that your code signing identity is correctly set for distribution (see Figure 13-21).

Figure 13-21. Checking the code signing identity

Then, in a similar fashion to how we made our ad hoc build in the previous section, select Product→Archive from the Xcode menu to build your application. The Organizer window should open automatically to the Archives tab as before, but if not, open it by selecting Window→Organizer (⇧⌘2) from the Xcode menu.

Click on the Validate button and you'll be asked to log in to iTunes Connect (see Figure 13-22). Xcode is going to validate your archive Bundle ID and other details against the details you provided to Apple in iTunes Connect. If they don't match, then validation will fail and you won't be able to upload your binary.

Enter your details and click on the Next button, you'll be presented with something a lot like Figure 13-23.

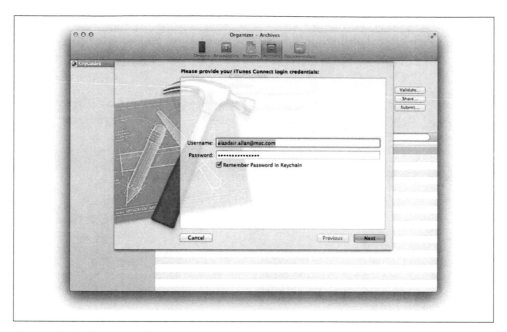

Figure 13-22. Log in to iTunes Connect

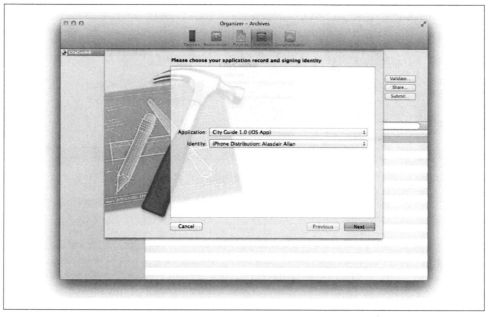

Figure 13-23. Choosing your application and identity

Choose your application from the drop-down, and select the signing identity we generated for App Store distribution (not the one we used for ad hoc—that isn't going to work).

 If you don't see the application, make sure you clicked on the Ready to Upload Binary button in iTunes Connect and that your application's status is Waiting For Upload.

If all goes well, you should see something much like Figure 13-24.

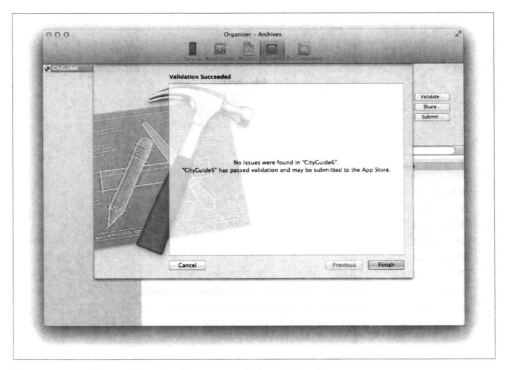

Figure 13-24. The application has successfully validated

 In the corner-case where you have never built the application for the device before, only for the simulator, make sure that you have selected Product→Build For→Build For Archiving from the Xcode menu before selecting Product→Archive. If you receive an error at this stage indicating a missing binary, this is probably what's happened.

Click Finish, and then on the Submit button. You'll be asked to sign into iTunes Connect one more time, and for validation, choose the application target and code signing identity. The application will then be uploaded directly to iTunes Connect. If you check on iTunes Connect, you should now see the application binary has been received (see Figure 13-25).

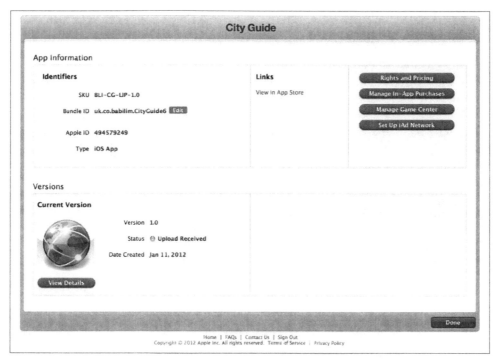

Figure 13-25. The application has been received by iTunes Connect

If you reload this page after a few minutes, you should see the status of your application change from Upload Received to Waiting for Review (see Figure 13-26).

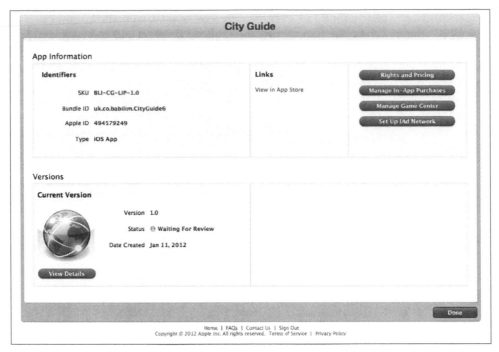

Figure 13-26. The application is Waiting for Review

Congratulations, your application is now in the queue for the review team.

 If you find a problem with your binary during the waiting period and need to upload a new version, click on View Details, then Binary Details, and then click on the Reject Binary button. The status of your application will change to Developer Rejected, and you can start the process again.

The App Store Resource Center

If you're confused about any aspect of distribution, you should make your way to the App Store Resource Center (*http://developer.apple.com/appstore/*). This site walks you through the process of preparing your application for submission, the App Store approval process itself, and how to manage your applications on the store once they're live.

Reasons for Rejection

The App Store review process is somewhat opaque, but generally, if your application is rejected, the review team will cite the specific section of the iOS Developer Program License Agreement that it violates in the rejection email. If you're careful, you can avoid most of the common pitfalls and save yourself, and the review team, a lot of time.

 Copies of the iOS Developer Program License Agreement—the agreement you signed with Apple to become an iOS developer—and the iOS Human Interface Guidelines are available for download from the App Store Resource Center in the App Store Approval Process section (*http://developer.apple.com/appstore*).

Some of the more common reasons for rejection concern the following:

Version number
Applications submitted with version numbers less than 1.0, or applications tagged as "beta" or "alpha," will be summarily rejected by the review team. Additionally, if there is any inconsistency in versioning—for instance, the version number in your application's About dialog does not match the version number in your *Info.plist* file (and the number you provided to iTunes Connect)—your application may be rejected.

Icons
The artwork for your 57×57-pixel icon must be identical to your 512×512 icon. Additionally, if you are uploading a free "lite" version of your application as well as a premium "pro" version, the application icons cannot be identical between the two versions.

Artwork
Using Apple's own graphics inside your application—for instance, logos or an image of an iOS device—is usually grounds for rejection.

Copyright material
Apple is extremely wary of allowing applications to make use of material (e.g., images, audio, and other media) that you do not have permission to use. Using material that might violate a trademark is similarly suspect.

Human Interface Guidelines
Violating the Human Interface Guidelines—for instance, using standard button icons for a nonstandard purpose, such as the Refresh, Organize, Trash, Reply, and Compose buttons—could be grounds for rejection.

Private frameworks

Applications published to the App Store are not allowed to link to private or third-party frameworks. Submitting applications for review that do link to such frameworks is an easy way to get your application rejected. Linking to third-party static libraries is a gray area, but is usually acceptable.

Existing functionality

Many applications have been rejected for duplicating existing functionality of a built-in app; applications that make extensive use of web browsers are particularly vulnerable to this accusation. Other obvious candidates are email clients and music player applications.

Table views

Improper handling of table view cells when the application has a table view in edit mode can be grounds for rejection, as can not deselecting table view cells appropriately after selecting them to perform some action.

Network reachability

Not testing for the presence of a network connection or not handling the loss of network connectivity correctly (and informing the user) is a common cause for rejection.

Bandwidth limitations

If your application makes use of large amounts of bandwidth, you need to make sure your current network connection is over the cellular network. Transferring large amounts of data over the cellular network can (sometimes) be grounds for rejection. So, if your application does that, you should disable, or throttle, data transfer when the device is on the cellular network.

Keyboard type

You should ensure that you are using the correct keyboard type when prompting for user input; using an inappropriate keyboard is usually grounds for rejection (e.g., using the keyboard designed to enter phone numbers for other purposes).

OS compatibility

If you claim that your application will run on OS 3.0 and later, you must ensure that it really does so. Apple will test your application with all of the versions of the OS between your minimum specified version and the current release. If the review team discovers that your application does not function correctly with a specific version of the OS, they will normally reject it. Unfortunately, it's fairly rare for them to tell you in which version of the OS the bug manifested. This can lead to the unfortunate situation where you cannot duplicate the bug since you and the reviewer are testing the application under different OS revisions.

Description

Do not include the price in your application description, as part of your icon, or anywhere in the UI. According to Apple, this may "potentially confuse users," as the text cannot be localized to all markets.

Crippled functionality

If you provide a free "lite" version of your application, it cannot have crippled functionality (e.g., obviously disabled buttons or menu items). It also cannot directly refer to the paid "pro" version of the application. Free or "lite" versions of an application are acceptable, but the application must be a fully functional application in itself and cannot reference features that are not implemented.

Minimal user functionality

If your application doesn't actually do very much, it might get rejected. However, there are numerous cases where applications that don't do very much have been accepted (e.g., flashlight applications).

Does not work as advertised

Applications that do not work as described in their application descriptions will be summarily rejected. You should therefore be careful when writing your application description when submitting your application to iTunes Connect.

CHAPTER 14

Going Further

We've managed to cover a lot of ground over the preceding 13 chapters, but there is still a lot more ground to go. While you should by now be confidently building solid applications for the iPhone, iPad, and iPod touch, there is still a lot to learn.

Cocoa and Objective-C

The Objective-C language has a number of powerful features, and the Cocoa framework that is layered on top of the language is extensive. I've obviously not had the time or space in this book to cover either one in the depth it really deserves.

If you intend to continue developing for the iPhone, you should consider reading further on Objective-C, especially if you're having difficulties with memory management or the Model-View-Controller pattern around which most iPhone application development revolves.

Apple provides some excellent tutorial material on its developer website, and that should certainly be your first port of call. I also recommend the books *Programming in Objective-C* by Stephen G. Kochan (Addison-Wesley) and *Cocoa and Objective-C: Up and Running* by Scott Stevenson (O'Reilly), for a more detailed look at the language. See also *Cocoa Design Patterns* by Erik M. Buck and Donald A. Yacktman (Addison-Wesley) for a detailed look at design patterns in Cocoa.

The iOS SDK

Predictably, I've focused on the parts of Cocoa and Objective-C that will be most helpful in allowing you to write your own applications for iOS. But even there I've left out a lot in an attempt to simplify and get you started quickly. A more in-depth look at the iOS SDK is available in *iOS SDK Development* (*http://pragprog.com/book/adios/ios-sdk-*

development) by Chris Adamson and Bill Dudney (Pragmatic Programmers), which covers many parts of the SDK that I've left out for brevity.

A good cookbook to help you solve specific problems is *The iOS 5 Developer's Cookbook: Core Concepts and Essential Recipes for iOS Programmers* by Erica Sadun (Addison-Wesley). Erica's book consists of an excellent collection of recipes that solve the vexing question: "How do I make my application do X, Y, or Z?" She provides some solid example code that you can lift off the page and use yourself, often without any modification, in your own applications. Alternatively, you might want to look at the *iOS 5 Programming Cookbook* by Vandad Nahavandipoor (O'Reilly).

Web Applications

This book looked at how to build native applications. As I mentioned in Chapter 1, there is an alternative: you can build your application as a web application, taking it entirely online and doing away with the native SDK altogether. However, many native iOS applications sit on a blurry line between the native and web worlds, wrapping custom content in a UIWebView inside the application, with much of the backend processing done "in the cloud." For instance, I know of several developers who are using Google App Engine to power their applications and store user data, with little or no number crunching actually going on in the iOS device. Knowing how to build web applications is a useful skill, even for a hardened Objective-C programmer building a native application.

If you're interested in building web applications for the iPhone, you should look at *Building iPhone Apps with HTML, CSS, and JavaScript* by Jonathan Stark (O'Reilly).

PhoneGap

PhoneGap (*http://www.phonegap.com/*), developed by Nitobi, is an open source development platform for building cross-platform mobile applications with JavaScript.

On iOS, it works by providing a prebuilt library containing Objective-C classes that wrap native capabilities (e.g., vibration and accelerometer support) and exposes these capabilities to JavaScript along with an Xcode project template that makes use of the library. You can then compile your application as a hybrid of native Objective-C and JavaScript inside Xcode.

The platform is device-agnostic, allowing you to build an application for the iOS, Android, BlackBerry, WebOS, WP7, and Symbian devices simultaneously. Developing applications using the PhoneGap framework is a reasonable alternative to building all-native applications in Objective-C.

In the past, submitting applications built around the PhoneGap platform to the App Store was problematic. However, since the 0.8.0 release of PhoneGap, this has been resolved, and Apple has approved Phone-Gap for building applications intended for the store.

If you're a web developer who wants to build mobile applications in HTML and Java-Script while still taking advantage of the hardware features on the iOS, you may want to take a look at the PhoneGap platform.

Core Data

One of the most important additions to the iOS SDK, at least from the perspective of the developer community, was Core Data. It is a powerful and efficient framework for data management and persistence, and while it was new to the iPhone at the time it was added, it had been available to developers on the Mac since the release of Mac OS X 10.4 (Tiger).

Core Data allows you to easily define your application's data model, creating a managed object model that allows you to specify an abstract definition of your model objects. In a similar fashion to how Interface Builder takes much of the heavy lifting out of building complicated user interfaces (the view), Core Data takes the heavy lifting out of building the model.

We didn't even touch on Core Data in this book; if you're interested in this framework, I recommend that you look at *Core Data: Apple's API for Persisting Data on Mac OS X* by Marcus S. Zarra (Pragmatic Programmers). I also recommend that you look at *Core Data for iPhone: Building Data-Driven Applications for the iPhone and iPod Touch* by Tim Isted (Addison-Wesley Professional).

In-App Purchase

The Store Kit Framework is an in-application payment engine for paid applications allowing you to request payment from your users (e.g., for accessing additional content).

You can also simplify your development by creating a single version of your application that uses In-App Purchase to unlock additional functionality, eliminating the need to create two versions of your application: a paid "pro" version and a free "lite" version. You can distribute your application for free, and then ask users to upgrade using In-App Purchase.

Only digital items may be sold using In-App Purchase, not physical goods or services, and these digital goods must be delivered to the application from which they were purchased (and in addition be available on all devices that the user may own). The framework leverages the App Store to collect payment, even sending the user the familiar App Store receipt email she would normally receive after purchasing.

 Details of the Store Kit framework and the In-App Purchase service are given in the Apple Store Kit Programming Guide, which can be found along with other useful information on the Apple Developer website (*http://developer.apple.com/appstore/resources/inapppurchase/*).

MKStoreKit

If you're finding the Store Kit framework hard to work with and your in-app purchases don't requite server-side hosting, then you might want to look at MKStoreKit by Mugunth Kumar, which is available at his GitHub site (*https://github.com/MugunthKumar/MKStoreKit*). It's a solid, well-supported wrapper library that has grown along with the in-app purchase capabilities provided by Apple. I use it myself and can recommend it thoroughly.

Core Animation

Built on top of the OpenGL libraries, Core Animation was designed from the ground up to allow developers to build lightweight but graphically rich UIs, and is the framework that underlies many of Apple's ubiquitous animation effects.

If you want to learn more about the Core Animation framework, I recommend *Graphics and Animation on iOS* by Vandad Nahavandipoor (O'Reilly). You might also want to take a look at *Core Animation for Mac OS X and the iPhone: Creating Compelling Dynamic User Interfaces* by Bill Dudley (Pragmatic Programmers) and *Core Animation* by Marcus Zarra and Matt Long (Addison-Wesley).

Game Kit

Despite the name, the Game Kit framework is not just for games, as it offers two important technologies to developers: peer-to-peer networking using Bonjour over Bluetooth, and in-application voice chat. Interestingly, the voice chat features included in Game Kit work over any network connection, not just the peer-to-peer Bluetooth connections established by the Game Kit framework.

A good general book on peer-to-peer networking with Bonjour, Apple's name for zero configuration networking, is *Zero Configuration Networking: The Definitive Guide* by Daniel Steinberg and Stuart Cheshire (O'Reilly). You can find some good iOS-specific examples using Game Kit in *iOS SDK Development* by Chris Adamson and Bill Dudley (Pragmatic Programmers).

Writing Games

Apple has advertised the iPod touch as "the funnest iPod ever" and is pushing it heavily as a game platform, competing directly with the Nintendo DS and Sony PSP platforms.

However, writing good games is a lot harder than most people would imagine, and is certainly not within the scope of a book such as this. If you're interested in developing games for the iOS platform, I recommend you look at *Tap, Move, Shake: Turning Your Game Ideas into iPhone & iPad Apps* by Todd Moore (O'Reilly).

If you're interested in developing games using the popular Cocos2D game engine, you might also want to take a look at *Learning Cocos2D: A Hands-On Guide to Building iOS Games with Cocos2D, Box2D, and Chipmunk* by Rod Strougo and Ray Wenderlich (Addison-Wesley Professional).

Look and Feel

Apple has become almost infamous for its strict adherence to its Human Interface Guidelines. Designed to present users with "a consistent visual and behavioral experience across applications and the operating system," the interface guidelines mean that (most) applications running on the Mac OS X desktop have a consistent look and feel, and behave in the same way. Long-time users of the platform generally view applications that don't adhere to the guidelines with some suspicion, and even novice users sometimes get the feeling that there is something "not quite right" about applications that break them.

Even for developers who are skeptical about whether they really need to strictly adhere to the guidelines, especially when Apple periodically steps outside them, the Human Interface Guidelines have remained a benchmark against which the user experience can be measured.

With the introduction of the iPhone and iPod touch, Apple had to draw up a radically different set of guidelines describing how user interactions should be managed on a platform radically unlike the traditional desktop environment.

I highly recommend that you read the mobile Human Interface Guidelines carefully, if only because violating them could lead to your application being rejected by the review team during the App Store approval process.

 A copy of the iOS Human Interface Guidelines (HIG) can be found in the iOS Developer Library (*http://developer.apple.com/library/ios/#doc umentation/UserExperience/Conceptual/MobileHIG/*).

Hardware Accessories

If you're interested in using the External Accessory framework to work with third-party hardware, you need to consider becoming a member of the Made for iPhone (MFi) Licensing Program.

Licensed developers gain access to technical documentation, hardware components, and technical support so that they can develop their own hardware and software in parallel. More information about this program is available on the Developer website (*http://developer.apple.com/programs/mfi/*).

However, if the thought of yet another set of NDAs is off-putting, you might be interested in *iOS Sensor Apps with Arduino*, also written by me (O'Reilly). In that book, I'll walk you through connecting your iOS hardware to an Arduino and other external hardware using an (already MFi approved) RS-232 adaptor.

Index

We'd like to hear your suggestions for improving our indexes. Send email to index@oreilly.com.

networks, 277

B

background modes, 281
backup, iCloud, 333–336
battery monitoring application, 129–139
    code, 134
    interface, 130
beta releases, 16
browsers (see web browsers)
building, 396–404
    ad hoc distribution, 397–403
        building your application, 400
        distributing a build, 402
        obtaining a distribution certificate, 397
        provisioning profile, 399
        registering devices, 399
    App Store distribution, 404
    developer-to-developer distribution, 403
    your application
        for ad hoc distribution, 400
        for App Store, 412–416

C

camera
    availability, 277
    using, 282
casting, defined, 28
certificates
    distribution certificates, 397
    preparing iOS devices, 16
city guide application
    data persistence, 269
    image picker view controller, 165–175
    view controller, 154–165
classes
    and objects, 26
    Apple Reachability class, 185–200
    application delegate class, 38
    class variables, 26
    declarations, 38
    delegate classes, 27
    methods, 27
    Objective-C, 53–60
        calling methods, 59
        declaring methods, 58
        declaring with an interface, 53
        defining with the implementation, 55

dot syntax, 58
object typing, 55, 55
properties, 56
synthesizing properties, 57
singleton classes, 130
UIDevice class, 130
CLPlacement objects, 307
CMMotionManager class, 283
Cocoa framework, 421
Cocoa Touch framework, MVC pattern, 65
compass, availability, 278
controllers, connecting to the model, 86–89
Core Animation framework, 424
Core Data, 274, 423
Core Location framework, 301–305
Core Motion framework, 283–297
    accelerometer, 285–290
    gyroscope, 291
    magnetometer, 294–297
    pulling motion data, 284
    pushing motion data, 284

D

data, 237–274
    capturing it table views, 119
    data entry, 237–241
        UITextField, 238
        UITextView, 240
    parsing JSON, 245–259
        JSON Framework, 247
        NSJSONSerialization, 245
        Social framework, 250
        Twitter Trends, 248, 251–259
    parsing XML, 242–245
        with libxml2, 242
        with NSXMLParser, 244
    pulling motion data, 284
    pushing motion data, 284
    regular expressions, 260–265
        NSRegularExpression, 261
        regex support, 264
        RegexKitLite, 262
    retrieving
        from the Internet, 217–236
        from UIWebView, 211
    storing, 265–274
        Core Data, 274
        flat files, 265
        SQL databases, 266–273

libxml2, parsing XML, 242
look and feel, 425

M

Mac Developer Program, 11
magnetometer
    availability, 278
    Core Motion framework, 294–297
MapKit, 317–332
marketing your application, 5
master-detail applications, 175–182
media playback, 373–378
memory management, 60–64
    alloc, retain, copy and release cycle, 62
    automatic reference counting, 63
    autorelease pool, 61
    creating objects, 61
    dealloc method, 64
    handling manually, 62
    Objective-C, 28
    warnings, 64
messages, defined, 27
metadata, 407
methods
    accessor methods, 56
    classes, 27, 58
    dealloc method, 64
MKStoreKit, 424
mobile provisioning profile, iOS devices, 21
modal view controllers, 154–165
MVC pattern
    about, 65
    Cocoa Touch framework, 65

N

names, display name, 393
native applications
    about, 1
    versus web applications, 5
Navigator window, 33
networks, 185–236
    availability, 277
    detecting network status, 185–200
    email, 211–217
    embedding a web browser in your application, 200–211
        displaying static HTML files, 210
        example, 200–209

        retrieving data from UIWebView, 211
    performance, 3
    retrieving data from the Internet, 217–236
        asynchronous requests, 218
        synchronous requests, 217
        Web services, 219–236
nib files, universal applications, 176
nil, calling methods on, 60
NSJSONSerialization, parsing JSON, 245
NSLog, debugging using, 48
NSRegularExpression, 261
NSXMLParser, parsing XML, 244

O

object typing, Objective-C, 55
object-oriented programing, Objective-C, 25–30
Objective-C, 25–30, 53–68
    classes, 53–60
        calling methods, 59
        declaring methods, 58
        declaring with an interface, 53
        defining with the implementation, 55
        dot syntax, 58
        object typing, 55
        properties, 56
        synthesizing properties, 57
    Cocoa framework, 421
    iOS design patterns, 64–68
        Delegates and DataSource pattern, 67
        MVC pattern, 65
        views and view controllers, 66
    memory management, 60–64
        alloc, retain, copy and release cycle, 62
        automatic reference counting, 63
        autorelease pool, 61
        creating objects, 61
        dealloc method, 64
        warnings, 64
    object model, 28
    object-oriented programing, 25–30
    root class, 54
    syntax, 29
objects
    autorelease objects, 62
    memory management, 61
OS X 10.6 (Snow Leopard), 8

instance variables, 26, 87
vibration, 300
view controllers, 127–183
    combining view controllers, 147–154
    image picker view controller, 165–175
    iOS design patterns, 66
    master-detail applications, 175–182
    modal view controllers, 154–165
    popover controllers, 182
    tab bar applications, 140–146
    utility applications, 127–139
    Xcode, 41

W

warnings, memory management, 64
Weather application, 305–316
    CLPlacement objects, 307
    forward geocoding, 307
    reverse geocoding, 306
Weather Underground service, 219
    building an application, 222
    parsing the XML document, 231
    populating the UI, 234
    tidying up, 235
web applications
    about, 422

versus native applications, 5
web browsers, embedding in applications, 200–211
web services, 219–236
    Weather Underground service, 219
        building an application, 222
        parsing the XML document, 231
        populating the UI, 234
        tidying up, 235
WiFi, 281
writability property, 56

X

Xcode, 34–42
    application delegate class, 38
    distribution of, 403
    iOS SDK, 11
    iPhone application, 36
    Utility Application template, 127
    view controller, 41
XML, parsing, 242–245
    about, 231
    with libxml2, 242
    with NSXMLParser, 244

About the Author

Alasdair Allan is the author of several books published by O'Reilly Media, including this one. He and Pete Warden (*http://petewarden.typepad.com/*) are somewhat infamous for causing a privacy scandal by uncovering that your iPhone was recording your location (*http://radar.oreilly.com/2011/04/apple-location-tracking.html*) all the time. This caused several class action lawsuits and a US Senate hearing. He isn't sure what to think about that. From time to time he stands in front of cameras (*http://shop.oreilly.com/product/0636920026457.do*), and you can often find him at conferences (*http://lanyrd.com/profile/aallan/*).

He runs a small technology consulting business (*http://babilim.co.uk/*) writing software, building hardware, and providing training; including a series of workshops on sensors (*http://sensorworkshops.com/*). He sporadically writes blog posts (*http://dailyack.com/*) about things that interest him, or more frequently provides commentary about them in 140 characters or less (*http://twitter.com/aallan*).

Alasdair is also a senior research fellow (*http://emps.exeter.ac.uk/physics-astronomy/staff/aa247*) at the University of Exeter (*http://www.exeter.ac.uk/*). As part of his work there he built a distributed peer-to-peer network of telescopes (*http://www.estar.org.uk/*) which, acting autonomously, reactively scheduled observations of time-critical events. Notable successes included contributing to the detection of the most distant object yet discovered, a gamma-ray burster at a redshift of 8.2 (*http://arxiv.org/abs/0906.1577*).

Colophon

The animal on the cover of *Learning iOS Programming* is a lapwing (*Vanellus vanellus*), also known as a northern lapwing, a peewit, or a green plover. This wading bird is 11–13 inches long with a 26–28 inch wingspan, a black crest, and rounded wings. Although its plumage is predominantly black and white, the upperparts are metallic green or bronze. The name lapwing may refer to the sound its wings make in flight, to its erratic flight pattern, or to its practice of pretending to have a broken wing in order to fool predators. The name peewit mimics the sound of its call. One of the lapwing's unique habits is the tumbling flight performed by the male during breeding season: it flies up, wheels, darts down, and climbs again, all while making its shrill cry.

The lapwing is common throughout the United Kingdom, Europe, and Asia, and occasionally makes its way to Alaska and Canada. It has an extensive range and may winter as far south as Africa, India, and China. The lapwing migrates in large flocks, which can be found on farmland, pastures, and wetlands searching for worms and insects.

Lapwing populations have declined since the 1980s, as the species has been affected by intensive agricultural practices, increases in grazing density, and climate change. It is now protected in the European Union, although parts of the Netherlands still enjoy the traditional hunt for the first lapwing egg of the year, thought to be a herald of spring. This hunt is allowed only from March 1 to April 9, and the actual collection of eggs is prohibited by law.

The cover image is from *The Riverside Natural History*. The cover font is Adobe ITC Garamond. The text font is Adobe Minion Pro; the heading font is Adobe Myriad Condensed; and the code font is Dalton Maag's Ubuntu Mono.

Get even more for your money.

Join the O'Reilly Community, and register the O'Reilly books you own. It's free, and you'll get:

- $4.99 ebook upgrade offer
- 40% upgrade offer on O'Reilly print books
- Membership discounts on books and events
- Free lifetime updates to ebooks and videos
- Multiple ebook formats, DRM FREE
- Participation in the O'Reilly community
- Newsletters
- Account management
- 100% Satisfaction Guarantee

Signing up is easy:

1. **Go to: oreilly.com/go/register**
2. **Create an O'Reilly login.**
3. **Provide your address.**
4. **Register your books.**

Note: English-language books only

To order books online:
oreilly.com/store

For questions about products or an order:
orders@oreilly.com

To sign up to get topic-specific email announcements and/or news about upcoming books, conferences, special offers, and new technologies:
elists@oreilly.com

For technical questions about book content:
booktech@oreilly.com

To submit new book proposals to our editors:
proposals@oreilly.com

O'Reilly books are available in multiple DRM-free ebook formats. For more information:
oreilly.com/ebooks

O'REILLY®

Spreading the knowledge of innovators   **oreilly.com**

CPSIA information can be obtained at www.ICGtesting.com
Printed in the USA
LVOW11s2247100913

351835LV00019B/957/P